There is a world referred to in the Scripture that is quite unseen, but also quite present and active. Michael Heiser's *The Unseen Realm* seeks to unmask this world. Heiser shows how important it is to understand this world and appreciate how its contribution helps to make sense of Scripture. The book is clear and well done, treating many ideas and themes that often go unseen themselves. With this book, such themes will no longer be neglected, so read it and discover a new realm for reflection about what Scripture teaches.

Darrell L. Bock, PhD
Executive Director for Cultural Engagement, Senior Research Professor of New Testament Studies, Howard G. Hendricks Center for Christian Leadership and Cultural Engagement

This is a provocative book that is badly needed. Many readers will be surprised by it—both its main theme and certain specific parts of it. This is because the author highlights the unseen realm as the Bible presents it in its ancient context, but this part of what the Bible teaches has not been well incorporated into either Christian theology or the preaching and teaching of the believing church (or at least many segments of it). We tend to ignore or downplay the many passages where the unseen realm is made visible, along with their implications. The author is enthusiastic about how his own eyes have been opened by the text, so he has written this book to open the eyes of his brothers and sisters in Christ to this same unseen (but very real!) realm.

Richard E. Averbeck, PhD
Director, Doctor of Philosophy (Theological Studies) Program, Professor of Old Testament and Semitic Languages, Trinity Evangelical Divinity School

The Unseen Realm is a spiritual game changer. Like Elisha's servant, you'll have your eyes opened to truths you've missed in the Bible that have been there all along. Heiser breathes new life into a biblical concept commonly misunderstood and misapplied in the evangelical world: spiritual warfare. He illumines the meaning of strange things in the Scriptures that Christians shy away from: the divine council, the sons of God, Watchers, Nephilim, giants. But he shows how these oddities are actually crucial to understanding the story line of God's redemptive plan for humanity. I am not exaggerating when I say that this book changed my understanding of God, the Bible, and my spiritual life. This is beautiful theology.

Brian Godawa
Author of the best-selling biblical fiction series Chronicles of the Nephilim

How was it possible that I had never seen that before? Dr. Heiser's survey of the complex reality of the supernatural world as the Scriptures portray it covers a subject that is strangely sidestepped. No one is going to agree with everything in his book, but the subject deserves careful study, and so does this book.

John Goldingay, PhD, DD
David Allan Hubbard Professor of Old Testament, School of Theology, Fuller Theological Seminary

Michael Heiser has written an incredibly accessible and well-researched work on some notoriously thorny biblical passages. Heiser's work on the divine council has earned him respect in the scholarly community for years, and he has now made this available to all. Without a doubt, *The Unseen Realm* will encourage, correct, and challenge many of our views on the spiritual realms revealed in the Bible—showing us the reality of things unseen!

William R. "Rusty" Osborne, MDiv
Assistant Professor of Biblical and Theological Studies, College of the Ozarks

This is a "big" book in the best sense of the term. It is big in its scope and in its depth of analysis. Michael Heiser is a scholar who knows Scripture intimately in its ancient cultural context. All—scholars, clergy, and laypeople—who read this profound and accessible book will grow in their understanding of both the Old and New Testaments, particularly as their eyes are opened to the Bible's "unseen world."

Tremper Longman III, PhD
Robert H. Gundry Professor of Biblical Studies, Westmont College

In this remarkable volume Michael Heiser not only opens our eyes to the unseen realm of the supernatural in the Scriptures, but also alerts us to the reality of supernatural forces in our own experience. Although based on exhaustive research in both primary biblical and ancient Near Eastern sources and secondary scholarly literature relevant to his project, Michael's book is written in a style that is accessible to scholars and laypeople alike. Even when readers disagree with his interpretation of specific biblical texts, they will be stimulated and inspired by fresh readings that he offers as he constructs a coherent picture of the role of the supernatural in biblical revelation.

Daniel I. Block, DPhil
Gunther H. Knoedler Professor of Old Testament, Wheaton College

THE
UNSEEN
REALM

Recovering the supernatural
worldview of the Bible

Michael S. Heiser

LEXHAM PRESS

To Roger

*Someday when the Lord sits me down to have a talk about this,
I'm going to remind him that you started it.*

Contents

FIRST THINGS

Reading Your Bible Again—
for the First Time

We all have watershed moments in life, critical turning points where, from that moment on, nothing will ever be the same.

One such moment in my own life—the catalyst behind this book—came on a Sunday morning in church while I was in graduate school. I was chatting with a friend who, like me, was working on a PhD in Hebrew studies, killing a few minutes before the service started. I don't recall much of the conversation, though I'm sure it was something about Old Testament theology. But I'll never forget how it ended. My friend handed me his Hebrew Bible, open to Psalm 82. He said simply, "Here, read that ... look at it closely."

The first verse hit me like a bolt of lightning:

God [*elohim*] stands in the divine assembly;
he administers judgment in the midst of the gods [*elohim*].[1]

I've indicated the Hebrew wording that caught my eye and put my heart in my throat. The word *elohim* occurs twice in this short verse. Other than the covenant name, Yahweh, it's the most common word in the Old Testament for God. And the first use of the word in this verse worked fine. But since I knew my Hebrew grammar, I saw immediately that the second instance needed to be translated as plural. There it was, plain as day: *The God of the Old Testament was part of an assembly—a pantheon—of other gods.*

Needless to say, I didn't hear a word of the sermon. My mind was reeling.

How was it possible that I'd never seen that before? I'd read through the Bible seven or eight times. I'd been to seminary. I'd studied Hebrew. I'd taught for five years at a Bible college.

---

1. Unless otherwise indicated, all Scripture quotations come from the *Lexham English Bible* (Bellingham, WA: Lexham Press, 2012). Typographical formatting used in the *Lexham English Bible* has been removed.

What did this do to my theology? I'd always thought—and had taught my students—that any other "gods" referenced in the Bible were just idols. As easy and comfortable as that explanation was, it didn't make sense here. The God of Israel isn't part of a group of idols. But I couldn't picture him running around with other real gods, either. This was the Bible, not Greek mythology. But there it was in black and white. The text had me by the throat, and I couldn't shake free.

I immediately set to work trying to find answers. I soon discovered that the ground I was exploring was a place where evangelicals had feared to tread. The explanations I found from evangelical scholars were disturbingly weak, mostly maintaining that the gods (*elohim*) in the verse were just men—Jewish elders—or that the verse was about the Trinity. I knew neither of those could be correct. Psalm 82 states that the gods were being condemned as corrupt in their administration of the nations of the earth. The Bible nowhere teaches that God appointed a council of Jewish elders to rule over foreign nations, and God certainly wouldn't be railing against the rest of the Trinity, Jesus and the Spirit, for being corrupt. Frankly, the answers just weren't honest with the straightforward words in the text of Psalm 82.

When I looked beyond the world of evangelical scholarship, I discovered that other scholars had churned out dozens of articles and books on Psalm 82 and Israelite religion. They'd left no stone unturned in ferreting out parallels between the psalm and its ideas and the literature of other civilizations of the biblical world—in some cases, matching the psalm's phrases word for word. Their research brought to light other biblical passages that echoed the content of Psalm 82. I came to realize that most of what I'd been taught about the unseen world in Bible college and seminary had been filtered by English translations or derived from sources like Milton's *Paradise Lost*.

That Sunday morning and its fallout forced a decision. My conscience wouldn't let me ignore my own Bible in order to retain the theology with which I was comfortable. Was my loyalty to the text or to Christian tradition? Did I really have to choose between the two? I wasn't sure, but I knew that what I was reading in Psalm 82, taken at face value, simply didn't fit the theological patterns I had always been taught. And yet there had to be answers. After all, the passages I had only now noticed had also been read by apostles like Paul—and by Jesus himself, for that matter. If I couldn't find help in finding those answers, I would just have to put the pieces together myself.

That journey has taken fifteen years, and it has led to this book. The path has not been easy. It came with risk and discomfort. Friends, pastors, and colleagues at times misunderstood my questions and my rebuttals of their proposed answers. Conversations didn't always end well. That sort of thing happens when you demand that creeds and traditions get in line behind the biblical text.

Clarity eventually prevailed. Psalm 82 became a focal point of my doctoral dissertation, which also examined the nature of Israelite monotheism and how the biblical writers really thought about the unseen spiritual realm. I wish I could say that I was just smart enough to figure things out on my own. But in reality, even though I believe I was providentially prepared for the academic task I faced, there were times in the process when the best description I can give is that I was *led* to answers.

I still believe in the uniqueness of the God of the Bible. I still embrace the deity of Christ. But if we're being honest when we affirm inspiration, then how we talk about those and other doctrines must take into account the biblical text.

What you'll read in this book won't overturn the important applecarts of Christian doctrine, but you'll come across plenty of mind grenades. Have no fear—it will be a fascinating, faith-building exercise. What you'll learn is that a theology of the unseen world that derives exclusively from the text understood through the lens of the ancient, premodern worldview of the authors informs *every* Bible doctrine in significant ways. If it sounds like I'm overpromising, just withhold judgment till you've read the rest of the book.

What you'll read in this book will change you. *You'll never be able to look at your Bible the same way again.* Hundreds of people who read the early drafts of this book over the past decade have told me so—and appreciated the experience deeply. I know they're right because I'm living that experience, too.

My goal is simple. When you open your Bible, I want you to be able to see it like ancient Israelites or first-century Jews saw it, to perceive and consider it as they would have. I want *their* supernatural worldview in *your* head.

You might find that experience uncomfortable in places. But it would be dishonest of us to claim that the biblical writers read and understood the text the way we do as modern people, or intended meanings that conform to theological systems created centuries after the text was written. *Our context is not their context.*

Seeing the Bible through the eyes of an ancient reader requires shedding the filters of our traditions and presumptions. They processed life in supernatural terms. Today's Christian processes it by a mixture of creedal statements and modern rationalism. I want to help you recover the supernatural worldview of the biblical writers—the people who produced the Bible. Obtaining and retaining that ancient mind-set requires observing a few ground rules, which we'll examine in the next chapter.

CHAPTER 2

Rules of Engagement

I've always been interested in anything old and weird. I was good at school, too. When I became a Christian in high school I felt like I'd been born for Bible study. I know—that level of interest in the Bible wasn't normal for a teenager. It was a bit of an obsession. I spent hours studying the Bible, as well as theology books. I took commentaries to study hall.

Since there was no 12-step program for my addiction, I went to Bible college to feed it. After that it was off to seminary. I wanted to be a biblical studies professor, so the next step was graduate school, where I finally focused on the Hebrew Bible and lots of dead ancient languages. I'd found biblical *nerdvana*, at least until that Sunday morning when I saw Psalm 82 without English camouflage.

Looking back, I can explain all my study, education, and learning before and after my Psalm 82 moment using two metaphors: a filter and a mosaic.

FILTERING THE TEXT

Filters are used to eliminate things in order to achieve a desired result. When we use them in cooking, the unwanted elements are dredged, strained, and discarded. When used in our cars, they prevent particles from interfering with performance. When we use them in email, they weed out what (or whom) we don't want to read. What's left is what we use—what contributes to our meal, our engine, or our sanity.

Most of my education was conducted in this way—using filters. It was no sinister plot. It was just what it was. The content I learned was filtered through certain presumptions and traditions that ordered the material for me, that put it into a system that made sense to my modern mind. Verses that didn't quite work with my tradition were "problem passages" that were either filtered out or consigned to the periphery of unimportance.

I understand that a lot of well-meaning Bible students, pastors, and professors don't look at how they approach the Bible that way. I know I didn't. But it's what happens. We view the Bible through the lens of what we know and what's familiar. Psalm 82 broke my filter. More importantly, it alerted me to the fact that I'd been using one. Our traditions, however honorable, are not intrinsic to the Bible. They are systems we invent to organize the Bible. They are artificial. They are *filters*.

Once I'd been awakened to this, it struck me as faithless to use a filter. But throwing away my filters cost me the systems with which I'd ordered Scripture and doctrine in my mind. I was left with lots of fragments. It didn't feel like it at the time, but that was the best thing that could have happened.

THE MOSAIC

The facts of the Bible are just pieces—bits of scattered data. Our tendency is to impose order, and to do that we apply a filter. But we gain a perspective that is both broader and deeper if we allow ourselves to see the pieces in their own wider context. We need to see the mosaic created by the pieces.

The Bible is really a theological and literary mosaic. The pattern in a mosaic often isn't clear up close. It may appear to be just a random assemblage of pieces. Only when you step back can you see the wondrous whole. Yes, the individual pieces are essential; without them there would be no mosaic. But the meaning of all the pieces is found in the *completed* mosaic. And a mosaic isn't imposed *on* the pieces; it derives *from* them.

I now view Psalm 82 not as a passage that shredded my filter but rather as an important piece of a larger, mesmerizing mosaic. Psalm 82 has at its core the unseen realm and its interaction with the human world. And that psalm isn't the only piece like that; there are lots of them. In fact, the intersection of our domain and the unseen world—which includes the triune God, but also a much more numerous cast—is at the heart of biblical theology.

My passion is to persuade you to remove your filter and begin to look at the pieces of Scripture as part of a mosaic so that this "big picture" can begin to take focus. If you do it, you'll find, as I did, that this approach leads you to the answers to questions like, "Why is *that* in the Bible?" and "How can I make sense of all this?" If you've spent serious time in Scripture, you know that there are many odd passages, curious phrases, troubling paradoxes, echoes of one event in another, connections within and between the testaments that can't be coincidental.

OBSTACLES AND PROTOCOLS

There are some serious obstacles to transitioning from seeing the Bible through filters to allowing all of its pieces to form a mosaic. I've experienced all of them.

*1. We've been trained to think that the history
    of Christianity is the true context of the Bible.*

We talk a lot about interpreting the Bible in context, but Christian history is *not* the context of the biblical writers. The proper context for interpreting the Bible is not Augustine or any other church father. It is not the Catholic Church. It is not the rabbinic movements of late antiquity and the Middle Ages. It is not the Reformation or the Puritans. It is not evangelicalism in any of its flavors. *It is not the modern world at all, or any period of its history.*

The proper context for interpreting the Bible is the context of the biblical writers—the context that *produced* the Bible.[1] Every other context is alien to the biblical writers and, therefore, to the Bible. *Yet there is a pervasive tendency in the believing Church to filter the Bible through creeds, confessions, and denominational preferences.*

I'm not arguing that we should ignore our Christian forefathers. I'm simply saying that we should give their words and their thought the proper perspective and priority. Creeds serve a useful purpose. They distill important, albeit carefully selected, theological ideas. But they are not inspired. They are no substitute for the biblical text.

The biblical text was produced by men who lived in the ancient Near East and Mediterranean between the second millennium BC and the first century AD. To understand how biblical writers thought, we need to tap into the intellectual output of that world. A vast amount of that material is available to us, thanks to modern technology. As our understanding of the worldview of the biblical writers grows, so does our understanding of what they intended to say—and the mosaic of their thinking takes shape in our minds.

*2. We've been desensitized to the vitality and
    theological importance of the unseen world.*

Modern Christianity suffers from two serious shortcomings when it comes to the supernatural world.

---

1. We do not share the cognitive framework of the biblical writers. While the implications may seem uncomfortable, it is hermeneutically pointless to pretend otherwise. See the companion website for examples of resistance to this transparently obvious fact.

First, many Christians claim to believe in the supernatural but think (and live) like skeptics. We find talk of the supernatural world uncomfortable. This is typical of denominations and evangelical congregations outside the charismatic movement—in other words, those from a background like the one I grew up in.

There are two basic reasons why noncharismatics tend to close the door on the supernatural world. One is their suspicion that charismatic practices are detached from sound exegesis of Scripture. As a biblical scholar, it's easy for me to agree with that suspicion—but over time it has widely degenerated into a closed-minded overreaction that is itself detached from the worldview of the biblical writers.

The other reason is less self-congratulatory. The believing church is bending under the weight of its own rationalism, a modern worldview that would be foreign to the biblical writers. Traditional Christian teaching has for centuries kept the unseen world at arm's length. We believe in the Godhead because there's no point to Christianity without it. The rest of the unseen world is handled with a whisper or a chuckle.

The second serious shortcoming is evident within the charismatic movement: the elevation of experience over Scripture. While that movement is predisposed to embrace the idea of an animate spiritual world, its conception of that world is framed largely by experience and an idiosyncratic reading of the book of Acts.

Those two shortcomings, while seemingly quite different, are actually born of the same fundamental, underlying problem: Modern Christianity's view of the unseen world isn't framed by the ancient worldview of the biblical writers. One segment wrongly consigns the invisible realm to the periphery of theological discussion. The other is so busy seeking some interaction with it that it has become unconcerned with its biblical moorings, resulting in a caricature.

I'm concerned about both shortcomings, but since this book derives from my own story, the problem of the Christian skeptic hits closer to home and is my greater concern.

If your background, like mine, is in the evangelical, noncharismatic branch of Protestantism, perhaps you consider yourself an exception to the patterns I've identified, or think that I've overstated the situation. But what would you think if a Christian friend confided to you that he believed he had been helped by a guardian angel, or that he had audibly heard a disembodied voice warning him of some danger? What if your friend claimed to have witnessed demonic possession, or was convinced that God had directed her life through a dream that included an appearance of Jesus?

Most of us noncharismatics would have to admit that our initial impulse would be to doubt. But we actually have a less transparent reflex. We would nod our head and listen politely to our friend's fervent story, but the whole time we would be seeking other possible explanations. That's because our modern inclination is to insist on evidence. Since we live in a scientific age, we are prone to think these kinds of experiences are actually emotional misinterpretations of the events—or, worse, something treatable with the right medication. And in any individual case, that might be so—but the truth is that our modern evangelical subculture has trained us to think that our theology *precludes* any experience of the unseen world. Consequently, it isn't an important part of our theology.

My contention is that, if our theology really derives from the biblical text, *we must reconsider our selective supernaturalism and recover a biblical theology of the unseen world.* This is not to suggest that the best interpretation of a passage is always the most supernatural one. But the biblical writers and those to whom they wrote were predisposed to supernaturalism. To ignore that outlook or marginalize it will produce Bible interpretation that reflects *our* mind-set more than that of the biblical writers.

*3. We assume that a lot of things in the Bible
    are too odd or peripheral to matter.*

Sometime after we moved to Wisconsin for my doctoral work, my wife and I found a church that felt as if it might become our new church home. The pastor had a degree from a well-known seminary. His first two sermons from 1 Peter were filled with solid exposition. I was excited about the prospects. By our third visit, he had reached 1 Peter 3:14–22 in his sermon series, a very odd passage that's also one of my favorites. What happened next is etched on my memory. The pastor took the pulpit and announced with complete sincerity, "We're going to skip this section of 1 Peter since it's just too strange." We didn't visit again.

I've seen this sort of evasion more than once. Usually it's not as dramatic. Pastors don't typically tell their people to skip part of the Bible. The more common strategy for "handling" strange passages is more subtle: Strip the bizarre passage of anything that makes it bizarre. The goal is to provide the most ordinary, comfortable interpretation possible.

This strategy is ironic to say the least. Why is it that Christians who would strenuously defend a belief in God or the virgin birth against charges that they are unscientific or irrational don't hesitate to call out academic SWAT teams to explain away "weird" biblical passages? The core doctrines of the faith are themselves neither ordinary nor a comfortable fit with empirical rationalism.

The odds are very high that you've never heard that Psalm 82 plays a pivotal role in biblical theology (including New Testament theology). I've been a Christian for over thirty years and I've never heard a sermon on it. There are many other passages whose content is curious or "doesn't make sense" and so are abandoned or glossed over. Here's a sampling of them:

• Gen 1:26	• 1 Sam 23:1–14	• 1 Cor 2:6–13
• Gen 3:5, 22	• 1 Kgs 22:1–23	• 1 Cor 5:4–5
• Gen 6:1–4	• 2 Kgs 5:17–19	• 1 Cor 6:3
• Gen 10–11	• Job 1–2	• 1 Cor 10:18–22
• Gen 15:1	• Pss 82, 68, 89	• Gal 3:19
• Gen 48:15–16	• Isa 14:12–15	• Eph 6:10–12
• Exod 3:1–14	• Ezek 28:11–19	• Heb 1–2
• Exod 23:20–23	• Dan 7	• 1 Pet 3:18–22
• Num 13:32–33	• Matt 16:13–23	• 2 Pet 1:3–4
• Deut 32:8–9[2]	• John 1:1–14	• 2 Pet 2:4–5
• Deut 32:17	• John 10:34–35	• Jude 5–7
• Judg 6	• Rom 8:18–24	• Rev 2:26–28
• 1 Sam 3	• Rom 15:24, 28	• Rev 3:21

Don't consider that a mere catalog. The list is deliberate, and all of those passages will be examined in this book. All are conceptually interconnected, and all help illuminate the more commonly studied passages—those that *do* "make sense." Look them up for a glimpse of what we'll be talking about.

How are we supposed to understand the identity of the "sons of God" in Genesis 6:1–4? Why did Jesus angrily rebuke Peter by saying "Get behind me, Satan"? Why does Paul tell the Corinthian church to stop arguing because they would someday "rule over angels"? There are lots of explanations offered by pastors and teachers of the Bible for these and other strange passages, but most are offered without consideration of how that explanation works with the rest of the Bible, with passages strange or not-so-strange.

In this book, I'll be offering my take on many "strange passages." Other scholars have done the same. But if mine are different, it's because they grow out of the perspective of the mosaic. They don't exist in isolation from other passages. They have explanatory power in more than one place.

My point is not to suggest that we can have absolute certainty in interpretation everywhere in the Bible. No one, including the present writer, is always right about what every passage means. I have a firm grasp of my own lack of

---

2. See the ESV or NRSV. These translations rightly incorporate the Dead Sea Scroll reading into the running text of the translation.

omniscience. (So does my wife, for the record.) Rather, my contention in this book is that *if it's weird, it's important.* Every passage plays a coherent role in the mosaic whole.

• • •

I've said that the mosaic of biblical theology gives coherence to the pieces of the Bible. But the Bible is a long, detailed work. One of the hardest parts about writing this book was deciding what to reserve for another book—how to be comprehensive without being exhaustive. I decided to cheat.

The present book is the culmination of years of my time spent reading and studying the biblical text and exploring the insights of other scholars. I've accumulated thousands of books and scholarly journal articles that relate in some way to the ancient biblical worldview that produces the mosaic. I've read nearly all of them in part or whole. My bibliography is nearly as long as this book. I mention this to make it clear that the ideas you'll read here are not contrived. All of them have survived what scholars call peer review. My main contribution is *synthesis* of the ideas and articulating a biblical theology not derived from tradition but rather framed exclusively in the context of the Bible's own ancient worldview.

The present book is academic in tone, but it's not necessarily a book for scholars. You don't need to have gone to seminary or earned an advanced degree to follow along. I've tried to reserve technical discussion to a companion website to this book that will provide fuller discussion on certain topics, additional bibliography, and "nuts and bolts" data from the original languages for those who desire that.[3]

For those for whom this book may feel too dense, I've written a less-detailed version entitled *Supernatural.* It covers the core concepts in this book with an orientation toward practical application of the supernatural worldview of the biblical writers—toward how the biblical mosaic presented here should change our spiritual lives and outlook.

The subtitle of this book ("Recovering the Supernatural Worldview of the Bible") captures the struggle of being a modern person with a believing heart trying to think like a premodern biblical writer. If you can feel even a little of that conflict, you're where I've been for a very long time. And I'm still on that journey. Somewhere along the way, I came to believe that I didn't need protection from my Bible. If you believe that too, you're good to go.

---

3. The companion website is www.moreunseenrealm.com.

PART 2

THE HOUSEHOLDS OF GOD

CHAPTER 3

God's Entourage

CHILDREN OFTEN ASK, "WHAT WAS THERE BEFORE GOD MADE THE WORLD?" The answer most adults would give is that *God* was there. That's true, but incomplete. God had company. And I'm not talking about the other members of the Trinity.

GOD'S FAMILY

The biblical answer is that the heavenly host was with God before creation. In fact, they witnessed it. What God says to Job in Job 38:4–7 is clear on that point:

> 4 "Where were you at my laying the foundation of the earth?
>   Tell me, if you possess understanding.
> 5 Who determined its measurement? Yes, you do know.
>   Or who stretched the measuring line upon it?
> 6 On what were its bases sunk?
>   Or who laid its cornerstone,
> 7 when the morning stars were singing together
>   and all the sons of God shouted for joy?

When God laid the foundations of the earth, the "sons of God" were there, shouting for joy. But who are the sons of God? Obviously, they aren't humans. This is *before* the creation of the world. We might think of them as angels, but that wouldn't be quite correct.

The unseen world has a hierarchy, something reflected in such terms as *archangel* versus *angel*. That hierarchy is sometimes difficult for us to discern in the Old Testament, since we aren't accustomed to viewing the unseen world like a dynastic household (more on that following), as an Israelite would have processed certain terms used to describe the hierarchy.[1] In the ancient Semitic world, *sons of God* (Hebrew: *beney elohim*) is a phrase used to identify divine beings with higher-level responsibilities or jurisdictions. The term *angel* (Hebrew: *mal'ak*) describes an important but still lesser task: delivering messages.[2]

In Job 38, the sons of God are referred to as "morning stars." That same description is found outside the Bible in ancient texts from the biblical world. Ancient people thought the stars were living entities.[3] Their reasoning was simple: Many stars moved. That was a sign of life to the ancient mind. Stars were the shining glory of living beings.

The stars also inhabited the divine realm—literally, in the sense that they existed off the earth. The ancients believed that divine beings lived far away from humans, in remote places where human habitation wasn't possible. The most remote place of all was the sky, the heavens.

Morning stars are the stars one sees over the horizon just before the sun appears in the morning. They signal new life—a new day. The label works. It conveys the right thought. The original morning stars, the sons of God, saw the beginning of life as we know it—the creation of earth.

Right from the start, then, God has company—other divine beings, the sons of God. Most discussions of what's around before creation omit the mem-

---

1. On the hierarchy of divine beings within the heavenly host, see E. Theodore Mullen Jr., "Divine Assembly," *The Anchor Yale Bible Dictionary*, vol. 2 (ed. David Noel Freedman; New York: Doubleday, 1992), 215–16; S. B. Parker, "Sons of (The) God(S)," in *Dictionary of Deities and Demons in the Bible*, 2nd ed. (ed. Karel van der Toorn, Bob Becking, and Pieter W. van der Horst; Leiden; Boston; Cologne; Grand Rapids, MI; Cambridge: Brill; Eerdmans, 1999), 798; Michael S. Heiser, "Divine Council," in *Lexham Bible Dictionary* (ed. John D. Barry and Lazarus Wentz; Bellingham, WA: Lexham Press, 2012); Michael S. Heiser, "Divine Council," in the *Dictionary of the Old Testament: Wisdom, Poetry, and Writings* (Downers Grove, IL: InterVarsity Press, 2008), 112–16; G. Cooke, "The Sons of (the) God(s)," *Zeitschrift für die alttestamentliche Wissenschaft* 35 (1964): 22–47.

2. This is why, in the Hebrew Bible, the sons of God are actually never called angels. That is, there are no passages in which *beney elohim* (and similar phrases) occur in parallel with *mal'akim* ("angels"). Later Jewish texts, such as the Septuagint, the Greek translation of the Hebrew Bible, in some instances rendered *beney elohim* as *angeloi* ("angels"), but such translation decisions are not driven by the distinctive Hebrew vocabulary.

3. Compare Isa 14:13–14. Astral religion and solar mythology were common in the ancient world. The notion that stars were animate divine beings was part of Israelite thinking. The stars had names (Psa 147:4), were created by God (Gen 1:16), were thought of as a divine army (Judg 5:20; Isa 40:25–26; Dan 8:10; Rev 12:1–9). The idea persisted well into the New Testament era. See Mark S. Smith, "Astral Religion and the Representation of Divinity: The Cases of Ugarit and Judah," *Prayer, Magic, and the Stars in the Ancient and Late Antique World* (ed. Scott Noegel, Joel Walker, Brannon Wheeler; University Park: Pennsylvania State University Press, 2003), 187–206; Alan Scott, *Origen and the Life of the Stars: A History of an Idea*, Oxford Early Christian Studies (Oxford: Oxford University Press, 1994); Elmer B. Smick, "Another Look at the Mythological Elements in the Book of Job," *Westminster Theological Journal* 40 (1978): 213–28; Ulf Oldenburg, "Above the Stars of El: El in Ancient South Arabic Religion," *Zeitschrift für die alttestamentliche Wissenschaft* 82 (1970): 187–208.

bers of the heavenly host. That's unfortunate, because God and the sons of God, the divine family, are the first pieces of the mosaic.

We've barely made it to creation so far, and already we've uncovered some important truths from Scripture that have the potential to affect our theology in simple but profound ways. Their importance, if it isn't clear yet, will become apparent soon.

First, we learned that the sons of God are divine, not human. The sons of God witnessed creation long before there were people. They are intelligent nonhuman beings. The reference to the sons of God as stars also makes it clear that they are divine. While the language is metaphorical, it is also more than metaphorical. In the next chapter we'll see other passages that tell us that the sons of God are real, divine entities created by Yahweh, the God of Israel.

Second, the label "sons" deserves attention. It's a family term, and that's neither coincidental nor inconsequential. God has an unseen family—in fact, it's his original family. The logic is the same as that behind Paul's words in Acts at Mars Hill (the Areopagus) that all humans are indeed God's offspring (Acts 17:28). God has created a host of nonhuman divine beings whose domain is (to human eyes) an unseen realm. And because he created them, he claims them as his sons, in the same way you claim your children as your sons and daughters because you played a part in their creation.

While it's clear that the sons of God were with God before creation, there's a lot about them that isn't clear. They're divine, but what does that really mean? How should we think of them in relation to God?

GOD'S HOUSEHOLD

The rulers of ancient Egypt were called pharaohs. In the language of ancient Egypt, the title was actually two words, *per a-a*, which meant "great house(hold)." The household concept for the ruling families of ancient Egypt was that of a dynastic bureaucracy. Pharaohs typically had large, extended families. They frequently appointed family members to key positions of authority in their administration. The elite staffing of the king's governing bureaucracy typically came from Pharaoh's household. They were administrators, not lowly messengers.

This concept and structure was well known throughout the ancient world. It spoke of layered authority: a high king, elite administrators who were often related to the king, and low-level personnel who served the higher levels of authority. Everyone in the system was part of the government, but authority and status were tiered.

Several Old Testament passages describe this administrative structure existing in the heavenly realm, as well. Psalm 82 is perhaps the clearest—and perhaps the most startling. As I related in the first chapter, it's the passage that opened my own eyes. The psalm refers to Yahweh's administration as a council.[4] The first verse reads:

God (*elohim*) stands in the divine assembly;
he administers judgment in the midst of the gods (*elohim*).

You no doubt noticed that, as I pointed out in chapter one, the word *elohim* occurs twice in this verse. You also probably recognize *elohim* as one of God's names, despite the fact that the form of the word is *plural*. In English we make words plural by adding -s or -es or -ies (*rats, horses, stories*). In Hebrew, plurals of masculine nouns end with -*im*.

While the word *elohim* is plural in form, its *meaning* can be either plural or singular. Most often (over 2,000 times) in the Hebrew Bible it is singular, referring to the God of Israel.

We have words like this in English. For example, the word *sheep* can be either singular or plural. When we see *sheep* by itself, we don't know if we should think of one sheep or a flock of sheep. If we put *sheep* into a sentence ("The sheep is lost"), we know that only one sheep is meant since the verb *is* requires a singular subject. Likewise, "The sheep are lost" informs us that the status of more than one sheep is being discussed. Grammar guides us. It's the same with Hebrew.

Psalm 82:1 is especially interesting since *elohim* occurs twice in that single verse. In Psalm 82:1, the first *elohim* must be singular, since the Hebrew grammar has the word as the subject of a singular verbal form ("stands"). The second *elohim* must be plural, since the preposition in front of it ("in the midst

---

4. The major scholarly works on the divine councils of Canaan, Ugarit, and Israel are E. Theodore Mullen Jr., *The Divine Council in Canaanite and Early Hebrew Literature*, Harvard Semitic Monographs 24 (Chico, CA: Scholars Press, 1980) and Lowell K. Handy, *Among the Host of Heaven: The Syro-Palestinian Pantheon as Bureaucracy* (Winona Lake, IN: Eisenbrauns, 1994); H. W. Robinson, "The Council of Yahweh," *Journal of Theological Studies* 45 (1944): 151–57; David Marron Fleming, "The Divine Council as Type Scene in the Hebrew Bible" (PhD diss., Southern Baptist Theological Seminary, 1989); Min Suc Kee, "The Heavenly Council and Its Type-Scene," *Journal for the Study of the Old Testament* 31.3 (2007): 259–73; Patrick D. Miller, "Cosmology and World Order in the Old Testament: The Divine Council as Cosmic-Political Symbol," *Horizons in Biblical Theology*, no. 2 (1987): 53–78; Ellen White, *Yahweh's Council: Its Structure and Membership* (Forschungen zum Alten Testament 65; Tübingen: Mohr Siebeck, 2014). See also my review of White's book on the companion website. For a general academic survey of the divine council, see Heiser, "Divine Council," in *Dictionary of the Old Testament*; Heiser, "Divine Council," in *Lexham Bible Dictionary*. On Psa 82 see Matitiahu Tsevat, "God and the Gods in Assembly," *Hebrew Union College Annual* 40–41 (1969–70): 123–37; James Stokes Ackerman, "An Exegetical Study of Psalm 82" (PhD diss., Harvard University, 1966); Willem S. Prinsloo, "Psalm 82: Once Again, Gods or Men?" *Biblica* vol. 76, no. 2 (1995): 219–28.

of") requires more than one. You can't be "in the *midst* of" *one*. The preposition calls for a group—as does the earlier noun, *assembly*. The meaning of the verse is inescapable: The singular *elohim* of Israel presides over an assembly of *elohim*.

A quick read of Psalm 82 informs us that God has called this council meeting to judge the *elohim* for corrupt rule of the nations. Verse 6 of the psalm declares that these *elohim* are sons of God. God says to them:

> I have said, "You are gods [*elohim*],
> and sons of the Most High [*beney elyon*], all of you.

To a biblical writer, the Most High (*elyon*) was the God of Israel. The Old Testament refers to him as Most High in several places (e.g., Gen 14:18–22; Num 24:16; Pss 7:17; 18:13; 47:2). The sons of God/the Most High here are clearly called *elohim*, as the pronoun "you" in verse 6 is a plural form in the Hebrew.

The text is not clear whether all of the *elohim* are under judgment or just some. The idea of *elohim* ruling the nations under God's authority is a biblical concept that is described in other passages we'll explore later. For now, it's sufficient that you see clearly that the sons of God are divine beings under the authority of the God of Israel.[5]

You see why the psalm threw me for a loop. The first verse has God presiding over an assembly of gods. Doesn't that sound like a pantheon—something we associate with polytheism and mythology? For that very reason, many English translations obscure the Hebrew in this verse. For example, the NASB translates it as: "God takes His stand in His own congregation; He judges in the midst of the rulers."

There's no need to camouflage what the Hebrew text says. People shouldn't be protected from the Bible. The biblical writers weren't polytheists. But since Psalm 82 generates questions and controversy, we need to spend some time on what it teaches and what it doesn't teach, along with other passages that inform us about the divine council. We'll do just that in the next chapter.

---

5. As we proceed, I'll be referring to the "divine council worldview" of the biblical writers. This phrase and others like it refer to God's rule over all things, visible or invisible, through his intelligent agents—his imagers—both human and nonhuman. Since, as we will discover, it was God's original intention for humanity (and thus humanity's original destiny) that they rule and reign with him as part of his heavenly nonhuman household, human affairs are encompassed in the divine council worldview. In biblical theology, there is a symbiosis of both realms, whether in loyal service to God, or in spiritual conflict in the wake of divine and human rebellions.

CHAPTER 4

God Alone

THERE'S NO DOUBT THAT PSALM 82 CAN ROCK YOUR BIBLICAL WORLDVIEW. Once I saw what it was actually saying, I was convinced that I needed to look at the Bible through ancient eyes, not my traditions. I had to navigate the questions that are probably floating around in your own head and heart now that you've read—really read—that passage.

First and foremost, you should be aware of some of the ways the clear meaning of Psalm 82 is distorted by interpreters and why it *isn't* teaching polytheism.

DIVINE BEINGS ARE NOT HUMAN

Many Christians who object to the plain meaning of the Hebrew text of Psalm 82 assert that this psalm is actually describing God the Father speaking to the other members of the Trinity. This view results in heresy. I'm confident you can see why—the psalm has God judging the other *elohim* for corruption (vv. 2–4). The corrupt *elohim* are sentenced to die like humans (v. 7). These observations alone should make any Christian who cares about the doctrine of God abandon this idea. It has other flaws. The end of the psalm makes it evident that the *elohim* being chastised were given some sort of authority over the nations of the earth, a task at which they failed. This doesn't fit the Trinity.

Other Christians who see the problems with this first idea try to argue that the sons of God are human beings—Jews to be specific. Some Jewish readers (who obviously would not be Trinitarian) also favor this view.

This "human view" is as flawed as the Trinitarian view.[1] At no point in

---

1. Space constraints make it impossible to fully address the flawed thinking behind the human explanation for *elohim* (in Psa 82 and elsewhere) in this chapter. In the discussion that proceeds, I touch on some of the more glaring logical and scriptural problems for this view. Arguments for the human view of *elohim* stemming from passages like Judg 18, Exod 22:7–9, Psa 45:7, or Jesus' quotation of Psa 82:6 in John 10:34 are dealt with at length on the companion website.

the Old Testament does the Scripture teach that Jews or Jewish leaders were put in authority over the other nations. The opposite is true—they were to be separate from other nations. The covenant with Abraham presupposed this separation: If Israel was wholly devoted to Yahweh, other nations would be blessed (Gen 12:1–3). Humans are also not by nature disembodied. The word *elohim* is a "place of residence" term. Our home is the world of embodiment; *elohim* by nature inhabit the spiritual world.

The real problem with the human view, though, is that it cannot be reconciled with other references in the Hebrew Old Testament that refer to a divine council of *elohim*.

Psalm 89:5–7 (Hebrew: vv. 6–8) explicitly contradicts the notion of a divine council in which the *elohim* are humans.

> ⁵ And so the heavens will praise your wonderful deed, O Yahweh,
>   even your faithfulness, in the assembly of the holy ones.
> ⁶ For who in the sky is equal to Yahweh?
>   Who is like Yahweh among the sons of God,
> ⁷ a God feared greatly in the council of the holy ones,
>   and awesome above all surrounding him?

God's divine council is an assembly *in the heavens*, not on earth. The language is unmistakable. This is precisely what we'd expect if we understand the *elohim* to be divine beings. It is utter nonsense if we think of them as humans. There is no reference in Scripture to a council of human beings serving Yahweh in the skies (Jews or otherwise).

What Psalms 82 and 89 describe is completely consistent with what we saw earlier in Job 38:7—a group of heavenly sons of God. It also accords perfectly with other references to the sons of God as plural *elohim*:

> The sons of God came to present themselves before Yahweh. (Job 1:6; 2:1)

> ¹ Ascribe to Yahweh, O sons of God,
>   ascribe to Yahweh glory and strength.
> ² Ascribe to Yahweh the glory due his name (Psa 29:1–2).

Do these references describe a group of Jewish leaders, among whom (in the passage from Job) Yahweh's great adversary appears, leading to Job's suffering? The conclusion is obvious.

PLURAL ELOHIM DOES NOT MEAN POLYTHEISM

Many scholars believe that Psalm 82 and other passages demonstrate that the religion of ancient Israel began as a polytheistic system and then evolved into monotheism. I reject that idea, along with any other explanations that seek to hide the plain reading of the text. In all such cases, the thinking is misguided.[2] The problem is rooted in a mistaken notion of what exactly the word *elohim* means.

Since *elohim* is so often translated *God*, we look at the Hebrew word the same way we look at capitalized G-o-d. When we see the word *God*, we instinctively think of a divine being with a unique set of attributes—omnipresence, omnipotence, sovereignty, and so on. But this is not how a biblical writer thought about the term. Biblical authors did not assign a specific set of attributes to the word *elohim*. That is evident when we observe how they used the word.

The biblical writers refer to a half-dozen different entities with the word *elohim*. By any religious accounting, the attributes of those entities are *not* equal.

- Yahweh, the God of Israel (thousands of times—e.g., Gen 2:4–5; Deut 4:35)
- The members of Yahweh's council (Psa 82:1, 6)
- Gods and goddesses of other nations (Judg 11:24; 1 Kgs 11:33)
- Demons (Hebrew: *shedim*—Deut 32:17)[3]
- The deceased Samuel (1 Sam 28:13)
- Angels or the Angel of Yahweh[4] (Gen 35:7)

The importance of this list can be summarized with one question: Would any Israelite, especially a biblical writer, really believe that the deceased human dead and demons are on the same level as Yahweh? No. The usage of the term *elohim* by biblical writers tells us very clearly that the term is not about a set of attributes. Even though when *we* see "G-o-d" we think of a unique set of attri-

---

2. I've written three technical articles that discuss this subject: "Are Yahweh and El Distinct Deities in Deut 32:8–9 and Psalm 82?" *HIPHIL* 3 (2006); "Monotheism, Polytheism, Monolatry, or Henotheism? Toward an Assessment of Divine Plurality in the Hebrew Bible," *Bulletin for Biblical Research* 18.1 (2008): 1–30; and "Does Divine Plurality in the Hebrew Bible Demonstrate an Evolution from Polytheism to Monotheism in Israelite Religion?" *Journal for the Evangelical Study of the Old Testament* 1.1 (2012): 1–24. The first and third articles are accessible online via the companion website. The third article addresses some recent articulations of the consensus view, that Psa 82 has Yahweh and El as separate deities. See the companion website for some excerpts from this article and further discussion.

3. There is much confusion about the term *demon* among both scholars and nonspecialists. The term in its ancient Near Eastern context doesn't align well with modern conceptions (from the Middle Ages onward). See the ensuing discussion and footnotes.

4. The choice between these two options depends on the interpretation of Gen 35:7 and the event(s) that form(s) the backdrop to that verse. Later chapters in this book will make it clear that I believe the Angel of Yahweh is Yahweh in visible form, and so that particular angel shares Yahweh's attributes. However, the rest of the discussion here makes clear that angels—in fact, all spiritual beings—are *elohim* due to the nature of what that term in fact denotes.

butes, when a biblical writer wrote *elohim*, he wasn't thinking that way. If he were, he'd never have used the term *elohim* to describe anything but Yahweh.

Consequently, there is no warrant for concluding that plural *elohim* produces a pantheon of interchangeable deities. There is no basis for concluding that the biblical writers would have viewed Yahweh as no better than another *elohim*. A biblical writer would not have presumed that Yahweh could be defeated on any given day by another *elohim*, or that another *elohim* (why not any of them?) had the same set of attributes. *That* is polytheistic thinking. It is not the biblical picture.

We can be confident of this conclusion by once again observing what the biblical writers say about Yahweh—and never say about another *elohim*. The biblical writers speak of Yahweh in ways that telegraph their belief in his uniqueness and incomparability:

> "Who is like you among the gods [*elim*], Yahweh?" (Exod 15:11)

> " 'What god [*el*] is there in the heaven or on the earth who can do according to your works and according to your mighty deeds?' " (Deut 3:24)

> "O Yahweh, God of Israel, there is no god [*elohim*] like you in the heavens above or on the earth beneath" (1 Kgs 8:23).

> For you, O Yahweh, are most high over all the earth.
> You are highly exalted above all gods [*elohim*] (Psalm 97:9).

Biblical writers also assign unique qualities to Yahweh. Yahweh is all-powerful (Jer 32:17, 27; Pss 72:18; 115:3), the sovereign king over the other *elohim* (Psa 95:3; Dan 4:35; 1 Kgs 22:19), the creator of the other members of his host-council (Psa 148:1–5; Neh 9:6; cf. Job 38:7; Deut 4:19–20; 17:3; 29:25–26; 32:17; Jas 1:17)[5] and the lone *elohim* who deserves worship from the other *elohim* (Psa 29:1). In fact, Nehemiah 9:6 explicitly declares that Yahweh is unique—there is only *one* Yahweh ("You alone are Yahweh").

The biblical use of *elohim* is not hard to understand once we know that it

---

5. Jas 1:17 calls God "the Father of lights," a phrase that points to God as the creator of celestial objects and all other heavenly beings. Like the cultures of the wider ancient world, Jewish thinking held that the stars were heavenly beings. The idea is found in the Old Testament, where the sons of God are metaphorically referred to as "the stars of God" (Job 38:7). James' description of God as the "Father of lights" therefore speaks of God as the creator of all heavenly beings. He alone is uncreated—they are created and, therefore, inferior. See P. W. van der Horst, "Father of the Lights," *Dictionary of Deities and Demons in the Bible*, 2nd ed. (ed. Karel van der Toorn, Bob Becking, and Pieter W. van der Horst; Leiden; Boston; Cologne; Grand Rapids, MI; Cambridge: Brill; Eerdmans, 1999), 328–29. The fact that, in biblical theology, there can by definition be only one uncreated being in turn means that all other *elohim* inhabitants of the spiritual realm are made of *something*. We often mistake invisibility with nonmateriality, but that is scientifically (materially) not the case.

isn't about attributes. *What all the figures on the list have in common is that they are inhabitants of the spiritual world.* In that realm there is hierarchy. For example, Yahweh possesses superior attributes with respect to all *elohim*. But God's attributes aren't what makes him an elohim, since inferior beings are members of that same group. The Old Testament writers understood that Yahweh was an *elohim*—but no other *elohim* was Yahweh. He was species-unique among all residents of the spiritual world.

This is not to say that an *elohim* could not interact with the human world. The Bible makes it clear that divine beings can (and did) assume physical human form, and even corporeal flesh, for interaction with people, but that is not their normal estate. Spiritual beings are "spirits" (1 Kgs 22:19–22; John 4:24; Heb 1:14; Rev 1:4). In like manner, humans can be transported to the divine realm (e.g., Isa 6), but that is not our normal plane of existence. As I explained earlier in this chapter, the word *elohim* is a "place of residence" term. It has nothing to do with a specific set of attributes.

Let's take a look at some other questions Psalm 82 raises.

WHAT DOES GOD NEED WITH A COUNCIL?

This is an obvious question. Its answer is just as obvious: God doesn't *need* a council. But it's scripturally clear that he has one. The question is actually similar to another one: *What does God need with people?* The answer is the same: God doesn't *need* people. But he uses them. God is not dependent on humans for his plans. God doesn't need us for evangelism. He could save all the people he wanted to by merely thinking about it. God could terminate evil in the blink of an eye and bring human history to the end he desires at any moment. But he doesn't. Instead, he works his plan for all things on earth by using human beings. He's also not incomplete without our worship, but he desires it.

I'm not saying that the question of whether God needs a council is pointless. I'm saying that it's no argument against the existence of a divine council.

ARE THE ELOHIM REAL?

Those who want to avoid the clarity of Psalm 82 argue that the gods are only idols. As such, they aren't real. This argument is flatly contradicted by Scripture. It's also illogical and shows a misunderstanding of the rationale of idolatry.

With respect to Scripture, one need look no further than Deuteronomy 32:17.

They [the Israelites] sacrificed to demons [*shedim*], not God [*eloah*], to gods [*elohim*] whom they had not known.

The verse explicitly calls the *elohim* that the Israelites perversely worshiped demons (*shedim*). This rarely used term (Deut 32:17; Psa 106:37) comes from the Akkadian *shedu*.[6] In the ancient Near East, the term *shedu* was neutral; it could speak of a good or malevolent spirit being. These Akkadian figures were often cast as guardians or protective entities, though the term was also used to describe the life force of a person.[7] In the context of Deuteronomy 32:17, *shedim* were *elohim*—spirit beings guarding foreign territory—who must not be worshiped.[8] Israel was supposed to worship her own God (here, *eloah*; cf. Deut 29:25).[9] One cannot deny the reality of the *elohim/shedim* in Deuteronomy 32:17 without denying the reality of demons.[10]

Scholars disagree over what kind of entity the *shedim* were. But whatever the correct understanding of *shedim* might be, they are not pieces of wood or stone.

---

6. Ludwig Koehler et al., *The Hebrew and Aramaic Lexicon of the Old Testament* (Leiden; New York: Brill, 1999), 1417.

7. "šedu," *The Assyrian Dictionary of the Oriental Institute of the University of Chicago*, Vol. 17: Š Part II (ed. John A. Brinkman, Miguel Civil, Ignace J. Gelb, A. Leo Oppenheim, Erica Reiner; Chicago: Oriental Institute, 1992), 256.

8. In the wider context of Deuteronomy as a whole, these *shedim/elohim* are the gods allotted to the nations (see chapters 14–15 of this book). Some recent evangelical treatments of the term *shedim*, most notably that of John Walton, contribute much to the discussion but seem to confuse language that identifies an entity as a member of the spiritual realm (*elohim*) with hierarchy in the divine council (see the companion website for specific interaction with John H. Walton, "Demons in Mesopotamia and Israel: Exploring the Category of Non-Divine but Supernatural Beings," in *Windows to the Ancient World of the Hebrew Bible: Essays in Honor of Samuel Greengus* [Winona Lake, IN: Eisenbrauns, 2014], 229–46). The biblical picture is simply not a neat one that conforms precisely to cognate material. All spiritual beings are, in biblical usage, labeled *elohim*. Terms like *beney elohim* or *beney elim* can either denote rank in the divine council (e.g., Job 1:6; 2:1; Psa 89:6 [Heb: 89:7]) or, more generally, speak of spiritual beings (Job 38:7; Psa 29:1). All spiritual beings are members of the heavenly host, the divine council (1 Kgs 22:19–23), in the sense that they all have some role to play. (There are no spiritual beings who operate alone. They are either under God's authority or in rebellion.) Some beings are distinguished by role, such as messengers (*mal'ak*, a term translated in many instances as "angel," but which means "messenger"). In ancient Near Eastern councils, messengers have low rank—but the term does not always denote low status. For example, at Ugarit the messengers (*mlkm*) of Baal are still referred to as gods (*'ilm*; *KTU* 1.3.iii:32). They are not "less divine" because of their role. Even Yahweh himself, when embodied or appearing in human form, takes that term ("angel [*mal'ak*] of Yahweh"; see chapters 16–18). Yahweh embodied in the Old Testament is not lesser than Yahweh invisible who is the sender. Hierarchy and identification are not completely interchangeable notions. For our purposes here, Deut 32:17 serves simply to point to the fact that the biblical writers understood the *elohim* as real beings. That Paul picks up on this passage to express fear of fellowship with demons (1 Cor 10:21–22; see chapter 38 of this book) informs us that he believed the *elohim* of Deut 32:17 were real spiritual beings.

9. This is the central point of the *shema*, the creed of ancient Israel (Deut 6:4). Despite its familiarity and centrality in Old Testament theology, the *shema* is one of the most notoriously difficult verses in the Bible to translate. See the companion website for discussion.

10. Deut 32:17 is poorly translated in a number of Bible versions. See Michael S. Heiser, "Does Deuteronomy 32:17 Assume or Deny the Reality of Other Gods?" *Bible Translator* 59.3 (July 2008): 137–45.

Scholars of Paul's first letter to the Corinthians know that, in the apostle's warning to not fellowship with demons (1 Cor 10:20), Paul's comments follow the history of the Israelites described in Deuteronomy 32.[11] He warns believers against fellowship with demons on the basis of Israel's failure in worshiping other gods. Paul uses the word *daimonion*, one of the words used frequently in the New Testament for evil spiritual beings, to translate *shedim* in Deuteronomy 32:17. Paul knew his Hebrew Bible and didn't deny the reality of the *shedim*, who are *elohim*.

"NO GODS BESIDES ME"?

Another misguided strategy is to argue that statements in the Old Testament that have God saying "there is none besides me" mean that no other *elohim* exist. This isn't the case. These phrases do not contradict Psalm 82 or others that, for example, say Yahweh is above all *elohim* or is the "God of gods [*elohim*]."

I've written a lot on this subject—it was a focus of my doctoral dissertation.[12] These "denial statements," as they are called by scholars, do not assert that there are no other *elohim*. In fact, some of them are found in chapters where the reality of other *elohim* is affirmed. We've already seen that Deuteronomy 32:17 refers to *elohim* that Paul believed existed. Deuteronomy 32:8–9 also refers to the sons of God. Deuteronomy 4:19–20 is a parallel to that passage, and yet Deuteronomy 4:35 says there is no god besides Yahweh. Is Scripture filled with contradictions?

No. These "denial statements" do not deny that other *elohim* exist. Rather, they deny that any *elohim* compares to Yahweh. They are statements of incom-

---

11. A good scholarly resource on this point is Guy Waters, *The End of Deuteronomy in the Epistles of Paul* (*Wissenschaftliche Untersuchungen zum Neuen Testament* 221; Tübingen: Mohr Siebeck, 2006). See especially footnote 12 on page 134, where Waters provides a list of commentators that argue Paul has Deut 32:17 explicitly in view in 1 Cor 10:20. Proving that the *elohim/shedim* of Deut 32:17 are not merely idols does not depend on 1 Cor 10:20. Their spiritual identity is evident after a trip through Deuteronomy. In Deut 32:8–9 (reading v. 8 with the Dead Sea Scrolls, as do the ESV and NRSV), when the nations were divided at the tower of Babel incident, the nations were placed by God under the authority of lesser *elohim*, the "sons of God" (see chapter 14 of this book for more detail). The parallel passage to that text is Deut 4:19–20. There the gods "allotted" to the other nations while Yahweh took Israel are called the "host of heaven." Worshiping them is forbidden. This is the same language as in 1 Kgs 22:13–23, where the prophet Micaiah has a vision of a divine council meeting (see chapter 7 of this book). These members of the "host of heaven" are called *elohim* in Deut 17:2–5, where Israel is again warned to not worship them. Unfortunately, Deut 29:25 informs us that Israelites did worship *elohim* that were not "allotted" to them. These passages, along with Deut 32:17, interchange the following terms or phrases: host of heaven, gods (*elohim*), and demons (*shedim*). This is where Paul got his theology. He isn't innovating—he knows Deuteronomy well.

12. See sections 1.2 and 1.3 of Heiser, "Monotheism, Polytheism, Monolatry, or Henotheism?" for a summary of the part of my dissertation that deals with this issue.

parability. This point is easily illustrated by noticing where else the same denial language shows up in the Bible. Isaiah 47:8 and Zephaniah 2:15 have, respectively, Babylon and Nineveh saying "there is none besides me." Are we to believe that the point of the phrase is to declare that no other cities *exist* except Babylon or Nineveh? That would be absurd. The point of the statement is that Babylon and Nineveh considered themselves *incomparable*, as though no other city could measure up to them. This is precisely the point when these same phrases are used of other gods—they cannot measure up to Yahweh. The Bible does not contradict itself on this point. Those who want to argue that the other *elohim* do not exist are at odds with the supernatural worldview of the biblical writers.

EXAMINING THE LOGIC

The denial that other *elohim* exist insults the sincerity of biblical writers and the glory of God. How is it coherent to say that verses extolling the superiority of Yahweh above all *elohim* (Psa 97:9) are really telling us Yahweh is greater than beings that don't exist? Where is God's glory in passages calling other *elim* to worship Yahweh (Psa 29:1–2) when the writers don't believe those beings are real? Were the writers inspired to lie or hoodwink us? To give us theological gibberish?

To my ear, it mocks God to say, "You're greater than something that doesn't exist." So is my dog. Saying, "Among the beings that we all know don't exist there is none like Yahweh" is tantamount to comparing Yahweh with Spiderman or Spongebob Squarepants. This reduces praise to a snicker. Why would the Holy Spirit inspire such nonsense?

MISUNDERSTANDING IDOLATRY

The biblical prophets love to make fun of idol making. It seems so stupid to carve an idol from wood or stone or make one from clay and then worship it. But ancient people did not believe that their gods were actually images of stone or wood. We misread the biblical writers if we think that.

What ancient idol worshippers believed was that the objects they made were *inhabited* by their gods. This is why they performed ceremonies to "open the mouth" of the statue.[13] The mouth (and nostrils) had to be ritually opened for the spirit of the deity to move in and occupy, a notion inspired by the idea

---

13. Edward M. Curtis, "Idol, Idolatry," in *The Anchor Yale Bible Dictionary* (ed. David Noel Freedman; New York: Doubleday, 1992), 377.

that one needs to breathe to live. The idol first had to be animated with the very real spiritual presence of the deity. Once that was done, the entity was localized for worship and bargaining.

This is easily proven from ancient texts. There are accounts, for example, of idols being destroyed. There is no sense of fear in those accounts that the god was dead.[14] Rather, there was only a need to make another idol.

Paul's warning in 1 Corinthians 10:18–22, alluded to previously, reflects this thinking. Earlier in the letter, he told the Corinthians that an idol had no power and was, in and of itself, nothing (1 Cor 8:4). While Gentiles had other lords and gods, for believers there was only one true God. But in chapter 10, he clarifies that he also knows that sacrifices to idols are actually sacrifices to demons—evil members of the spiritual world.

WHAT ABOUT JESUS?

Readers of Psalm 82 often raise a specific question about Jesus. If there are other divine sons of God, what do we make of the description of Jesus as the "only begotten" son of God (John 1:14, 18; 3:16, 18; 1 John 4:9)? How could Jesus be the *only* divine son when there were others?

"Only begotten" is an unfortunately confusing translation, especially to modern ears. Not only does the translation "only begotten" seem to contradict the obvious statements in the Old Testament about other sons of God, it implies that there was a time when the Son did not exist—that he had a beginning.

The Greek word translated by this phrase is *monogenes*. It doesn't mean "only begotten" in some sort of "birthing" sense. The confusion extends from an old misunderstanding of the root of the Greek word. For years *monogenes* was thought to have derived from two Greek terms, *monos* ("only") and *gennao* ("to beget, bear"). Greek scholars later discovered that the second part of the word *monogenes* does not come from the Greek verb *gennao*, but rather from the noun *genos* ("class, kind"). The term literally means "one of a kind" or "unique" without connotation of created origin. Consequently, since Jesus

---

14. Michael Dick, a scholar who has devoted two decades of attention to the subject of idolatry in Israel and the ancient Near East, agrees. In his scholarly work on the subject, Dick cites a number of texts where the ancient idolater used deity language for the product of his hands, but also made an intellectual distinction between the statue and the deity it represented, or which was thought to take residence in the statue. See Michael P. Dick, *Born in Heaven, Made on Earth: The Making of the Cult Image in the Ancient Near East* (Winona Lake, IN: Eisenbrauns, 1999), 33–34. In one telling citation referenced by Dick, the destruction of the statue of Shamash of Sippar was not regarded as the death of Shamash. Indeed, Shamash could still be worshiped.

is indeed identified with Yahweh and is therefore, with Yahweh, unique among the *elohim* that serve God, the term *monogenes* does not contradict the Old Testament language.

The validity of this understanding is borne out by the New Testament itself. In Hebrews 11:17, Isaac is called Abraham's *monogenes*. If you know your Old Testament you know that Isaac was *not* the "only begotten" son of Abraham. Abraham had earlier fathered Ishmael (cf. Gen 16:15; 21:3). The term must mean that Isaac was Abraham's *unique* son, for he was the son of the covenant promises. Isaac's genealogical line would be the one through which Messiah would come. Just as Yahweh is an *elohim*, and no other *elohim* are Yahweh, so Jesus is the unique Son, and no other sons of God are like him.

We've already encountered a lot of material that needs careful thought—and we've barely begun this epic story. The sons of God watched as God laid the foundations of the earth (Job 38:7). We're about to see, as they did long ago, exactly what their Maker was up to.

CHAPTER 5

As in Heaven, So on Earth

THE SAYING "AS IN HEAVEN, SO ON EARTH" IS FAMILIAR TO CHRISTIANS. IT'S part of the Lord's Prayer (Matt 6:9–15). In that prayer, we learn what the saying means: "your kingdom come, your will be done" (6:10). The kingdom of God is the rule of God. God desires to rule over *all* he has created: the invisible spiritual realm and the visible earthly realm. He will have his way in both domains.

In the next three chapters, I'll explain how the ancient biblical writers originally conceived this kingship from the beginning of creation. What we'll discover amounts to the real focus of the Bible—its theological center, if you will. I'd put it this way:

> The story of the Bible is about God's will for, and rule of, the realms he has created, visible and invisible, through the imagers he has created, human and nonhuman. This divine agenda is played out in both realms, in deliberate tandem.

The term *imager* may be unfamiliar. Later in this chapter I'll explain what it means to be one.

The part of the story we know most about is the one we're in—the visible, terrestrial world. Naturally, that's the one that gets the most attention from pastors and theologians. The invisible realm is regularly overlooked, or talked about only in relation to God, Jesus, and the Holy Spirit. The two realms are not mutually exclusive or peripheral to each other; they are integrally connected—by design. That point is telegraphed very early in the biblical story.

CREATOR OR CREATORS?

The "as in heaven, so on Earth" idea is much older than the Lord's prayer. It begins in Genesis. The first chapter of Genesis is easily misinterpreted by one not yet acquainted with God's original family and household, the divine council. Note carefully the emphasis in bold I've placed in Genesis 1:26–28:

[26]And God said, "Let **us** make humankind in **our** image and according to **our** likeness, and let them rule over the fish of the sea, and over the birds of heaven, and over the cattle, and over all the earth, and over every moving thing that moves upon the earth." [27]So God created humankind in **his** image, in the likeness of God **he** created him, male and female **he** created them. [28]And God blessed them, and God said to them, "Be fruitful and multiply, and fill the earth and subdue it, and rule over the fish of the sea and the birds of heaven, and over every animal that moves upon the earth."

Many Bible readers note the *plural* pronouns (*us*; *our*) with curiosity. They might suggest that the plurals refer to the Trinity, but technical research in Hebrew grammar and exegesis has shown that the Trinity is not a coherent explanation.[1] The solution is much more straightforward, one that an ancient Israelite would have readily discerned. What we have is a single person (God) addressing a group—the members of his divine council.

It's like me going into a room of friends and saying, "Hey, let's go get some pizza!" I'm the one speaking. A group is hearing what I say. Similarly, God comes to the divine council with an exciting announcement: "Let's create humankind!"

But if God is speaking to his divine council here, does that suggest that humankind was created by more than one *elohim*? Was the creation of humankind a group project? Not at all. Back to my pizza illustration: If I am the one

---

1. The most exhaustive scholarly treatment of the plural language and the image is W. Randall Garr, *In His Own Image and Likeness: Humanity, Divinity, and Monotheism* (Culture and History of the Ancient Near East 15; Leiden: Brill, 2003). See especially pp. 17–94. Seeing the Trinity in Gen 1:26 is reading the New Testament back into the Old Testament, something that isn't a sound interpretive method for discerning what an Old Testament writer was thinking. Unlike the New Testament, the Old Testament has no Trinitarian phrases (e.g., "Father, Son, and Holy Spirit"; cf. Matt 28:19–20). The triune godhead idea is never transparently expressed in the Old Testament. Since, as we saw in chapter 3, other references to divine plurality involve divine beings who are lesser than Yahweh, we must be careful about attributing the language of divine plurality to the Trinity. Doing so will get us into theological trouble in other passages. As we'll see in chapters 17 and 18, Israelites and first-century Jewish writers *did* discern a *two-person* Godhead in the Old Testament. I believe that the evidence for a two-person Godhead discussed in those chapters can in places reveal a third person in the Old Testament (see the companion website). In chapter 33 we'll see how New Testament writers used the two-person Godhead perspective of the Old Testament to talk about Jesus as God and to articulate the belief that the Spirit was part of the Godhead as well. The answer to the plurality language is also *not* the "plural of majesty." As Joüon-Muraoka notes, "The *we* of majesty does not exist in Hebrew" (Paul Joüon and Takamitsu Muraoka, *A Grammar of Biblical Hebrew* (Rome: Pontificio Istituto Biblico, 2003), 2:375–76 (par. 114.e). The plural of majesty does exist for nouns (see Joüon-Muraoka, par. 136.d), but Gen 1:26 is not about the nouns—the issue is the verbal forms. See also John C. Beckman, "*Pluralis Majestatis*: Biblical Hebrew," *Encyclopedia of Hebrew Language and Linguistics*, vol. 3 (P-Z) (ed. Geoffrey Khan; Leiden: Brill, 2013), 145–46.

paying for the pizza—making the plan happen after announcing it—then I retain both the inspiration and the initiative for the entire project. That's how Genesis 1:26 works.

Genesis 1:27 tells us clearly that only God himself does the creating. In the Hebrew, all the verbs of creation in the passage are singular in form: "So God created humankind in his image, in the likeness of God he created him." The other members of the council do not participate in the creation of humankind. They watch, just as they did when God laid the foundations of the earth (Job 38:7).

You might wonder at this point why the language changes from plural in verse 26 ("Let *us* make humankind in *our* image and according to *our* likeness") to singular in verse 27 ("So God created humankind in *his* image, in the likeness of God he created him"). Does the Bible contradict itself here? No. But understanding the switch requires understanding what the "image" language means.

IMAGE OR IMAGER?

Identifying the nature of the divine image has preoccupied students and pastors for a long time. Chances are you've heard a sermon or two on the topic. I'm willing to bet that what you've heard is that the image of God is similar to something in this list:

- Intelligence
- Reasoning ability
- Emotions
- The ability to commune with God
- Self-awareness (sentience)
- Language/communication ability
- The presence of a soul or spirit (or both)
- The conscience
- Free will

All those things sound like possibilities, but they're not. The image of God means none of those things. If it did, then Bible-believers ought to abandon the idea of the sanctity of human life in the womb. That assertion may jar you, but it's quite evident once you really consider that list in light of how Scripture talks about the image of God.

Genesis teaches us several things about the image of God—what I call "divine image bearing." All of what we learn from the text must be accounted for in any discussion of what the image means.

1. Both men and women are equally included.

2. Divine image bearing is what makes humankind distinct from the rest of *earthly* creation (i.e., plants and animals). The text of Genesis 1:26 does *not* inform us that divine image bearing makes us distinct from heavenly beings, those sons of God who were already in existence at the time of creation. The plurals in Genesis 1:26 mean that, in some way, we share something with them when it comes to bearing God's image.

3. There is something about the image that makes humankind "like" God in some way.

4. There is nothing in the text to suggest that the image has been or can be bestowed incrementally or partially. You're either created as God's image bearer or you aren't. One cannot speak of being *partly* or *potentially* bearing God's image.

Among the list of proposed answers to what image bearing means are a number of *abilities* or *properties*: intelligence, reasoning ability, emotions, communing with God, self-awareness, language/communication ability, and free will. The problem with defining the image by any of these qualities is that, on one hand, nonhuman beings like animals possess *some* of these abilities, although not to the same extent as humans. If one animal anywhere, at any time, learned anything contrary to instinct, or communicated intelligently (to us or within species), or displayed an emotional response (again to us or other creatures), those items must be ruled out as image bearing. We know certain animals have these abilities because of carefully conducted research in the field of animal cognition. Artificial intelligence is on the verge of similar breakthroughs. And if intelligent extraterrestrial life is ever discovered, that would also undermine such definitions.

Defining image bearing as *any* ability is a flawed approach. This brings me back to my pro-life assertion. The pro-life position is based on the proposition that human life (and so, personhood) begins at conception (the point when the female egg is fertilized by the male sperm). The simple-celled zygote inside the woman's womb, which pro-lifers believe to be a human person, is not self-aware; it has no intelligence, rational thought processes, or emotions; it cannot speak or communicate; it cannot commune with God or pray; and it cannot exercise its will or respond to the conscience. If you want to argue that those things are there *potentially*, then that means that you have only a potential person. That's actually the pro-choice position. *Potential* personhood is not *actual* personhood. This thought process would mean that abortion is not killing until personhood is achieved, which nearly all pro-choicers would certainly consider to be after birth.

Even the soul idea fails the uniqueness and actuality tests. This notion derives from the traditional rendering of Genesis 2:7 in the King James Version ("and the man became a living *soul*"). The Hebrew word translated "soul" is *nephesh*. According to the Bible, animals also possess the *nephesh*. For example, in Genesis 1:20, when we read that God made swarms of "living creatures," the Hebrew text underlying "creatures" is *nephesh*. Genesis 1:30 tells us the "living *nephesh*" is in animals.

The term *nephesh* in these passages means *conscious life* or *animate life* (as opposed to something like plant life). Humans share a basic consciousness with certain animals, though the nature of that consciousness varies widely.

We also cannot appeal to a *spirit* being the meaning of image bearing. The word *nephesh* we just considered is used interchangeably with the Hebrew word for spirit (*ruach*). Examples include 1 Samuel 1:15 and Job 7:11. Both terms speak of an inner life where thinking, reason, and emotions occur, along with their use in activities like prayer and decision making. The point is that the Old Testament does not distinguish between soul and spirit.[2] All these qualities associated with spirit require cognitive function, and so cannot be relevant until after brain formation (and use) in the fetus.

So how do we understand divine image bearing in a way that does not stumble over these issues and yet aligns with the description in Genesis? Hebrew grammar is the key. The turning point is the meaning of the preposition *in* with respect to the phrase "*in* the image of God." In English we use the preposition *in* to denote many different ideas. That is, *in* doesn't always mean the same thing when we use that word. For example, if I say, "put the dishes *in* the sink," I am using the preposition to denote *location*. If I say, "I broke the mirror *in* pieces," I am using *in* to denote the *result* of some action. If I say, "I work *in* education," I am using the preposition to denote that I work *as* a teacher or principal, or in some other educational capacity.

This last example directs us to what the Hebrew preposition translated *in* means in Genesis 1:26. Humankind was created *as* God's image. If we think of imaging as a verb or function, that translation makes sense. We are created to image God, to be his imagers. It is what we are by definition. The image is

---

2. Only one passage in the New Testament suggests a differentiation between body, soul, and spirit: 1 Thess 5:23. Since the Old Testament clearly sees two parts to humans (body and soul/spirit; material and immaterial), it is best to interpret this single verse the same way for theological consistency. Many scholars do not consider soul and spirit in this verse as discrete, separate items. This verse is similar to the *shema* (Deut 6:4; cf. Matt 22:37; Mark 12:29–30), which tells us to love God with all our heart, soul, and might. The point is *totality*, not that heart, soul, might (and mind in the gospel references) are separable. The Old Testament uses both *nephesh* and *ruach* to describe the source of these inner parts. Totality is also the point of Heb 4:12 (which actually uses four items, not three).

not an ability we have, but a status. We are God's representatives on earth. To *be* human is to image God.

This is why Genesis 1:26–27 is followed by what theologians call the "dominion mandate" in verse 28. The verse informs us that God intends us to be him on this planet. We are to create more imagers ("be fruitful and multiply ... fill") in order to oversee the earth by stewarding its resources and harnessing them for the benefit of all human imagers ("subdue ... rule over").

GOD'S TWO FAMILY-HOUSEHOLD-COUNCILS

Understanding that we are God's imagers on earth helps to parse the plurals in Genesis 1:26 and the change to singular language in the next verse. God alone created humankind to function as his administrators on earth. But he has also created the other *elohim* of the unseen realm. They are also like him. They carry out his will in that realm, acting as his representatives. They are his heavenly council in the unseen world. We are God's council and administration in this realm. Consequently, the plurals inform us that both God's families—the human and the nonhuman—share imaging status, though the realms are different. As in heaven, so on Earth.

This biblical theology sets the table for understanding other passages and concepts in both testaments. The logic of idolatry we talked about earlier takes on new irony. Humans after the fall will resort to making objects of wood and stone that they must ceremonially animate to draw the deity into the artifact. But from the beginning, God created his own imagers—humankind, male and female. His desire was to live among them, and for them to rule and reign with him.

After the fall that plan was not altered. Eventually, God would decide to tabernacle *within* humans, through his Spirit. Language describing believers as sons or children of God (John 1:12; 1 John 3:1–3), or as "adopted" into God's family (Gal 4:5; Eph 1:5) is neither accidental nor pragmatic. *It reflects the original vision of Genesis.* And once we are glorified, the two council-families will be one—in a new Eden. We'll discover more about all those themes as we proceed.

This is what Eden was about ... as in heaven, so on Earth. The original intent becomes even clearer once we understand the ancient conception of Eden.

CHAPTER 6

Gardens and Mountains

WE'VE LEARNED THAT THE OLD TESTAMENT DESCRIBES TWO HOUSE-hold-families of God, one human and the other nonhuman. Those two families were created as God's representatives to serve him in different realms. In this chapter we'll explore how descriptions of Eden reinforce these concepts.

We usually think of Eden as it's described in Genesis 2:8, the place the first humans called home: "Yahweh God planted a garden in Eden in the east, and there he put the man whom he had formed." But the description of Eden as the home of humankind deflects our attention away from Eden's primary status.

Eden was *God's* home on earth. It was his residence. And where the King lives, his council meets. As modern readers, we don't see how that thinking is telegraphed in the biblical text. Ancient readers couldn't miss it.

THE ANCIENT CONTEXT

Eden can only be properly understood in light of the worldview the biblical writers shared with other people of the ancient Near East. Like Israel, the people of ancient Egypt and Mesopotamia, for example, also believed in an unseen spiritual world that was governed by a divine council. The divine abodes of gods—the places they lived and where they met for governing the affairs of the human world—were portrayed in several ways. Two of the most common were gardens and mountains. Eden is described as both in the Old Testament.

Ancient people thought of their gods living in luxuriant gardens or mountains for simple reasons. It made sense that the gods would have the best lifestyle because, well, they're *gods*. Cosmic celebrities can't possibly live like we do.

The ancient Near East was primarily an agrarian culture where most people subsisted day-to-day, hand-to-mouth. The few who didn't live that way were kings or priests—and thinking as the ancients did, those few had been chosen for that elevated status by the gods. The environment was hot and arid. Life depended on finding water and harnessing its power. That's why the world's first civilizations were founded along rivers (e.g., the Nile, the Tigris, and the Euphrates). Surely the gods lived in a place where water was abundant, where life-sustaining vegetation and fruit grew everywhere, where an abundance of animals were nourished to fatness. The gods lived in places where there was no conceivable lack. Paradise.

Mountain peaks were the domain of gods because no humans lived there. Ancient times were not like modern times. People didn't recreationally climb mountains. They had no equipment with which to get very far if they tried. Mountains were remote and forbidding—the perfect places for gods to get away from pesky humans. Mountain peaks touched the heavens, which was obviously the domain of the gods.

This sort of thinking in part explains why Egypt's temples are carved and painted with the imagery of luscious gardens, or why pyramids and ziggurats were built. These structures were mountains made by human hands which served as gateways to the spiritual world, the realm of the gods, in life or in death. They were metaphors in stone.

ANCIENT UGARIT

For our purposes, though, it is the less grandiose ancient civilization of Ugarit, a city-state in ancient Syria, just to the north of Israel, which is particularly relevant.[1]

The site of Ugarit was discovered in 1928 and excavated in the decades that followed. One of the major finds was a library containing thousands of clay tablets, roughly 1400 of which were in an alphabetic language (now called Ugaritic) that was closer to biblical Hebrew than any other ancient language. The vocabulary and grammar are in many instances virtually identical.

Scholars have learned a lot from this library, about both Ugarit and the content of the Old Testament. The chief deity of Ugarit was El—one of the

---

1. The best scholarly resources on the garden and mountain imagery at Ugarit and the Old Testament are Richard J. Clifford, *The Cosmic Mountain in Canaan and the Old Testament*, Harvard Semitic Monographs 4 (Cambridge: Harvard University Press, 1972; repr., Eugene, OR: Wipf & Stock, 2010); L. Michael Morales, *The Tabernacle Pre-Figured: Cosmic Mountain Ideology in Genesis and Exodus* (Biblical Tools and Studies 15; Leuven: Peeters, 2012); Daniel T. Lioy, "The Garden of Eden as a Primordial Temple or Sacred Space for Humankind," *Conspectus: The Journal of the South African Theological Seminary* 10 (2010): 25–57; Gordon Wenham, "Sanctuary Symbolism in the Garden of Eden Story," in *Cult and Cosmos: Tilting toward a Temple-Centered Biblical Theology* (ed. L. Michael Morales; Biblical Tools and Studies 18; Leuven: Peeters, 2014), 161–66.

names that appear in the Old Testament for the God of Israel. El had a divine council whose members were "the sons of El," and he had a coruler, Baal. Since El's and Baal's duties sometimes appeared to overlap, and since Ugarit was so geographically close to Israel, it was small wonder that Baal worship was such a problem in Israel. The discoveries at Ugarit put all of that Old Testament history in context.

El and Baal were, to say the least, markedly different in behavior from Yahweh of Israel. But the literature of Ugarit proved very illuminating in other respects, especially as to where El, Baal, and the Ugaritic divine council lived and held court. At Ugarit the divine council had three levels: the highest authority (El, who did most of his ruling through a coruling vizier, Baal), the "sons of El," and messenger gods (*mal'akim*).

The council of El met on a mountain or lush garden. These were not different places. Rather, the same place was described in two different ways. The abode of El had an abundant water supply, as it was situated at the "source of the two rivers" in the "midst of the fountains of the double-deep." The divine council met in a place called *Tsapanu*, the remote heights of the north (*tsapanu* means "north").

Council meetings were held in "the tents of El" or El's "tent shrine," whence divine decrees were issued. At times Baal's palace was in view, with its "paved bricks" that gave his house "the clearness of lapis lazuli."

YAHWEH'S ABODE

All of this will sound familiar to someone who has read the Old Testament closely. The Hebrew Bible uses these same descriptions for the abode and throne room of Yahweh. And where Yahweh is, he is surrounded by his heavenly assembly, ready to conduct business (cf. Isa 6; 1 Kgs 22:13–28). The Old Testament has a three-tiered council structure like that at Ugarit. Yahweh is at the top.[2] His family-household ("sons of God") are next in hierarchy. The lowest level is reserved for *elohim* messengers—*mal'akim* (the word translated "angels").

The Tabernacle tent structure and the Tent of Meeting, both of which are mentioned throughout the books of Exodus through Judges, are clear parallels to places where God dwells and hands down his decrees. Yahweh could also be found on mountains (Sinai or Zion). In Psalm 48:1–2, Jerusalem, the city of

---

2. We will see in later chapters that Yahweh too has a coregent or vizier, just as the council at Ugarit. But that figure is not another created *elohim*—it is Yahweh himself in a second personage. This is the backdrop to the idea of a Godhead that Christians often only associate with the New Testament.

God, is said to be located in the "heights of the north" (*tsaphon* in Hebrew).[3] Mount Zion is the "mountain of assembly," again located in the "heights of the north" (Isa 14:13). At Sinai, Moses and others saw the seated God of Israel, under whose feet was a pavement "like sapphire tile work and like the very heavens for clearness" (Exod 24:9–10).

The garden of Eden, of course, is a lush, well-watered habitation (Gen 2:5– 14). Ezekiel 28:13 mentions the garden of Eden ("garden of God"), but then adds the description that the garden of God is "God's holy mountain" (Ezek 28:14).[4] We naturally think of God's mountain as Mount Sinai or Mount Zion. When it comes to garden imagery, the latter is spoken of in Edenic terms. Like Eden, Mount Zion is also described as a watery habitation (Isa 33:20–22; Ezek 47:1–12; Zech 14:8; Joel 3:18). Whether Sinai or Zion, the mountain of God is, in effect, his temple.[5]

IMPLICATIONS

An ancient Israelite would have thought of Eden as the dwelling of God and the place from which God and his council direct the affairs of humanity. The imagery is completely consistent with how Israel's neighbors thought about their gods.[6] But in biblical theology, there is additional messaging.

As we'll see in the ensuing chapters, *the biblical version of the divine council at the divine abode includes a human presence.* The theological message is that the God of Israel created this place not just as his own domain, but because he desires to live among his people. Yahweh desires a kingdom rule on this new Earth that he has created, and that rule will be shared with humanity. Since the heavenly council is also where Yahweh is, both family-households should

---

3. "Heights of the north" is my own translation, deliberately more literal than phrases like "far north" in many English translations. The phrase points to the mountainous regions to the north of Canaan, well-known in Canaanite religion as Zaphon, the mountain dwelling of the Canaanite (Ugaritic) divine council. See "Zaphon," in *Dictionary of Deities and Demons in the Bible*, 2nd ed. (ed. Karel van der Toorn, Bob Becking, and Pieter W. van der Horst; Leiden; Boston; Cologne; Grand Rapids, MI; Cambridge: Brill; Eerdmans, 1999), 927.

4. That Ezekiel's "garden of God" and "holy mountain of God" are to be identified with each other as the same divine abode is presumed by all interpreters I know of for a straightforward reason. God is addressing a single divine resident ("you") concerning his living space throughout. There is no way to grammatically justify the notion God is speaking to different individuals in Ezek 28, and so the range of descriptions for that figure's dwelling speaks of one location.

5. See Ronald E. Clements, "Sacred Mountains, Temples, and the Presence of God," in Morales, *Cult and Cosmos*, 69–85; Richard J. Clifford, "The Temple and the Holy Mountain," in ibid., 85–98.

6. Eden and its environs have received a good deal of attention in scholarship. Noteworthy studies include Geo Widengren, *The King and the Tree of Life in Ancient Near Eastern Religion* (King and Saviour 4; Wiesbaden: Otto Harrassowitz, 1951); Tryggve N. D. Mettinger, *The Eden Narrative: A Literary and Religio-Historical Study of Genesis 2–3* (American Oriental Society; Winona Lake, Ind.: Eisenbrauns, 2007).

function together. Had the fall not occurred, humanity would have been glorified and made part of the council.

This is not speculation. In the last chapter we saw the beginning of the theological idea that humans are the children of God. It was God's original intent to make them part of his family. The failure in Eden would alienate God from man, but God would make a way of salvation to bring believers back into that family (John 1:12; 1 John 3:1–3). We also saw that humanity's presence showed that God's original desire was for his human children to participate in his rule. Both of these theological threads wind through the Old Testament and create the context from which New Testament writers will talk about the kingdom and the glorification of believers. These are ideas we'll return to in future chapters.

One more verse about Eden—one that will vault us into the next chapter: Eden is described in Ezekiel 28:2 as the "seat of the gods." The phrase should be familiar to modern readers. It speaks of governing authority ("county seat"; "Congressional seat"). Ezekiel's words draw attention to Eden as a seat of authority and action. There was work to be done. God had plans for the whole planet, not just Eden.

CHAPTER 7

Eden—
Like No Place on Earth

GOD DOES NOT ACT WITHOUT PURPOSE. HE CREATED THE HEAVENLY HOST, intending that they carry out his will. Did he create them to meet some need in him? No. A complete, perfect being has no deficiencies. God has no need of a council, but he uses one. Similarly, God did not need humans to steward his creation or, later on, to reveal that Messiah had come. But those were his choices as well. God delighted in creating proxies to represent him and carry out his wishes. His decisions in that regard have ramifications.

EARTH WAS NOT EDEN

The first observation is one that is transparent from the biblical text, but somehow missed by many: *Not all the world was Eden*. It's important to establish that Eden was, rather than the entire earthly creation, only a tiny part of it. This distinction will become important in future chapters. The text tells us this in several ways.

Eden was actually a tiny plot on Earth. Its location is circumscribed by geographical markers (Gen 2:8–14). In the last chapter we saw that the Ugaritic council met in a garden where two rivers intersected ("in the midst of the fountains of the double deep"). Eden is described with four water sources:

> [10] Now a river flowed out from Eden that watered the garden, and from there it diverged and became four branches. [11] The name of the first is the Pishon. It went around all the land of Havilah, where there is gold. [12] (The gold of that land is good; bdellium and onyx stones are there.) [13] And the name of the second is the Gihon. It went around all the land of Cush. [14] And the name of the third is Tigris. It flows east of Assyria. And the fourth river is the Euphrates (Gen 2:10–14).

This description alone tells us quite clearly the earth was not Eden. There are other indicators.

In Genesis 1:26–27 God made humankind as his imagers, his representatives in this new domain. This functional view of the image becomes clear in the commands of verse 28:

> And God blessed them, and God said to them, "Be fruitful and multiply, and fill the earth and subdue it, and rule over the fish of the sea and the birds of heaven, and over every animal that moves upon the earth."

Notice that verse 28 says that the *earth* needed filling. This does not refer to Eden. Eden has not even appeared yet in the Genesis story. Its first mention comes in Genesis 2:8:

> And Yahweh God planted a garden in Eden in the east, and there he put the man whom he had formed.

The garden of Eden is said to be *in the east*. The directional word informs us that there were other parts of the earth. God "planted" this garden. We know from Genesis 1 that the dry land (called "earth") already existed. It had to in order for God to plant a garden in it to the east.

Genesis 2:15 is also of interest. The man God has made is put in the garden for a reason: "And Yahweh God took the man and set him in the garden of Eden to cultivate it and to keep it." The man's job is to take care of the garden. Earlier in Genesis 1:28, his job was to "be fruitful and multiply, and fill the earth and subdue it, and rule…." Of course the man needs a woman for that, but she hasn't even been created yet in Genesis 2 when God puts the man in the garden. Cultivation of the garden and subduing the earth are not the same tasks.

Genesis 1 and 2 aren't intended to be chronological in their relationship. What they reveal is that the man's original task was to care for the garden, where he lived (Gen 2). After he gets a partner (Gen 1), God says to both of them (the commands are plural in Hebrew) to be fruitful, multiply, fill the earth, subdue it, and rule over its creatures.

We can see that the tasks of humanity, taken in tandem with the earlier observations that require Eden and Earth to be distinct, distinguish Eden and the earth. It makes no sense to subdue the garden of God. It's already what God wants it to be. There's no place on Earth like it. If it needed subjugation, that would imply imperfection. That's something that cannot be said about Eden, but it's true of the rest of the world. For sure God was happy with the whole creation. He pronounced it "very good" (Gen 1:31). But "very good" is not perfect.[1]

Lastly, Eden and Earth must be distinct since, after the fall, Adam and Eve are expelled from it and have to live elsewhere. Unless you believe that they were sent into outer space, you must acknowledge Eden and Earth as distinct.

Observing this distinction affects a range of biblical concepts and provides solutions to a few thorny theological problems. But I'm only concerned with one issue here. The distinction helps us see that *the original task of humanity was to make the entire Earth like Eden.*

Adam and Eve lived in the garden. They cared for it. But the rest of the earth needed subduing. It wasn't awful—in fact Genesis 1 tells us that it was habitable. But it wasn't quite what Eden was. The *whole world* needs to be like God's home. He could do the job himself, but he chose to create human imagers to do it for him. He issued the decree; they were supposed to make it happen. They were to do that by multiplying and following God's direction.

Eden is where the idea of the kingdom of God begins. And it's no coincidence that the Bible ends with the vision of a new Edenic Earth (Rev 21–22).

PROCLAMATION AND PARTNERSHIP

The working relationship between God and humankind, before and after the fall, involves genuine, meaningful participation on the part of God's human

---

1. In context, describing the creation as "very good" means that the creation was fit for human habitation and the perpetuation and survival of Earth's creatures. Had the biblical writer wanted to convey a situation of perfection—where nothing was lacking or in need of any improvement—he would have chosen a word other than *ṭob* ("good"). Hebrew words such as *tōm* convey completeness (see *The Hebrew and Aramaic Lexicon of the Old Testament* [Leiden; New York: Brill, 1999], 1743). The idea that the pronouncement of Gen 1:31 ("And God saw everything that he had made and, behold, *it was* very good") means that earth was created in a state of perfection is a common one, found very early on in the early church fathers. There are a number of problems with this assumption, of which I only mention a handful here. The claim here is not that creation failed to conform to God's will. Indeed, the creation was precisely what God wanted at the time. Rather, creation was not all that Eden was, a contrast that God intended and which informs the biblical-theological story. For a full treatment of this issue, see Hulisani Ramantswana, "God Saw That It Was Good, Not Perfect: A Canonical-Dialogic Reading of Genesis 1–3" (PhD diss., Westminster Theological Seminary, 2010). A dissertation by Eric M. Vail also offers some insights: "Using 'Chaos' in Articulating the Relationship of God and Creation in God's Creative Activity" (PhD diss., Marquette University, 2009). The concepts of chaos and disorder and the presentation of Genesis cosmology as bringing order, both in terms of human habitation and divine temple-building for Yahweh's rest and habitation, are subjects I have elected to reserve for a second volume. These subjects are accessible in the meantime in many works. See for example, William P. Brown, *The Seven Pillars of Creation: The Bible, Science, and the Ecology of Wonder* (Oxford: Oxford University Press, 2010), esp. chapter 3, "The Cosmic Temple: Cosmogony according to Genesis 1:1–2:3"; John H. Walton, *The Lost World of Genesis One: Ancient Cosmology and the Origins Debate* (Downers Grove, IL: InterVarsity Press, 2009); Moshe Weinfeld, "Sabbath, Temple and the Enthronement of the Lord," *Mélanges bibliques et orientaux en l'honneur de M. Henri Cazelles* (ed. A. Caquot, and M. Delcor; Alter Orient und Altes Testament 212; Kevelaer and Neukirchen-Vluyn, 1981), 501–12.

imagers. This is most transparently seen as God works through figures like Moses, Joshua, David, Solomon, the prophets, and the apostles. But the pattern extends to us, to all believers. There is nothing we do that God could not accomplish himself. But he has not chosen that method. Rather, he tells us what his will is and commands his loyal children to get the job done.

We saw in an earlier chapter that imaging status is something shared by human and nonhuman, divine beings. This fact is reflected in the plural language of Genesis 1:26, when God said, "Let us make humankind." The ensuing singular forms guided us to conclude that the passage has humankind created by a single creator, the God of Israel, who creates humans as his imagers. The prior plural language was a clue that God's other family, the divine sons of God created sometime earlier, were also imagers of their creator.

Given this connection and backdrop, the participatory nature of the working relationship between God and his human imagers is no surprise. The heavenly council works under the same kind of arrangement. God decrees his will and leaves it to his administrative household to carry out those decrees. That's apparent from two Old Testament passages.

First Kings 22 provides a revealing glimpse into a divine council meeting. The first fifteen verses set the context. After three years of peace between Syria and Israel, King Jehoshaphat of Judah, the southern Israelite kingdom, paid a visit to Ahab, the king of Israel, the northern kingdom that had broken away from the tribes loyal to David's dynasty. The northern kings were described throughout the Old Testament as spiritually apostate. Ahab was arguably the worst of the bunch.

Ahab wanted Jehoshaphat to join forces with him in a plan to break the peace by attacking Ramoth-Gilead, which was under Syrian control. Ramoth-Gilead was part of the original tribal land of Gad and a Levitical city of refuge (Josh 20:8; 21:38; 1 Chr 6:80; Deut 4:43). It didn't legitimately belong to the Syrians. That was Ahab's leverage.

Jehoshaphat agreed with this reasoning, but wanted to know whether Yahweh approved. The apostate king of Israel summoned about four hundred of his prophets, who told the kings they would win the battle. Suspicious, Jehoshaphat asked if there were any other prophets around to consult. Yes, there is one, Ahab answered—and made no secret of his hatred of that prophet. Micaiah, the prophet of Yahweh, always told Ahab things he didn't want to hear—like the truth.

Micaiah was summoned and asked whether the kings should go to war. At first he mocked Ahab, pretending to be like the other prophets, but Ahab wasn't stupid. Here's what happened next:

¹⁶Then the king [Ahab] said to him, "How many times must I make you swear that you shall not tell me anything but truth in the name of Yahweh?" ¹⁷So he [Micaiah] said, "I saw all of Israel scattering to the mountains, like sheep without a shepherd. Yahweh also said, 'There are no masters for these, let them return in peace, each to his house.'" ¹⁸Then the king of Israel said to Jehoshaphat, "Did I not say to you that he would not prophesy good concerning me, but disaster?"

¹⁹And he [Micaiah] said, "Therefore, hear the word of Yahweh. I saw Yahweh sitting on his throne with all the hosts of heaven standing beside him from his right hand and from his left hand. ²⁰And Yahweh said, 'Who will entice Ahab so that he will go up and fall at Ramoth-Gilead?' Then this one was saying one thing and the other one was saying another. ²¹Then a spirit came out and stood before Yahweh and said, 'I will entice him,' and Yahweh said to him, 'How?' ²²He said, 'I will go out and I will be a false spirit in the mouth of all his prophets.' And he said, 'You shall entice and succeed, go out and do so.' ²³So then, see that Yahweh has placed a false spirit in the mouth of all of these your prophets, and Yahweh has spoken disaster concerning you" (1 Kgs 22:16–23).

This passage, specifically verses 19–22, describes a meeting between God and his divine council. Verse 20 tells us plainly that God had decided it was time for Ahab to die. God then asked the host of heaven standing in attendance *how Ahab's death should be accomplished*. God had decreed Ahab was going to die at Ramoth-Gilead, but the means of his death was not decreed. The council debated the matter until one of the spiritual beings came forward with a proposition (vv. 21–22): "I will go out and I will be a false spirit in the mouth of all his prophets." Upon hearing this, God said (paraphrasing), "Good. I know that will work—go get it done."

There are other glimpses of this kind of divine decision making, where God's decree and genuine participation on the part of his council are both evident.

In Daniel 4 Nebuchadnezzar relates a dream wherein he saw an enormous tree that reached into the heavens. Nebuchadnezzar tells Daniel that in the dream he saw a watcher—a term for a divine being (a "holy one") in this chapter of Daniel (Dan 4:13, 17, 23). The watcher proclaims that the tree will be chopped down, leaving only its stump. The tree and the stump are symbols for Nebuchadnezzar, who, the watcher announces, will lose his mind and become like an animal (Dan 4:13–16).

In verse 17 readers discover who decreed this fate for Nebuchadnezzar:

The sentence is by the decree of the watchers,
  and the decision by the command of the holy ones,

in order that the living will know
    that the Most High is sovereign over the kingdom of humankind,
and to whomever he wills he gives it (Dan 4:17).

What's fascinating here is that the source of the decree is said to be the watchers, but sovereignty belongs to the singular Most High. Later, when Daniel interprets the dream, he says:

This is the explanation, O king, and it *is* a decree of the Most High that has come upon my lord the king (Dan 4:24).

Here we see that the ultimate authority behind the decree is God, the Most High, and yet the watcher who delivered the decree in verse 17 said "the sentence is by decree of the watchers." Both God and his divine agents were involved in the decision.

Daniel adds a few details as he continues. Note the emphasis in bold carefully:

²⁵you [Nebuchadnezzar] will be driven away from human society and you will dwell with the animals of the field, and you will be caused to graze grass like the oxen yourself, and you will be watered with the dew of heaven, and seven periods of time will pass over you until that you have acknowledged that **the Most High is sovereign** over the kingdom of humankind, and to whom he wills he gives it. ²⁶And in that they said to leave alone the stump of the tree's root, so your kingdom will be restored for you when you acknowledge that **heaven is sovereign** (Dan 4:25–26).

Verse 25 says very plainly that the Most High is sovereign. It is clearly singular. The phrase "heaven is sovereign" is interesting because the Aramaic word translated heaven (*shemayin*) is plural and is accompanied by a plural verb. The plurality of *shemayin* can point to either the members of the council or the council as a collective. In any event, the wording is suggestive of the interchange between council and Most High earlier in Daniel 4.

The takeaway is that God rules over the heavenly realm and the earthly realm with the genuine assistance of his imager-representatives. He decrees and they carry out his commands. These points are clear. What is perhaps less clear is that the way God's will is carried out and accomplished is open—imagers can make free decisions to accomplish God's will. God decrees the ends, but the means can be (and apparently are at times) left up to the imagers.

This balance of sovereignty and free will is essential for understanding what happened in Eden. The choices made by human and nonhuman beings described in Genesis 3 were neither coerced nor needed by Yahweh for sake of his greater plan. The risk of creating image bearers who might freely choose rebellion was something God foresaw but did not decree. We'll examine all that in more detail in the next chapter.

CHAPTER 8

Only God Is Perfect

LIKE THE CREATION STORY, THE STORY OF THE FALL IN GENESIS 3 IS ONE OF those episodes in Scripture that anyone acquainted with the Bible seems to know. But there's more to the story than meets the eye. Over the next few chapters I'll draw attention to some often-overlooked details in the story and the questions they raise.

What we've covered in earlier chapters serves as crucial backdrop for understanding the fall. Eden was both the divine abode and the nerve center for God's plan for Earth. The worldview of the biblical writer was: Where Yahweh is, so is his council.

Yahweh had announced his intention to create humankind as his imagers (Gen 1:26). The council members heard that these humans, new members in Yahweh's family, would be tasked with overspreading the earth, advancing God's kingdom rule. They were Yahweh's choice to be steward-kings over a global Eden under his authority.

We'll soon see that one divine being dissented. But how could there be trouble in paradise? *How could things have gone so wrong?*

The book of Job contains some of the clues.

THE BACKDROP

Job is an odd book. That's part of what makes it so interesting. The story opens with a divine council scene—the sons of God appear before Yahweh (Job 1:6). During the council meeting the *satan* shows up. His rank is not clear. The language is ambiguous with respect to whether he is of the same level as the sons of God or is on the scene as a servant official to the council. The lower status is more likely, given what we learn about his job.

I use the phrase "the *satan*" deliberately. The Hebrew (*satan*) means something like "adversary," "prosecutor," or "challenger." It speaks of an official legal function within a ruling body—in this case, Yahweh's council. When Yahweh asks the *satan* where he has been, we learn that his job involves investigating what is happening on earth (Job 1:7). He is, so to speak, Yahweh's eyes and ears on the ground, reporting what he has seen and heard.

The *satan* in Job 1–2 is not a villain. He's doing the job assigned to him by God. The book of Job does not identify the *satan* in this scene as the serpent of Genesis 3, the figure known in the New Testament as the devil. The Old Testament never uses the word *satan* of the serpent figure from Genesis 3. In fact, the word *satan* is not a proper personal noun in the Old Testament.[1]

Old Testament scholars are well aware of all this. Their conclusion that *satan* is not a proper personal name in the Old Testament is driven by Hebrew grammar. Like English, Hebrew does not attach the definite article (the word "the") to proper personal nouns. English speakers do not refer to themselves (or to another person) with phrases like "the Tom" or "the Sally." I'm not "the Mike." English doesn't use the definite article with personal names. Neither does Hebrew.

Most of the twenty-seven occurrences of *satan* in the Hebrew Bible, however, do indeed have the definite article—including all the places English readers presume the devil is present (Job 1:6–9, 12; 2:1–4, 6–7; Zech 3:1–2). The *satan* described in these passages is not the devil. Rather, he's an anonymous prosecutor, as it were, fulfilling a role in Yahweh's council—bringing an accusatory report. The instances of *satan* in the Old Testament that lack the definite article also don't refer to the devil or the serpent figure. Those occurrences describe either humans or the Angel of Yahweh, who is occasionally sent by God to "oppose" someone or execute judgment (e.g., Num 22:22–23).

The *function* of the office of the *satan* is why later Jewish writings began to adopt it as a proper name for the serpent figure from Genesis 3 who brought ruin to Eden. That figure opposed God's choices for his human imagers. The dark figure of Genesis 3 was eventually thought of as the "mother of all adversaries," and so the label *satan* got stuck to him. He deserves it. The point here is only that the Old Testament doesn't use that term for the divine criminal of Eden.

In Job 1 the *satan* and God converse about Job. The *satan* gets a bit uppity, challenging God about Job's integrity. We know the rest of the story—God gives the *satan* enough latitude to prove himself wrong, albeit at Job's expense.

---

1. See Peggy Day, *An Adversary in Heaven: śāṭān in the Hebrew Bible* (Harvard Semitic Monographs 43; Atlanta: Scholars Press, 1988); John H. Walton, "Satan," *Dictionary of the Old Testament: Wisdom, Poetry, and Writings* (Downers Grove, IL: InterVarsity Press, 2008): 714–17.

The beginning of Job is of interest to us because of two statements later in the book. In Job 4, one of Job's friends, Eliphaz, responds to Job's lament and wish for death (Job 3:11). He's not much of a comfort. He questions Job's belief that he has done nothing deserving of suffering (Job 4:6), something the reader knows is actually true (Job 1:8). Eliphaz says at one point:

> ¹⁷ Can a human being be more righteous than God,
>   or can a man be more pure than his Maker?
> ¹⁸ Look, he does not trust in his servants
>   and he charges his angels with error.
> ¹⁹ How much more dwellers in clay houses,
>   whose foundation is in the dust?
>   They are crushed like a moth (Job 4:17–19).

Who do you think you are, Job! A man isn't more righteous than his Maker! Why would God consider you blameless when he doesn't even look at his heavenly messengers that way? Eliphaz repeats the thought in Job 15:14–15:

> ¹⁴ What is a human being, that he can be clean,
>   Or that one born of a woman can be righteous?
> ¹⁵ Look, he does not trust his holy ones,
>   and the heavens are not clean in his eyes.

What Eliphaz says is significant. Here are two scriptural statements that *God's heavenly council members are corruptible; they are not perfect.*

That's not terribly profound on the surface. The only truly perfect Being is God himself. God never actually said that Job was incorruptible and perfect, only that he was blameless at the time of the council meeting. God knows that Job could indeed fail—just like the divine beings in his council. Even the lesser *elohim* cannot be completely trusted.

FREE IMAGERS

God knows that none of his imagers, divine or human, can be completely trusted. The reason is straightforward. Though imagers are like God, they aren't God. That's a truth we know all too well from our own struggles and experiences in a fallen world.

Without genuine free will, imagers cannot truly represent God. We saw earlier that the image of God is not an attribute or ability. Rather, it is a status conferred by God on all humans, that of representing God. God created humankind to extend Eden over all the earth. That's what the commands of

Genesis 1:28, collectively referred to by theologians as the dominion mandate, are about. Humanity was to multiply, steward the creation, and govern on God's behalf. The goal was to care for the earth and harness its gifts for the betterment of fellow human imagers, all the while enjoying the presence of God.

How all that happens in our postfall world varies from person to person. In our experience, humans have widely differing abilities. Some never see birth due to natural death or abortion. Others manifest in their bodies the effects of a world that isn't Eden. Some human beings have severe mental and physical defects that impede or prevent representing God according to the original vision. And even if we're blessed with what we consider normal health, we're all subject to disease, injury, aging, and the weakness of a world subject to corruption. But imaging is bound to our humanity. Regardless of ability or stage, human life is sacred precisely because we are the creatures God put on earth to represent him.

Humans who survive birth without suffering severe impairment, however, are able to represent God as originally intended. They do so by means of a spectrum of abilities we have as humans. These abilities are part of our being like God. They are attributes we share with God, such as intelligence and creativity. The attributes God shared with us are the *means* to imaging, not the image status itself. Imaging status and our attributes are related but not identical concepts.

One of these attributes is freedom—free will that reveals itself in decision making. If humanity had not been created with genuine freedom, representation of God would have been impossible. Humans would not mirror their Maker. They could not accurately *image* him. God is no robot. We are reflections of a free Being, not a cosmic automaton.

Put another way, God did not intend to create imagers that did nothing. True, even if an imager accomplished nothing (say, an aborted human fetus), they would still be an imager. But God's original intent was to arm his imagers with both the will and the ability to carry out his decrees. Representation of God as his imagers and possession of free will are inextricably related.

Since the lesser *elohim* were also created as God's imagers, they too must have free will. Both human and nonhuman imagers are less than their Maker. Only God is perfect in the possession and exercise of his attributes. Every lesser being is imperfect. The only perfect Being is God. *This* is why things could, and did, go wrong in Eden.

If that was true even in Eden—the place on earth where the council was present—then *being in the presence of God is no guarantee that free-will beings will never stray or act out of self-will.* Only God is perfect. Beings that are lesser than God, whether human or divine, are not perfect. The potential for error and disobedience is by definition possible.[2] Trouble *could* happen in paradise, and of course it did. God's decision to create free imagers involved that risk.

You might think that all the risk was ours—after all, the world of humanity has suffered in its wake. But the only way in which there was no risk involved for God is if you define risk as the threat of harm. God cannot be harmed. But he can be grieved. He is moved by human sin and suffering (Gen 6:6; Isa 54:6–7). God was willing to risk that to have humanity.

What we've learned leaves us with important questions. Even though free will is necessitated by imaging and representation, is *risk* the right word to use of God's decision? If God foreknew all the things that would happen as a result of his decision, didn't he also predestine those things? But if he did, how can we even talk about free will? How are Adam and Eve truly responsible? What about the notion that they would "know good and evil" (Gen 3:5) and be like God—does that mean God has an evil streak in him?

These questions have long been debated. It may therefore surprise you when I say they all have straightforward answers. What we've seen in this and earlier chapters about Eden, God, and his divine council prepares us for the answers. God does not delight in evil and suffering. Nor does he need it for his sovereign plan. The conundrums evaporate if we just allow the text to say what it says. We need to lay our theological systems aside, answer these questions like an ancient Israelite would have, and embrace the results.

---

2. The kingdom of God and its residents (believers) will be restored and glorified after the final judgment. In the last chapter of this book we'll discuss how the new Eden and its occupants are the same and yet superior to the original Edenic situation.

CHAPTER 9

Peril and Providence

We closed the last chapter with a series of questions. How is it appropriate to talk about God's decisions involving risk? If God knew what was going to happen—and if he predestines the events—where's the risk? Perhaps Adam and Eve needed to be taught a lesson about good and evil. Surely God didn't learn anything. But how do we get God off the moral hook when it comes to the appearance of sin and evil?

An ancient Israelite would have thought differently about these questions than most believers do today. One reason is that we have layers of tradition that filter the Bible in our thinking. It's time to peel those layers away.

GOD'S GIFT

We might wonder why God doesn't do away with evil and suffering on earth. The answer sounds paradoxical: He *can't*—because that would require elimination of all his imagers. But he will at the last day. For evil to be eliminated, Earth and humanity as we know it would have to end. God has a chronology, a plan, for this ultimate development. It could be no other way, given his decision to create time-bound humans as the vehicles for his rule. But in the meantime, we experience the positive wonders of life as well. Though God knew the risk of Eden, he deemed the existence of humankind preferable to our eternal absence.

Despite the risk of evil, free will is a wonderful gift. God's decision was a loving one. Understanding that requires only a consideration of the two alternatives: (1) not having life at all, and (2) being a mindless robot, capable only of obeying commands and responding to programming.

If our decisions were all coerced, how authentic would those "decisions" actually be? If love is coerced or programmed, is it really love? Is *any* such decision really a genuine *decision* at all? It isn't. For a decision to be real, it must be made against an alternative that could be chosen.

We all know the difference between freedom and coercion. The IRS doesn't tell you that you *may perhaps* pay your taxes by April 15. When you behave wrongly, where would the emotional healing of forgiveness be if the person you offended was merely programmed to say those words, or coerced to say them? Free will is a gift, despite the risk.

KNOWING GOOD AND EVIL

Several phrases in Genesis 3:5, 22 that have puzzled interpreters become more understandable in light of what we've been discussing.

In Genesis 3:5 the serpent (Hebrew: *nachash*) says to Eve: "For God (*elohim*) knows that on the day you *both* eat from it, then your eyes will be opened and you *both* shall be like gods (*elohim*), knowing good and evil." This verse is like Psalm 82:1. The word *elohim* occurs two times in the same verse. The first instance is singular because of grammar (the verbal "knows" is singular in form). While most English translations render the second instance as "God," it should be plural because of the context supplied by Genesis 3:22. That verse reads: "And Yahweh God said, "Look—the man has become **as one of us**, to know good and evil." The phrase "one of us" informs us that, as in Genesis 1:26, God is speaking to his council members—the *elohim*. This tells us clearly that the second instance of *elohim* in Genesis 3:5 should be plural.

This fits well with Psalm 8:5, where the psalmist notes that humankind was created "a little lower than *elohim*." We aren't a "little" lower than God—we're light years lower. Relatively speaking, the gap is narrower if we assume the reference in the psalm is plural ("a little lower than the *elohim*"). This is the way the writer of Hebrews takes the phrase. In Hebrews 2:7 the writer quotes Psalm 8:5 from the Septuagint. That translation reads the plural "angels" for *elohim*, a clear plural.

In Genesis 3:5, Eve is being told that if she violates God's command, she and Adam will become as *elohim*, knowing good and evil. Notice that the phrase is "*knowing* good and evil," not *will be capable of* good and evil. As free-will beings, Adam and Eve were already capable of disobedience. Like God's holy ones in council, they were imperfect. But Adam and Eve had not yet experienced evil—either by their own commission or as bystanders.

The "knowing good and evil" phrase with the same Hebrew vocabulary occurs elsewhere. Deuteronomy 1:39 says:

And your little children, who you thought shall become plunder, and your sons, who do not today **know good or bad**, shall themselves go there, and I will give it to them, and they shall take possession of it.

The little children referred to here are the generation of Israelites that would arise after the original generation that had escaped from Egypt at the exodus. That first generation had been sentenced by God to wander in the desert for forty years until they died off for their refusal to enter the promised land in conquest (Num 14). The new generation did not know good or evil and would be allowed entrance into the land.

The meaning is clearly that the second generation *was not held morally accountable* for the sins of their parents. Though as children they were under the authority of their parents, they had no decision-making authority in the matter and were thus not willing participants. Therefore they were not considered liable. They were *innocent.*

The same perspective makes sense in Genesis 3. Prior to knowing good and evil, Adam and Eve were innocent. They had never made a willing, conscious decision to disobey God. They had never seen an act of disobedience, either. When they fell, that changed. They did indeed know good and evil, just as God and the rest of his heavenly council members—including the *nachash* ("serpent").[1]

EVIL AND FOREKNOWLEDGE

Acknowledging God's foreknowledge and also the genuine free will of humankind, especially with respect to the fall, raises obvious questions: Was the fall predestined? If so, how was the disobedience of Adam and Eve free? How are they truly responsible?

Since we aren't told much in Genesis about how human freedom works in relation to divine attributes like foreknowledge, predestination, and omniscience, we need to look elsewhere in Scripture for some clarification. Let's look at 1 Samuel 23:1–13. Note the bold words carefully.

[1] Now they told David, "Look, the Philistines are fighting in Keilah and they are raiding the threshing floors." [2] So David inquired of Yahweh, saying, "Shall I go and attack these Philistines?" And Yahweh said to David, "Go and attack the Philistines and save Keilah." [3] But David's men said to him, "Look, we are afraid here in Judah. How much more if we go to Keilah to the battle lines of the Philistines?" [4] So David again inquired of Yahweh, and Yahweh answered

---

1. See chapters 10 and 11 on the nachash as a divine being, a member of the council.

him and said, "Get up, go down to Keilah, for I am giving the Philistines into your hand." **⁵**So David and his men went to Keilah and fought with the Philistines. They drove off their livestock and dealt them a heavy blow. So David saved the inhabitants of Keilah. **⁶**Now when Abiathar the son of Ahimelech fled to David at Keilah, he went down with an ephod in his hand. **⁷**When it was told to Saul that David had gone to Keilah, Saul said, "God has given him into my hand, because he has shut himself in by going into a city with two barred gates. **⁸**Saul then summoned all of the army for the battle, to go down to Keilah to lay a siege against David and his men. **⁹**When David learned that Saul was plotting evil against him, he said to Abiathar the priest, "Bring the ephod here." **¹⁰**And David said, "**O Yahweh, God of Israel**, your servant has clearly heard that Saul is seeking to come to Keilah to destroy the city because of me. **¹¹Will the rulers of Keilah deliver me into his hand? Will Saul come down** as your servant has heard? O Yahweh, God of Israel, please tell your servant!" **And Yahweh said, "He will come down." ¹²**Then David said, "**Will the rulers of Keilah deliver me and my men into the hand of Saul?**" And **Yahweh said, "They will deliver you." ¹³**So **David and his men got up**, about six hundred men, and **went out from Keilah** and wandered wherever they could go. When it was told to Saul that **David had escaped from Keilah**, **he stopped his pursuit.**

In this account, David appeals to the omniscient God to tell him about the future. In the first instance (23:1–5), David asks God whether he should go to the city of Keilah and whether he'll successfully defeat the Philistines there. God answers in the affirmative in both cases. David goes to Keilah and indeed defeats the Philistines.

In the second section (23:6–13), David asks the Lord two questions: (1) will his nemesis Saul come to Keilah and threaten the city on account of David's presence? And (2) will the people of Keilah turn him over to Saul to avoid Saul's wrath? Again, God answers both questions affirmatively: "He will come down," and "They will deliver you."

Neither of these events that God foresaw ever actually happened. Once David hears God's answers, he and his men leave the city. When Saul discovers this fact (v. 13), he *abandons* his trip to Keilah. Saul never made it to the city. The men of Keilah never turned David over to Saul.

Why is this significant? *This passage clearly establishes that divine foreknowledge does not necessitate divine predestination.* God foreknew what Saul would do and what the people of Keilah would do given a set of circumstances. In other words, God foreknew a *possibility*—but this foreknowledge did not mandate that the possibility was actually predestined to happen. The events never happened, so by definition they could not have been predestined. And yet the omniscient God did indeed foresee them. Predestination and foreknowledge are *separable*.

The theological point can be put this way:

That which never happens can be foreknown by God, but it is not predestined, since it never happened.

But what about things that *do* happen? They can obviously be foreknown, but were they predestined?

Since we have seen above that foreknowledge *in itself* does not necessitate predestination, all that foreknowledge truly guarantees is that something is foreknown. If God foreknows some event that happens, then he *may have* predestined that event. But the fact that he foreknew an event does not require its predestination if it happens. The only guarantee is that God foreknew it correctly, whether it turns out to be an actual event or a merely possible event.

The theological point can be put this way:

Since foreknowledge doesn't require predestination, foreknown events that happen may or may not have been predestined.

This set of ideas goes against the grain of several modern theological systems. Some of those systems presume that foreknowledge requires predestination, and so everything must be predestined—all the way from the fall to the holocaust, to what you'll choose off a dinner menu. Others dilute foreknowledge by proposing that God doesn't foreknow all possibilities, since all possibilities cannot happen. Or they posit other universes where all the possibilities happen. These ideas are unnecessary in light of 1 Samuel 23 and other passages that echo the same fundamental idea: foreknowledge does not necessitate predestination.

Things we discussed earlier in this book allow us to take the discussion further. God may foreknow an event and predestine that event, but such predestination does not necessarily include decisions that lead up to that event. In other words, God may know and predestine the end—that something is ultimately going to happen—without predestining the means to that end.

We saw this precise relationship when we looked at decision making in God's divine council. The passages in 1 Kings 22:13–23 and Daniel 4 informed us that God can decree something and then leave the means up to the decisions of other free-will agents. The end is sovereignly ordained; the means to that end may or may not be.

IMPLICATIONS

An ancient Israelite would have embraced this parsing of foreknowledge, predestination, sovereignty, and free will. He would not have been encumbered by a theological tradition. She would have understood that *this is the way God himself has decided his rule over human affairs will work*. These are *Yahweh's* decisions, and we accept them.

This has significant implications for not only the fall, but the presence of evil in our world in general. God is not evil. There is no biblical reason to argue that God predestined the fall, though he foreknew it. There is no biblical reason to assert that God predestined all the evil events throughout human history simply because he foreknew them.

There is also no biblical coherence to the idea that God factored all evil acts into his grand plan for the ages. This is a common, but flawed, softer perspective, adopted to avoid the previous notion that God directly predestines evil events. It unknowingly implies that God's "perfect" plan *needed* to incorporate evil acts because—well, because we see them every day, and surely they can't just *happen*, since God foreknows everything. Therefore (says this flawed perspective) they must just be part of how God decided best to direct history.

God does not *need* the rape of a child to happen so that good may come. His foreknowledge didn't require the holocaust as part of a plan that would give us the kingdom on earth. *God does not need evil as a means to accomplish anything.*

God foreknew the fall. That foreknowledge did not propel the event. God also foreknew a solution to the fall that he himself would guarantee, a solution that entered his mind long before he laid the foundations of the earth. God was ready. The risk was awful, but he loved the notion of humanity too much to call the whole thing off.

Evil does not flow from a first domino that God himself toppled. Rather, evil is the perversion of God's good gift of free will. It arises from the choices made by imperfect imagers, not from God's prompting or predestination. God does not need evil, but he has the power to take the evil that flows from free-will decisions—human or otherwise—and use it to produce good and his glory through the obedience of his loyal imagers, who are his hands and feet on the ground *now*.

All of this means that what we choose to do is an important part of how things will turn out. What we do *matters*. God has decreed the ends to which all things will come. As believers, we are prompted by his Spirit to be the good means to those decreed ends.

But the Spirit is not the only influence. The experiences of our lives involve other imagers, both good and evil, including divine imagers we cannot see. The worldview of the biblical author was an animate one, where the members of the unseen world interact with humans. Loyal members of God's "congregation" (council), sent to minister to us (Heb 1:14), have embraced God's Edenic vision—we are brothers and sisters (Heb 2:10–18).

Other divine beings would oppose God's plan. The original dissident takes center stage in the next chapter.

Section Summary

We're just at the beginning of our journey. But we've learned some key concepts already—concepts that will emerge elsewhere in the Bible to form patterns. Other ideas will accrue to these concepts, and the mosaic will start to take form.

There are several takeaways from this first section of the book that will take on more shape and definition as we proceed.

First, God has a divine family—a heavenly assembly, or council, of *elohim*. These *elohim* are not a replacement for the Trinity, nor do they add to it. Yahweh is among the *elohim*, but he is superior to all other *elohim*. He is their creator and sovereign master. He is unique. Since Jesus is Yahweh in flesh, he too is distinct from, and superior to, all *elohim*. While God has no need of a council, Scripture makes it clear that he uses one. His divine family is his divine administration. The *elohim* serve him to carry out his decrees.

God also has a human family and administration. Their status and function mirror the divine family-administration. Just as with the members of the divine council who represent God in what they are tasked to do, so humans are God's imaging representatives. Just as God doesn't need a divine council, he doesn't need humans, either—but he has chosen to use them to further his intentions for Earth.

Heaven and Earth are separate but connected realms. God's households operate in tandem toward a mutual destiny. Their points of intersection along the way inform many other threads of biblical theology.

With Eden the divine had come to earth, and earth would be brought into conformity. Humans were created to enjoy everlasting access to God's presence, working side by side with God's loyal *elohim*. But this yearning of God's came with risk, a risk that was fully known by him and accepted. Free will in the hearts and hands of imperfect beings, whether human or divine, means imagers can opt for their own authority in place of God's.

Sadly, that will also become a pattern. Both of God's households will experience rebellion. The result will be the commencement of a long war against God's original intention. The good news is that there will be an equally committed effort on God's part to preserve what he began.

PART 3

DIVINE TRANSGRESSIONS

CHAPTER 10

Trouble in Paradise

THE STORY OF THE FALL OF HUMANITY IN GENESIS 3 SEEMS STRAIGHTFOR-
ward, perhaps because we've heard it told so many times. The truth is that the
passage presents a lot of interpretive questions. We've devoted some time to
a couple of them in the previous chapter. Now it's time to examine the main
character, the serpent. Once again, there's a lot more than meets the eye here.

One of the things that always bothered me about the story was why Eve
wasn't scared witless when the serpent spoke to her. There's no indication
that she thought the incident unusual. I've run into some odd explanations
for that, such as, "Maybe animals back then could walk and talk." That sort
of speculation is aimed at preserving an overliteralized view of the text, and
it's often accompanied by an appeal to science—a claim that snake anatomy
shows snakes once had legs. It's a bit misguided when someone attempts to
defend biblical literalism by appealing to the evolutionary history of snakes.
And anyway, the whole approach misses the point. It also presumes that the
villain was simply an animal. He wasn't.

The truth is that an ancient reader would not have expected Eve to be
frightened. Given the context—she was in Eden, the realm of Yahweh and
his *elohim* council—it would have been clear that she was conversing with
a divine being. As we've seen in earlier chapters, the biblical author has telegraphed that Eve was on divine turf.

GENESIS 3 IN CONTEXT

In ancient Near Eastern literature of the Old Testament world, animal speech
is not uncommon. The context for such speaking is that of magic, which of
course is tied to the world of the gods, or direct divine intervention. No Egyptian, for example, would have presumed that the animals they experienced

in their normal lives could talk. But when the gods or magical forces were in view, that was a different story. Animals were often the vehicle for manifesting a divine presence or power in a story. The kind of animal would often depend on characteristics associated with that animal, or on the status of that animal in a culture's religion.

Consequently, the point of Genesis 3 is not to inform us about ancient zoology or a time when animals could talk. We're not in the realm of science *by design*. Genesis telegraphed simple but profound ideas to Israelite readers: The world you experience was created by an all-powerful God; human beings are his created representatives; Eden was his abode; he was accompanied by a supernatural host; one member of that divine entourage was not pleased by God's decisions to create humanity and give them dominion. All that leads to how humanity got into the mess it's in.

In some respects, we *know* that the Genesis "serpent" wasn't *really* a member of the animal kingdom. We have other passages to help us grasp that point, particularly in the New Testament. We understand that, even though New Testament writers refer to the serpent back in Eden, they are really referring to a supernatural entity—not a mere member of the animal kingdom (2 Cor 11:3; 1 Thess 3:5; Rev 12:9).

This is how we need to think about the story of Genesis 3. An Israelite would have known that the episode described interference in the human drama by a divine being, a malcontent from within Yahweh's council.[1] The vocabulary used by the writer reveals several things about the divine enemy that has emerged from the council. If we're thinking only in terms of a snake, we'll miss the messaging.

My task in this chapter and the next is to help you think beyond the literalness of the serpent language. If it's true that the enemy in the garden was a supernatural being, then he wasn't a snake.[2]

But it's also true that the story is told as it is for a reason. As odd as it sounds, the vocabulary and the imagery are designed to alert readers to the presence of a divine being, not a literal snake. Making that case will involve comparing Genesis 3 to other Old Testament passages. But to see that those

---

1. I refer to the divine council broadly here, as roughly equivalent to the heavenly host. In what follows, readers will discover I consider the divine rebel's description to be one of a divine throne guardian. The divine council need not *necessarily* be conceptually restricted to decision makers. Indeed, the analogy of human government in civilizations that had a conception of a divine council makes the point clear. Not all members of a king's "government" would be directly involved in decision making, but they still worked for the high sovereign.

2. Other scholars have taken the same view, notably van Dijk (*Ezekiel's Prophecy on Tyre (Ez. 26:1–28:19): A New Approach*), cited more fully in the ensuing discussion.

passages are indeed conceptually linked to Genesis 3, we need to review some things we've learned.

Eden was the divine abode and, therefore, the place where Yahweh held council meetings. Here are some of the terms and verses associated with Eden we briefly noted in an earlier chapter. I've added the Hebrew words behind the English.

Hebrew Term	English Meaning	Concept	Important Verses
elim, elohim (plural)	"gods"	council members	Gen 3:5, 22
gan	"garden"	Divine abode, council meeting place	Gen 2:8–10, 15–16 Gen 3:1–3, 8, 10, 23–24
'ed nahar yamim	"(watery) mist" "river" "seas, waters"	description of the well-watered garden of the council	Gen 2:6, 10–14; Ezek 28:2
har	"mount, mountain"	mountain range where divine council met	Ezek 28:13
moshab elohim	"seat of the gods" (place of governing authority)	the divine assembly	Ezek 28:2

You can see quickly that, other than Genesis 2–3, the other source of verse citations is Ezekiel 28. That's one of the chapters conceptually linked to Genesis 3. Its connection is explicit. Ezekiel 28:13–14 refers to "Eden, the garden of God … God's holy mountain."

The table does not list all the points of connection between the two. There are a number of others, most of them hotly debated by scholars.[3] Back in the first chapter I told you that there are many interpretations for strange passages in the Bible, but the best ones are those that make sense in the context of many others—the mosaic. The relationship of Genesis 3 to Ezekiel 28 and other passages is going to illustrate that point.

EZEKIEL 28

Ezekiel 28 is not specifically about the fall of humankind. It's also not a commentary on Genesis 3. The chapter begins with God chastising the prince of Tyre (Ezek 28:1–8). God accuses this prince of extraordinary arrogance. In

---

3. The debate over the relationship of Ezek 28 and Gen 3 quickly becomes very technical. This chapter and the next introduce a few selective points of connection and issues relevant to those connections. See the companion website for more detailed analysis of the grammatical, text-critical, and conceptual issues related to the Edenic referents in Ezek 28.

verse 2 the prince considers himself a god (*el*), who sits in the seat of the gods (*moshab elohim*), a term associated with the divine council.[4]

The choice of *el* for who the prince considers himself to be is interesting. It also appears in verse 9, where it is in parallel to *elohim*. The word *el* is another word that means "god" in Hebrew and other Semitic languages. The people of Ugarit called their high god El—they used the term as a proper name. So did the people of Tyre, which was a Phoenician city. The Phoenician religion had a divine council led by El, who was also called *elyon* ("Most High") in Phoenician texts and considered the creator of the earth.

To the ancient reader familiar with El, the notion that the prince of Tyre would think himself fit to rule in El's place (or even to be a more generic deity-participant in the divine council) would be ludicrous. For biblical writers, the idea was also offensive. For them Yahweh was Most High—the true king of all gods and creator of heaven and earth. This is why the biblical writers refer to Yahweh as *el-elyon* ("God Most High"; Gen 14:20, 22). The point of assigning *el* and *elyon* to Yahweh was not to endorse how Phoenicians and residents of Ugarit thought about their gods, but to assert Yahweh's superiority. He was incomparable among spiritual beings; the others were pretenders. Consequently, the biblical writers would have viewed the human arrogance of the prince of Tyre as an affront to the God of Israel.

---

4. Both phrases, "seat of the gods" and "heart of the seas," point to the place of divine authority, the throne room of the divine council. Ugaritic yields a close parallel to *moshab elohim* (Ugar. *m[t]b il*, "seat of El"; *KTU* 1.4.i.13). See Richard J. Clifford, *The Cosmic Mountain in Canaan and the Old Testament* (Harvard Semitic Monographs 4; Cambridge: Harvard University Press, 1972; reprinted by Wipf and Stock, 2010; but page numbers refer to the original edition, not the reprint by Wipf and Stock), 170; E. Theodore Mullen Jr., *The Divine Council in Canaanite and Early Hebrew Literature* (Harvard Semitic Monographs 24; Chico, CA: Scholars Press, 1980), 150–55. Block seeks to deny a number of connections back to the divine council in this passage on the basis that an orthodox Yahwist wouldn't have drawn the analogies Block does (Daniel Isaac Block, *The Book of Ezekiel, Chapters 25–48* [The New International Commentary on the Old Testament; Grand Rapids, MI: Eerdmans, 1997], 94–95). This is misguided in my judgment. There is nothing unorthodox about a biblical writer's repurposing of Ugaritic terms and ideas. Their use wasn't an endorsement of the theology of Ugarit. Their purpose is quite the opposite: to typecast a villain by comparing his arrogance to a supernatural rebellion against Yahweh. W. Hermann summarizes the view of most scholars in this regard: "The residence of El (*mtb il*) is referred to in *KTU* 1.3 iv:48; v:39; 1.4 i:12; iv:52. El's mythic dwelling is situated at *mbk nhrm / apq thmtm*, 'the fountainhead of the two rivers / bedding of the two floods' (e.g. *KTU* 1.2 iii:4; 1.6 i:33–34)" ("El," in *Dictionary of Deities and Demons in the Bible*, 2nd ed. [ed. Karel van der Toorn, Bob Becking, and Pieter W. van der Horst; Leiden: Brill, 1995], 278). Biblical writers draw on ancient Near Eastern religious material dozens, perhaps hundreds, of times to make their own theological points, not endorse foreign ones. The Hebrew Bible uses *moshab* of Zion, the place of Yahweh's rule and governance (Psa 132:13). Likewise Zion is called the "heights of the north" (Psa 48:2), a phrase recognized by Semitics scholars as being drawn from the description of Baal's abode (*KTU* 1.3 i:21–22; iii:29, 47–iv:1; iv: 19–20, 37–38; 1.4 iv:19; v:23, 55; 1.5 i:10–11; 1.6 vi:12–13; 1.10 iii:27–37). As Niehr notes: "Nearly always in the mythological texts Mount Zaphon is mentioned together with Baal because mount Zaphon is his divine abode" ("Zaphon," in *Dictionary of Deities and Demons in the Bible*, 928).

God proceeds to acknowledge the great intelligence of this prince, but reminds him that he is no god, and certainly not the Most High (Ezek 28:2–6). This sort of arrogance must be punished. Judgment will come. God asks sarcastically (v. 9), "Will you indeed still say 'I am a god!' before the face of your killers?"

In verse 10 God adds a strange detail: "You will die the death of the uncircumcised by the hand of strangers." Since the prince of Tyre is an uncircumcised Gentile anyway, the phrasing seems to lack coherence. If we read a little further in Ezekiel, the point would be clear to an ancient reader. The underworld realm of the dead, Sheol, is described by Ezekiel as the place where the uncircumcised warrior-king enemies of Israel find themselves (Ezek 32:21, 24–30, 32; Isa 14:9). This is the place of the Rephaim dead, quasi-supernatural beings we'll encounter later.

It is at this point that God has the prophet raise a lament over the prince of Tyre, the brilliant prince whose arrogance led to his fall, not only to the earth but *under* the earth. God, through the prophet, begins:

> ¹² You were a perfect model of an example,
>> full of wisdom and perfect of beauty.
> ¹³ You were in Eden, the garden of God,
>> and every precious stone was your adornment:
> carnelian, topaz and moonstone,
>> turquoise, onyx and jasper,
> sapphire, malachite and emerald.
>> And gold was the craftsmanship of your settings
> and your mountings in you;
>> on the day when you were created they were prepared (Ezek 28:12–13).

These verses raise questions. The prince of Tyre wasn't in Eden—he was in Tyre. We see now that, although Ezekiel 28 is about the prince of Tyre, in describing this prince's arrogance, downfall, and original state, the prophet utilizes an older tale of a downfall *in Eden*.

THE HUBRIS OF ADAM?

Many scholars argue that the Edenic figure in view is Adam. This view depends on rejecting the traditional Hebrew text of the passage. If one prefers the Septuagint here, then God is speaking to an individual who is "with the anointed cherub"—as opposed to speaking directly to the anointed cherub. The more coherent alternative is that the cherub is the serpent—more pointedly, a divine being who has forgotten his place in the pecking order.

But where do we see a serpent in Ezekiel 28? Let's look first at what's clear before addressing that question.

This "prince" was in Eden, the garden of God (v. 13). He is beautiful—words like *shining* or *radiant* are what come to mind when reading about the panoply of gems that were his "adornment" (vv. 12b–13).

Some have taken this language to refer to a literal jewel-encrusted garment worn by the human prince. They in turn argue that the prince of Eden was Adam. They also note that many of the jewels listed here correspond to the jewels on the breastplate of the Israelite high priest (Exod 28:17–20; 39:10–13). The picture, they say, is Adam as priest-king of Eden. Since Jesus was the second Adam and a priest-king, the analogy fits. The backdrop to the prince of Tyre's arrogance is the rebellious Adam, not the serpent.

This sounds reasonable until you start looking at how "Adam" is characterized in the verses that follow.

> [14] You were an anointed guardian cherub,
>> and I placed you on God's holy mountain;
> you walked in the midst of stones of fire.
> [15]   You were blameless in your ways
> from the day when you were created,
>> until wickedness was found in you.
> [16] In the abundance of your trading,
>> they filled the midst of you with violence, and you sinned;
> and I cast you as a profane thing from the mountain of God,
>> and I expelled you, the guardian cherub,
>> from the midst of the stones of fire.
> [17] Your heart was proud because of your beauty;
>> you ruined your wisdom because of your splendor.
> I threw you on the ground before kings;
>> I have exposed you for viewing (Ezek 28:14–17).

Was Adam with an "anointed guardian cherub"? Where do we read in Genesis 3 that Adam was filled with violence, or that his sin was propelled by the fact he was egotistically enamored of his own beauty and splendor? When was Adam cast to the ground to be exposed before kings (v. 17)?

All of the phrases alluded to in the questions above are important. Dealing with them will take the rest of this chapter and the next. The key question that frames any discussion of them is this: Is Ezekiel drawing on a tale about the rebellion of a *divine* being against God, or about *Adam's* rebellion against God? I believe the former is more coherent, a decision that links what's going on here back to the only *divine* rebel in Genesis 3—the serpent. In what remains of this chapter, I'll begin to explain my reasoning, and then continue that exploration in the next chapter.[5]

ANOTHER APPROACH

Ezekiel 28:12b addresses the prince of Tyre this way: "You were a perfect model of an example." Some translations have "You were the signet of perfection." This line is one of the more troublesome in the book for translation. Some scholars go as far as to list it among the more problematic in the entire Old Testament.[6] The Hebrew word behind "perfect model" or "signet ring" (*ch-w-t-m*) is the crux of the problem. The word is not a noun, but a participle that literally means "the sealer." A translation of "signet ring" takes the term to denote some object, but the term is addressed as a person ("You"). The fact that this "sealer" is described as being "full of wisdom" and "perfect in beauty" also makes it clear that an object is not in view, but some intelligent person or entity.

The question of course is just how this entity should be identified. Ultimately, the answer to this question derives from the answer to the previous question of whether Ezekiel is drawing on a story about a divine rebel or a human one. That question is the focus of the next chapter. But there are certain observations that can be made here that will help frame that discussion.

Let's reconsider the gemstones that describe the appearance of the "the sealer" in Ezekiel 28:13. As I mentioned earlier, proponents of the view that Ezekiel is drawing on Adam's rebellion for his analogous portrayal of the prince of Tyre want to argue that the gemstones point to a human priest-king. But the "adornment" can quite easily be telegraphing something else—divinity. All of the gems have one thing in common—they shine or sparkle. Luminescence is a characteristic of divine beings or divine presence across the ancient Near Eastern world and the Old Testament (e.g., Ezek 1:4–7, 27–28 [cf. Ezek 10:19–20]; Dan 10:6; Rev 1:15). This description of the divine cherub in Eden is designed to convey divinity—a shining presence.

There are more details. The anointed cherub ultimately gets cast out of Eden, out from "the midst of the stones of fire." We already know from other data that Eden is the place of the council. The "stones of fire" is another clue

---

5. Again, the companion website provides much greater detail and depth of analysis for the points made here and in the next chapter.

6. See H. J. van Dijk, *Ezekiel's Prophecy on Tyre (Ez. 26:1–28:19): A New Approach* (Biblica et orientalia 20; Rome: Pontifical Biblical Institute, 1968), 113–14. This is a technical work. Van Dijk argues for a divine serpentine figure in Ezek 28:12–19 against the Adam explanation. See the companion website for more of his thoughts.

in that direction. This phrase is associated in other Jewish texts (1 Enoch 18:6–11; 1 Enoch 24–25) with the supernatural, mountainous dwelling of God and the divine council.[7]

It may be objected here that Eden was the dwelling place of God and so the "stones of fire" do not only point to the divine beings of Yahweh's council. That much is true, but there's more to the phrase than a dwelling place. Other scholars have also drawn attention to the ancient Near Eastern propensity to describe divine beings as stars. Job 38:7 refers to the sons of God as "stars," and Isaiah 14:12–13 refers to a being fallen from heaven as the "Day Star, son of Dawn" (ESV) who wanted to ascend above the "stars of God" in the divine realm. The "stones of fire" therefore do not only describe an abode, but also divine entities in that abode.[8]

The "ground" to which this haughty divine being is cast and where he is disgraced is also of interest. The Hebrew word translated "ground" is *ʾerets*. It is a common term for the earth under our feet. But it is also a word that is

---

7. See Kelley Coblentz Bautch, *A Study of the Geography of 1 Enoch 17–19: 'No One Has Seen What I Have Seen'* (Leiden: Brill, 2003), 107–15. Bautch's work also discusses Mesopotamian backgrounds to 1 Enoch 18:1–6. See van Dijk and his footnoted references in *Ezekiel's Prophecy on Tyre*, 118–23, for Mesopotamian connections to the motifs in Ezek 28:12–19. The Septuagint translation of Ezek 28 provides another indication that the "stones of fire" refers to the divine abode. All the stones in Ezek 28:13 except one are used elsewhere to describe the supernatural Jerusalem (Rev 21), which is obviously the divine abode and throne room. This is entirely consistent with the portrayal of divinity in terms of luminescence. The lone exception is the Septuagint's ἄνθραξ (for Hebrew תַּרְשִׁישׁ). That word is used elsewhere in Ezekiel to describe the divine throne (Ezek 10:9) as well as in Isaiah to describe the new Jerusalem (Isa 54:11). Readers who check the Greek closely may presume a point of incongruence with one other item in the Septuagint rendering of Ezek 28:13—ὀνύχιον (for Hebrew בָּרְקַת) is not found in Rev 21. The supposed discrepancy is a misperception. The word ὀνύχιον is "a kind of *onyx*, Thphr.*Lap*.31, LxxEx.28.20: as Adj. ὀνύχιος (sc. λίθος), Suid" (Henry George Liddell et al., *A Greek-English Lexicon* [Oxford: Clarendon Press, 1996], 1234). Instead of ὀνύχιον we see σαρδόνυξ in Rev 21:19. Both terms describe the gem onyx, thus allowing an identification of all the gemstones in Ezek 28 (Septuagint) with the description of the supernatural Jerusalem in Rev 21. See James Harrell, "Gemstones," *UCLA Encyclopedia of Egyptology* 1.1 (2012): 5 (table 1, pts. 5–6). Harrell notes that both onyx and sardonyx were referred to by ὀνύχιον. Several other scholars have argued for a close connection between the gemstone description of Rev 21 and Ezek 28: F. Petrie, "Precious Stones," *Dictionary of the Bible*, vol. 4 (ed. J. Hastings; New York: Scribner, 1919), 619–21; J. L. Myres, "Stones (Precious)," *Encyclopedia Biblica*, vol. 4 (ed. T. K. Cheyne and J. S. Black; New York: Macmillan, 1903), 4799–4812; and E. F. Jourdain, "The Twelve Stones in the Apocalypse," *Expository Times* 22 (1911): 448–50. Daniel Block appears to misidentify the LXX rendering of בָּרְקַת when he says the word is "a derivation from *bāraq*, 'to flash, shine,' [which] connects the word with 'lightning.' In Exod 28:17 LXX renders it σμάραγδος, which is probably to be identified with emerald." See Block, *Book of Ezekiel, Chapters 25–48*, 109. For the equation of בָּרְקַת with ὀνύχιον, see Emanuel Tov, *The Parallel Aligned Hebrew-Aramaic and Greek Texts of Jewish Scripture* (Bellingham, WA: Logos Bible Software, 2003). See the companion website for further discussion.

8. Clifford's treatment of the astral language of Ezek 28 and Isa 14:4b–21 in his work on the cosmic mountain and divine council is illustrative of the clear connections between the terminology and divine beings. See Clifford, *Cosmic Mountain*, 160–73. See also John Gray, "The Desert God 'Athtar in the Literature and Religion of Canaan," *Journal of Near Eastern Studies* 78 (1949): 72–83; Ulf Oldenburg, "Above the Stars of El: El in Ancient South Arabic Religion," *Zeitschrift für die alttestamentliche Wissenschaft* 82 (1970): 187–208.

used to refer to the underworld, the realm of the dead (e.g., Jonah 2:6), where ancient warrior-kings await their comrades in death (Ezek 32:21, 24–30, 32; Isa 14:9). Adam, of course, was already on earth, so he couldn't be sentenced there. And he didn't wind up in the underworld. Yet this is the sort of language we would expect if the point was the expulsion of a heavenly being from the divine council.

Lastly, some scholars have suggested that the problematic term "sealer" (Hebrew *ch-w-t-m*) might be a cryptic reference to the serpent figure of Genesis 3. If their suggestion is correct, the point of confusion becomes a clever signal that Adam is not in view.[9]

There is a rare phenomenon in ancient Semitic languages where the final letter *m* is silent (the "enclitic *mem*").[10] If the *m* is made silent in (in effect, removed from) our confusing word, the word becomes *ch-w-t*, which means "serpent" in Phoenician and other Semitic languages.[11] That noun in its lemma form is *ch-w-h*.[12]

Though the case for this reading cannot be made conclusively, its message would be to read Ezekiel 28:11–19 in light of Genesis 3 and its serpent.[13] It

---

9. What follows is a summation of this alternative. For more technical discussion, see the companion website.

10. An analogy in English spelling, though imprecise, would be the silent *e*. In English, silent *e* serves to telegraph that the preceding vowel sound is long. Enclitic *mem* is considered a particle directing attention to the word for emphasis. Scholars have debated the reality of the enclitic *mem* in biblical Hebrew. See Horace D. Hummel, "Enclitic mem in Early Northwest Semitic, Especially Hebrew," *Journal of Biblical Literature* LXXVI (1957): 85–107; Mitchell Dahood, "Enclitic *mem* and emphatic *lamedh* in Psalm 85," *Biblica* 37, no. 3 (1956): 338–40; J. A. Emerton, "Are There Examples of Enclitic *mem* in the Hebrew Bible?" in *Texts, Temples, and Traditions: A Tribute to Menaham Haran* (ed. Menaham Haran and Michael V. Fox; Winona Lake, IN: Eisenbrauns, 1996): 321–38; C. Cohen, "The Enclitic *mem* in Biblical Hebrew: Its Existence and Initial Discovery," in *Sefer Moshe: The Moshe Weinfeld Jubilee Volume; Studies in the Bible and the Ancient Near East, Qumran, and Post-Biblical Judaism* (ed. Chaim Cohen, Avi Hurvitz, and Shalom M. Paul; Winona Lake, IN: Eisenbrauns, 2004), 231–60. One clear example is the *mem* at the end of the phrase בני אלם (*bny 'lm*) in Psa 29:1. This phrase was long considered to read "sons of El/God" (בני אלים) but has recently been changed in modern editions of the Hebrew text to "sons of the gods" (בני אלים). David N. Freedman writes: "The elim in the first line is to be read as El with enclitic *mem*: eli-m, i.e., the sons of El, the gods" (David N. Freedman, "Archaic Forms in Hebrew Poetry," *Zeitschrift für die alttestamentliche Wissenschaft* 31 [1960]: 101–7 [esp. 104]).

11. See Jacob Hoftijzer, Karel Jongeling, Richard C. Steiner, Adina Mosak Moshavi, and Bezalel Porten, *Dictionary of the North-West Semitic Inscriptions*, 2 vols. (Leiden: Brill, 1995), 2:726 (*nḥš₆*), 353.

12. The Hebrew consonants are חוה. A lemma is the form of a word without suffix endings or prefixes, or any sort of alteration. It is the most basic form. For example, one would not find "running" as a headword in a dictionary. Rather, you would find "run"—the most basic form. "Run" is a lemma.

13. As the next chapter and the companion website discuss, my view of the relationship between Gen 3, Ezek 28, and Isa 14 does not depend on this reconstruction. There are many points of intersection between the three chapters. Ultimately, the issue comes down to whether a backdrop of a divine rebellion or human rebellion has more comprehensive explanatory power for all the interconnections. My view is that the latter view, though the majority view in biblical scholarship, cannot account for certain connections and is therefore less coherent (see note 14 below).

produces a play on words that takes us directly back to the scene of the fall in Eden. Since we know that we are not dealing with a mere animal in Genesis 3, but rather a divine being that is cast as creaturely, the description that this figure in the garden was an "anointed guardian cherub" makes sense. A cherub was a *divine* throne guardian in the ancient Near Eastern worldview.[14] Ancient Near Eastern art and engravings have many examples of such throne guardians as animals, including serpents. There is little coherence to viewing the guardian cherub in Ezekiel 28 as the human Adam.

Let's summarize where this leaves us. Ezekiel 28 browbeats the prince of Tyre using an ancient tale of divine arrogance in Eden, where a member of Yahweh's council thought himself on par with the Most High. This divine throne guardian was expelled from Eden to the "ground" or underworld.

These elements show up in another passage: Isaiah 14.[15] We'll consider what Isaiah says next and then take a fresh look at what went on in Eden.

---

14. See Alice Wood, *Of Wings and Wheels: A Synthetic Study of the Biblical Cherubim* (Beihefte zur Zeitschrift für die alttestamentliche Wissenschaft 385; Berlin: Walter de Gruyter, 2008). Wood provides an excellent concise summary of the morphological, grammatical, and text-critical difficulties in Ezek 28:11–19 that become part of the effort to identify the figure (divine or human?) lurking in the background of this passage. See the companion website for interaction with her work. Bernard F. Batto takes a similar perspective. He describes the Edenic rebel this way: "The 'serpent' [was] a semi-divine creature with wings and feet like the seraphs in Isa 6:2, whose function was to guard sacred persons and sacred objects such as the tree of divine wisdom" (*In the Beginning: Essays on Creation Motifs in the Bible and the Ancient Near East* [Siphrut: Literature and Theology of the Hebrew Scriptures 9; Winona Lake, IN: Eisenbrauns, 2013], 47).

15. One of the significant weaknesses of identifying the Edenic rebel lurking in the background of Ezek 28 as Adam is the relationship between Ezek 28 and Isa 14. Scholars acknowledge that the two passages have clear, undeniable conceptual overlaps—yet they do not posit Adam in Isa 14. Instead, they posit a divine rebellion tale as the conceptual source of Isaiah's portrait of the king of Babylon while positing Adam as the rebel behind Ezek 28. This divergence in approach to two passages that contain clear points of overlap is methodologically inconsistent. See the companion website for a discussion of how an ancient tale of divine rebellion accounts for all the elements in both passages.

CHAPTER 11

Like the Most High?

IN THE PREVIOUS CHAPTER, WE SAW THAT EZEKIEL 28 PRESENTS US WITH the tragic portrait of the prince of Tyre. The prophet uses the literary strategy of drawing on an ancient story of a divine being in Eden who thought himself heading "the seat of the gods" (Ezek 28:2), the divine council. This being was punished with expulsion from Eden to the underworld. The portrait of this being as a divine guardian cherub, using the imagery of brilliant, shining gems and a serpent, has conceptual links to Genesis 3.

These elements also show up in Isaiah 14. We'll consider that passage and then take another look at the serpent in Eden.

ISAIAH 14

In Isaiah 14:4, God tells the prophet to take up a "taunt" (Hebrew: *mashal*) against the king of Babylon. A *mashal* is better described as a comparative parable. The question to keep in mind as we proceed is, to whom is the king of Babylon being compared?[1]

---

1. The *mashal* of Isa 14 has several points of correlation with a Ugaritic divine council scene involving a lesser deity snubbing El. See Michael S. Heiser, "The Mythological Provenance of Isaiah 14:12–15: A Reconsideration of the Ugaritic Material," *Vetus Testamentum* 51.3 (Fall 2001): 354–69. I noted at the end of the last chapter that it is inconsistent to see a human rebellion (Adam) as the backdrop for Ezek 28 but a divine rebellion behind Isa 14 when all scholars agree they are conceptually related. Among the treatments of Isa 14 that explore some sort of divine rebellion as the backdrop to Isa 14, see Joseph Jensen, "Helel Ben Shahar (Isaiah 14.12–15) in Bible and Tradition," in *Writing and Reading the Scroll of Isaiah: Studies of an Interpretive Tradition* (Supplements to Vetus Testamentum 70; Leiden: Brill, 1997), 339–57; J. W. McKay, "Helel and the Dawn-Goddess: A Re-Examination of the Myth in Isaiah XIV 12–15," *Vetus Testamentum* 20 (1970): 451–64; Peter C. Craigie, "Helel, Athtar and Phaethon (Jes 14 12–15)," *Zeitschrift für die alttestamentliche Wissenschaft* 85 (1973): 223–25; W. S. Prinsloo, "Isaiah 14 12–15: Humiliation, Hubris, Humiliation," *Zeitschrift für die alttestamentliche Wissenschaft* 93.3 (1981): 432–38; Ulf Oldenburg, "Above the Stars of El: El in Ancient South Arabic Religion," *Zeitschrift für die alttestamentliche Wissenschaft* 82 (1970): 187–208. With such an abundance of possible correlations to a divine rebellion story as the backdrop of Isa 14, why look to Adam in Ezek 28, which is so closely related to Isa 14? The major recent work on this is Hugh R.

The beginning of the parable sounds as unfavorable to the king of Babylon as Ezekiel's description of the prince of Tyre is to that ruler. The king of Babylon is called an "oppressor" (ESV; v. 4) who ruthlessly persecuted the nations (vv. 5–6). The world will finally be at rest when the oppressor is "laid low" (ESV; vv. 7–8). In anticipation of the joy of finally being rid of the king of Babylon, the prophet writes:

> [9] Sheol below is getting excited over you,
>   to meet you when you come;
> it arouses the dead spirits [*rephaim*] for you,
>   all of the leaders of the earth [*'erets*].
>   It raises all of the kings of the nations from their thrones.
> [10] All of them will respond and say to you,
>   "You yourself also were made weak like us!
>   You have become the same as us!"
> [11] Your pride is brought down to Sheol,
>   and the sound of your harps;
> maggots are spread out beneath you like a bed,
>   and your covering is worms (Isa 14:9–11).

As in Ezekiel 28, the figure in Isaiah 14 who is the target of its diatribe goes to Sheol, the underworld. The Rephaim are there, here identified again as the dead warrior-kings ("you have become the same as us"). The king of Babylon will be one of these living dead, just like the prince of Tyre.

Recall that Ezekiel 28 shifted from the prince of Tyre to a divine figure in Eden. That shift informed us that the writer was using a story of cosmic, divine rebellion to, by comparison, portray the arrogance of the earthly prince. After verse 11, Isaiah 14 shifts to a divine context with clear links to Ezekiel 28. Those connections in turn take us conceptually back to Genesis 3.

Isaiah 14:12–15 reads:

> [12]   How you have fallen from heaven, morning star, son of dawn!
>   You are cut down to the ground, conqueror of nations!
>
> [13] And you yourself said in your heart,
>
>   "I will ascend to heaven;
>   I will raise up my throne above the stars of God;

Page, *The Myth of Cosmic Rebellion: A Study of Its Reflexes in Ugaritic and Biblical Literature* (Supplements to Vetus Testamentum 65; Leiden: Brill, 1996). My conclusions will differ at points with Page's. He prefers the Keret Epic (which involves a human king) as the backdrop to Ezek 28. As I show on the companion website, all the evidences he draws for this proposal can also be found in myths of a rebellion of a *divine* being. In short, divine rebellion motifs account for all the elements in *both* biblical passages (which have clear touch-points to the *nachash* of Gen 3), but the same cannot be said for appeals to Adam or the Keret Epic. See the companion website for more detailed discussion on this point.

and I will sit on the mountain of assembly
on the summit of Zaphon;

¹⁴ I will ascend to the high places of the clouds,
I will make myself like the Most High."

¹⁵ But you are brought down to Sheol,
to the depths of the pit (Isa 14:12–15).

The divine council context is transparent. You've already seen much of the terminology in chapter 6 about divine gardens and mountains.

The figure to whom the king of Babylon is being compared is a divine being fallen "from heaven" (v. 12). He is called the "morning star, son of dawn." The language takes us back to Job 38:7, where the sons of God were called "morning stars." But the Hebrew terms in Isaiah 14:12 are different than those in Job 38:7.

"Morning star, son of dawn" is an English rendering of the Hebrew *helel ben-shachar*, which literally means "shining one, son of the dawn." When we talked about Job 38:7 in chapter 3, I noted that "morning stars" were the visible bright stars seen on the horizon as the sun rose. Astronomers (ancient and modern) knew another celestial object that behaved the same way—an object so bright it could still be seen as the sun rose. That object was Venus, and so Venus, though a planet, became known to the ancients as the "bright morning star."

In essence, borrowing the language of Ezekiel 28, Isaiah portrays this particular divine being as hopelessly enamored of his own brilliance. So great was his arrogance that he declared himself above all the "stars of God" (*kokebey el*), the other members of the divine council (Job 38:7).

That this "shining one" sought superiority over the other members of the divine council is indicated by the phrase "raise … my throne" and his desire to "sit" on "the mountain of assembly." That this "mountain of assembly" speaks of the divine council is clear from its location in "Zaphon" ("the north"; *tsaphon*) and the clouds. The "seat" language is familiar from Ezekiel 28:2 (the "seat of the gods"). Isaiah 14 reads like an attempted coup in the divine council. *Helel ben-shachar* wanted his seat in the divine assembly on the divine mountain to be above all others. He wanted to be "like the Most High" (*elyon*). But there can be only one of those.

It's no surprise that *helel ben-shachar*, the shining one, meets the same end as the divine throne guardian in Ezekiel 28. In three places we see his fate. You've seen two of the verses already. Take note of the emphasis in bold:

⁹ **Sheol below** is getting excited over you,
to meet you when you come;

it arouses the **dead spirits** for you,
> all of the leaders of the earth.
> It raises all of the kings of the nations from their thrones....

¹² "How you have fallen from heaven,
> morningstar, son of dawn!
> You are **cut down to the ground** [*'erets*]....

¹⁵ But you are **brought down to Sheol**,
> to the **depths of the pit** (Isa 14:9, 12, 15).

The punishment of *helel* is to live in the realm of the dead. *Helel* ends up in Sheol, the pit (*bor*); brought down to earth (*'erets*) by God, the truly Most High.

The table below expands on the one we began in the previous chapter. As we move forward, I'll add terms and verses to those from Ezekiel 28. I'll focus on divine council connections between that chapter and Isaiah 14 and Genesis 3, but will include references from elsewhere when appropriate.

THE DIVINE COUNCIL CONTEXT			
Hebrew Term	**English Meaning**	**Concept**	**Important Verses**
elim, elohim (plural)	"gods"	council members	Gen 3:5, 22; Psa 82:1, 6; Ezek 28:2
beney elim *beney elohim* *kokebey boqer* *kokebey el* *helel ben-shachar*	"sons of God" "morning stars" "stars of God" "shining one, son of the dawn"	council members shining appearance	Job 38:7; Pss 29:1; 89:6; Isa 14:13; Ezek 28:13 (gems)
gan	"garden"	divine abode, council meeting place	Gen 2:8–10, 15–16 Gen 3:1–3, 8, 10, 23–24 Ezek 28:13
'ed *nahar* *yamim*	"(watery) mist" "river" "seas, waters"	description of the well-watered garden of the council	Gen 2:6, 10–14 (Zion); Ezek 47:1–12 (Jerusalem temple; cf. Zech 14:8); Ezek 28:2
tsaphon *yarketey tsaphon* *bamot*	"north" "heights of the north" "heights"	mountain range where divine council met	Psa 48:1–2 (Jerusalem temple; cf. Ezek 40:2); Isa 14:13–14
har	"mount, mountain"	mountain range where divine council met	Exod 24:15 (Sinai; cf. Psa 68:15–17; Deut 33:1–2); Isa 14:13; 27:13 (Zion); Ezek 47:1–12 (Jerusalem temple)
adat *sod* *mo'ed* *moshab*	"assembly" "council" "meeting" "seat" (governing)	the divine assembly	Pss 82:1; 89:7; Isa 14:13; Ezek 28:2

THE NACHASH OF GENESIS 3

The pivotal character of Genesis 3 is the serpent. The Hebrew word translated *serpent* is *nachash*. The word is both plain and elastic.

The most straightforward meaning is the one virtually all translators and interpreters opt for: serpent. When the Hebrew root letters *n-ch-sh* are a noun, that's the meaning.

But *n-ch-sh* are also the consonants of a verb. If we changed the vowels to a verbal form (recall that Hebrew originally had no vowels), we would have *nochesh*, which means "the diviner." Divination refers to communication with the supernatural world. A diviner in the ancient world was one who foretold omens or gave out divine information (oracles). We can see that element in the story. Eve is getting information from this being.

The consonants *n-ch-sh* may also form an alternative noun, *nachash*, which is at times used descriptively, like an adjective. This term is used in place names outside the Bible and once within the Old Testament. First Chronicles 4:12 refers to "Tehinnah, father of *Ir-Nachash*." The otherwise unknown Tehinnah is regarded in this verse as the founder of the city (Hebrew: *ir*) of *nachash*.

This city has yet to be securely identified by archaeologists. The phrase means "the city of copper/bronze (smiths)." Hebrew words like *nechosheth* ("bronze"; "copper") are derived from this noun. *Ir-nachash* was a place known for copper and bronze metallurgy. The option is interesting because copper and bronze are *shiny* when polished. In fact, the Old Testament uses *nechosheth* to describe divine beings (Dan 10:6).

We have words with such elasticity in English, where meaning depends on the part of speech. For example:

(Noun): "*Running* is a good form of exercise."

(Verb): "The engine is *running* on diesel."

(Adjective): "*Running* paint is an eyesore."

Sometimes writers, when they use a term, want their readers to think about *all* possible meanings and nuances. If I ask, "How has your reading been?" the reader is forced to think about all three. Do I mean the latest assignment (noun)? Am I wondering if you got the right glasses (adjective)? Or am I referencing the process (verb)? What I'm suggesting is that, since there are immediate clues in the story that the serpent is more than a mere snake, that he may be a *divine* adversary, the term *nachash* is a triple entendre. The writer wants his readers to consider all the possible nuances in their interpretive, intellectual experience. All of them carry theological weight.[2]

The serpent (*nachash*) was an image commonly used in reference to a divine throne guardian. Given the context of Eden, that helps identify the villain as a divine being. The divine adversary dispenses divine information, using it to goad Eve. He gives her an oracle (or, an omen!): You won't really die. God knows when you eat you will be like one of the *elohim*. Lastly, a shining appearance conveys a divine nature. All the meanings telegraph something important. They are also consistent with the imagery from Isaiah 14 and Ezekiel 28.

DIVINE JUDGMENT

I tend to be sympathetic toward Eve. She all too often gets cast as stupid and naïve. Given the divine council context of her status as God's imager and new member of his family, what the *nachash* said to her had the ring of validity. Of course God wants us to be like the *elohim*—we're all one family. We all represent the creator, don't we? Why would we die?

This doesn't excuse Eve (or Adam). Their disobedience had dire consequences. But while the reason for God's judgment is transparent, the meanings of that judgment beg for some careful thought. Entire books have been written on the implications of God's response, so my thoughts will be very selective.[3]

The curse levied at Adam (Gen 3:17–19) did not supersede God's mandate to subdue the earth and take dominion. But it did make the task harder. The expulsion of humankind from Eden (Gen 3:22–25) turned a glorious dominion mission into mundane drudgery. We know that God would take steps to

---

2. I am not arguing that *nachash* should not be translated "serpent." It is not the translation that matters, but the recognition that the story is not about a mere animal. The serpent is actually a divine being. Rather, I am suggesting that, to literate readers of the Hebrew Bible, the lemma *nachash* would have (intentionally so) brought to mind other elements of the cognitive framework of the original readers: the dispensing of divine knowledge (the verb form) and luminescence (*nachash* is of the same root as *nechoshet* ["copper, bronze"] in biblical Hebrew). With respect to the latter, given the Babylonian/Aramaic context for other portions of Gen 1–11 (see chapters 12–15 in this book), it is worth noting that Aramaic *n-ch-sh* also refers to "copper, shining bronze," evoking the same sense of radiance or brilliance. See Marcus Jastrow, *A Dictionary of the Targumim, the Talmud Babli and Yerushalmi, and the Midrashic Literature, Vol. I and II* (London; New York: Luzac & Co.; G. P. Putnam's Sons, 1903), 896 (נחש II); Jacob Hoftijzer, Karel Jongeling, Richard C. Steiner, Adina Mosak Moshavi, and Bezalel Porten, *Dictionary of the North-West Semitic Inscriptions*, 2 vols. (Leiden: Brill, 1995), 2:726 (*nḥš₆*).

3. I prefer the term "judgment" to "curse" when it comes to God's response to Adam and Eve, reserving the term "curse" for the serpent. I agree with Wenham's assessment: "It should be noted that neither the man nor the woman are cursed: only the snake (v 14) and the soil (v 17) are cursed because of man. The sentences on the man and woman take the form of a disruption of their appointed roles" (Gordon J. Wenham, *Genesis 1–15* [vol. 1; Word Biblical Commentary; Dallas: Word, Incorporated, 1998], 81).

restore his rule, and that descendants of Adam (especially one of them—Gen 3:15) would be critical to that kingdom. The human yearning for utopia is interesting in this light. We seem to have an inner sense of need to restore something that was lost, but Eden cannot return on purely human terms.[4]

God's judgment of Eve is in some sense entwined with the curse of the *nachash*. Eve would suffer intensified pain in childbirth (Gen 3:16: "I will *multiply* your pain."). There is no indication that, had she borne children before the fall, Eve would have felt no pain at all. She was human. And it was important that she bear children, since her childbearing would have some relationship to the destiny of the *nachash* and his deed.

> [15]I will put enmity between you and the woman,
> and between your offspring and her offspring;
> he shall bruise your head,
> and you shall bruise his heel (Gen 3:15 ESV).

The wording of Gen 3:15 is veiled. For reasons that I'll make clear later, I believe prophecies like this that ultimately move in a messianic direction were deliberately cryptic. At the very least the verse tells us that God was not done with humanity yet. The goal of his rule on earth *through humanity* would not be abandoned. A descendant of Eve would come forth who would someday undo the damage caused by the divine rebel, the *nachash*. That this descendant is linked to Eve implies that the score will be settled through her bloodline.

This human threat to the *nachash* is fitting. The seduction to sin meant that Yahweh would have to be true to his word and eliminate humanity. The *nachash* counted on the justice of God to eliminate his rivals. God was just in this regard. Elimination from Eden did indeed mean death, but not in the sense of immediate annihilation. God would see to it that their lives ended, but not before continuing his plan. Humanity would die, but it would also, at some point, produce a descendant who would ultimately restore God's Edenic vision and destroy the *nachash*.

Adam and Eve had contingent immortality prior to the fall. They had

---

4. Utopianism is a familiar theme in classic literary works of Western civilization. Plato's *Republic*, Augustine's *City of God*, and Thomas More's *Utopia* are the more obvious examples. In the Christian context, utopian communities that sought to separate from the world or reform the culture according to Christian ideals include Calvin's Geneva, the Shaker movement, and the Ephrata Cloister. The Transcendental movement and sociopolitical ideologies like Marxism are also well-known secular examples. All attempts at creating a perfect harmonious society are doomed because people are imperfect, and total conformity is contrary to human nature. See Frank Edward Manuel, Fritzie Prigohzy Manuel, and Frank Edward Manuel, *Utopian Thought in the Western World* (Cambridge: Harvard University Press, 2009); Michael Fellman, *The Unbounded Frame: Freedom and Community in Nineteenth Century American Utopianism* (Westport, CT: Greenwood Press, 1973).

never-ending life, depending on certain circumstances. The imagery of Eden, home of the life-giver, and its tree of life convey the notion that, so long as Adam and Eve ate from the tree of life, called Eden their home, and didn't do anything that resulted in mortal injury (they were truly human after all), they would live.[5] Protected in their perfect environment, they could multiply and carry out their tasks as God's representatives on earth until the job was done.

All of that goes by the wayside once they are removed from Eden. God even takes the extra step of preventing them from returning to Eden's tree of life (Gen 3:24). Had they access to it, they would have gone on living, despite what had happened. After the fall, the only way to extend the work of God's human council-family was childbirth. Eve was redeemed through childbearing (1 Tim 2:15). So were the rest of us, in the sense that that is the only way God's original plan remained viable. Where there are no offspring, there can be no human imaging and no kingdom.

But the judgment on Eve also tells us that the *nachash* would have offspring as well. The rest of the biblical story doesn't consist of humans battling snake people. That's no surprise, since the enemy of humanity wasn't a mere snake. The Bible does, however, describe an ongoing conflict between followers of Yahweh and human and divine beings who follow the spiritual path of the *nachash*. All who oppose God's kingdom plan are the seed of the *nachash*.

Many readers who still feel the urge to see only a snake in Eden would no doubt contend that the curse pronounced on the *nachash* requires that. I disagree. Literal readings are inadequate to convey the full theological messaging and the entirety of the worldview context.

Consider what happens to the *nachash* against the backdrop of the judgment language found in Ezekiel 28 and Isaiah 14:

SERPENT/SHINING ONE IMAGERY & PUNISHMENT			
Hebrew Term	English Meaning	Concept	Important Verses
nachash	"serpent" (noun) "to use divination, give omens" (verb) "bronze, brazen" (adj)	word play; triple entendre Image of serpent (divine throne guardian), information from divine realm (divination), shining appearance associated with divinity (brazen)	Gen 3:1–2, 4, 13–14
chawwat	"serpent"		Ezek 28:12 (with silent *m*)
helel ben-shachar	"shining one, son of the dawn"	shining appearance associated with divinity	Isa 14:12 Ezek 28:13 (gems)

---

5. See the companion website for the theological messaging of the tree of life imagery.

Hebrew Term	English Meaning	Concept	Important Verses
yarad gada' shalak	"brought down" "cut down" "cast down"	an expulsion from the divine presence and former service role to Yahweh[6]	Ezek 28:8, 17 Isa 14:11–12, 15
'erets sheol	"earth, ground" (abstractly): underworld realm of the dead Sheol; realm of the dead	underworld, realm of the dead NOTE: the nachash of Gen 3 is made to crawl on his belly, put on the ground, under the feet of animals (Gen 3:14)	Ezek 28:17 Isa 14:9, 11–12, 15
rephaim melakim	Rephaim; the "shades"; the dead in the underworld "kings" (fallen enemies)	underworld occupants	Ezek 28:17 Isa 14:9

The *nachash* was cursed to crawl on its belly, imagery that conveyed being *cast down* (Ezek 28:8, 17; Isa 14:11–12, 15) to the ground. In Ezekiel 28 and Isaiah 14, we saw the villain cast down to the *'erets*, a term that refers literally to the dirt and metaphorically to the underworld (Ezek 28:17; Isa 14:9, 11–12, 15). The curse also had him "eating dirt," clearly a metaphorical reference, since snakes don't really eat dirt as food for nutrition. It isn't part of the "natural snake diet." The point being made by the curse is that the *nachash*, who wanted to be "most high," will be "most low" instead—cast away from God and the council to earth, and even under the earth. In the underworld, the *nachash* is even lower than the beasts of the field. He is hidden from view and from life in God's world. His domain is death.

After the fall, though humankind was estranged from God and no longer immortal, the plan of God was not extinguished. Genesis 3 tells us why we die, why we need redemption and salvation, and why we cannot save ourselves. It also tells us that God's plan has only been delayed—not defeated—and that the human story will be both a tragic struggle and a miraculous, providential saga.

But the situation is going to get worse before it gets better.

---

6. The satan of Job 1–2 is not the *nachash* of Eden. See the discussion in Chapter 8. The divine rebel of Eden lost his role as Yahweh's throne guardian and, consequently, access to Yahweh's council. As will be noted in subsequent chapters, as lord of the dead, the *nachash* (later called Satan in the New Testament) has claim over humanity through death, since human immortality in the presence of God was disrupted by human sin in Eden, necessitating redemption to once again be part of God's eternal family.

CHAPTER 12

Divine Transgression

AFTER THE RUINATION OF EDEN, THE HUMAN STORY HEADS SOUTH IN A hurry. That's to be expected. The curses that followed the events in the garden bound the fate of humanity together with the seed of the *nachash*, all those who oppose the rule of God in either the earthly or the spiritual realm. The rule of God known as Eden would disappear, kept alive only through a fledgling humanity to whom God extended mercy.

The seed of the *nachash* is therefore literal (people and divine beings are real) and spiritual (the lineage is one of spiritual rebellion). This description has secure biblical roots. Jesus told the Pharisees, "You are of your father the devil, and you want to do the desires of your father" (John 8:44), and called them "serpents" and "offspring of vipers" (Matt 23:33). In 1 John 3 the apostle John expressed the notion of spiritual seed—good or evil—manifesting itself in the human heart when he wrote:

> [8] The one who practices sin is of the devil, because the devil has been sinning from the beginning. For this reason the Son of God was revealed: in order to destroy the works of the devil. [9] Everyone who is fathered by God does not practice sin, because his seed resides in him, and he is not able to sin, because he has been fathered by God. [10] By this the children of God and the children of the devil are evident: everyone who does not practice righteousness is not of God, namely, the one who does not love his brother.
>
> [11] For this is the message that you have heard from the beginning: that we should love one another, [12] not as Cain, who was of the evil one and violently murdered his brother. And for what reason did he violently murder him? Because his deeds were evil and the deeds of his brother were righteous (1 John 3:8–12).

This passage describes people whose lives are characterized by wickedness as "children of the devil," a contrast to the spiritual "children of God." This is a spiritual lineage, since the children of God have "God's seed" abiding in them, a reference to the Holy Spirit. Peter echoes the same thought in 1 Peter 1:23, where he describes those born again (literally, born "from above") as being born not as mortal offspring or seed, but of "imperishable seed," through the word of God. The language, then, points toward the spiritual—following Yahweh or following the example of the original rebel, the *nachash*.

Interestingly, John mentions Cain specifically. Cain murdered Abel sometime after their parents were expelled from Eden, the point at which we've arrived in our exploration. Cain's spiritual father was the *nachash*. They walked the same path.

Things eventually got so bad that in Genesis 6:5 we read, "And Yahweh saw that the evil of humankind *was* great upon the earth, and every inclination of the thoughts of his heart was always only evil." But that verdict is preceded by four verses that describe a different kind of rebellion—a divine one. There were those in that realm who, as the *nachash* had done, made a free choice that violated God's design and strategy for his rule on earth.

In what remains of this chapter, we'll take a closer look at this divine transgression, focusing on how the account has been stripped of its supernatural features—and therefore its intended meaning—by most Christian interpreters. We'll continue the discussion in the two chapters that follow, where we'll examine how the original context and intent of the passage compels a supernatural interpretation and then explore that interpretation's implications.

PRECURSOR TO THE FLOOD: Divine Rebellion

Genesis 6:1–4 is one of those texts that many readers and pastors would rather skip. Not here. Its theological message is important.

> [1]And it happened that, when humankind began to multiply on the face of the ground, daughters were born to them. [2]Then the sons of God saw the daughters of humankind, that they were beautiful. And they took for themselves wives from all that they chose. [3]And Yahweh said, "My Spirit shall not abide with humankind forever in that he is also flesh. And his days shall be one hundred and twenty years." [4]The Nephilim were upon the earth in those days, and also afterward, when the sons of God went into the daughters of humankind, and they bore children to them. These were the mighty warriors that were from ancient times, men of renown.

There are few Bible passages that raise as many questions as this one.[1] Who are

---

1. There is a substantial body of scholarly literature on Gen 6:1–4. The issues are many and complex. See the companion website.

the sons of God? Are they divine or human? Who were the Nephilim? How do these verses relate to the human evil described in Genesis 6:5?

Before we start tackling these questions and others,[2] we need to learn how *not* to interpret this passage.

THE SETHITE INTERPRETATION

This interpretation of Genesis 6:1–4 is the one most commonly taught in Christian churches, evangelical or otherwise. It has been the dominant Christian position since the late fourth century AD.[3]

In this approach, the sons of God in Genesis 6:1–4 are merely human beings, men from the line of Seth, Adam and Eve's son who was born after Cain murdered Abel (Gen 4:25–26; 5:3–4). Presumably, these four verses describe forbidden intermarriage between the godly men of Seth's lineage ("sons of God") and the ungodly women of Cain's line ("daughters of humankind"). In this reading, everyone who lived on earth ultimately came from these two lines, both of them lines descended from Adam and Eve's children.[4] In this way, the Bible distinguished the godly from the ungodly. Part of the rationale for this view comes from Genesis 4:26, where, depending on the translation, we read that either Seth or humankind "began to call on the name of the Lord" (NIV).[5] The line of Seth was to remain pure and separate from evil lineage. The marriages of Genesis 6:1–4 erased this separation and incurred the wrath of God in the flood.

Exposing the deficiencies of the Sethite view isn't difficult. The position is deeply flawed.

First, Genesis 4:26 never says the *only* people who "called on the name of the

---

2. The questions listed here are addressed in this chapter and the next. Other questions include how to think about the sexual element of the story and how, if everyone but Noah and his family is wiped out by the flood, Nephilim could show up on the earth after the flood. Those questions will be addressed in chapter 23.

3. The history of how Gen 6:1–4 has been interpreted is chronicled in detail in Annette Yoshiko Reed, *Fallen Angels and the History of Judaism and Christianity: The Reception of Enochic Literature* (Cambridge: Cambridge University Press, 2005).

4. One wonders how only women could produce a "line."

5. The verb form ("began") is third masculine singular. Since the word *'adam*, which is often rendered "mankind" or "humankind" in modern translations (e.g., Gen 1:26), does not actually appear in the verse, the most natural rendering would be that *Seth* began to call on the name of the Lord. If this is the case, then the Sethite view needs to extrapolate Seth's faith to only *men* from that point on, since it is the "sons" of God who must be spiritually distinct from the "daughters" of humankind. One way around this is to argue that Gen 6:1–4 describes godly Sethite men marrying ungodly non-Sethite women. The passage of course never says that, and it presumes that, by definition, the only godly women on the planet were those related to Seth. Those who insert "humankind" into the verse ("humankind began to call on the name of the Lord") undermine the Sethite view with that decision, as it would have humans from other lineages, not just that of Seth, calling on the name of the Lord.

Lord" were men from Seth's lineage. That idea is imposed on the text. Second, as we'll see in the next chapter, the view fails miserably in explaining the Nephilim. Third, the text never calls the women in the episode "daughters of Cain." Rather, they are "daughters of humankind." There is no actual link in the text to Cain. This means that the Sethite view of the text is supported by something *not* present in the text, which is the very antithesis of exegesis. Fourth, there is no command in the text regarding marriages or any prohibition against marrying certain persons. There are no "Jews and Gentiles" at this time.[6] Fifth, nothing in Genesis 6:1–4 or anywhere else in the Bible identifies people who come from Seth's lineage with the descriptive phrase "sons of God." That connection is purely an assumption through which the story is filtered by those who hold the Sethite view.

A close reading of Genesis 6:1–4 makes it clear that a contrast is being created between two classes of individuals, one human and the other divine. When speaking of how humanity was multiplying on earth (v. 1), the text mentions only daughters ("daughters were born to them"). The point is not literally that every birth in the history of the earth after Cain and Abel resulted in a girl.[7] Rather, the writer is setting up a contrast of two groups. The first group is human and female (the "daughters of humankind"). Verse 2 introduces the other group for the contrast: the sons of God. That group is not human, but divine.

There are more deficiencies in this viewpoint than I will take time here to expose, but the point is evident. The Sethite hypothesis collapses under the weight of its own incoherence.

DIVINIZED HUMAN RULERS

Another approach that argues the "sons of God" in Genesis 6:1–4 are human suggests that they should be understood as divinized human rulers. A survey of the academic literature arguing this perspective reveals that it springs from the following: (1) taking the phrase "sons of the Most High" in Psalm 82:6 as referring to humans, then reading that back into Genesis 6:1–4; (2) noting language where God refers to humans as his sons (Exod 4:23; Psa 2:7), which, it is argued, is parallel to ancient Near Eastern beliefs that kings were thought

---

6. It is also misguided to argue that the Sethite view is valid because the writers and editors of the Torah were living under the law. There are near-relation marriages in the Genesis story prior to the Sinai legislation. For example, Abraham and Sarah had the same father, but different mothers, a forbidden sexual relationship in the Torah (Gen 20:12; cf. Lev 18:9, 11; 20:17; Deut 27:22). In other words, the later legal backdrop of Sinai isn't being presumed elsewhere in Genesis, so it cannot be presumed as the backdrop for Gen 6:1–4. There simply is no support for condemned human intermarriage in the text.

7. This sort of awkward overliteralizing cannot explain, for example, where Noah got his sons.

to be divine offspring; and (3) arguing that the evil marriages condemned in the verses were human polygamy on the part of these divinized rulers.

We have already seen how the human view of the plural *elohim* language in Psalm 82 fails, so that fundamental flaw need not be reiterated here. But there are other flaws in this approach.

First, the text of Genesis 6 never says the marriages were polygamous. That idea must be read into the passage. Second, ancient parallels restrict divine sonship language to kings. Consequently, the idea of a *group* of sons of God lacks a coherent ancient Near Eastern parallel. The precise plural phrase refers to divine beings elsewhere in the Old Testament, not kings (Job 1:6; 2:1; 38:7; Pss 29:1; 82:6 [cf. 82:1b]; 89:6 [Hebrew: 89:7]).[8] Third, the broad idea of "human divine kingship" elsewhere in the Old Testament is not a coherent argument against a supernatural view of Genesis 6. It was God's original design for his human children to be servant rulers over the earth under his authority as his representatives—*in the presence of his glory*. Restoring the loss of the Edenic vision eventually involves creating a people known as Israel and giving them a king (David), who is the template for messiah. In the final eschatological outcome, the messiah is the ultimate Davidic king, and all *glorified* believers share that rule in a new, global Eden.[9] But it is flawed hermeneutics to read either ancient kingship or the glorification of believers back into

---

8. The divinized kingship view is also defended by contending that there are no examples in ancient Near Eastern materials of divine beings "marrying" human women, while there are examples of kings claiming mixed ancestry from gods and humans. This of course presumes Gen 6:1–4 is describing matrimonial unions. This is playing word games, since the "marriage" idea derives from English translations. The word translated "wife" is simply the normal plural for "women" (*nashim*). The biblical euphemisms of "taking" (Gen 6:2) or "going in to" a woman (Gen 6:4) are not exclusively used for marriage. They are also used to describe the sexual act outside a marriage bond. That is, "taking" a woman can describe an illicit sexual relationship (Gen 38:2; Lev 18:17; 20:17, 21; 21:7), as can "coming/going in to" (Gen 38:2; 39:14; Lev 21:11; Judg 16:1; Amos 2:7). The point of the language of Gen 6:1–4 is a sexual relationship, not matrimony. This objection is therefore a distinction without a difference. This view also fails logically. The objection about the lack of divine-human *marriages* is aimed at eliminating the divine element from Gen 6:1–4, thus reducing the episode to purely human relationships (albeit with divine kings as focus). But on what logical basis would multiple marriages between kings and women bring the world into chaos, necessitating God's judgment in a catastrophic flood?

9. Rev 2:7, 26–28; 3:21; 5:10; 21:24 ["kings" = rulers]. The idea of believers ruling over nations must be read in the context of the reclamation of the nations disinherited by God in Deut 32:8–9 (see chapter 15 and the final chapter of this book). The eschatological portrayal of glorified human rulers in a global Eden is why Hos 1:10 cannot be used to argue that the sons of God in Gen 6:1–4 are human. First, the phrase is not a precise parallel. Second, that passage must be viewed in the larger context of biblical theology. Hos 1:10 is *eschatological*. It looks to a distant future time when the *northern* kingdom of Israel will be restored as people of God. That eschatological event coincides with the ultimate glorification of believers—who are, and will be, children of the living God, ruling and reigning with Yahweh, as originally intended, in a new, global Eden. The fact that God will see his human family fulfill the original Edenic goal does not overturn the fact that God also has a divine family. At the last day, when human believers are glorified, the two families and councils *merge*. One family of God doesn't erase the other.

Genesis 6. The reason is obvious: the marriages in Genesis 6:1–4 corrupt the earth in the prelude to the flood story. A biblical theology of divinized human rulership in the restored Eden would not be corruptive and evil.

In summary, the plurality of the phrase "sons of God" and the heavenly contexts of its use elsewhere show us there is no *exegetical* reason to exclude the occurrences of the phrase in Genesis 6:2, 4 from the list of supernatural beings. What drives this choice is apprehension about the alternative.

PETER AND JUDE

Peter and Jude did not fear the alternative. They embraced a supernatural view of Genesis 6:1–4. Two passages are especially relevant.

> [1] But there were also false prophets among the people … [3] And in greediness they will exploit you with false words, whose condemnation from long ago is not idle, and their destruction is not asleep. [4] For if God did not spare **the angels who sinned**, but **held them captive in Tartarus with chains of darkness and handed them over to be kept for judgment,** [5] and **did not spare the ancient world, but preserved Noah,** a proclaimer of righteousness, and seven others when he brought a flood on the world of the ungodly, [6] and condemned the cities of Sodom and Gomorrah to destruction, reducing them to ashes, having appointed them as an example for those who are going to be ungodly, [7] and rescued righteous Lot, worn down by the way of life of lawless persons in licentiousness [8] (for that righteous man, as he lived among them day after day, was tormenting his righteous soul by the lawless deeds he was seeing and hearing), [9] then the Lord knows how to rescue the godly from trials and to reserve the unrighteous to be punished at the day of judgment, [10] and **especially those who go after the flesh in defiling lust and who despise authority** (2 Peter 2:1–10).

> [5] Now I want to remind you, although you know everything once and for all, that Jesus, having saved the people out of the land of Egypt, the second time destroyed those who did not believe. [6] And **the angels who did not keep to their own domain but deserted their proper dwelling place, he has kept in eternal bonds under deep gloom for the judgment of the great day,** [7] as Sodom and Gomorrah and the towns around them indulged in sexual immorality and pursued unnatural desire **in the same way as these,** are exhibited as an example by undergoing the punishment of eternal fire (Jude 5–7).

Scholars agree that the passages are about the same subject matter.[10] They

---

10. See, for example, Peter H. Davids, *The Letters of 2 Peter and Jude* (Pillar New Testament Commentary;

describe an episode from the time of Noah and the flood where "angels" sinned.[11] That sin, which precipitated the flood, was sexual in nature; it is placed in the same category as the sin which prompted the judgment of Sodom and Gomorrah. The transgression was interpreted by Peter and Jude as evidence of despising authority and the boundaries of "proper dwelling" for the parties concerned. All of those elements are transparent in Genesis 6:1–4. There is simply no other sin in the Old Testament that meets these specific details—and no other "angelic" sin *at all* in the Old Testament that might be the referent.[12]

The punishment for the transgression, however, is not mentioned in Genesis 6:1–4. Peter has the divine sons of God held captive in "Tartarus" in chains of darkness until a time of judgment.[13] Jude echoes the thought and clarifies the judgment as the day of the Lord ("the great day"; cf. Zeph 1:1–7; Rev 16:14). These elements come from Jewish literature written between our Old and New Testaments (the "Second Temple" period) that retell the Genesis 6 episode. The most famous of these is 1 Enoch. That book informed the thinking of Peter and Jude; it was part of their intellectual worldview.[14] The inspired

---

Grand Rapids, MI: Eerdmans, 2006), 3; Michael Green, *2 Peter and Jude: An Introduction and Commentary* (Tyndale New Testament Commentaries 18; Downers Grove, IL: InterVarsity Press, 1987), 68; Jerome H. Neyrey, *2 Peter, Jude: A New Translation with Introduction and Commentary* (Anchor Yale Bible 37C; New Haven; London: Yale University Press, 2008), 120–22.

11. The word choice ("angels") comes from the Septuagint. Despite its imprecision, the divine orientation is clear.

12. Some interpreters imagine a prefall rebellion of angels that might fit with 2 Peter. The Bible records no such event. The closest one that comes to it is in Rev 12:7–9. Not only is Revelation the last book of the Bible written, which means it cannot be the referent of 2 Peter, but Rev 12:7–9 associates the war in heaven with the first coming of the messiah, not events before the flood. There is no biblical evidence for a prefall angelic rebellion. The idea comes from Milton's *Paradise Lost*, not the Bible.

13. The phrase "held captive in Tartarus" in 2 Pet 2:4 is the translation of a verb lemma (ταρταρόω) that points to the term from classical Greek literature for the destination of the divine Titans, a term that is also used of their semidivine offspring. The terminology clearly informs us that, for Peter and Jude, an antisupernaturalist interpretation of Gen 6:1–4 was not in view. See G. Mussies, "Titans," in *Dictionary of Deities and Demons in the Bible*, 2nd ed. (ed. Karel van der Toorn, Bob Becking, and Pieter W. van der Horst; Leiden; Boston; Cologne; Grand Rapids, MI; Cambridge: Brill; Eerdmans, 1999), 872–874; G. Mussies, "Giants," in ibid., 343–345; David M. Johnson, "Hesiod's Descriptions of Tartarus (*Theogony* 721–819)," *The Phoenix* 53:1–2 (1999): 8–28; J. Daryl Charles, "The Angels under Reserve in 2 Peter and Jude," *Bulletin for Biblical Research* 15.1 (2005): 39–48.

14. This sort of thing is common in human experience. For example, anyone who has read John Calvin's thoughts on predestination, or a dispensationalist's take on prophecy, will find it next to impossible to eliminate that material from their thinking while reading, respectively, the book of Romans or Revelation. First Enoch and other works are part of the thinking of Peter and Jude because they were well known and taken seriously by contemporaries. The content of 1 Enoch shows up elsewhere in these epistles. It is obvious to those who study all these texts, especially in Greek, that Peter and Jude knew 1 Enoch very well. Scholars have devoted considerable attention to parallels between that book and the epistles of Peter and Jude. See George W. E. Nickelsburg, *1 Enoch: A Commentary on the Book of 1 Enoch 1–36, 81–108* (Minneapolis: Fortress, 2001), 83–87, 560; Pieter G. R. de Villiers, ed., *Studies in 1 Enoch and the New Testament*

New Testament writers were perfectly comfortable referencing content found in 1 Enoch and other Jewish books to articulate their theology.[15] These observations are important. All Jewish traditions before the New Testament era took a supernatural view of Genesis 6:1–4.[16] In other words, they were in line with 2 Peter and Jude. The interpretation of the passage, at least with respect to its supernatural orientation, was not an issue until the late fourth century AD, when it fell out of favor with some influential church fathers, especially Augustine.

But biblical theology does not derive from the church fathers. It derives from the biblical text, framed in its own context. Scholars agree that the Second Temple Jewish literature that influenced Peter and Jude shows intimate familiarity with the original Mesopotamian context of Genesis 6:1–4.[17] For the person who considers the Old and New Testament to be equally inspired, interpreting Genesis 6:1–4 "in context" means analyzing it in light of its Mesopotamian background as well as 2 Peter and Jude, whose content utilizes

---

(= *Neotestamentica* 17; Stellenbosch: University of Stellenbosch Press, 1983); and Richard J. Bauckham, *2 Peter, Jude* (Word Biblical Commentary, vol. 50; Dallas: Word, 1998), 139–40.

15. None of this means 1 Enoch should be considered inspired. It shouldn't and wasn't. A handful of leaders in the early church gave it that status, and those who did eventually abandoned the idea. See James C. VanderKam, "1 Enoch, Enochic Motifs, and Enoch in Early Christian Literature," in *The Jewish Apocalyptic Heritage in Early Christianity* (ed. James C. VanderKam and William Adler; Minneapolis: Fortress, 1996), 33–101.

16. The well-known texts of 1 Enoch have the offenders of Gen 6 as divine (the sons of God are called Watchers in 1 Enoch, a term that, as our next chapter shows, derives from a Mesopotamian context) and their offspring as giants. First Enoch connects this to demonology in that, when a giant was killed, its "Watcher spirit" is referred to as a demon. Hence in Gen 6 divine-human cohabitation is the answer to where demons come from in Second Temple Jewish thinking. On that subject, see Reed, *Fallen Angels*; Archie T. Wright, *The Origin of Evil Spirits: The Reception of Genesis 6:1–4 in Early Jewish Literature* (*Wissenschaftliche Untersuchungen zum Neuen Testament* 198, second series; Tübingen: Mohr Siebeck, 2013). There are several other Second Temple Jewish texts that take the same perspective (and none that oppose it to my knowledge). For instance, several Dead Sea Scrolls refer to demons as "bastard spirits" (4Q510 [=4QShir[a]] frag. 1:5; 4Q511 [=4QShir[b]] frag. 35:7; 4Q204 [=4QEnoch[c] ar], Col V:2–3). Another scroll (11QapocPsa[=11Q11] refers to demons in Col II:3 and then later calls the demons "offspring of man and the seed of the holy ones" (Col V:6). See the companion website for those texts. This is a clear indication of how Second Temple Jews understood Gen 6:1–4, which was in turn based on a grasp of the original polemic context of Gen 6:1–4. See chapter 13 for more on that context. On the Qumran scrolls mentioned above, see Loren T. Stuckenbruck, "The 'Angels' and 'Giants' of Genesis 6:1–4 in Second and Third Century BCE Jewish Interpretation: Reflections on the Posture of Early Apocalyptic Traditions," *Dead Sea Discoveries* 7.3 (2000): 354–77; Ida Fröhlich, "Theology and Demonology in Qumran Texts," *Henoch* 32.1 (2010):101–128; Hermann Lichtenberger, "Spirits and Demons in the Dead Sea Scrolls," in *The Holy Spirit and Christian Origins: Essays in Honor of James D. G. Dunn* (ed. James D. G. Dunn, Graham Stanton, Bruce W. Longenecker, and Stephen C. Barton; Grand Rapids, MI: Eerdmans, 2004), 22–40.

17. See Amar Annus, "On the Origin of the Watchers: A Comparative Study of the Antediluvian Wisdom in Mesopotamian and Jewish Traditions," *Journal for the Study of the Pseudepigrapha* 19.4 (2010): 277–320, and Ida Frölich, "Mesopotamian Elements and the Watchers Traditions," in *The Watchers in Jewish and Christian Traditions* (ed. Angela Kim Hawkins, Kelley Coblentz Bautch, and John Endres; Minneapolis: Fortress, 2014), 11–24.

supernatural interpretations from Jewish theology of their own day. Filtering Genesis 6:1–4 through Christian tradition that arose centuries after the New Testament period cannot honestly be considered interpreting Genesis 6:1–4 in context.

Our next step is to build on what we've learned. In the next chapter, we'll take a closer look at how the ancient contexts of Genesis 6:1–4 demand a supernatural outlook for the passage. Doing so will enable us to understand its message and role in the larger biblical narrative.

The Bad Seed

IN THE LAST CHAPTER WE LEARNED THAT NEW TESTAMENT WRITERS PARtook of the intellectual climate of their own Jewish community, a community that flourished in the period between the Old and New Testament. It might seem unnecessary to mention this, given the enthusiasm many Bible readers have today for tapping into the Jewish mind to understand the words of Jesus and the apostles. When it comes to Genesis 6:1–4, though, that enthusiasm often sours, since the result doesn't support the most comfortable modern Christian interpretation.

The truth is that the writers of the New Testament knew nothing of the Sethite view, nor of any view that makes the sons of God in Genesis 6:1–4 humans. Our goal in this chapter is to revisit the passage and dig deeper. When we take it on its own terms, we can determine its character and meaning.

THE ANCIENT NEAR EASTERN CONTEXT

That Genesis 1–11 has many connections to Mesopotamian literature is not disputed by scholars, evangelical or otherwise. The story of creation, the genealogies before the flood, the flood itself, and the tower of Babel incident all have secure connections to Mesopotamian material that is much older than the Old Testament.[1]

---

1. The literature on these connections is voluminous. Mesopotamian epics such as *Enuma Elish* ("The Epic of Creation"), the *Eridu Genesis*, the *Tale of Adapa*, the Sumerian King List, *Atrahasis*, the *Epic of Gilgamesh*, and *Enmerkar and the Lord of Aratta* all contain close parallels to what we read in Gen 1–11. There are many more texts that do as well, including texts from Egypt and Canaan. To learn about these connections, see John H. Walton, *Ancient Israelite Literature in Its Cultural Context* (Grand Rapids, MI: Zondervan, 1994), and Bill Arnold and Brian Beyer, *Readings from the Ancient Near East: Primary Sources for Old Testament Study* (Grand Rapids, MI: Baker Book House, 2002). A more scholarly volume is Richard S. Hess and David Toshio Tsumura, eds., *I Studied Inscriptions from before the Flood: Ancient Near Eastern, Literary, and Linguistic Approaches to Genesis 1–11*, Sources for Biblical and Theological Study 4 (Winona Lake, IN: Eisenbrauns, 1994).

Genesis 6:1–4, too, has deep Mesopotamian roots that, until very recently, have not been fully recognized or appreciated.[2] Jewish literature like 1 Enoch that retold the story shows a keen awareness of that Mesopotamian context. This awareness shows us that Jewish thinkers of the Second Temple period understood, correctly, that the story involved divine beings and giant off-spring.[3] That understanding is essential to grasping what the biblical writers were trying to communicate.

Genesis 6:1–4 is a polemic; it is a literary and theological effort to undermine the credibility of Mesopotamian gods and other aspects of that culture's worldview. Biblical writers do this frequently. The strategy often involves borrowing lines and motifs from the literature of the target civilization to articulate correct theology about Yahweh and to show contempt for other gods. Genesis 6:1–4 is a case study in this technique.

Mesopotamia had several versions of the story of a catastrophic flood, complete with a large boat that saves animals and humans.[4] They include mention of a group of sages (the *apkallus*), possessors of great knowledge, in the period before the flood. These *apkallus* were divine beings. Many *apkallus* were considered evil; those *apkallus* are integral to Mesopotamian demonology. After the flood, offspring of the *apkallus* were said to be human in descent (i.e., having a human parent) and "two-thirds *apkallu*."[5] In other words, the *apkallus* mated with human women and produced quasi-divine offspring.

---

2. The single best study in this regard is Amar Annus, "On the Watchers: A Comparative Study of the Antediluvian Wisdom in Mesopotamian and Jewish Traditions," *Journal for the Study of the Pseudepigrapha* 19.4 (2010): 277–320. Other works that deserve accolades include Helge S. Kvanvig, *Roots of Apocalyptic: The Mesopotamian Background of the Enoch Figure and the Son of Man* (Wissenschaftliche Monographien zum Alten und Neuen Testament 61; Neukirchen-Vluyn: Neukirchener Verlag, 1988); Kvanvig, *Primeval History: Babylonian, Biblical, and Enochic* (Supplements to the Journal for the Study of Judaism 149; Leiden: Brill, 2011); and S. Bhayro, *The Shemihazah and Asael Narrative of 1 Enoch 6–11: Introduction, Text, Translation and Commentary with Reference to Ancient Near Eastern Antecedents* (Alter Orient und Altes Testament 322; Münster: Ugarit Verlag, 2005).

3. *First Enoch* is witnessed in other manuscripts besides those known from Qumran. The Qumran material is in part important because it was held in high regard by certain Jewish sects. See George W. E. Nickelsburg, "Scripture in *1 Enoch* and *1 Enoch* as Scripture," in *Texts and Contexts: Biblical Texts in Their Textual and Situational Contexts: Essays in Honor of Lars Hartman* (Oslo: Scandinavian University Press, 1995), 333–54.

4. See Victor Matthews, *Old Testament Parallels* (rev. and exp. ed.; Mahwah, NJ: Paulist Press, 2007), 21–42, and Stephanie Dalley, *Myths from Mesopotamia: Creation, Flood, Gilgamesh, and Others* (Oxford: Oxford University Press, 1998). The standard scholarly discussion is Alan Millard and W. G. Lambert, *Atra-Hasis: The Babylonian Story of the Flood with the Sumerian Flood Story* (Winona Lake, IN: Eisenbrauns, 2010).

5. More specifically, the last of the postflood *apkallus* in Mesopotamian tradition (Lu-Nanna) was only two-thirds *apkallu* (see Anne Draffkorn Kilmer, "The Mesopotamian Counterparts of the Biblical Nepilim," in *Perspectives on Language and Text: Essays and Poems in Honor of Francis I. Andersen's Sixtieth Birthday, July 28, 1985* (ed. Edgar W. Conrad and Edward G. Newing; Winona Lake, IN: Eisenbrauns, 1987): 39–44

The parallels to Genesis 6:1–4 are impossible to miss. The "two-thirds divine" description is especially noteworthy, since it precisely matches the description of the Mesopotamian hero Gilgamesh. Recent critical work on the cuneiform tablets of the *Epic of Gilgamesh* has revealed that Gilgamesh was considered a giant who retained knowledge from before the flood.[6]

Other connections: In the Mesopotamian flood story found in a text now known as the *Erra Epic*, the Babylonian high god Marduk punishes the evil *apkallus* with banishment to the subterranean waters deep inside the earth, which were known as Apsu.[7] The Apsu was also considered part of the under-world.[8] Marduk commanded that they never come up again. The parallels are clear and unmistakable. The banishment of these sinister divine beings to beneath the earth is significant. In the last chapter, I noted that this element of the story, found in 2 Peter and Jude, is not found in the Old Testament. The presence of this item in books like 1 Enoch and, subsequently, in the New Testament, is a clear indication that Jewish writers between the testaments were aware of the Mesopotamian context of Genesis 6:1–4.[9]

There are two other features to highlight in our discussion before we discuss what it all means.

THE SONS OF GOD:
Watchers, Sons of Heaven, Holy Ones

The divine transgression before the flood is retold in several Jewish texts from the intertestamental period. At least one has the divine offenders coming to earth to "fix" the mess that was humankind—to provide direction and

---

(esp. 41). Annus ("Origin of the Watchers," 282) notes that this description "exactly matches the status of Gilgamesh in the post-diluvian world, as he also was 'two-thirds divine, and one-third human.'"

6. See Andrew George, *The Babylonian Gilgamesh Epic: Introduction, Critical Edition and Cuneiform Texts* (Oxford: Oxford University Press, 2003); George, "The Gilgamesh Epic at Ugarit," *Aula Orientalis* 25 (2007): 237–54. The relevant lines in the *Gilgamesh Epic* are tablet 1, lines 8, 48.

7. Annus is unclear on this issue, as is his wording regarding the *apkallu* and the Apsu. In some places he has the *apkallu* sages sent to the Apsu; in others he refers to this assertion as a speculation (e.g., pp. 309–10). The line from the *Erra Epic* confirms the *apkallu* sages were sent to the Apsu. Marduk says: "I made those (original) Craftsmen [the seven sages] go down to the Apsu, and I said they were not to come back up" (William W. Hallo and K. Lawson Younger, *The Context of Scripture* [Leiden; New York: Brill, 1997–], 1:407. See footnote 19 at the end of the line from *Erra* for the identification of the craftsmen as the *apkallu* sages).

8. See Wayne Horowitz, *Mesopotamian Cosmic Geography* (Winona Lake, IN: Eisenbrauns, 1998), 342–44.

9. As we saw in the previous chapter, 2 Pet 2:4 has the guilty divine beings imprisoned in "Tartarus." This Greek word is the precise term used in classical Greek myths of ancient Titans and giants. The two groups are different but also conflated by classical Greek writers. However, both groups *were divine in origin* in Greek mythology. For our purposes, Peter's word choice here points very specifically to the divine nature of the sons of God in Gen 6:1–4.

leadership through their knowledge. They were trying to help, but once they had assumed flesh, they failed to resist its urges.[10] The more common version of events, one with a more sinister flavor, is found in 1 Enoch 6–11. This is the reading that informed Peter and Jude. The story begins very much like Genesis 6:

> And when the sons of men had multiplied, in those days, beautiful and comely daughters were born to them. And the watchers, the sons of heaven, saw them and desired them. And they said to one another, "Come, let us choose for ourselves wives from the daughters of men, and let us beget for ourselves children."

The account has the Watchers descending to Mount Hermon, a site that will factor into the biblical epic in unexpected ways. *Watcher*, the English translation of Aramaic *'ir*, is not new to us. In an earlier chapter about how God and his council participate together in decision making, we looked at part of Daniel 4, one of the sections of Daniel written in Aramaic, not Hebrew. Daniel 4 is the only biblical passage to specifically use the term *watcher* to describe the divine "holy ones" of Yahweh's council.[11] The geographical context of Daniel is of course Babylon (Dan 1:1–7), which is in Mesopotamia.

The offspring of the Watchers (sons of God) in 1 Enoch were giants (1 Enoch 7). Some fragments of 1 Enoch among the Dead Sea Scrolls give names for some of the giants. Other texts that retell the story and are thus related to 1 Enoch do the same. The most startling of these is known today by scholars as *The Book of Giants*. It exists only in fragments, but names of several giants, offspring of the Watchers, have survived. One of the names is Gilgamesh, the main character of the Mesopotamian *Epic of Gilgamesh*.[12]

Figurines of *apkallus*, the Mesopotamian counterparts to the sons of God, are known through the work of Mesopotamian archaeologists. They were buried in rows of boxes as parts of foundation walls for Mesopotamian buildings

---

10. The best scholarly survey of Second Temple retellings of Gen 6 is Loren T. Stuckenbruck, "The 'Angels' and 'Giants' of Genesis 6:1–4 in Second and Third Century BCE Jewish Interpretation: Reflections on the Posture of Early Apocalyptic Traditions," *Dead Sea Discoveries* 7.3 (2000): 354–77.

11. In Jewish literature from the era of Daniel through the Second Temple period, *watcher* is a common term for the heavenly sons of God. See John C. Collins, "Watcher," in *Dictionary of Deities and Demons in the Bible*, 2nd ed. (ed. Karel van der Toorn, Bob Becking, and Pieter W. van der Horst; Grand Rapids, MI; Eerdmans, 1999), 893–895.

12. Humbaba (Aramaic: *Chobabish*) and Utnapishtim, the Babylonian Noah, are others. Scholars of this material believe that Utnapishtim is the name from which a third giant's name (Atambish) is derived. See J. C. Reeves, "Utnapishtim in the Book of the Giants?" *Journal of Biblical Literature* 112 (1993): 110–15; Matthew Goff, "Gilgamesh the Giant: The Qumran *Book of Giants'* Appropriation of Gilgamesh Motifs," *Dead Sea Discoveries* 16.2 (2009): 221–53.

to ward off evil powers.[13] These boxes were referred to by Mesopotamians as *mats-tsarey*, which means "watchers."[14] The connection is explicit and direct.

THE NEPHILIM

One of the great debates over Genesis 6:1–4 is the meaning of the word *nephilim*. We've seen from the Mesopotamian context that the *apkallus* were divine, mated with human women, and produced giant offspring. We've also seen that Jewish thinkers in the Second Temple period viewed the offspring of Genesis 6:1–4 in the same way—as giants. Any analysis of the term *nephilim* must account for, not ignore or violate, these contexts.

Interpretation of the term *nephilim* must also account for another Jewish phenomenon between the testaments—translation of the Old Testament into Greek. I speak here of the Septuagint. The word *nephilim* occurs twice in the Hebrew Bible (Gen 6:4; Num 13:33). In both cases the Septuagint translated the term with *gigas* ("giant").[15]

Given the backdrop we've covered, it would seem obvious that *nephilim* ought to be understood as "giants." But many commentators resist the rendering, arguing that it should be read as "fallen ones" or "those who fall upon" (a battle expression). These options are based on the idea that the word derives from the Hebrew verb *n-p-l* (*naphal*, "to fall"). More importantly, those who argue that *nephilim* should be translated with one of these expressions rather than "giants" do so to avoid the quasi-divine nature of the Nephilim. That in turn makes it easier for them to argue that the sons of God were human.

In reality, it doesn't matter whether "fallen ones" is the translation. In both the Mesopotamian context and the context of later Second Temple Jewish thought, their fathers are divine and the *nephilim* (however translated) *are still described as giants*.[16] Consequently, insisting that the name means "fallen" produces no argument to counter a supernatural interpretation.

Despite the uselessness of the argument, I'm not inclined to concede the point. I don't think *nephilim* means "fallen ones."[17] Jewish writers and

---

13. As is the case with biblical *elohim*, some *apkallus* were good and fought against the demonic powers.

14. See the discussion in Annus, "On the Watchers."

15. The plural forms in context are, respectively, *gigantes* and *gigantas*.

16. As was the case with the Septuagint, the Greek manuscripts of 1 Enoch use *gigas* ("giant") when describing the offspring of the Watchers. See 1 Enoch 7:2, 4; 9:9.

17. The translation "fallen ones" is based on a characterization of the behavior of the giants, not on any passage that informs us this is what *nephilim* means. One Dead Sea Scrolls text says that the Watchers "fell" from right standing with God and that their offspring followed in their footsteps (CD [*Damascus Document*] II:19–19). Note that while the verb *naphal* appears in this verse, the word *nephilim* does not. That is, the "fallen state" is not attributed to the name itself. The word *nephilim* occurs only twice in the Dead Sea

translators habitually think "giants" when they use or translate the term. I think there's a reason for that.

Explaining my own view of what the term means involves Hebrew morphology, the way words are spelled or formed in Hebrew. Since that discussion gets technical very quickly, I've elected to put those details elsewhere, at least for the most part.[18] But since I don't like to leave questions unanswered, we need to devote some attention to it here.

The spelling of the word *nephilim* provides a clue to what root word the term is derived from. *Nephilim* is spelled two different ways in the Hebrew Bible: *nephilim* and *nephiylim*. The difference between them is the "y" in the second spelling. Hebrew originally had no vowels. All words were written with consonants only. As time went on, Hebrew scribes started to use some of the consonants to mark long vowel sounds. English does this with the "y" consonant—sometimes it's a vowel. Hebrew does that with its "y" letter, too (the *yod*).

The takeaway is that the second spelling (*nephiylim*) tells us that the root behind the term had a long-i (y) in it before the plural ending (-*im*) was added. That in turn helps us determine that the word does not mean "those who fall." If that were the case, the word would have been spelled *nophelim*. A translation of "fallen" from the verb *naphal* is also weakened by the "y" spelling form. If the word came from the verb *naphal*, we'd expect a spelling of *nephulim* for "fallen."

However, there's another possible defense for the meaning "fallen." Instead of coming from the verb *naphal*, the word might come from a noun that has a long-i vowel in the second syllable. This kind of noun is called a *qatiyl* noun. Although there is no such noun as *naphiyl* in the Hebrew Bible, the hypothetical plural form would be *nephiylim*, which is the long spelling we see in Numbers 13:33.

This option solves the spelling problem, but it fails to explain everything else: the Mesopotamian context, the Second Temple Jewish recognition of that

---

Scrolls. Neither instance makes a connection to any behavior. In fact, no explanation of the term is ever offered. Certain English translations of the Dead Sea Scrolls will occasionally have this "fallen" language elsewhere, but such instances are bracketed—they have been supplied by translators but without any manuscript support (e.g., 4Q266 Frag. 2 ii:18). The most recent scholarly work on the Nephilim and the later giant clans is the recent Harvard dissertation by Brian Doak (published as *The Last of the Rephaim: Conquest and Cataclysm in the Heroic Ages of Ancient Israel*, Ilex Series 7 [Cambridge: Harvard University Press, 2013]). Despite its many merits, Doak's book on the giants fails with respect to the meaning of *nephilim*. Annus's ground-breaking article does not appear in either Doak's dissertation bibliography or that of his book. The article likely appeared after Doak had finished his dissertation work. See the companion website for some discussion of Doak's work.

18. See the companion website.

context, the connection of the term to Anakim giants (Num 13:33; Deut 2–3), and the fact that the Septuagint translators interpreted the word as "giants."

So where does the spelling *nephiylim* come from? Is there an answer that would simultaneously explain why the translators were consistently thinking "giants"?

There is indeed.

Recall that the Old Testament tells us that Jewish intellectuals were taken to Babylon. During those seventy years, the Jews learned to speak Aramaic. They later brought it back to Judah. This is how Aramaic became the primary language in Judea by the time of Jesus.

The point of Genesis 6:1–4 was to express contempt for the divine Mesopotamian *apkallus* and their giant offspring. Biblical writers had an easy choice of vocabulary for divine beings: sons of God. Their readers would know that the phrase pointed to divine beings, and other passages in the Torah (Deut 32:17) labeled other divine beings as demons (*shedim*). But these writers needed a good word to villainize the giant offspring. "Fallen ones" doesn't telegraph giantism, so that didn't help them make the point.

My view is that, to solve this messaging problem, the Jewish scribes adopted an Aramaic noun: *naphiyla*—which means "giant." When you import that word and pluralize it for Hebrew, you get *nephiylim*, just what we see in Numbers 13:33. This is the only explanation to the meaning of the word that accounts for all the contexts and all the details.

THE STRATEGY OF GENESIS 6

But what does it all mean? Why is Genesis 6:1–4 in the Bible? What was its theological message? I've already noted that the goal was polemic—a dismissal of Mesopotamian religion. But that's a little vague. Let's explore it.

Because the content of Genesis 1–11 has so many deep, specific touchpoints with Mesopotamian literary works, many scholars believe that these chapters either were written during the exile in Babylon or were edited at that time.[19] The scribes wanted to make it clear that certain religious ideas about the gods and the world were misguided or false.

Think about the setting. The Jews, followers of Yahweh, were in Babylon, deported against their will by the greatest empire in their known world.

---

19. The issue of the Mesopotamian contexts for so much of Gen 1–11 naturally relates to the debate over Mosaic authorship of the Torah (and what that actually means). The issue is complex. I've read or met hundreds of evangelical scholars over my career. Very few would have any trouble with the notion of the Torah reaching its final form during the exile whether they embrace Mosaic authorship in whole or in part.

Though captives, prophets like Ezekiel (and Jeremiah before him) had told the people that their situation was temporary—that the God of Israel remained the real sovereign. He was fully in control and was the true God. They would be set free and Babylon would crumble. For Jewish scribes, their work during the exile was an opportunity to set the record straight for posterity. And that they did.

Babylonian intellectuals (mostly, the priestly class) presumed that civilization in Mesopotamia before the flood had been handed down by their gods. For that reason, they wanted to connect themselves and their intellectual achievements with knowledge from before the flood. It was their way of claiming that their knowledge and skills were divine and, therefore, superior to those of the nations they had conquered. That in turn meant that the gods of those nations were inferior to the gods of Babylon.

The *apkallus* were the great culture-heroes of preflood knowledge. They were the divine sages of a glorious bygone era. Babylonian kings claimed to be descended from the *apkallus* and other divine figures from before the flood. The collective claim was that glorious Babylonia was the sole possessor of divine knowledge, and that that empire's rule had the approval of the gods.

The biblical writers and later Jews disagreed. They saw Babylonian knowledge as having demonic origins—in large part because the *apkallus* themselves were so intertwined with Mesopotamian demonology. The Babylonian elite taught that the divine knowledge of the *apkallus* had survived the flood through a succeeding postflood generation of *apkallus*—giant, quasi-divine offspring fathered by the original preflood *apkallus*.

The biblical writers took what Babylonians thought was proof of their own divine heritage and told a different story. Yes, there were giants, renowned men, both before and after the flood (Gen 6:4). But those offspring and their knowledge were not of the true God—they were the result of rebellion against Yahweh by lesser divine beings. Genesis 6:1–4, along with 2 Peter and Jude, portrays Babylon's boast as a horrific transgression and, even worse, the catalyst that spread corruption throughout humankind. Genesis 6:5 is essentially a summary of the *effect* of the transgression. It gets little space—it's a restrained account. The later Second Temple Jewish literature goes after it full bore.

First Enoch 8 goes on to elaborate how certain watchers corrupted humankind by means of forbidden divine knowledge, practices largely drawn from Babylonian sciences, another clear indication that the intellectual context of the story was known to Second Temple authors. Since the Babylonian *apkallus* were considered demonic, it is no mystery why Peter and Jude link the events of Genesis 6:1–4 to false teachers (2 Pet 2:1–4). While attacking their aberrant knowledge, Peter and Jude evoke the imagery of Genesis 6. False teachers are "licentious" men who indulge in "defiling lusts" (2 Pet 2:2, 10; Jude 8). Like the divine beings of Genesis 6 who "did not keep to their own domain" (Jude 6), defecting from the loyal *elohim* of Yahweh's council, false teachers "despise authority" and "blaspheme majestic beings" whom angels dare not rebuke (2 Pet 2:9–11; Jude 8–10).

Less obvious is the implication of the incident with respect to the promised seed of Eve. The biblical writers draw attention to Noah's blamelessness (Gen 6:9). Scripture does not specifically exempt Noah and his family from the sinful cohabitation of Genesis 6:1–4, but since the event was so heinous, it would be absurd to presume otherwise.[20] As concepts like divine sonship began to appear in the Bible with respect to Yahweh's people Israel (Exod 4:23), the Israelite king (Psa 2:7), and, ultimately, the messiah, the theological messaging became important. Noah is in the line of Christ (Luke 3:36; cf. 3:38). At no point could it be claimed that the ultimate seed of Eve, the messianic deliverer, was the son of any *elohim* besides Yahweh.[21]

Genesis 6:1–4 is far from being peripheral in importance. It furthers the theme of conflict between divine rebels (the "seed of the *nachash*") and humanity that will impede the progress of Eden's restoration. It is one of two passages in the Old Testament that fundamentally frame the history of Israel as a people and a land. The other one is the subject of the next chapter.

---

20. The quandary of how anyone, including the giants, had survived the flood led some Jewish writers to speculate that Noah himself had been fathered by a Watcher. One Dead Sea scroll, *The Genesis Apocryphon*, has Noah's father challenging his wife, the mother of Noah, about whether her pregnancy was the work of one of the Watchers (*Genesis Apocryphon* [=1QapGen] 1:1–5:27). She vehemently denies the charge. See chapter 23 for a discussion of Nephilim after the flood.

21. Infecting the messianic line is never a stated goal of the Watchers in any Jewish text. Nevertheless, the theological messaging is the important issue—the messiah is Yahweh's son; there is no divine rival claim on that heritage.

CHAPTER 14

Divine Allotment

The divine transgressions of Genesis 3 and 6 are part of a theological prelude that frames the rest of the Bible. These two episodes, along with a third we'll cover in this chapter, are core components of the supernatural worldview of ancient Israelites and the Jewish community in which Christianity was born.

Taken together, these episodes are a theological morality tale about the futility and danger of trying to recover Eden on any terms other than those God has set. After Eden, God still intended to dwell with humanity. But there would be opposition. Divine beings in service to Yahweh could defect. Enemies of Yahweh and his rule, from the human to the divine to something in between, lurked over the horizon. Heaven and earth were destined to be reunited, but it would be a titanic struggle.

In the meantime, any effort to recapture God's original intent apart from God's own strategy and will for restoring Eden would end in disaster. There would be no Edenic utopia revived by human beings or other gods. It would be a painful lesson.

FROM THE FLOOD TO BABEL

There are several features of Genesis 6 that an Israelite would have picked up on that informed his reading of other passages in the Torah. Verse 4 is especially noteworthy:

> The Nephilim were upon the earth in those days, and also afterward, when the sons of God went into the daughters of humankind, and they bore children to them. These were the mighty warriors that were from ancient times, men of renown.

The Nephilim are cast as "mighty warriors" (*gibborim*) and "men of renown"—

literally, "men of the name (*shem*)."[1] The terms *gibbor*(*im*) and *shem* appear in several places in the Old Testament story.[2]

Immediately after the flood, Nimrod (whose name most likely means "rebellion") is called a *gibbor*.[3] Nimrod is cast as the progenitor of the civilizations of Assyria and Babylon (Gen 10:6–12). Once again, as with Genesis 6, the Mesopotamian context is transparent. Assyria and Babylon are the two civilizations that will later destroy the dream of the earthly kingdom of God in Israel, dismantling, respectively, the northern kingdom (Israel) and southern kingdom (Judah).

The language is not coincidental. It links Babylon back to Genesis 6 and its divine transgression. The Nimrod description in Genesis 10, in the so-called Table of Nations, is therefore a theological bridge between the violation of Genesis 6:1–4 and the next momentous event in the Torah that will frame the entire story of Israel.[4]

---

1. I am aware that the terms *nephilim* and *gibborim* could be distinguished, and that certain Jewish texts and translations take that route (see Stuckenbruck, "The 'Angels' and 'Giants' of Genesis 6:1–4 in Second and Third Century BCE Jewish Interpretation: Reflections on the Posture of Early Apocalyptic Traditions," *Dead Sea Discoveries* 7.3 [2000]: 354–77, and Brian Doak, *The Last of the Rephaim: Conquest and Cataclysm in the Heroic Ages of Ancient Israel*, Ilex Series 7, Ilex Foundation; Center for Hellenic Studies [Cambridge: Harvard University Press, 2013]). Viewing the terms as labels for one group is also grammatically and syntactically viable. That option is preferable, and really the only coherent choice, given the Mesopotamian context for Gen 6:1–4 we've discussed earlier. The *apkallus* were *both* giant in stature and the culture heroes who transmitted the sacred divine knowledge that resulted in civilization. It makes sense to see the biblical writer, as he created a polemic against them, using both terms of one group.

2. The word *gibbor* is the singular of *gibborim*.

3. See the companion website for more on Nimrod in Gen 10. Nimrod has not successfully been identified with a known historical figure from Mesopotamian texts. Other scholars consider the name a wordplay on rebellion and consider the description of him as a *gibbor* to be a clue to another polemic against Babylon. In other words, Nimrod would not be a historical figure but a theological swipe at Babylon and her gods, since the name and the word *gibbor* point back to the Nephilim/*apkallu* polemic. The parenthetical comment about Nimrod would be the biblical writer's way of saying that Babylon and her religious knowledge that survived after the flood are evil. Nimrod has also been identified with the constellation Orion—the giant hunter in the sky, the realm of the gods. The connection of Nimrod to the giant Nephilim is the backdrop to several odd Jewish traditions about Abraham, including that his family lineage went back to the giants (Pseudo-Eupolemos, quoted from Alexander Polyhistor by Eusebius, *Praeparatio Evangelica* 9.18.2). An excellent essay on Nimrod traditions is Karel van der Toorn, "Nimrod before and after the Bible," *Harvard Theological Review* 83.1 (1990): 1–29.

4. The language also points forward. After Yahweh divides the nations "among the sons of God" at Babel and declares Israel his own "portion" (Deut 32:8–9), he calls Abram. The intention is not only to start over with a people through whom God will restart the rule of God on earth. In Gen 12:1–3 we learn that Yahweh will make Abram's name (*shem*) great. This is but one aspect of the Abrahamic covenant. Other parts of the covenant description connect a "great name" to divine protection and blessing. The lemmas used in the covenant language appear in the meeting between Abram and Melchizedek (Gen 14) and in the patriarchal blessing of Judah by Jacob, in which the well-known prophecy of kingship is found (Gen 49:10). See the companion website for discussion. The Nephilim, called *gibborim* and "men of the name," are the ancestors of the giant clans encountered by Moses and Joshua centuries later in the struggle to claim the land Yahweh had allotted as the inheritance of his people (Num 13:32–33; 21:31–35; Deut 1–3; Josh 11:21–22; 14:12–15). See chapters 23–25.

THE TOWER OF BABEL

The famous story of the building of the Tower of Babel is about much more than an ill-fated construction project and language confusion. The episode is at the heart of the Old Testament worldview. It was at Babylon where people sought to "make a name (*shem*) for themselves" by building a tower that reached to the heavens, the realm of the gods. The city is once again cast as the source of sinister activity and knowledge.

Genesis 11:1–9 reads:

> ¹Now the whole earth had one language and the same words. ²And as people migrated from the east they found a plain in the land of Shinar and settled there. ³And they said to each other, "Come, let us make bricks and burn them thoroughly." And they had brick for stone and they had tar for mortar. ⁴And they said, "Come, let us build ourselves a city and a tower whose top reaches to the heavens. And let us make a name for ourselves, lest we be scattered over the face of the whole earth."
>
> ⁵Then Yahweh came down to see the city and the tower that humankind was building. ⁶And Yahweh said, "Behold, they are one people with one language, and this is only the beginning of what they will do. So now nothing that they intend to do will be impossible for them. ⁷Come, let us go down and confuse their language there, so that they will not understand each other's language." ⁸So Yahweh scattered them from there over the face of the whole earth, and they stopped building the city. ⁹Therefore its name was called Babel, for there Yahweh confused the language of the whole earth, and there Yahweh scattered them over the face of the whole earth.

You'll notice right away that there's the same sort of "plural exhortation" going on in verse 7 as we saw in Genesis 1:26. The verse has Yahweh proclaiming, "Let *us* go down and confuse their language." As was the case in Genesis 1:26, the plural announcement is followed by the actions of only one being, Yahweh: "So Yahweh scattered them" (11:8).

It's at this point that most Bible readers presume there's nothing more to think about. That's because other Old Testament passages that speak of this event tend to be omitted from the discussion. The most important of these is Deuteronomy 32:8–9 (ESV):

> ⁸When the Most High gave to the nations their inheritance,
>   when he divided mankind,
>   he fixed the borders of the peoples
>   according to the number of the sons of God.

⁹But the Lᴏʀᴅ's portion is his people,
    Jacob his allotted heritage.

Deuteronomy 32:8–9 describes how Yahweh's dispersal of the nations at Babel resulted in his *disinheriting* those nations as his people. This is the Old Testament equivalent of Romans 1:18–25, a familiar passage wherein God "gave [humankind] over" to their persistent rebellion. The statement in Deuteronomy 32:9 that "the Lᴏʀᴅ's [i.e., Yahweh's] portion is his people, Jacob his allotted heritage" tips us off that a contrast in affection and ownership is intended. Yahweh in effect decided that the people of the world's nations were no longer going to be in relationship to him. He would begin anew. He would enter into covenant relationship with a new people that did not yet exist: Israel.

The implications of this decision and this passage are crucial to understanding much of what's in the Old Testament.[5]

Most English Bibles do not read "according to the number of the sons of God" in Deuteronomy 32:8. Rather, they read "according to the number of the sons of Israel." The difference derives from disagreements between manuscripts of the Old Testament. "Sons of God" is the correct reading, as is now known from the Dead Sea Scrolls.[6]

Frankly, you don't need to know all the technical reasons for why the "sons of God" reading in Deuteronomy 32:8–9 is what the verse originally said. You just need to think a bit about the *wrong* reading, the "sons of Israel." Deuteronomy 32:8–9 harks back to events at the Tower of Babel, an event that occurred *before* the call of Abraham, the father of the nation of Israel. This means that the nations of the earth were divided at Babel *before Israel even existed as a people*. It would make no sense for God to divide up the nations of the earth "according to the number of the sons of Israel" if there was no Israel. This point is also brought home in another way, namely by the fact that Israel is not listed in the Table of Nations.

THE DEUTERONOMY 32 WORLDVIEW

So what happened to the other nations? What does it mean that they were apportioned as an inheritance according to the number of the sons of God?

---

5. As we'll see in later chapters, the worldview that extends from this passage factors into Israelite ritual, sacred space, wars of conquest, the destiny of the nations, and the progression of the gospel and the nature of the church in the New Testament.

6. For a discussion of the Hebrew text and manuscript support for "sons of God," see Michael S. Heiser, "Deuteronomy 32:8 and the Sons of God," *Bibliotheca Sacra* 158 (January-March 2001): 52–74. The ᴇsᴠ and ɴʀsᴠ have incorporated the reading of the scrolls into the running translation. Other English translations leave it in a footnote.

As odd as it sounds, the rest of the nations were placed under the authority of members of Yahweh's divine council.[7] The other nations were assigned to lesser *elohim* as a judgment from the Most High, Yahweh.

That this interpretation is sound is made clear by an explicit parallel passage, Deuteronomy 4:19–20. There Moses says to the Israelites:

> [19] And do this so that you do not lift your eyes *toward* heaven and observe the sun and the moon and the stars, all the host of the heaven, and be led astray and bow down to them and serve them, things that Yahweh your God has allotted to all *of* the peoples under all *of* the heaven. [20] But Yahweh has taken you and brought you out from the furnace of iron, from Egypt, to be a people of inheritance to him, as it is this day.

Deuteronomy 4:19–20 is the other side of God's punitive coin. Whereas in Deuteronomy 32:8–9 God apportioned or handed out the nations to the sons of God, here we are told God "allotted" the gods to those nations. God decreed, in the wake of Babel, that the other nations he had forsaken would have other gods besides himself to worship. It is as though God was saying, "If you don't want to obey me, I'm not interested in being your god—I'll match you up with some other god." Psalm 82, where we started our divine council discussion, echoes this decision. That psalm has Yahweh judging other *elohim*, sons of the Most High, for their corruption in administering the nations. The psalm ends with the psalmist pleading, "Rise up, O God, judge the earth, because you shall inherit all the nations."

It might seem that God's response at the tower of Babel incident was overly severe. But consider the context. The point is not that Yahweh was a glorified building inspector.

As we noted in an earlier chapter, gods were perceived to live on mountains. The tower of Babel is regarded by all scholars as one of Mesopotamia's famous man-made sacred mountains—a ziggurat. Ziggurats were divine abodes, places where Mesopotamians believed heaven and earth intersected.[8] The nature of this structure makes evident the purpose in building it—to bring the divine down to earth.

The biblical writer wastes no time in linking this act to the earlier divine

---

7. It is interesting to note that the number of the nations listed in Gen 10 is seventy (see Nahum M. Sarna, *Genesis* [JPS Torah Commentary; Philadelphia: Jewish Publication Society, 1989], 69). This is precisely the number of the sons of El in the divine council at Ugarit. This number, in the context of the disinheritance of the nations, will surface later in our discussion of the Gospels.

8. As Nahum Sarna notes, the ziggurats at Nippur and Asshur were, respectively, named "The House of the Mountain" and "The House of the Mountain of Heaven and Earth." The ziggurat at Babylon was named "The House of the Foundation of Heaven and Earth" (Sarna, *Genesis*, 82).

transgression of Genesis 6:1–4. That passage sought to portray the giant quasi-divine Babylonian culture heroes (the *apkallus*) who survived the flood as "men of renown" or, more literally, "men of the name [*shem*]." Those who built the tower of Babel wanted to do so to "make a name [*shem*]" for themselves. The building of the tower of Babel meant perpetuating Babylonian religious knowledge and substituting the rule of Babel's gods for rule by Yahweh.

Yahweh would have none of it. After the flood God had commanded humanity once again to "be fruitful and multiply, and fill the earth" (Gen 9:1). These words reiterated the original Edenic intention. But instead of obeying and having Yahweh be their god, the people gathered to build the tower. The theological messaging of the story is clear. Humanity had shunned Yahweh and his plan to restore Eden through them, so he would shun *them* and start again.

While the decision was harsh, the other nations are not *completely* forsaken. Yahweh disinherited the nations, and in the very next chapter of Genesis, he calls Abram out of—you guessed it—Mesopotamia. Again, this is not accidental. Yahweh would take a man from the heart of the rebellion and make a new nation, Israel. But in his covenant with Abram, God said that all the nations of the earth would be blessed through Abram, through his descendants (Gen 12:1–3).

The covenant language reveals that it was God's intention, right on the heels of his decision to punish the nations, that the Israelites would serve as a conduit for their return to the true God. This is one of the reasons Israel is later called "a kingdom of priests" (Exod 19:6). Israel would be in covenant with "the God of gods" and the "Lord of lords" (Deut 10:17). Those disinherited would be in spiritual bondage to the corrupt sons of God. But Israel would be a conduit, a mediator. Yahweh would leave a spiritual bread-crumb trail back to himself. That path would wind through Israel and, ultimately, Israel's messiah.

From the fateful decision at Babel onward, the story of the Old Testament is about Israel versus the disinherited nations, and Yahweh versus the corrupt, rebel *elohim* of those nations. The division of the nations and their allotment under other *elohim* is behind the scenes in all sorts of places in biblical history. I'll give you a glimpse of what I mean in the next chapter.

CHAPTER 15

Cosmic Geography

In the last chapter we got our first exposure to Deuteronomy 32:8–9, Yahweh's disinheritance of the nations. This was the theological lens through which an ancient Israelite viewed her own nation with respect to all others, and her *elohim*, Yahweh, against the gods of those nations. By definition Yahweh was superior. He was Most High (*elyon*)—the title used in Deuteronomy 32:8–9.[1]

The Old Testament therefore describes a world where cosmic-geographical lines have been drawn. Israel was holy ground because it was Yahweh's "inheritance," in the language of Deuteronomy 32:8–9. The territory of other nations belonged to other *elohim* because Yahweh had decreed it. Psalm 82 told us that these lesser *elohim* were corrupt.[2] We aren't told how the *elohim* Yahweh assigned to the nations became corrupt, only that they were. It is clear from Deuteronomy 4:19–20; 17:3; 29:25; and 32:17 that these *elohim* were illegitimate for Israelite worship.

This cosmic-geographical perspective explains several odd passages in the Bible, and provides dramatic theological backdrop to others. Some of the most startling are in the New Testament. I'll hold those until we reach the time of Jesus and the apostles. For now I'll illustrate the point with some short, but fascinating, examples.

---

1. Most critical scholars believe Israel's faith evolved from polytheism and contend that Yahweh and Elyon (Most High) are separate deities in Deut 32:8–9. Though some critical evangelical scholars would file that idea under "progressive revelation," I reject the evolutionary idea. For a discussion of the issue, see Michael S. Heiser, "Does Divine Plurality in the Hebrew Bible Demonstrate an Evolution from Polytheism to Monotheism in Israelite Religion?" *Journal for the Evangelical Study of the Old Testament* 1.1 (2012): 1–24.

2. As we'll see in subsequent chapters, particularly when we discuss the conquest under Joshua, the Old Testament also makes it clear that the descendants of Nephilim of Gen 6:4 occupied territory within those nations.

DAVID'S PREDICAMENT

After his anointing by Samuel and victory over Goliath (1 Sam 16–18), David spends a good deal of time trying to escape the blind rage of King Saul. During the time he's on the run, David occasionally must flee into territory outside the borders of Israel. In one of the episodes where David finds Saul in a vulnerable situation and could have killed his pursuer, we read the following conversation:

> [17] Then Saul recognized David's voice and said, "Is this your voice, my son David?" And David said, "It is my voice, my lord the king." [18] Then he said, "Why is my lord pursuing after his servant? For what have I done? And what evil is in my hand? [19] And so then, please let my lord the king listen to the words of his servant: If Yahweh has incited you against me, may he delight in an offering; but if it is mortals, may they be accursed before Yahweh, for they have driven me away today from sharing in the inheritance of Yahweh, saying, 'Go, serve other gods!' (1 Sam 26:17–19).

One of the points of David's distress is that he has been driven away "from sharing in the inheritance of Yahweh." The "inheritance" language is the same as that found in Deuteronomy 32:8–9, where Jacob (Israel) is Yahweh's inheritance, the land and the people Yahweh "took" for himself (Deut 4:19–20).

Is David ignorant of the fact that the God who made heaven and earth can be anywhere? No. In David's mind, being driven outside Israel meant not being able to worship Yahweh. Note that he does not complain of being driven from the Ark of the Covenant, located at Kiriath Jearim (1 Sam 7:2), or from the Tabernacle, apparently located at Nob (1 Sam 21–22). His complaint is being expelled from the "inheritance" of Yahweh—the holy land of his God. David can't worship as he should if he is not on holy ground. The lands outside Israel belong to other gods.

NAAMAN ASKS FOR DIRT

Another fascinating story that illustrates the Israelite cosmic-geographical worldview is the story of Naaman, the commander of the army of Syria, a foreign country just beyond Israel's northern border. Naaman also happened to be afflicted with leprosy.

According to 2 Kings 5, at the suggestion of a captive Israelite servant girl, Naaman decides to seek the prophet Elisha for a cure for his condition. He travels to Israel, but Elisha doesn't even come out to talk to him in person.

He sends a messenger to tell the military hero to wash himself in the Jordan seven times if he wants to be healed. Insulted, Naaman at first resists, then relents at the encouragement of his servants. He does as instructed and emerges cleansed from the skin disease. Naaman returned to the prophet, who this time chose to speak with the Syrian. Picking up the story:

> [15] When he returned to the man of God, he and all of his army, he came and stood before him and said, "Please now, I know that there is no God in all of the world except in Israel. So then, please take a gift from your servant." [16] And he said, "As Yahweh lives, before whom I stand, I surely will not take it." Still he urged him to take it, but he refused. [17] Then Naaman said, "If not, then please let a load of soil on a pair of mules be given to your servants, for your servant will never again bring a burnt offering and sacrifice to other gods, but only to Yahweh. [18] As far as this matter, may Yahweh pardon your servant when my master goes into the house of Rimmon to worship there, and he is leaning himself on my arm, that I also bow down in the house of Rimmon: when I bow down in the house of Rimmon, may Yahweh please pardon your servant in this matter." [19] He said to him, "Go in peace" (2 Kgs 5:15–19).

The brief trip into Israel and the encounter with Yahweh's prophet have taught Naaman some good theology. He affirms that "there is no God in all of the world except in Israel" (v. 15). From henceforth he will sacrifice only to Yahweh. But how can he keep that vow after returning to Syria? Simple—*he pleads for dirt to take home.* Naaman views the land of Israel as holy ground—it is Yahweh's territory. Naaman takes as much dirt as his mules can carry so he can worship Yahweh on Yahweh's own territory, even though Naaman lives in the domain of the god Rimmon.

We aren't told if Naaman went home and spread dirt on the floor of a room in his home. We don't know how he handled his duty to accompany his aged king into Rimmon's temple. Perhaps he carried dirt with him as a pledge of his believing loyalty to Yahweh. What we do know is that the dirt was a theological statement. Dirt from Israel was the means by which Naaman showed his faith and kept his vow to the true God, Yahweh.

DANIEL AND PAUL

Another passage in the Old Testament, Daniel 10, presumes the Deuteronomy 32 worldview. In Daniel 10 we read about a vision of the prophet. Daniel sees a "man" dressed in linen, whom he describes this way:

> Now his body was like turquoise, and his face was like the appearance of light-

ning, and his eyes were like torches of fire, and his arms and his legs were like the gleam of polished bronze, and the sound of his words was like the sound of a multitude (Dan 10:6).

We've seen before that shininess or brilliant luminescence is a stock description for a divine being. The radiant figure, who is never identified in the passage, says to Daniel:

> [12]You must not fear, Daniel, for from the first day that you set your heart to understand and to humble yourself before your God, your words were heard, and I myself have come because of your words. [13]But the prince of the kingdom of Persia stood before me for twenty-one days. And look, Michael, one of the chief princes, came to assist me, and I left him there beside the king of the Persians. [14]And I have come to instruct you about what will happen to your people in the future, for there is a further vision here for the future (vv. 12–14).

The figure later adds, before ending the conversation:

> [20]And now I return to fight against the prince of Persia and I myself am going, and look, the prince of Javan[3] will come. [21]However, I will tell you what is inscribed in the book of truth, and there is not one who contends with me against these beings except Michael, your prince (vv. 20 and 21).

Biblical scholars are in unanimous agreement that the "princes" referred to in Daniel 10 are divine beings, not humans. This is transparent from the mention of Michael in 10:13 and 10:21, who is called "prince" (cf. Dan 12:1). They are also agreed that the concept is based on Deuteronomy 32:8–9.[4]

This passage, along with Deuteronomy 32:8–9, is the foundation for Paul's theology of the unseen world.[5] This is made clear in an overarching sense in Acts 17:26–27, where Luke records Paul's speech at the Areopagus. In talking about God's salvation plan, Paul says:

> [26]And he [God] made from one *man* every nation of humanity to live on all the face of the earth, determining *their* fixed times and the fixed boundaries of

---

3. Javan is the Hebrew term for the land of Greece.

4. For example: "*The Prince of the kingdom of Persia:* This indicates the patron angel of Persia. The notion that different nations were allotted to different gods or heavenly beings was widespread in the ancient world. In Deut 32:8–9 we read that 'When the Most High gave to the nations their inheritance, when he separated the sons of men, he fixed the bounds of the peoples according to the number of the sons of God.' The origin of this idea is to be sought in the ancient Near Eastern concept of the divine council" (John Joseph Collins and Adela Yarbro Collins, *Daniel: A Commentary on the Book of Daniel* [Hermeneia: A Critical and Historical Commentary on the Bible; Minneapolis: Fortress, 1993], 374).

5. See Ronn Johnson, "The Old Testament Background for Paul's Principalities and Powers," (PhD diss., Dallas Theological Seminary, 2004).

their habitation, [27] to search for God, if perhaps indeed they might feel around for him and find *him*. And indeed he is not far away from each one of us (Acts 17:26–27).

Paul quite clearly alludes to the situation with the nations produced by God's judgment at Babel, the Deuteronomy 32:8–9 worldview. God had disinherited the nations as his people and made a new people for himself, Israel, his own "portion" (Deut 32:9). Immediately after the judgment at Babel (Gen 11:1–9), God called Abraham for that purpose, initiating a covenant relationship with Abraham and his yet unborn descendants. That covenant relationship included the idea Paul refers to in Acts 17:27, the drawing of the disinherited Gentile nations (Gen 12:3). Paul's rationale for his own ministry to the Gentiles was that it was God's intention to reclaim the nations to restore the original Edenic vision.[6] Every person in every nation was given the opportunity to repent and believe in the risen Christ (Acts 17:30–31). Salvation was not only for the physical children of Abraham, but for anyone who would believe (Gal 3:26–29).

More pointedly, Paul's terminology for the powers of darkness reflects the cosmic-geographical worldview arising from Deuteronomy 32:8–9. The Hebrew word for "prince" used throughout Daniel 10 is *sar*. In Daniel 10:13, where Michael is called "one of the chief princes," the Septuagint refers to Michael as one of the chief *archontōn*.[7] In another Greek translation of Daniel, a text many scholars consider even older than the Septuagint currently in use, the prince of Persia and Israel's prince, Michael, are both described with the Greek word *archōn*.[8] These are the terms Paul uses when describing the

---

6. See chapters 32, 35–36.

7. Recall that the Septuagint is the ancient Greek translation of the Old Testament. It was heavily used by the New Testament writers. Since the New Testament was composed in Greek, the majority of the quotations of the Old Testament by New Testament writers reflect the Septuagint, not the traditional Hebrew text.

8. See Theodotian's Greek text of Daniel. Michael is also called an *archangel* in Jude 9. The term refers to one who outranks other angels (i.e., has ruling authority over them; see J. W. van Henten, "Archangel," in *Dictionary of Deities and Demons in the Bible*, 2nd ed. (ed. Karel van der Toorn, Bob Becking, and Pieter W. van der Horst; Leiden; Boston; Cologne; Grand Rapids, MI; Cambridge: Brill; Eerdmans, 1999], 80–82). But Michael is not the only archangel. First Thess 4:16 lacks the definite article before ἀρχαγγέλου. That passage also distinguishes the term from the returning Jesus. In chapters 16–18 I discuss the evidence for the concept of a Godhead in the Old Testament—the evidence for *two* Yahweh figures in various passages who were interchangeable yet distinct. The second Yahweh is visible and embodied in human form. The most telling evidence is that of the Angel of Yahweh, in whom resided the very presence of Yahweh (the "name"). The motifs associated with this second Yahweh in human form lay the groundwork for the incarnation of Yahweh as Jesus. I raise the issue of this content here because I do not consider Michael to be this second Yahweh figure. Briefly, I reject this equation for the following reasons. Michael is referred to as the prince of Israel (Dan 10:21; 12:1) and *one* of an unidentified number of "chief princes" (Dan 10:13). These statements must inform our reading of Dan 8:11, where the little horn of Daniel's vision "became great, even as great as the Prince *of the host*" (italics mine). The phrase "prince of the host" transparently describes a leader of the entire heavenly host (i.e., all divine beings besides Yahweh). It is never used of

"rulers of this age" (1 Cor 2:6, 8), the rulers "in heavenly places" (Eph 3:10) and "the ruler of the authority of the air" (Eph 2:2).

Paul often interchanged these terms with others that are familiar to most Bible students:

- "principalities" (*archē*)
- "powers"/"authorities" (*exousia*)
- "powers" (*dynamis*)
- "dominions"/"lords" (*kyrios*)
- "thrones" (*thronos*)

These terms have something in common—they were used in both the New Testament and other Greek literature for *geographical domain rulership*. This is the divine dominion concept of Deuteronomy 32:8–9. At times these terms are used of humans, but several instances demonstrate that Paul had spiritual beings in mind.

The first three terms are found in Ephesians 6:12 ("Our struggle is not against blood and flesh, but against the rulers, against the authorities, against the world rulers of this darkness, against the spiritual forces of wickedness in the heavenly places"). Paul tells us in Ephesians 1:20–21 that when God raised Jesus from the dead, "he seated him at his right hand in the heavenly places, far above all rule and authority and power and dominion" (ESV). It was only

---

Michael in the Bible. Dan 8:11 leaves this figure unidentified. Consequently, linking Michael to this phrase is arbitrary. This fact is important in view of Dan 8:25, where the earlier "prince of the host" is called "the prince of princes." In Dan 8, this figure, exalted above all divine beings under Yahweh, is assaulted by the little horn. Dan 11:36 describes this same assault with slightly different language. There the earthly "king" who is the analogy to the little horn "shall exalt himself and magnify himself above every god, and shall speak astonishing things against the God of gods" (RSV). Since Dan 8's "prince of the host" who is "prince of princes" is correlated with "God of gods" in Dan 11:36, it would be coherent to see this unidentified figure as a second Yahweh figure who, as I describe in detail later, is identified with Jesus. In fact, in the Septuagint, the "commander of Yahweh's army" (Josh 5:13–15) is described with *archistratēgos*, a word that occurs as a synonym for *archangelos* in Second Temple Jewish literature (e.g., *Testament of Abraham*, long rescension 1:4 and 14:10; 3 Baruch (Greek Apocalypse) 11:8). I will argue in chapters 16–18 that this figure is the second embodied Yahweh. But none of this fits Michael. The phrases of Dan 8 are never used of Michael, and so an identification of Michael with this figure (and therefore "the God of gods" and Jesus) lacks scriptural support. Michael is merely one of several chief princes (Dan 10:13). He is not exalted over all other princes (Dan 8:11, 25). The most complete recent scholarly survey of Michael in Jewish and Christian tradition is Darrell D. Hannah, *Michael and Christ: Michael Traditions and Angel Christology in Early Christianity* (*Wissenschaftliche Untersuchungen zum Neuen Testament* 109, second series; Tübingen: Mohr Siebeck, 1999). See also Gillian Bampfylde, "The Prince of the Host in the Book of Daniel and the Dead Sea Scrolls," *Journal for the Study of Judaism in the Persian, Hellenistic, and Roman Periods* 14.2 (1983): 129–34; Benedikt Otzen, "Michael and Gabriel: Angelological Problems in the Book of Daniel," in *The Scriptures and the Scrolls: Studies in Honor of A. S. van der Woude on the Occasion of his 65th Birthday* (ed. F. Garcia Martinez, A. Hilhorst, and C. J. Labuschagne; Leiden: Brill, 1992), 114–24. On the efforts of some to divorce the son of man of Dan 7:13 from the prince of the host (and, by extension, Jesus), see chapter 7 of my dissertation on the companion website.

after Christ had risen that God's plan was "made known … to the rulers and the authorities in the heavenly places" (Eph 3:10). These cosmic forces are "the rulers and the authorities" disarmed and put to shame by the cross (Col 2:15).

The incident at Babel and God's decision to disinherit the nations drew up the battle lines for a cosmic turf war for the planet. The corruption of the *elohim* sons of God set over the nations meant that Yahweh's vision of a global Eden would be met with divine force. Every inch outside Israel would be contested, and Israel itself was fair game for hostile conquest. The gods would not surrender their inheritances back to Yahweh; he would have to reclaim them. God would take the first step in that campaign immediately after Babel.

Section Summary

God's plan that all the earth be Eden came to a screeching halt almost as soon as it began. The *nachash* arrogantly sought to be the Most High. His transgression succeeded in undermining the fulfillment of God's original intention for humanity but failed to result in human destruction. The rebel inserted himself into the role of Most High, casting himself as God's mouthpiece, but wound up as lord of the dead.

In some respects, the *nachash* took humanity with him when Adam and Eve were barred from the presence of God and the tree of life, imagery that telegraphed the theological message that humans are mortal and that everlasting life in God's presence could come only through God's grace and mercy. Without saving grace, humanity was now the rightful property of death and its lord.

God, the Life-giver, forgave Adam and Eve. They were not destroyed. Humanity *would* survive. They would bear children to perpetuate their line and, with it, keep God's original intention alive. The rule of God would someday return to earth—in his time and by his methods. Evil would impede, but not defeat, God's purpose. This new circumstance—this gracious *good news*—would demand that humanity make the choice rejected in Eden. From this point forward, dwelling forever as a member of God's family-council requires choosing loyalty to him above any other divine voice.

Free-will rebellion didn't end with Eden. It was only the beginning—for both divine and human imagers. Transgressions before (Gen 6:1–4) and after (Gen 11:1–9; Deut 32:8–9) the flood are cases in point, as well as points of reference. They set the stage for the rest of the Old Testament.

Yahweh's portion would be Israel. He cast off the other nations and assigned them to lesser gods. Those gods become divine rivals, not servants, of Yahweh. Their rule is corrupt (Psa 82). The rest of the Old Testament pits Yahweh against those gods and Israel against their nations. To make matters worse, the residue of Genesis 6 lived among the inhabitants of those nations, on the ground that Yahweh had promised to Abraham. Yahweh's chosen portion of land would be contested. War loomed.

But first Yahweh's portion, his people, would have to take root. Yahweh would initiate a relationship with Abraham, and that required a meeting. That presented a fundamental problem for God. He is so unlike anything in human experience that his pure presence cannot be processed by the human senses. It would, in fact, be lethal. God's solution was to veil himself for human protection and detection. This was necessary even in Eden, where the writer casts God as a man, walking through the garden, searching for his fallen imagers (Gen 3:8). That, too, will emerge as a pattern hidden in plain sight.

PART 4

YAHWEH AND HIS PORTION

CHAPTER 16

Abraham's Word

We learned from Deuteronomy 32:8–9 that Yahweh placed the nations under the governance of junior *elohim*—the sons of God of his divine council. Having disinherited humanity, unwilling as it was to fulfill the mandate of Eden to overspread the earth, he decided it was time to start over. The reader of Genesis gets the feeling that the new beginning was almost immediate, as the Tower of Babel story is immediately followed by the call of Abram.

Abram was, of course, the original name of Abraham. God called this Mesopotamian man, seemingly out of the blue, to leave his extended family and journey to a foreign locale. God entered into a covenant with him, changed his name to Abraham,[1] and then enabled him and his wife to produce a son, Isaac, in their advanced age. Isaac in turn became the father of Jacob, whose name was later changed to Israel.

Simple, right? It won't surprise you when I say there's much more going on than meets the eye. Abraham is about to meet his God—but for Abraham's protection, God must come to the man in a way that blunts the light of his own glory and helps Abraham process him as a person.

THE JOY OF ABRAHAM

We first encounter God's covenant promises to Abraham in Genesis 12. But that chapter isn't the beginning of God's dealing with Abraham. In Genesis 12, Abraham is not in Mesopotamia; he's in a place north of Canaan called Haran (Gen 12:4). To understand the real beginning of God's contact with Abraham, let's back up.

After the Babel episode, the remainder of Genesis 11 is devoted to a genealogy—the genealogy of Abram (Abraham) back to Noah's son Shem.

---

1. As a matter of convenience I'll be using "Abraham" throughout the rest of this chapter and the book.

Genealogies often contain something important or interesting, and this one is no exception. Compare the last two verses of Abraham's genealogical roots (Gen 11:31–32) with Acts 7:2–4, and you'll discover that Yahweh first contacted Abraham before he got to Haran—and it was more than a conversation in his head. In Acts 7:2–4, Stephen says:

> The God of glory appeared to our father Abraham while he was in Mesopotamia, before he settled in Haran, ³and said to him, "Go out from your land and from your relatives and come to the land that I will show you." ⁴Then he went out from the land of the Chaldeans and settled in Haran. And from there, after his father died, he caused him to move to this land in which you now live.

The important element to catch here is in the first line: Yahweh *appeared* to Abraham. Abraham's first divine encounter in Mesopotamia involved *a visible appearance* of Yahweh. Genesis 12 is a follow-up. Abraham and Yahweh had talked before—face to face.

That's also what happened in Genesis 12. We're most familiar with the first three verses:

> ¹And Yahweh said to Abram, "Go out from your land and from your relatives, and from the house of your father, to the land that I will show you. ²And I will make you a great nation, and I will bless you, and I will make your name great. And you will be a blessing. ³And I will bless those who bless you, and those who curse you I will curse. And all families of the earth will be blessed in you" (Gen 12:1–3).

But verses 6–7 deserve closer attention:

> ⁶And Abram traveled through the land up to the place of Shechem, to the Oak of Moreh. Now the Canaanites *were* in the land at that time. ⁷And Yahweh appeared to Abram and said, "To your offspring I will give this land." And he built an altar there to Yahweh, who had appeared to him (vv. 6–7).

Twice in these two verses we read that Yahweh *appeared* to Abraham.[2] A close reading of Genesis chapters 12 through 50 tells us that visible manifestation is the normal choice of Yahweh with respect to Abraham and his descendants, the patriarchs.

This brings us to Genesis 15:1–6, where the covenant of Genesis 12:1–3 is repeated and ratified by a covenantal ceremony. The description of the person speaking to Abraham here is even more startling. Note the emphasis in bold:

---

2. The idea of visible appearances of Yahweh as a man, including corporeal embodiment, is not novel. See Esther J. Hamori, *"When Gods Were Men": The Embodied God in Biblical and Near Eastern Literature* (Beihefte zur Zeitschrift für die alttestamentliche Wissenschaft 384; Berlin: Walter deGruyter, 2008).

¹After these things **the word of Yahweh came to Abram in a vision**, saying: "Do not be afraid, Abram; I am your shield, and your reward shall be very great." ²Then Abram said, "O Yahweh, my Lord, what will you give me? I continue to be childless, and my heir is Eliezer of Damascus." ³And Abram said, "Look, you have not given me a descendant, and here, a member of my household is my heir." ⁴And behold, **the word of Yahweh** came to him saying, "This person will not be your heir, but your own son will be your heir." ⁵And **he brought him outside** and said, "Look toward the heavens and count the stars if you are able to count them." And he said to him, "So shall your offspring be." ⁶And he believed in Yahweh, and he reckoned it to him as righteousness (Gen 15:1–6).

This is a fascinating text. Notice right from the start that it is the "Word of Yahweh" who comes to Abraham *in a vision*.³ As before, the encounter was a visible manifestation of Yahweh. The Word here is something that can be *seen*—why else call it a *vision*?⁴ In verse 4 we read that the Word "*brought him [Abraham] outside*" to continue the conversation. This isn't the kind of language one would expect if Abraham was hearing only a sound.

These appearances of the Word of Yahweh are the conceptual backdrop to the apostle John's language in his gospel that Jesus was the Word. The most familiar instance is John 1:1 ("In the beginning was the Word, and the Word was with God, and the Word was God") and John 1:14 ("And the Word became flesh and took up residence among us, and we saw his glory, glory as of the one and only from the Father, full of grace and truth").⁵ But John says some equally dramatic things in connection with this idea that are less familiar.

In John 8:56, Jesus, the incarnate Word, informs his Jewish antagonists *that he appeared to Abraham prior to his incarnation*: "Abraham your father rejoiced that he would see my day, and he saw it and was glad." The Jews object vehemently to this claim, whereupon Jesus utters his famous statement, "Before Abraham was, I am" (John 8:58). Only Genesis 12 and 15 provide the coherent backdrop to this claim.⁶

---

3. I will capitalize *Word* when I have a visible divine manifestation in mind by its use.

4. Our discussion of the Word of the Lord here and elsewhere is not to suggest that every time this phrase occurs in the Bible a visible figure is involved. In most cases, there is no suggestion in the context for that conclusion. At other times, such as the instances I'll highlight, the context drives that conclusion. The point of course is that this language—Yahweh is the visible Word, even to the point of embodiment—is the conceptual backdrop for John's language about Jesus.

5. John's theology of the visible and embodied Word was also influenced by Aramaic translations (Targums) of the Old Testament widely used in the Jewish communities of his day. See John Ronning, *The Jewish Targums and John's Logos Theology* (Grand Rapids, MI: Baker Academic, 2010).

6. Commentators often miss or omit the Old Testament context for the phrasing. While it's true that the language John uses in John 8:56–58 points to more than just the visible appearance of Yahweh as the Word, it is illegitimate to exclude the visible-Word-as-Yahweh element from analysis of John. For example, when

I hope you grasp the significance of the interchange. Since the Word is clearly *equated with* and *identified as* Yahweh in Genesis 12 and 15, when the New Testament has Jesus saying "that was me," he is claiming to be the Word of the Old Testament, who was the visible Yahweh.

This understanding is also behind some of the things Paul says about Abraham and Jesus. In Galatians 3:8 Paul says that the gospel—that God would justify the Gentile nations—*was preached to Abraham*. This is a clear reference to the content of the Abrahamic covenant, delivered personally and visibly by the Word.

YAHWEH VISIBLE AND EMBODIED

The fact that the Old Testament at times has Yahweh appearing in visible form should now be on your radar. We're going to see a lot more of him (pun intended).

One of my favorite passages that features Yahweh made visible is 1 Samuel 3, the story of the young soon-to-be prophet, Samuel. Many readers will no doubt be familiar with it. The chapter opens with the cryptic statement, "The word of Yahweh was rare in those days; visions were not widespread." The reader is predisposed by the comment to expect a *vision* of the "Word of Yahweh." Samuel keeps hearing *a voice* calling his name while he's trying to sleep. He assumes it's the voice of the priest Eli and goes to the elderly man, but it was not Eli who spoke. After hearing the voice a third time, Eli realizes that it is Yahweh who is calling and instructs Samuel how to respond if it happens again.

Samuel goes back to bed. The narrative resumes in verse 10: "Then Yahweh came and stood *there* and called out as before, 'Samuel! Samuel!' And Samuel said, 'Speak, because your servant *is* listening.'" The description has Yahweh standing before Samuel. That he is clearly visible is made known by the ending of the chapter:

> [19]And Samuel grew up, and Yahweh was with him. He did not allow any of his prophecies to go unfulfilled. [20]All Israel from Dan to Beersheba realized that

---

Jesus says "I am" (instead of the expected, "I was"), he is taking for himself the name of God revealed to Moses in Exod 3 at the burning bush incident. There God said his name was "I am" (Exod 3:14). As we'll see, the burning bush incident also involved a *visible* appearance (Exod 3:1–3). The Jewish audience of Jesus was not averse to the idea that Abraham saw the messiah (see Andreas J. Köstenberger, *John* [Baker Exegetical Commentary on the New Testament; Grand Rapids, MI: Baker Academic, 2004], 271–72; George R. Beasley-Murray, *John* [Word Biblical Commentary 36; Dallas: Word, 2002], 138). The offense was that Jesus was inserting himself into this categorization.

Samuel was faithful as a prophet to Yahweh. [21] And Yahweh appeared again in Shiloh, for Yahweh revealed himself to Samuel in Shiloh through the word of Yahweh (1 Sam 3:19–21).

I was amazed the first time I saw this passage for what it was really saying. Yahweh "appeared" to Samuel with regularity in verse 21. The first verse of the chapter makes a clear association between the Word of the Lord and a *visionary* experience—not a mere auditory event. The idea of the visible Word—the visible Yahweh—in human form is nailed down by the "standing" language.

Some passages go beyond presenting Yahweh in visible, human form. Genesis 18 is perhaps the most startling example where Yahweh is not only visible, but embodied.

> [1] And Yahweh appeared to [Abraham] by the oaks of Mamre. And he was sitting in the doorway of the tent at the heat of the day. [2] And he lifted up his eyes and saw, and behold, three men were standing near him. And he saw them and ran from the doorway of the tent to meet them. And he bowed down to the ground. [3] And he said, "My lord, if I have found favor in your eyes do not pass by your servant. [4] Let a little water be brought and wash your feet, and rest under the tree. [5] And let me bring a piece of bread, then refresh yourselves. Afterward you can pass on, once you have passed by with your servant." Then they said, "Do so as you have said" (Gen 18:1–5).

That one of these three men is Yahweh is evident from the first verse. That the appearance of Yahweh and his two companions is physical is telegraphed by the request to wash their feet and partake in a meal (vv. 4–5), which they subsequently do (v. 8).

The narrator and the reader of course know that one of the men is Yahweh, but does Abraham? That he does is made clear from the conversation he has with the embodied Yahweh. After their meal the other two men (who we discover are angels in Gen 19) leave to go to Sodom. Once Abraham discerns that the destruction of Sodom and Gomorrah is imminent, he objects out of concern for his nephew Lot, a resident of Sodom. Addressing the Yahweh figure Abraham says in verse 25, "Far be it from you to do such a thing as this, to kill the righteous with the wicked, that the righteous would be as the wicked! Far be it from you! Will not the Judge of all the earth do justice?" Abraham knows the person before him is the "Judge of all the earth" since he addresses his plea directly. He addresses the figure as "you" twice before the rhetorical question that invokes the divine title.

How did Abraham know that the figure before whom he stood was

Yahweh? The chronology of his encounters in Genesis would tell us that he had heard Yahweh's voice before. This aural recognition is present in other passages involving Abraham that we'll see in a moment. But I also think Abraham *visually* recognized his visitor from those previous encounters.[7]

One final example from the Old Testament of an embodied Yahweh who is the "Word" is far less known, but no less dramatic. In Jeremiah 1 the prophet is called to service. He writes that "The word of Yahweh" came to him and said, "Before I formed you in the womb I knew you, and before you came out from the womb I consecrated you; I appointed you as a prophet to the nations."

Jeremiah identifies this Word as Yahweh himself when he replies, "Ah, Lord Yahweh! I do not know how to speak, for I am a youth" (v. 6). Yahweh—the Word—tells him to not be afraid, and then something shocking happens. Jeremiah writes in verse 9 that Yahweh, the Word, "stretched out his hand and he touched my mouth."

Sounds don't reach out and touch people. This is the language of a physical, embodied presence.

WHISPERS OF A GODHEAD

These passages raise three questions.

First, it's one thing to see that Yahweh appears in human form even to the point of embodiment, but what is the logic of this language? In other words, why do this?

Second, how is it that, if this Word was Yahweh, and the Word was visible and embodied, Jews of Jesus' day could tolerate the notion that Jesus was Yahweh incarnate on earth—while Yahweh was still in heaven? After all, Jesus prayed to the Father and spoke of the Father, Yahweh of Israel, in the third person. How could a Jew accommodate this "binitarian" idea—that, essen-

---

7. Many scholars resist saying Abraham knew that he was speaking to Yahweh because in vv. 3, 27–32 he addresses the figure as *adonai*—not with the divine name, Yahweh. Abraham did address Yahweh by name earlier (Gen 15:2, 8). Sarai refers to God by this name as well (Gen 16:2, 5). Readers of Gen 18, of course, know immediately (v. 1) that the figure who appears to Abraham at Mamre is Yahweh. This "problem" is misleading. That Abraham knew the divine name in the biblical text as we have it (cf. Exod 6:3) is no requirement that he use it in every exchange. The term *adonai* was a culturally proper term of reception of a guest or person due respect (e.g., Gen 19:18; 23:6; 24:18; 32:4; 33:8, 13). That Abraham understood who his guest was is suggested by Gen 18:25. When Abraham learns the fate that awaits Sodom and Gomorrah (the reader is not told how he learns that), he says to Yahweh, "Far be it from you! Will not the Judge of all the earth do justice?" Note that the statement correlates *the Judge of all the earth* with *you*. While it is possible from the language to say that Abraham could have viewed the three men as equals and the Judge of all the earth as a fourth person removed from the scene, that option is not compelling, nor is it consistent with the earlier encounters. There is no textual reason that forbids the notion that Abraham recognized the lead figure as Yahweh.

tially, there were two Yahwehs, one invisible and in heaven, the other on earth in visible form?[8]

Third, does this help or harm the New Testament articulation of a Trinity? Was the Trinity a new idea?

The answers to these questions are all found in the Old Testament. What we've begun to uncover in this chapter are whispers of the idea of a Godhead—in the Old Testament, the Bible of Judaism. Those whispers will get much louder as we continue.

---

8. The subject matter of the next two chapters does not argue for an Israelite Godhead on the basis of illeism—the use of the third person by God/Yahweh to God/Yahweh. While this phenomenon, evidenced in several passages of the Old Testament, was part of the two-powers-in-heaven discussion within Judaism, I will follow different, more substantive trajectories. On illeism in the Old Testament, see Andrew S. Malone, "God the Illeist: Third-Person Self-References and Trinitarian Hints in the Old Testament," *Journal of the Evangelical Theological Society* 52.3 (2009): 499–518.

CHAPTER 17

Yahweh Visible and Invisible

AT THE CLOSE OF THE LAST CHAPTER I NOTED THAT THE "WORD OF YAH-weh" being a visible appearance of God as a man raised certain questions. One of those was how a first-century Jew would have parsed the idea of Jesus being the "Word made flesh." True, there was Old Testament precedent for Yahweh being visible and embodied. That phenomenon would have helped a Jew accept at least the idea that God could show up in human form.

But it was more complicated than that. When Jesus referred to God in the third person, or prayed to God, what then? Would a Jew have been able to wrap her mind around that one? How could God be here (visibly and physically) and still be in heaven? Today, this apparent conundrum is what keeps many Jews from embracing Christianity—it feels like polytheism to them. Given this context, it's amazing how first-century Jews could embrace Jesus as Yahweh and not feel as if they were betraying the God of Israel. In fact, these same Jews were willing to die instead of worshiping the gods of the Greeks and the Romans.

We could also ask certain questions about readers of the Old Testament prior to the time of Jesus. When ancient Israelites read the passages we looked at in the last chapter, did they imagine that Yahweh was localized in only one place? Had he left heaven? Was he no longer omnipresent?

The startling reality is that long before Jesus and the New Testament, careful readers of the Old Testament would not have been troubled by the notion of, essentially, two Yahwehs—one invisible and in heaven, the other manifest on earth in a variety of visible forms, including that of a man. In some instances the two Yahweh figures are found *together in the same scene*. In this and the chapter that follows, we'll see that the "Word" was just one expression of a visible Yahweh in human form.[1]

---

1. The Jewish community that inherited the Old Testament was well aware of this. For centuries Judaism

The concept of a Godhead in the Old Testament has many facets and layers.[2] After the birth of his promised son, Isaac, Abraham's spiritual journey includes a divine figure that is integral to Israelite Godhead thinking: the Angel of Yahweh. Although the most telling passages that show this angel as a visible embodiment of the very presence of Yahweh occur later than the time of Abraham, there are early hints of his nature during the lifetimes of Abraham and his sons.

THE ANGEL OF YAHWEH

The heart-wrenching story of Genesis 22, where Abraham was prepared to sacrifice his covenant son Isaac, is our next stop. It's something of a transitional passage. We've seen that Abraham has had several encounters with Yahweh. The expression used to convey the visible, physical nature of those encounters has, to this point, been "the word of Yahweh." Genesis 22 marks a shift in the language for a visible Yahweh figure to the "Angel of Yahweh."

Although the Angel of Yahweh appears earlier than Genesis 22 (Gen 16:7–11; 21:17), this particular appearance begins to blur the identities of Yahweh and his angel. Genesis 22:1–9 relates how Abraham has taken Isaac, at the bizarre command of Yahweh, to Mount Moriah to offer his son as a burnt offering. We pick up the story in verse 10.

> [10]And Abraham stretched out his hand and took the knife to slaughter his son. [11]And the angel of Yahweh called to him from heaven and said, "Abraham! Abraham!" And he said, "Here I am." [12]And he said, "Do not stretch out your hand against the boy; do not do anything to him. For now I know that

---

felt no discomfort with the notion of two Yahweh figures. The idea was referred to as the "two powers in heaven" and was endorsed within Judaism until the second century AD. It is important to note that the two powers were both holy. This is not dualism, where two equal deities exist, one good, the other evil. The major work on Judaism's two-powers teaching was published originally in 1971 by the late Alan Segal. Segal was Jewish and his career focused on Second Temple and Rabbinic Judaism. His work documents how the two-powers idea became a heresy in Judaism in the second century AD. It was recently reprinted. See Alan F. Segal, *Two Powers in Heaven: Early Rabbinic Reports about Christianity and Gnosticism* (reprint, Waco, TX: Baylor University Press, 2012). The Old Testament roots of the two-powers doctrine were one of the major focus points of my doctoral dissertation. The logic of the two Yahweh figures in the Old Testament reflects an Israelite adaptation of the Canaanite structuring of the top tier of the Canaanite divine council. See Michael S. Heiser, "The Divine Council in Late Canonical and Non-Canonical Second Temple Jewish Literature" (PhD diss., University of Wisconsin–Madison, 2004).

2. The conception of a Godhead in orthodox Israelite thought, interpreted in the context of the wider Canaanite environment, was a focus of my dissertation. That material has been revised and put forth in an article accepted for publication at the time of this writing: Michael S. Heiser, "Co-Regency in Ancient Israel's Divine Council as the Conceptual Backdrop to Ancient Jewish Binitarian Monotheism," (forthcoming in the *Bulletin for Biblical Research*). I will post that article (presuming permission from *BBR*) on the companion website when it appears. The data and discussion go considerably beyond what appears in this book.

you are one who fears God, since you have not withheld your son, your only child, from me." [13]And Abraham lifted up his eyes and looked. And behold, a ram was caught in the thicket by his horns. And Abraham went and took the ram, and offered it as a burnt offering in place of his son. [14]And Abraham called the name of that place "Yahweh will provide," for which reason it is said today, "on the mountain of Yahweh it shall be provided." [15]And the angel of Yahweh called to Abraham a second time from heaven. [16]And he said, "I swear by myself, declares Yahweh, that because you have done this thing and have not withheld your son, your only child, [17]that I will certainly bless you and greatly multiply your offspring as the stars of heaven, and as the sand that is by the shore of the sea. And your offspring will take possession of the gate of his enemies. [18]All the nations of the earth will be blessed through your offspring, because you have listened to my voice" (Gen 22:10–18).

The first thing to notice is that when the angel of Yahweh speaks to Abraham, Abraham recognizes the voice. He does not ask the identity of the speaker, as though the voice is unfamiliar. He does not fear that he is harkening to the voice of another god. The reader, however, knows that the source is not Yahweh per se, but the angel of Yahweh. The word translated "angel" here is the Hebrew word *mal'ak*, which simply means "messenger."

The next observation is very important. The Angel speaks to Abraham in verse 11, and so is distinguished from God. But immediately after doing so, he commends Abraham for not withholding Isaac "from *me*." There is a switch to the first person which, given that God himself had told Abraham to sacrifice Isaac (Gen 22:1–2), seems to require seeing Yahweh as the speaker.

Many scholars would say that this is due to the Angel being Yahweh's mouthpiece, standing in Yahweh's place as it were. But that idea is conveyed only *later* in the passage when (v. 16) the angel prefaces his words with "declares Yahweh." In verse 11 there is no such clarification. The wording of the text *blurs the distinction* between Yahweh and the angel by swapping the angel into the role of the person who initially demanded the sacrifice as a test—Yahweh himself (Gen 22:1–2). Consequently the biblical writer had the opportunity to make sure Yahweh and the angel were distinguished, but did not do so. This "failure" occurs in several other places in the Old Testament even more overtly. It's not really a failure. It's not a careless oversight. The wording is *designed* to blur the two persons.

THE GODS OF ISAAC AND JACOB

Genesis 26:1–5 marks Yahweh's first visible *appearance* to Isaac ("And Isaac went … to Gerar … and Yahweh appeared to him"). It is a sign to Isaac that the covenant made with his father will be carried on through him. Yahweh repeats the words of the covenant to Isaac (vv. 3–4): "I will establish the oath that I swore to Abraham your father. And I will multiply your descendants like the stars of heaven, and I will give to your descendants all these lands. And all nations of the earth will be blessed through your offspring." Later in Genesis 26 (vv. 23–25) Yahweh appears to Isaac again. The baton has been passed.

Isaac's son Jacob receives the same divine approval in a series of visual encounters with Yahweh. The first instance is the well-known story of "Jacob's Ladder" in Genesis 28:10–22. Several details of the vision are noteworthy for continuing our discussion.

Jacob is on the way to Haran (vv. 1–2), the place from which his ancestor Abraham had departed years earlier at Yahweh's command. Jacob is fleeing the wrath of his brother Esau after stealing the birthright through deception (Gen 27). Scholars generally agree that the "ladder" is probably some sort of stair-step structure that (in Jacob's dream) connected heaven and earth, perhaps a ziggurat.[3] Jacob sees "angels of God" going up and down the structure, an indication of the presence of the divine council. Jacob also sees the visible Yahweh standing beside him (28:13)—the familiar language for Yahweh in human form we noted with Abraham.[4] In verse 15 Yahweh promises protection for Jacob and pledges to bring the man back to this location, the land promised to Abraham. Jacob names the place Bethel, "house of God" (v. 19), and erects a pillar to commemorate his conversation with Yahweh (vv. 18–19).

Jacob saw the visible Yahweh at Bethel. Given what we've already seen in Genesis, this isn't unusual. Things get more interesting in Genesis 31, the story of how Jacob became wealthy at the expense of his uncle, Laban. Jacob's flocks had multiplied supernaturally despite Laban's attempt to cheat him. As their relationship soured, Jacob had a dream. The wording is significant:

---

3. The term is difficult since it is a *hapax legomenon* in the Hebrew Bible (a word that occurs only once). Cognate material has yielded suggestive, but not certain, options for assistance in discerning its meaning. Aside from a ziggurat, another interpretive option is a "standing stone" (Hebrew: *maṣṣebah*). Both options are consistent with a conceptual or theological connection between God and human mortals. See Alan R. Millard, "The Celestial Ladder and the Gate of Heaven (Gen 28:12, 17)," *Expository Times* 78 (1966/1967): 86–87; C. Houtman, "What Did Jacob See in His Dream at Bethel? Some Remarks on Gen 28:10–22," *Vetus Testamentum* 27 (1977): 337–51.

4. The phrase in Gen 28:13 translated "beside him" in LEB and other English translations can also be translated "beside it" (i.e., the stairway structure) or "above it" (with the same referent).

[11] Then the angel of God said to me in the dream, "Jacob," and I said, "Here I am." [12] And he said, "Lift up your eyes and see—all the rams mounting the flock are streaked, speckled, and dappled, for I have seen all that Laban is doing to you. [13] I am the God of Bethel where you anointed a stone pillar, where you made a vow to me. Now get up, go out from this land and return to the land of your birth" (Gen 31:11–13).

The angel of God explicitly tells Jacob in verse 13 that he was the God of Bethel. Jacob had seen angels at Bethel and one lone deity—Yahweh, the God of Abraham. It was Yahweh who had promised protection, and to whom Jacob had erected the stone pillar. This passage fuses the two figures. This fusion is helpful for parsing Jacob's subsequent divine encounters.

As Jacob's life proceeds, he's in and out of trouble. Yet Yahweh is with him. After he succeeds in fleeing from his uncle Laban, Jacob learns in the course of his travels that he will soon be coming face-to-face with Esau, the brother from whom he had stolen his father's blessing years ago. At the time of Jacob's trickery, Esau had sought to kill him, and so now Jacob is wondering whether his brother is still holding a grudge. That meeting occurs in Genesis 33. But it's what happens to Jacob in the preceding chapter that draws our attention.

In Genesis 32 we learn a lot about Jacob's state of mind—and God's loyalty to him. In Genesis 32:1 God sends angels to meet him. This time it is no dream. Nevertheless, Jacob can't set aside his anxiety. He takes steps to bribe Esau, sending extravagant gifts ahead of the caravan. He removes his children and their four mothers to the other side of the Jabbok, a small stream (Gen 32:22–23). Alone, that night he has his most famous encounter with God—or maybe someone else who was also God. The story reads:

[24] And Jacob remained alone, and a man wrestled with him until the breaking of the dawn. [25] And when he saw that he could not prevail against him, he struck his hip socket, so that Jacob's hip socket was sprained as he wrestled with him. [26] Then he said, "Let me go, for dawn is breaking." But he answered, "I will not let you go unless you bless me." [27] Then he said to him, "What is your name?" And he said, "Jacob." [28] And he said, "Your name shall no longer be called Jacob, but Israel, for you have struggled with God and with men and have prevailed." [29] Then Jacob asked and said, "Please tell me your name." And he said, "Why do you ask this—for my name?" And he blessed him there. [30] Then Jacob called the name of the place Peniel which means "I have seen God face to face and my life was spared" (Gen 32:24–30).

Genesis 32:28–29 makes it apparent that the "man" with whom Jacob wrestled was a divine being. The mysterious combatant himself says "you have striven with *elohim*," a term we know can be translated either "God" or "a god." The narrative nowhere says Jacob's encounter was only a vision. This *elohim* is tangible and corporeal. Hosea 12:3–4 confirms the divine identity of Jacob's opponent—but then adds two surprising details.[5] Note the way Hosea uses parallelism to express the thought:

> [3] In the womb he [Jacob] deceived his brother,
> and in his manhood **he struggled** [Hebrew, *sarah*] **with God** [*elohim*].
> > [4] **He struggled** [Hebrew, *yasar*] **with the angel**
> > and prevailed:
> he pleaded for his mercy.
> He met him at Bethel, and there he spoke with him.[6]

Not only does Hosea describe Jacob's *elohim* opponent as an angel, but the last line of this quotation identifies this angel *with Bethel*. Curiously, we know from Genesis 32 that this incident did not occur at Bethel—it was at the waters of the Jabbok. Hosea's inspired commentary on the incident isn't about geography, though. He's telling us that Jacob wrestled with God himself, physically embodied—and identifies God with the angel who said he was the God of Bethel.[7]

We've seen this "confusion" of God with an angel before. It is deliberate. The point is not that Yahweh, the God of Israel, is a mere angel. The reverse is the case. *This angel is Yahweh.*

We have one more passage to consider. The way it fuses Yahweh and the angel is nothing short of amazing.

Genesis 48 records Jacob's deathbed words of blessing to Joseph's children. The passage references the God who had appeared to him at Bethel, who, readers know from Genesis 31:13, is called an angel. It's all set up for the thunderbolt in the section in bold below (vv. 15–16):

> [1] And it happened that after these things, it was said to Joseph, "Behold, your father is ill." And he took his two sons with him, Ephraim and Manasseh. [2] And it was told to Jacob, "Behold, your son Joseph has come to you." Then Israel strengthened himself and he sat up in the bed. [3] Then Jacob said to

---

5. Verses 4–5 in the Hebrew text.

6. This is the LEB rendering. The final word ("him") is interpretive. The Hebrew text, however, has a plural pronoun ("us"). The plural pronoun ("us") preserves the duality of the figures. That duality will be tightly merged in Genesis 48:15–16, explored in the ensuing discussion.

7. See the companion website for a discussion of Gen 35:1–7. Verse 7 is one of the rare instances where the word *elohim* is the grammatical subject of a *plural* verb. That construction has ramifications for the discussion here. See also my article on this grammatical issue: Michael S. Heiser, "Should *elohim* with Plural Predication Be Translated 'Gods'?" *Bible Translator* 61.3 (July 2010): 123–36.

Joseph, "El-Shaddai appeared to me in Luz [Bethel],[8] in the land of Canaan, and blessed me, [4]and said to me, 'Behold, I will make you fruitful and make you numerous, and will make you a company of nations. And I will give this land to your offspring after you as an everlasting possession.' …

[14]And Israel stretched out his right hand and put it on the head of Ephraim (now he was the younger), and his left hand on the head of Manasseh, crossing his hands, for Manasseh was the firstborn. [15]**And he blessed Joseph and said,**

> **"The God [*elohim*] before whom my fathers, Abraham and Isaac, walked,**
> **The God [*elohim*] who shepherded me all my life unto this day,**
> [16]**The angel [*mal'ak*] who redeemed me from all evil,**
> **may he bless the boys** (Gen 48:1–4, 14–16).

The parallel position of *elohim* and *mal'ak* ("angel") is unmistakable. Since the Bible very clearly teaches that God is eternal and existed before all things, and that angels are created beings, the point of this explicit parallel is not to say that God is an angel. On the other hand, it affirms that *this* angel *is* God.[9] But the most striking feature is the verb ("may *he* bless"). In Hebrew, the verb "bless" in this passage *is not grammatically plural*, which would indicate two different persons are being asked to bless the boys. Rather, *it is singular*, thereby telegraphing a tight *fusion* of the two divine beings on the part of the author. In other words, the writer had a clear opportunity to distinguish the God of Israel from the angel, but instead *merges their identities*.

As we leave this chapter, the implications of what we've seen are staggering. The patriarchal stories create an astonishing picture for us. If there is only one God—one Yahweh—then why does the writer fuse Yahweh and the angel in some passages, but have the angel refer to God in the third person in others? Why blur the distinction between Yahweh and this angel and yet keep them distinct? What's being communicated?

When the biblical text does this, it pushes us to wonder whether there are two Yahwehs, one invisible in heaven and one visible on earth. We'll see next that this is precisely the point. The God of Israel is God, but in more than one person.

---

8. Luz is Bethel, as is demonstrated by comparing Gen 28:19; 35:6; 48:3; Judg 1:23.

9. See the companion website for more discussion of the Hebrew text. It contains other indications that the two figures are to be linked together.

CHAPTER 18

What's in a Name?

We've seen some unusual things in the last two chapters. First, Yahweh called Abraham into covenant relationship with him, then he continued that relationship with Isaac and Jacob, whose name became Israel. The descendants of Israel were Yahweh's portion of humanity.

But the interactions between Yahweh and the patriarchs seemed convoluted. Sometimes Yahweh came visible as "the Word." At other times he came as an angel, apparently sent by Yahweh! Still other times there was only Yahweh in human form without any descriptive label. The language created questions about whether Israelites affirmed or denied omnipresence, and about their conception of Yahweh's identity.

In this chapter we'll be introduced to another expression for Yahweh. Its use in several passages makes it clear that the biblical writers conceived of two Yahwehs—one invisible and always present in the spiritual realm ("the heavens"), the other brought forth to interact with humanity on earth, most typically as a man. That there must be two is indicated by their simultaneous presence in some familiar stories.[1]

THE BURNING BUSH

The story of the exodus from Egypt really begins in chapter 3 of the book by that name. Moses' encounter with God at the burning bush has been etched into our minds by Sunday school teachers, ministers, and of course Cecil B. DeMille's

---

1. See chapter 17, footnote 1. The notion that gods can be more than one "personage" and in more than one place at one time is not unique to the Bible. The idea is also evident in ancient Near Eastern literature. The notion was not viewed as incompatible with embodiment. The most recent scholarly work documenting these ideas is that of Benjamin D. Sommer, *The Bodies of God and the World of Ancient Israel* (Cambridge: Cambridge University Press, 2009).

epic film *The Ten Commandments*. But there's something you may have never noticed about the bush. Hollywood certainly missed it.

> [1]And Moses was a shepherd with the flock of Jethro, his father-in-law, the priest of Midian, and he led the flock to the west *of* the desert, and he came to the mountain of God, to Horeb. [2]And the angel of Yahweh appeared to him in a flame of fire from the midst of a bush, and he looked, and there was the bush burning with fire, but the bush was not being consumed. [3]And Moses said, "Let me turn aside and see this great sight. Why does the bush not burn up?" [4]And Yahweh saw that he turned aside to see, and God called to him from the midst of the bush, and he said, "Moses, Moses." And he said, "Here I *am*." [5]And he said, "You must not come near to here. Take off your sandals from on your feet, because the place on which you *are* standing, it *is* holy ground." [6]And he said, "I am the God of your father, the God of Abraham, the God of Isaac, and the God of Jacob." And Moses hid his face because he was afraid of looking at God (Exod 3:1–6).

The text quite clearly states that "the angel of Yahweh" was in the bush (v. 2). But when Moses turns to look at the bush (v. 3), the text has Yahweh observing him and calling to him—"from the midst of the bush" (v. 4). Both the Angel— the visible Yahweh in human form—and the invisible Yahweh are characters in the burning bush scene. Interestingly, verse 6 tells us that Moses was afraid to look at God. This suggests that he had discerned something other than fire in the bush—most likely, the human form of the angel. The New Testament affirms this description in Acts 7:30–35. The martyr Stephen twice tells us that there was an angel in the bush (vv. 30, 35).

In the conversation that ensues, Yahweh (v. 7) reveals his covenant name to Moses: I AM (Exod 3:14). If Yahweh is speaking to Moses, one has to wonder why the Angel was needed. If Yahweh is doing the talking, why does he need a messenger? Or perhaps when the writer says Yahweh is speaking, he means the Angel. Like the passages in Genesis we've already seen, Exodus 3 includes Yahweh and his angel in the same scene as distinct figures, but then creates ambiguity between them. Are there two or one? Are the two the same but different? The reader is being prepped for something dramatic to come. He won't have long to wait.

THE ANGEL, THE NAME, THE PRESENCE

We know what happens after the burning bush. Yahweh, through Moses, delivers Israel from Egypt. Moses leads the people to Sinai to meet their God, receive the law, and prepare for the journey to the promised land. There's a short conversation between God and Moses about that task that is habitually overlooked by Bible readers. In Exodus 23 God says:

> [20] " 'Look, I *am about to* send an angel before you to guard you on the way and to bring you to the place that I have prepared. [21] Be attentive to him and listen to his voice; do not rebel against him, because he will not forgive your transgression, for my name is in him. [22] But if you listen attentively to his voice and do all that I say, I will be an enemy to your enemies and a foe to your foes" (Exod 23:20–22).

There's something strange about God's description to Moses that tells us that this is no ordinary angel. This angel has the authority to pardon sins or not, a status that belongs to God. More specifically, God tells Moses that the reason this angel has this authority is "my name is in him" (v. 21).

What does this curious phrase mean? Moses knew instantly. Anyone thinking of the burning bush account does as well. When God told Moses that his name was in this angel, he was saying that *he was in this angel*—his very presence or essence. The I AM of the burning bush would accompany Moses and the Israelites to the promised land and fight for them. Only he could defeat the gods of the nations and the descendants of the Nephilim whom Moses and Joshua would find there.

Other passages confirm that this reading is correct. This angel is Yahweh. Perhaps the easiest way to demonstrate this is to compare Old Testament passages about who it was that brought Israel out of Egypt and into the promised land.

> I *am* Yahweh, who brought you up from the land of Egypt to be for you as God (Lev 11:45).

> [35] You yourselves were shown this wonder in order for you to acknowledge that Yahweh is the God; there is no other God besides him. [36] From heaven he made you hear his voice to teach you, and on the earth he showed you his great fire, and you heard his words from the midst of the fire. [37] And because he loved your ancestors he chose their descendants after them. And he brought you forth from Egypt with his own presence, by his great strength, [38] to drive out nations greater and more numerous than you from before you, to bring you and to give to you their land as an inheritance, as it is this day[2] (Deut 4:35–38).

---

2. Exod 33:12–14 repeats that the very presence (*panim*) of God will go with Moses as he leads the people to Canaan. This passage follows Exod 23 in the text, but Moses seems completely unaware of the earlier conversation. Source critical scholars and literary-critical scholars have different explanations for the convoluted ordering, all of which is beyond the scope of this book.

Yahweh our God brought us and our ancestors from the land of Egypt, from the house of slavery, and did these great signs before our eyes. He protected us along the entire way that we went, and among all the peoples through whose midst we passed. And Yahweh drove out all the people before us (Josh 24:17–18a).

And the angel of Yahweh went up from Gilgal to Bokim and said, "I brought you up from Egypt, and I brought you to the land that I had promised to your ancestors" (Judg 2:1).

These passages interchange Yahweh, the Angel of Yahweh, and the "presence" (*panim*) of God as the identity of the divine deliverer of Israel from Egypt. There weren't three different deliverers. They are all the same. One of them, the angel, takes human form. If Deuteronomy 4:37 is read in light of Exodus 23:20–23, then the presence and the Angel are co-identified. This makes good sense in view of the meaning of the "Name" which was in the Angel.

THE NAME

Some readers with Jewish friends or a Jewish background know that even today the phrase "the Name" (*ha-shem*) is used by many Jews in the place of the divine name Yahweh.[3] The biblical passages we've seen above show that there is biblical precedent for the practice. In other passages, "the Name" functions as a substitute word for Yahweh. In several the Name is personified—the Name is *a person*. Isaiah 30:27–28 is quite striking in this regard:

> [27] Look! The name of Yahweh comes from afar,
>> burning with his anger and heaviness of cloud.
> His lips are full of indignation,
>> and his tongue is like a devouring fire.
> [28] And his breath is like an overflowing river;
>> it reaches up to the neck.

The Name is clearly cast as an entity, as Yahweh himself, in this text. In Psalm 20:1, 7, this is explicit:

> [1] May Yahweh answer you in the day of trouble.
> May the name of Jacob's God protect you.
>
> [7] Some boast in chariots and others in horses,
>> but we boast in the name of Yahweh, our God.

---

3. I've chosen to capitalize the Name from this point onward when I take the term to be a substitute for Yahweh's presence.

How is it that the psalmist would pray that "the Name" protect anyone? Israelites wouldn't get much protection from a string of consonants (Y-H-W-H). The point of the psalm is that trusting in the Name means trusting in Yahweh himself—*he is the Name.*

Deuteronomy has a lot to say about the Name, especially with respect to the Name being the very presence of God that will reside in the Tabernacle, the holy city, and eventually the Temple.[4] Deuteronomy 12 is representative (note the emphasis in bold):

> [2] You must completely demolish all of the places there where they served their gods, that is, the **nations** whom you are about to dispossess.... [4] You shall not worship Yahweh your God like this. [5] But only to the place that Yahweh your God will choose from all of your tribes **to place his name there** as his dwelling shall you seek, and there you shall go... [11] and then at the place that Yahweh your God will choose, **to let his name dwell there**, there you shall bring all the things I am commanding you (Deut 12:2, 4–5, 11).

THE COMMANDER OF YAHWEH'S ARMY

Readers may have already anticipated that the angel in whom Yahweh's name, his presence, dwells can be identified as the mysterious figure encountered by Joshua just before the wars of conquest. I would agree. Here is the passage in Joshua 5:

> [13] And it happened, when Joshua was by Jericho, he looked up, and he saw a man standing opposite him with his sword drawn in his hand. And Joshua went to him and said, "Are you with us, or with our adversaries?" [14] And he said, "Neither. I have come now as the commander of Yahweh's army." And Joshua fell on his face to the earth, and he bowed down and said to him, "What

---

4. There has been a good bit of recent scholarly work on the Name phenomenon in Israelite religion and the biblical text. Sandra Richter's work is critical of the idea that the Name is cast as an entity (Sandra L. Richter, *The Deuteronomistic History and the Name Theology: lešakkēn šemô šām in the Bible and the Ancient Near East* (Beihefte zur Zeitschrift für die alttestamentliche Wissenschaft 318; Berlin: Walter de Gruyter, 2002). In most basic terms, Richter argues that the "name theology" of Deuteronomy signifies only Yahweh's ownership, not that the name is a person or manifestation of Yahweh's essence. Richter's work was keenly critiqued in this regard by Tryggve Mettinger (www.bookreviews.org, 2004). Some of Mettinger's criticisms were anticipated by publications that preceded Richter's work (Gordon J. Wenham, "Deuteronomy and the Central Sanctuary," *Tyndale Bulletin* 22 (1971): 103–18; Ian Wilson, *Out of the Midst of the Fire: Divine Presence in Deuteronomy* [SBL Dissertation Series 151; Atlanta: Scholars Press, 1995]). The most thorough rebuttals, however, are Michael B. Hundley, "To Be or Not to Be: A Reexamination of Name Language in Deuteronomy and the Deuteronomistic History," *Vetus Testamentum* 59 (2009): 533–55; and Hundley, *Keeping Heaven on Earth: Safeguarding the Divine Presence in the Priestly Tabernacle* (Forschungen zum Alten Testament 50, second series; Tübingen: Mohr Siebeck, 2011).

is my lord commanding his servant?" [15]The commander of Yahweh's army said to Joshua, "Take off your sandals from your feet, for the place where you are standing is holy." And Joshua did so (Josh 5:13–15).

An important clue to identifying this "man" as the angel of Yahweh is the drawn sword in his hand. The Hebrew phrase here occurs only two other times: Numbers 22:23 and 1 Chronicles 21:16. Both explicitly name the Angel of Yahweh as the one with "drawn sword" in hand.

The connection is unmistakable on two other counts. Joshua bows to the man, an instinctive reaction to the divine presence. The commander orders Joshua, "Take off your sandals from your feet, for the place where you are standing is holy." The wording comes from Exodus 3:5, the burning bush passage. The angel of Yahweh was in that bush.[5]

AN INTRIGUING CONVERSATION

The angel of Exodus 23:20–23 did indeed go with Moses and Joshua to claim the promised land. In the wake of Joshua's death, however, Israel failed to complete the task. The Angel of Yahweh appeared in Judges 2 bringing news no one wanted to hear:

> [1]And the angel of Yahweh went up from Gilgal to Bokim and said, "I brought you up from Egypt, and I brought you to the land that I had promised to your ancestors. I said, 'I will never break my covenant with you. [2]And as for you, do not make a covenant with the inhabitants of this land; break down their altars.' But you did not listen to my voice. Why would you do such a thing? [3]Now I say, I will not drive them out from before you; they will become as thorns for you, and their gods will be a trap for you." [4]And as the angel of Yahweh spoke these words to all the Israelites, the people wept bitterly (Judg 2:1–4).

The angel of Yahweh's departure signaled an end to the regular presence of Yahweh with Israel. But even in the dark period of the judges he wouldn't stay away completely. The call of Gideon in Judges 6 includes one appearance during this period. The passage is lengthy, so the important items are in bold.

---

5. It is interesting to speculate on how Joshua was able to discern that this "man" was the angel of Yahweh. He bows down immediately upon hearing the commander's voice. It would seem that he recognizes the voice. Having accompanied Moses into the proximity of the divine presence on a number of occasions, this seems a reasonable explanation. However, the incident may only be a literary-theological way of partnering the angel with Joshua once Moses has died. Joshua had been commissioned in Num 27:18–23. The message in Joshua 5 to readers would be that, as Yahweh's presence in the angel was with Moses, so would he be with Joshua. Joshua's performance to this point in the wake of Moses' death had Yahweh's endorsement. See the companion website.

11 The angel of Yahweh came and sat under the oak that was at Ophrah that belonged to Jehoash the Abiezrite; and Gideon his son was threshing wheat in the winepress to hide it from the Midianites. **12 The angel of Yahweh appeared to him** and said to him, "**Yahweh is with you**, you mighty warrior." 13 Gideon said to him, "Excuse me, my lord. If Yahweh is with us, why then has all this happened to us? Where are all his wonderful deeds that our ancestors recounted to us, saying, 'Did not Yahweh bring us up from Egypt?' But now Yahweh has forsaken us; he has given us into the palm of Midian." **14 And Yahweh turned to him and said**, "Go in this your strength, and you will deliver Israel from the palm of Midian. Did I not send you?" **15 He [Gideon] said to him**, "Excuse me, my lord. How will I deliver Israel? Look, my clan is the weakest in Manasseh, and I am the youngest in my father's house." **16 And Yahweh said to him**, "But I will be with you, and you will defeat Midian as if they are one man." 17 And he said to him, "Please, if I have found favor in your eyes, show me a sign that you are speaking with me. **18 Please, do not depart from here** until I come back to you and bring out my gift and set it out before you." And he said, "**I will stay** until you return."

19 And Gideon went and prepared a young goat and unleavened cakes from an ephah of flour; he put meat in a basket, and the broth he put in a pot, and **he brought them to him under the oak** and presented them. **20 The angel of God said to him**, "Take the meat and the unleavened cakes and put them on this rock; pour the broth over it." And he did so. 21 Then the **angel of Yahweh** reached out the tip of the staff that was in his hand, and he touched the meat and the unleavened cakes; and fire went up from the rock and consumed the meat and the unleavened cakes. And **the angel of Yahweh went from his sight**. 22 And Gideon realized that he was the angel of Yahweh; and Gideon said, "Oh, my lord Yahweh! For now I have seen the angel of Yahweh face to face." 23 And **Yahweh said to him**, "Peace be with you. Do not fear; you will not die." 24 And Gideon built there an altar to Yahweh, and he called it "Yahweh is peace." To this day it is still in Ophrah of the Abiezrites (Judg 6:11–24).

This is a fascinating passage. In verse 11 the angel sits down under the oak tree for the conversation. He makes his visible presence known to Gideon in verse 12. There is no indication that Gideon considers his presence at all strange. Gideon's disgruntled reference to Yahweh in verse 13 makes it clear he doesn't know the man is Yahweh. The reader, however, knows that, since the narrator has *Yahweh* taking part in the conversation (vv. 14–16).

The scene is reminiscent of the burning bush (Exod 3) except that both Yahwehs have speaking roles. This serves to put the two characters on the same level to the reader. That tactic is by now familiar—putting both figures on par to blur the distinction. But in the case of Judges 6, the writer also makes them clearly separate.

That there are two clearly separate Yahweh figures becomes more dramatic after verse 19. Gideon asks the man (who is logically the angel of Yahweh) to stay put while Gideon makes a meal for him. The stranger agrees. When Gideon returns, he brings the meal to the tree (v. 19). The narrator has the Angel of God receiving it. Again that's logical, since the angel had sat there at the beginning of the story.

Now comes the shocker. The angel of Yahweh burns up the sacrifice and then leaves (v. 21). But we learn in verse 23 that *Yahweh is still there* and speaks to Gideon after the Angel's departure. Not only did the writer blur the distinction between the two figures, but he had them both in the same scene.

RAMIFICATIONS

The most familiar way to process what we've seen is to think about the way we talk about Jesus. Christians affirm that God is more than one Person, but that each of those Persons is the same in essence. We affirm that Jesus is one of those Persons. He is God. But in another respect, Jesus isn't God—he is not the Father. The Father is not the Son, and the Son is not the Father. Nevertheless, they are the same in essence.

This theology did not originate in the New Testament. You've now been exposed to its Old Testament roots. There are two Yahweh figures in Old Testament thinking—one invisible, the other visible and human in form. Judaism before the first century, the time of Jesus, knew this teaching. That's why ancient Jewish theology once embraced two Yahweh figures (the "two powers").[6] But once this teaching came to involve the risen Jesus of Nazareth, Judaism could no longer tolerate it.

We'll see specifically how New Testament writers repurposed the two-Yahwehs theology in later chapters. For now, we need to pay a visit to Sinai. Yahweh needs to lay down the law ... with the help of his angel and the divine council.

---

6. I mentioned Alan Segal's work in this regard in the first footnote of the previous chapter: Alan F. Segal, *Two Powers in Heaven: Early Rabbinic Reports about Christianity and Gnosticism* (reprint, Waco, TX: Baylor University Press, 2012). In addition to Segal, the following scholarly studies are noteworthy in regard to Judaism's two-powers teaching: Daniel Boyarin, "The Gospel of the Memra: Jewish Binitarianism and the Prologue to John," *Harvard Theological Review* 94.3 (2001): 243–84; Boyarin, "Beyond Judaisms: Met at ron and the Divine Polymorphy of Ancient Judaism," *Journal for the Study of Judaism in the Persian, Hellenistic, and Roman Periods* 41 (2010): 323–65.

CHAPTER 19

Who Is like Yahweh?

YAHWEH, THE MOST HIGH, THE GOD OF GODS, SHUNNED THE NATIONS. HE made himself known to his chosen people, his earthly portion, in the form of a man. The revelation began with Abraham and was repeated to Isaac and Jacob, Abraham's son and grandson. The Angel who was Yahweh in human form changed Jacob's name to Israel (Gen 32:27–28). Jacob's sons would eventually engage in a treachery against Joseph, one of their own, that would providentially place Israel in Egypt.

Many Bible readers wonder why God would have allowed (much less instructed, as in Gen 46:3–4) Israel to go to Egypt. The question becomes even more pressing given what I've called the "Deuteronomy 32 worldview," where the nations and their gods are pitted against Israel and Yahweh. The human propensity toward evil seems to explain why the Egyptians feared and then enslaved the Israelites after the death of Joseph, resorting even to murder to control the population (Exod 1–2). There's more to it than that.

THE VOICE OF PROVIDENCE

The story of Yahweh's disinheritance of the nations would have been passed on orally through generations of Israelites during the bondage in Egypt. Every Israelite child would have learned about Abraham, Isaac, Jacob, and Joseph. They would learn that their very existence was the result of a supernatural act, given that Isaac was born by supernatural intervention. They had life because of Isaac's life.

But the story produced a conundrum: *Why doesn't this God of gods deliver us?* Oral tradition would have preserved such a promise. Yahweh had sent Joseph into Egypt to preserve Israel from famine and had promised both

Abraham and Jacob that he would bring them back to the land he had promised them (Gen 15:13–16; 46:4).

The deliverance from Egypt would resolve that issue—and that wasn't the only question God's providential acts would address. The Israelites asked "*Where* is Yahweh?" in the wake of God's decision to send them into hostile territory. But Pharaoh and his people—and all the nations—asked a different question: "*Who* is Yahweh?" (Exod 5:2). They would find out the hard way.

The reason for Israel's circumstances was that it wasn't sufficient that only Israel knew Yahweh was Most High among all gods, and that Israel was his portion. The other nations had to know that as well. Scripture makes it clear that Israel's deliverance had that effect. Israel was in Egypt precisely so that Yahweh could deliver them—thereby conveying this theological message.

YAHWEH AND THE GODS OF EGYPT

Gentiles back in Canaan heard about what Yahweh had done (Josh 2:8–10; cf. Exod 15:16–18; Josh 9:9). In Midian, Jethro, Moses' father-in-law, put the impact in no uncertain terms: "Now I know that Yahweh is greater than all the gods, even in the matter where they the Egyptians dealt arrogantly against the Israelites" (Exod 18:11). Yahweh's reputation among the nations was linked to Israel's exodus and transplantation in the land (Num 14:15–16; Deut 9:28; Josh 7:9; 2 Sam 7:23).

This backdrop is why the exodus event is repeatedly cast as a conflict between Yahweh and the gods. Pharaoh, as we know, was unresponsive to the command of God through Moses to let his people go. In Exodus 5:2, Pharaoh had sarcastically asked Moses, "Who is Yahweh that I should listen to his voice to release Israel?" His answer came in a series of horrible plagues.

The Bible tells us the plagues were aimed at Egypt's gods (Exod 12:12; Num 33:4), the *elohim* who had been given their authority by Yahweh and who were supposed to govern Egypt on his behalf. The idea is not that each plague neatly corresponds to an Egyptian deity, only that the powerful acts of Yahweh went beyond the power of the gods of Egypt and their divine representative-son, Pharaoh.[1]

---

1. See the discussion of the plagues and their theological messaging in James K. Hoffmeier, *Israel in Egypt: The Evidence for Authenticity of the Exodus Tradition* (Oxford: Oxford University Press, 1996), 149–53. Hoffmeier introduces the notion that the plagues targeted Pharaoh's role as the representative god of the Egyptian state (p. 151), an approach he developed elsewhere: "Egypt, Plagues In," in *The Anchor Yale Bible Dictionary* (ed. David Noel Freedman; New York: Doubleday, 1992), 374–76. On the divinity of Pharaoh, see David P. Silverman, "Kingship and Divinity," in *Religion in Ancient Egypt: Gods, Myths, and Personal Practice* (ed. Byron Esely Shafer, Leonard H. Lesko, and David P. Silverman; Ithaca, NY: Cornell University Press, 1991), 58–87.

Egyptian theology linked Pharaoh and Egypt's pantheon. From the fourth dynasty onward in Egypt, Pharaoh was considered the son of the high God Re. He was, to borrow the biblical expression, Re's image on earth, the maintainer of the cosmic order established by Re and his pantheon at the creation.

Pharaoh was the son of Re. Israel was explicitly called the son of Yahweh in the confrontation with Pharaoh (Exod 4:23; cf. Hos 11:1). Yahweh and his son would defeat the high god of Egypt and his son. God against god, son against son, imager against imager. In that context, the plagues are spiritual warfare. Yahweh will undo the cosmic order, throwing the land into chaos.[2]

The final plague in particular, the death of the firstborn, was aimed at Egypt's gods. God told Moses, "And I will go through the land of Egypt during this night, and I will strike all of the firstborn in the land of Egypt, from human to animal, and I will do punishments among all of the gods of Egypt. I am Yahweh" (Exod 12:12).

The spiritual conflict is brought into vivid and tragic focus in this last plague. Yahweh would act directly, in the form of his angel, against the gods and people of Egypt. We read in Exodus 12:23 (ESV), "For the LORD will pass through to strike the Egyptians, and when he sees the blood on the lintel and on the two doorposts, the LORD will pass over the door and will not allow the destroyer [*mashkhit*] to enter your houses to strike you."

There is no explicit reference to the Angel here. However, the word translated "destroyer" (*mashkhit*) gives us a clue as to who the destroyer was. The term *mashkhit* is employed in only three passages to describe divine judgment: here in Exodus 12:23; 2 Samuel 24:16; and 1 Chronicles 21:15. These last two instances describe the same event—the judgment for David's sin carried out by the Angel of Yahweh. 2 Samuel 24:16–17a reads:

> [16] When the angel stretched out his hand to destroy Jerusalem, Yahweh regretted about the evil, and he said to the angel who brought destruction [*mashkhit*] among the people, "Enough, now relax your hand." Now the angel of Yahweh was at the threshing floor of Araunah the Jebusite. [17] David spoke to Yahweh when he saw the angel destroying among the people.

An identification of the destroyer with the Angel of the LORD is also perhaps suggested by Zechariah 12:8–10. In the context of the eschatological Day of the LORD we read:

---

2. See Thomas Dozeman, "The Song of the Sea and Salvation History," in *On the Way to Nineveh: Studies in Honor of George M. Landes*, American Schools of Oriental Research 4 (ed. S. L. Cook and S. C. Winter; Atlanta: Scholars Press, 1999), 94–113; and L. Michael Morales, *The Tabernacle Pre-Figured: Cosmic Mountain Ideology in Genesis and Exodus*, Biblical Tools and Studies 15 (Leuven: Peeters, 2012), 196–205, for the cosmic implications of the exodus event.

⁸On that day Yahweh will put a shield around the inhabitants of Jerusalem, and the one who stumbles among them on that day will be like David, and the house of David will be like God, like the angel of Yahweh, before them. ⁹And then on that day I will seek to destroy all the nations coming against Jerusalem. ¹⁰I will pour on the house of David and on the inhabitants of Jerusalem a spirit of grace and supplication, and they will look to me whom they pierced, and they shall mourn over him, as one wails over an only child, and they will grieve bitterly over him as one grieves bitterly over a firstborn (Zech 12:8–10).

The passage clearly identifies the angel with Yahweh, who seeks to destroy all the nations coming against Jerusalem and his people. The reference to those who suffer as grieving over a firstborn is a striking allusion back to the last plague against Egypt and the death angel.

That the destroyer is Yahweh's special angel should be no surprise. We've already looked ahead at his appearance to Joshua as commander of Yahweh's host. Yahweh comes in human form to be among his people and to fight for them, judging those who sought his people's enslavement and death (Exod 1–2; 13–14). The visible Yahweh would later do the same to other enemies, like the Assyrians (Isa 37:36).

WHO IS LIKE YAHWEH AMONG THE GODS?

On the other side of the Red Sea crossing, this earthly judgment of Egypt is clearly viewed as a victorious outcome of a cosmic conflict in the unseen world. As we've seen so often before, behind a familiar story much is missed without a grasp of the ancient cosmic worldview.

Having crossed the watery chasm[3] on dry land, Moses and the people of Israel sang the praises of the unmatchable Yahweh. This song is recorded for us in Exodus 15. Moses asks, "Who is like Yahweh, among the gods [*elim*]?" The answer to the rhetorical question is obvious. Yahweh is incomparable. *No*

---

3. The Israelites crossed through the waters of the "Red Sea" (Exod 15:4). The biblical phrase is *yam suph*, translated by most scholars as "sea of reeds" (the word "red" in Hebrew is *edom*, which does not occur with *yam*, "sea"). The phrasing and its translation has led to voluminous debate over the location of the crossing. To make matters more confusing, Num 33:8 says the Israelites "went through the midst of the sea into the desert" and has the Israelites at the "Red Sea" (*yam suph*) days *later* (Num 33:10–11). Scholars have offered a number of ways to reconcile the accounts, though all of them depend at some point on speculation. For our purposes, the proposal that *yam suph* describes both a real location and the primeval waters of chaos is most interesting, particularly in light of the ensuing discussion of Psa 74. See the companion website for my interaction with the following two articles: N. H. Snaith, "סוף ים: The Sea of Reeds; The Red Sea," *Vetus Testamentum* 15.3 (July 1965): 395–98 (note that the Hebrew pointing in the article title is that of Snaith); Bernard F. Batto, "The Reed Sea: *Requiescat in Pace*," *Journal of Biblical Literature* 102.1 (1983): 27–35.

other god is like him. As I noted earlier, if the other gods were considered fairy tales by Israelites, this statement is at best a joke and at worst a lie.

Why is it, then, that Psalm 74:12–17 describes the crossing as involving the defeat of a sea monster?

> ¹² But God has been my king from long ago,
> working salvation in the midst of the earth.
> ¹³ You split open the sea [*yam*] by your strength;
> You broke the heads of the sea monsters [*tanninim*] in the waters.
> ¹⁴ You crushed the heads of Leviathan [*liwyatan*];
> you gave him as food to the desert dwelling creatures.
> ¹⁵ You split open spring and wadi.
> You dried up ever-flowing rivers.
> ¹⁶ Yours is the day, yours is the night also.
> You established light and the sun.
> ¹⁷ You defined all the boundaries of the earth;
> Summer and winter—you formed them.

Did you catch the language? God "split open the sea" and crushed the heads of "sea monsters" (*tanninim*) and Leviathan (*liwyatan*), giving the beasts as food for "*desert dwelling creatures*." God split open the "spring and wadi," two terms frequently associated with desert water sources, and dried up "rivers." What happened to the *sea*?

To make things even more confusing, the psalm has a number of allusions to Genesis 1. In the original creation chapter, God also "divided the waters" (Gen 1:6–7). Virtually all of the language in verses Psalm 74:16–17 can be found in Genesis 1 (Gen 1:4–5, 9–10, 14–18).

Confusing? An ancient Israelite would have no trouble deciphering the messaging in Psalm 74 and recognizing that it ties the exodus crossing to creation—and then links both events to slaying a sea monster known as Leviathan.[4]

The symbolic imagery of Leviathan and the "sea" (*yam*) is well known from the ancient literature of Ugarit, a city-state in ancient Syria.[5] Of the stories that have survived from Ugarit, one of the most famous describes how Baal became king of the gods. This story is the backdrop for Psalm 74.

The epic tale describes how Baal battles against *Yamm*, a deity symbolized as a chaotic, violent force, often depicted as a dragon-like sea monster. In the

---

4. I've omitted a discussion of the forces of chaos—the point of the well-known Leviathan symbol in antiquity—and biblical creation accounts. See the companion website.

5. I mentioned and described Ugarit in chapter 6.

guise of this sea beast, *Yamm* was also referred to by the names *Tannun* or *Litanu*. The overlap with the biblical terminology is transparent. Baal defeated the raging sea and the sea monster, earning "everlasting dominion" over the gods. The moral of the Ugaritic story is that the high king of the gods (Baal) has power over the unpredictable forces of nature.[6]

Genesis 1 and 2 don't provide the Bible's only creation story. Psalm 74 describes creation as well—as Yahweh's victory over the forces of primeval chaos. Yahweh brought the world into order, making it habitable for humanity, his people as it were. The creation act as described in Psalm 74 was theologically crucial for establishing Yahweh's superiority over all other gods. Baal was not king of the gods, as the Ugaritic story proclaimed—Yahweh was.

Neither was Pharaoh, or any other Egyptian deity. By linking the exodus event—the taming of the chaotic waters so that Yahweh's people could pass through them untouched—with the creation story, the biblical writers were telegraphing a simple, potent message. Yahweh is king of all gods. He is lord of creation—not Pharaoh, who, in Egyptian theology, was responsible for maintaining creation order. The same God who created also maintains that creation, and calls it into his service when needed.[7]

It's no wonder that Exodus 15:11 has Moses, on the other side of the waters, ask: *Who is like you among the gods, Yahweh?*

No one in the ancient world, Israelite or otherwise, would have missed the theological punch. These passages left no question as to who was king of the unseen realm, and whose side that king was on. As creator, Yahweh had made the world habitable for all humanity. But the nations had been forsaken. Now the same God once again was described as subduing the forces of chaos to deliver his portion, Israel, for whom he had prepared a place of habitation—the promised land.

But before getting to the land, Yahweh needed to teach his people a few things. It's time for some theology lessons at a place called Mount Sinai, Yahweh's new earthly abode, headquarters of his unseen council.

---

6. Other passages in the Old Testament refer to Leviathan using descriptions found in Ugaritic tablets. In some Ugaritic stories *Litanu* is described as a "twisting serpent" and "fleeing serpent." Those exact phrases are used of Leviathan in Isa 27:1 and Job 26:13.

7. Yahweh frequently appears in a whirlwind with fire, lightning, and tempest, thereby identifying himself as the source and controller of all these forces (Job 22:14; 38:1; Pss 97:2; 104:3; Nah 1:3). He is Lord of the hosts of heaven, king of all gods (Deut 10:17; 2 Chr 2:5; Pss 86:8; 95:3; 96:4; 136:2).

CHAPTER 20

Retooling the Template

The exodus event, the deliverance from bondage in Egypt, was the catalyst for Israel's transition from a people to a nation. Any good commentary or guide to the Bible will flag that. But there's a good deal more going on. Over the next three chapters we'll see that events shortly after the exodus hark back to Eden and the divine council backdrop in some amazing ways.

God's Edenic vision began with his announcement that humankind was his image. Yahweh had divine sons; he would also have a human family. Genesis told us that God had a divine council of imagers who represented his authority in the unseen realm and participated in his rule. It also showed us that God planned a mirror-council on earth, this time composed of human imagers. These two family-administrations were together in his presence. Heaven had come to earth at Eden. Humanity was charged with extending the earthly presence and rule of God throughout the whole earth. God wanted to live and rule with all his children in his new creation.

Genesis 3–11 makes it clear that humanity failed miserably. Free will in the hands of imperfect beings comes with that risk. But the incident at Babel, foolish and self-willed as it was, shows us that there's an Edenic yearning in the human heart, a desire for utopia and a sense of divine presence. But God would not trade his own version of Eden for humanity's. He punished the nations with disinheritance. He would create a new people as his own portion. That inheritance was begun in covenant with Abraham and passed on through his family.

God delivered that family from bondage under Moses. Egypt and its gods were defeated. What was corrupted in Eden and counterfeited in the days of the flood and Babel was quickened to life on the other side of the waters of chaos.

ISRAEL IS MY SON

Yahweh's perception of Israel is clear: "Israel is my son, my firstborn" (Exod 4:22); "Out of Egypt I called my son" (Hos 11:1). As Abraham, Yahweh's portion (Deut 32:9), had been the new Adam, so Israel, the collective progeny of Abraham, was also the new Adam. Adam was Yahweh's son. Israel was Yahweh's son.

That may not seem profound, but it is. Once you realize that this pattern continues through the remainder of the Bible, the messaging becomes clear. Eventually, God will refer to the king of Israel as his son (Psa 2:7). The ultimate future king, the messiah, since he will sit on the seat of David, must be Yahweh's son as well. And since we, glorified believers, will sit on that throne too, sharing that rule (Rev 3:21), we are God's sons, his children. Every believer is also Abraham's offspring by faith (Gal 3:26–29). We are the current *and* eschatological sons of God. Our status began with Adam, was rescued in Abraham, and was fulfilled in Jesus, heir to David's throne.

These connections are actually among the more obvious. There is more that extends from Israel's sonship all the way to our glory.

BELIEVING ISRAEL: God's Earthly Council

Recall that in our discussion of Deuteronomy 32:8–9 I mentioned that the number of nations disinherited by Yahweh at the judgment of Babel was seventy.[1] The number is telling. Israel's nearest religious competition, the worship of El, Baal, and Asherah at Ugarit and in Canaan, held that their divine council had seventy sons. When Yahweh disinherited the nations and allotted them to the sons of God, a theological gauntlet was thrown down: Yahweh *alone* commands the nations and their gods. Other gods serve *him*.

The exodus story follows that theological punch in the nose with another. Not only is Israel Yahweh's son and portion on earth, but Israel is to be governed by a special group of *seventy* under Moses and, later, the Israelite king who is Yahweh's enthroned son.

Shortly after crossing through the sea, Moses and Israel encountered Jethro. The account is recorded in Exodus 18. Seeing the throngs, Jethro advises Moses to select men to help him govern the people. No number is given in that passage, but later, in Exodus 24, we read:

[1]And to Moses he [Yahweh] said, "Go up to Yahweh—you and Aaron, Nadab

---

1. See chapter 14.

and Abihu, and seventy from the elders of Israel—and you will worship at a distance. [2] And Moses alone will come near to Yahweh, and they will not come near, and the people will not go up with him.…

[9] And Moses and Aaron, Nadab and Abihu, and seventy from the elders of Israel went up. [10] And they saw the God of Israel, and what was under his feet was like sapphire tile work and like the very heavens for clearness (Exod 24:1–2, 9–10).

The wording suggests that these seventy elders were drawn from a larger group—as were the *elohim* of Yahweh's council, who were given different ranks and tasks. Not every member of the divine council has equal rank.[2] The sons of God with authority over the nations were assigned that role, but they became corrupt and are the object of the sentencing of Psalm 82.[3]

The correspondences are deliberate. The seventy nations were placed under the dominion of lesser gods in the wake of Yahweh's judgment of the nations at the Tower of Babel. Yahweh's own kingdom is structured with a single leader (Moses for now), with whom he speaks directly, and a council of seventy. Historically, this leadership structure would continue into Jesus' day, as the Jewish Sanhedrin, led by the high priest, numbered seventy.

We're more interested in the theological messaging. In terms of biblical theology, the imagery has a distinct meaning. God is starting his intended Edenic rule with Israel. Israel will have a single earthly leader (eventually the messianic king, the ultimate offspring of Eve) and a council of seventy. The number telegraphs that, as the kingdom of God is re-established on earth, the seventy nations will be reclaimed, a process that began with the ministry of Jesus and will continue to the end of days.[4]

The ultimate outcome of the reclaiming of the nations under Yahweh is suggested in passages that transparently relate to the divine council. Loyal members of Yahweh's council are themselves referred to as his elders in Isaiah 24:23, the context of which is clearly eschatological:

[21] "On that day the LORD will punish the host of heaven, in heaven, and the kings of the earth, on the earth.… [23] Then the moon will be confounded and

---

2. See the companion website for more discussion on the tiers of Yahweh's council and those of other cultures, such as Ugarit.

3. See chapter 30 on the judgment of the gods of Yahweh's council.

4. See the discussion in chapters 32, 37, 40–42. The number of the nations in Genesis reflects the known world at the time the biblical writers produced the Bible. When the Church inherits the promises of Abraham and Jesus sends out the seventy (Luke 10:1), and then all believers in the Great Commission, the language of reclaiming the nations becomes more encompassing. In our day, the messaging is the same: All nations belong to Yahweh; the dominions of darkness will be broken.

the sun ashamed, for the LORD of hosts reigns on Mount Zion and in Jerusalem, and his glory will be before his elders"(Isa 24:21, 23 ESV).[5]

That setting makes sense, given the divine council scene of Revelation 4–5, where the twenty-four *elders* surround God's throne.[6] The teaching point is profound: The corrupt sons of God who currently dominate the nations will be replaced by loyal members of God's family.

But which family? The New Testament explains that.

HEIRS OF THE COSMOS

Since the Church, the corporate body of believers, inherited the promises given to Abraham (Gal 3:26–29), believers are the "true Israel" the New Testament talks about. When we inherit rule of the nations with Jesus at the end of days (Rev 3:21), we will displace the corrupted divine sons of God presently ruling the nations, who are under judgment (Psa 82). We are already, but not yet, Yahweh's new council on earth. The apostle John captures the spirit of the point:

> But as many as received him—to those who believe in his name—he gave to them authority to become children of God (John 1:12).

> See what sort of love the Father has given to us: that we should be called children of God, and we are! (1 John 3:1).

This structuring helps us make sense of something else Paul said. The rulership of the nations was a higher-ranking task than being a messenger (the meaning of the word *angel*). The destiny of believers who will share Jesus' throne and the rule of nations is the backdrop for Paul's statement that Christians should stop letting the world's courts resolve their disputes. In 1 Corinthians 6:3 he protests: "Do you not know that we will judge angels?" When we are made divine (glorified) on the new earth, *we will outrank angels*. Believers are

---

5. Timothy M. Willis, "Yahweh's Elders (Isa 24, 23): Senior Officials of the Divine Court," *Zeitschrift für die alttestamentliche Wissenschaft* 103.3 (1991): 375–85. Isaiah 24 is part of the section of Isaiah that scholars refer to as the "little apocalypse" or the "Isaiah apocalypse" (chs. 24–27). See T. J. Johnson, "Apocalypticism, Apocalyptic Literature," in *Dictionary of the Old Testament: Prophets* (ed. Mark J. Boda and Gordon J. McConville; Downers Grove, IL; Nottingham, England: IVP Academic; Inter-Varsity Press, 2012), 41.

6. See the discussion of Rev 4–5 in chapter 39. The community of believers, the elder motif, and the heavenly assembly are also connected to the heavenly throne room vision of Rev 4–5. See Jürgen Roloff, *The Revelation of John: A Continental Commentary* (trans. John E. Alsup; Minneapolis: Fortress, 1993), 69; David E. Aune, *Revelation 1–5*, Word Biblical Commentary 52A (Dallas: Word, 1998), 277; Joseph M. Baumgarten, "The Duodecimal Courts of Qumran, Revelation, and the Sanhedrin," *Journal of Biblical Literature* 95 (1976): 59–78; Larry W. Hurtado, "Revelation 4–5 in the Light of Jewish Apocalyptic Analogies," *Journal for the Study of the New Testament* 25 (1985): 105–24.

God's once and future family, once and future council, once and future rulers with Jesus over all the nations. Israel's release propels this theology.

The glorified, divine aspect of Yahweh's human family-council is telegraphed in other ways.

The divine sons of God are called the "morning stars" in Job 38:7 and "the stars of God" in Isaiah 14:13. The imagery of Joseph's dream, where the sons of Jacob (Israel) are stars (Gen 37:9), is no accident. Neither is it a coincidence that Abraham's offspring will be "as the stars." While that phrase speaks of a numerical multitude of offspring, that isn't its *only* message.

Star language speaks of divinity or glorification elsewhere. In Revelation, Jesus himself, the morning star, and angels are identified with star language to denote their divine, nonearthly, nature (Rev 1:20; 22:16; cf. 2:28). As Daniel says, the righteous will "shine like the brightness of the sky above ... like the stars, forever and ever" (Dan 12:2–3). Our inheritance of the nations with Jesus at the end of days (Rev 3:21) is in a glorified, resurrected—divine—state. The star language of Genesis 15 has an eschatological connotation.

In Romans, Paul was tracking on this idea. Scholars have noticed with interest his slight change of the language of Genesis 15, God's promises to Abraham, in Romans 4.[7] In Genesis 15:5 the embodied Yahweh "brought [Abraham] outside and said, 'Look toward the heavens and count the stars if you are able to count them.' And he said to him, 'So shall your offspring be.'" Paul refers to the verse twice in Romans 4.

So that [Abraham] became the father of many nations, according to what was said, "so will your descendants be" (Rom 4:18).

---

7. This interpretive trajectory is part of New Testament and Second Temple period Jewish thinking on the glorification (also called "angelification," "apotheosis," and "deification") of believers. Second Temple period examples of this approach include Philo of Alexandria (*Who Is the Heir of Divine Things* 86–87, 280–83; *Questions and Answers in Genesis* 4.181; *On the Posterity of Cain* 89; *The Special Laws* 1.13–19); Sirach 44:21. See David Burnett, "'So Shall Your Seed Be': Paul's Use of Genesis 15:5 in Romans 4:18 in Light of Early Jewish Deification Traditions" (paper presented at the Annual Meeting of the Society of Biblical Literature, San Diego, CA, November 22–25, 2014; forthcoming in *Journal for the Study of Paul and His Letters*); M. David Litwa, *We Are Being Transformed: Deification in Paul's Soteriology, Beihefte zur Zeitschrift für die neutestamentliche Wissenschaft* 187 (Berlin: Walter de Gruyter, 2012); Devorah Dimant, "Men as Angels: The Self-Image of the Qumran Community," in *Religion and Politics in the Ancient Near East,* Studies in Jewish History and Culture (ed. Adele Berlin; Bethesda, MD: University Press of America, 1996), 93–103; James Tabor, "Firstborn of Many Brothers: A Pauline Notion of Apotheosis," in *Society of Biblical Literature Seminar Papers* 1984, 295–303. The eschatological ramifications of that thinking are the coherent outcome of the Deuteronomy 32 worldview's final resolution in biblical theology. Burnett's essay is particularly powerful in that it demonstrates a clear Jewish intellectual trajectory (especially Philo) that links the glorification of Abraham's seed (all believers, via Gal 3:26–29) to the divine sons of God. Glorified believers are Yahweh's household-council reconstituted to displace and replace the rebellious sons of God over the nations who now resist the advance of Yahweh's kingdom and reclamation of the nations. See the companion website for more discussion.

For the promise to Abraham or to his descendants, that he would be heir of the world [Greek: *kosmos*], was not through the law, but through the righteousness by faith (Rom 4:13).

A few observations are in order. For Paul, Abraham did not become the father of just Israel, but of *many nations*. The point of course harks back to his theology in Galatians 3, where all believers, Jew or Gentile, are "Abraham's seed" (Gal 3:26–29).

The notion of Abraham's offspring becoming "heir of the world" speaks to rulership of the nations by those offspring. The corrupt divine sons of God of Deuteronomy 32:8 would be displaced by new divine sons of God—glorified believers.[8]

Paul's logic makes sense if believers are Yahweh's children, especially given the merging of humanity with the divine presence back in Eden. Even now we are "sharers of the divine nature" (2 Pet 1:4), but one day we will be made like Jesus (1 John 3:1–3; 1 Cor 15:35–49) and rule with him over the nations. Believers, the spiritual offspring of Abraham, will ultimately reverse the disinheritance of the nations along with the curse of death that extended from Eden's failure.

EDEN AND SINAI

In Genesis, Eden was Yahweh's home and the meeting place of his divine council. God had since changed addresses. Sinai was now his domain—and where Israel was now headed.

Earlier we discovered that Eden was the dwelling place and headquarters of the divine council.[9] We were reminded of the description of Eden in Genesis as a lush *garden* with four rivers (Gen 2:10–14). Eden was also a *mountain* (Ezek 28:13–14), the administrative "seat of the gods" (Ezek 28:2), situated in "the heart of the seas" (Ezek 28:2), a description that reiterated the well-watered imagery of the council headquarters. The gods lived in the best or most remote places. That earlier discussion noted some connections between Eden and Mount Zion. It's time to take a look at connections with Sinai.[10]

---

8. See chapters 35–36, 42.

9. See chapter 6.

10. On Eden-Sinai connections, see Morales, "Mountain of God in the Wilderness," ch. 4 in L. Michael Morales, *The Tabernacle Prefigured: Cosmic Mountain Ideology in Genesis and Exodus* (Biblical Tools and Studies 15; Leuven: Peeters, 2012); Richard J. Clifford, "The Temple and the Holy Mountain," in *Cult and Cosmos: Tilting Toward a Temple-Centered Biblical Theology*, Biblical Tools and Books 18 (ed. L. Michael Morales; Leuven: Peeters, 2014), 85–98; D. W. Parry, "Sinai as Sanctuary and Mountain of God," in *By Study and Also by Faith*, vol. 1 in *Essays in Honor of Hugh Nibley on the Occasion of His Eightieth Birthday*

The fact that Eden is referred to as both a garden and a mountain in Ezekiel 28:13–14 is significant. It provides a clear conceptual link between Eden and the holy mountain of God, Sinai.[11]

We've actually already gotten a hint that Sinai is God's home and meeting place. In the passage about the seventy elders (Exod 24:9–11), Yahweh appeared in human form, as he had to the patriarchs and Moses. But this time the seventy earthly elders are along for the meeting. The council room has been reserved for the seventy from Israel.

Sinai as Yahweh's throne room is telegraphed in other ways. Exodus 24 notes that Yahweh was seated and that under his feet was a pavement of shining sapphire stone, "like the very heavens for clearness" (Exod 24:10). Again, light speaks of divine presence. This imagery is repeated in other passages and expanded to include fire, smoke, flashing light, lightning, and loud noises (Exod 19:16, 18; 20:18; Deut 5:4–5, 22–26).

All of these elements are found in familiar visions of Yahweh on his throne (Isa 6; Ezek 1; Dan 7; Psa 18). These passages employ the same imagery whether Yahweh is enthroned in the spiritual realm or on earth. Heaven and earth are connected. Yahweh rules both.

Some of these passages have the divine council, the heavenly host, present. That's to be expected in view of other Eden-Sinai connections. For example, in the throne room scene of Daniel 7 we read:

> [9]As I looked,
>
> > thrones were placed,
> > > and the Ancient of Days took his seat;
> > his clothing was white as snow,
> > > and the hair of his head like pure wool;
> > his throne was fiery flames;
> > > its wheels were burning fire.
> [10]   A stream of fire issued
> > > and came out from before him;
> > a thousand thousands served him,
> > > and ten thousand times ten thousand stood before him;
> > the court sat in judgment,
> > > and the books were opened (vv. 9–10 ESV).

(Provo, UT: Brigham Young University Press, 1990), 482–500; and Daniel C. Timmer, *Creation, Tabernacle, and Sabbath: The Sabbath Frame of Exodus 31:12–17; 35:1–3 in Exegetical and Theological Perspective* (Forschungen zur Religion und Literatur des Alten und Neuen Testaments 227;Göttingen: Vandenhoeck & Ruprecht, 2009).

11. Mount Sinai is also called Mount Horeb in the Old Testament. For example, see Exod 3:1–3; Deut 4:15; 5:2; 1 Kgs 8:9.

This is one of the more explicit divine council texts in the Old Testament. There are *multiple thrones* in this heavenly scene, along with the single throne occupied by the Ancient of Days, the God of Israel.[12] There is a clear reference to the council—the word translated "court" here refers to a judicial body.[13]

There's another fascinating Sinai passage that links the divine council to the mountain and also the thing that the mountain is perhaps best known for—the giving of the law. That might sound odd. In my experience, most people have Charlton Heston in their mind's eye when you bring up Sinai and the law, and there aren't any angels in that scene. But if the divine council isn't associated with the law, how do we handle verses like these?

> [52] Which of the prophets did your fathers not persecute? And they killed those who announced beforehand the coming of the Righteous One, whom you have now betrayed and murdered, [53] you who received the law as delivered by angels and did not keep it (Acts 7:52–53 ESV).

> [1] Therefore we must pay much closer attention to what we have heard, lest we drift away from it. [2] For since the message declared by angels proved to be reliable, and every transgression or disobedience received a just retribution, [3] how shall we escape if we neglect such a great salvation? (Heb 2:1–3a ESV).

The Law delivered by angels? Hollywood wasn't exactly following the biblical script very closely. We'll set the record straight in the next chapter.

---

12. Some Jewish interpreters say the plural "thrones" refers to only two thrones—that of the God of Israel and the other for King David, whom they identify with the Son of Man in this passage. There are several problems with that view, namely the passage's clear literary parallels to divine council scenes from the Ugaritic Baal Cycle and the fact that the Son of Man neither takes a seat nor has one offered to him when he approaches the Ancient of Days. See the discussion in chapter 29. It also cannot be argued that the plural seats are for human Jewish elders, since the court/council in Dan 7 is clearly in heaven and is making a decision *for* the human holy people at the time when the kingdom of the Son of Man is established; cf. Dan 7:22. See the sixth chapter ("The Divine Council in the book of Daniel") in Michael S. Heiser, "The Divine Council in Late Canonical and Non-Canonical Second Temple Jewish Literature," (PhD diss., University of Wisconsin–Madison, 2004). The dissertation is available on the companion website.

13. The court is seated at this point in the narrative (v. 10). God, the presiding judge, is already seated (v. 9).

CHAPTER 21

God's Law, God's Council

I'LL ADMIT, IT'S A LITTLE HARD TO GET EXCITED ABOUT THE LAW OF GOD. How many of us would echo Paul's sentiment, that he delighted in the law of God in his heart (Rom 7:22)? We certainly don't think of the law like David did:

> [7] The law of Yahweh is perfect, reviving life.
> The testimony of Yahweh is firm, making wise the simple.
> [8] The precepts of Yahweh are right, making the heart rejoice.
> The command of Yahweh is pure, enlightening the eyes (Psa 19:7–8).

We tend to think of the law as though every one of its 613 commands were an oppressive lynchpin in a relationship to Yahweh. We tend to view the law negatively, as though it were given to produce feelings of guilt or to frustrate Israelites with the impossibility of pleasing God. This is misguided. The laws of the Torah broadly deal with a person's relationship to Yahweh (e.g., worship, access to sacred space),[1] relationships with fellow Israelites or outsiders (e.g., sex, business, property), and the nation's covenantal bond with her God. The law was not a means of *meriting* salvation. An Israelite would have known that believing was at the heart of right relationship with Yahweh, not mere mechanical observance of a list of do's and don'ts. For sure some Israelites would have lapsed into this mistaken thinking, particularly after the shock of the exile, but that wasn't what the law was about.[2]

---

1. See chapter 22 for these concepts.

2. The Torah was clear that possession of the promised land was linked to obedience, particularly in regard to rejecting the worship of other gods and idolatry (e.g., Lev 26; Deut 4:25–27, 39–40; 11:18–24). The preaching of the prophets, the destruction of the temple, and expulsion from the land itself jolted the exiled Israelites to the realization that their exile was due to disobedience. Consequently, the Torah became the central focus of the surviving community. In exile, the teaching of the law in the new institution of the synagogue replaced temple ritual in the religious life of the community. Synagogues and the focus on the law were retained even after the return to the land and the building of a new temple. With Israel determined to never be driven from the land again, the law became the orientation point for Judaism. The

In other words, legalism was not intrinsic to a biblical theology of the law. The heart of salvation in biblical theology—across both testaments—is *believing loyalty* to Yahweh. That orientation extends from Eden and has deep roots in what happened at Sinai. It is no coincidence that when Israel, Yahweh's portion, met with him at Sinai, the result was a second covenant involving laws binding Israel and Yahweh in faithfulness, witnessed by the members of Yahweh's divine council.

THE COSMIC MOUNTAIN: Birthplace of the Law

In the last chapter we were introduced to the connections between Eden and Sinai. Both were sacred places where Yahweh's children saw him in human form (Gen 3:8; Exod 24:9–11). We ended our discussion with the provocative notion that the divine council was present at God's mountain, specifically during the giving of the law.

The link between the law and the heavenly council is noted several times in the New Testament, which uses for the divine council the umbrella term "angels." I closed the last chapter with two passages that described the law as "delivered by angels" (Acts 7:53) and "declared by angels" (Heb 2:2).[3]

When I first came across these New Testament verses, I had read a lot of the Old Testament and had never before seen this idea, so I naturally won-

---

focus on obedience to the law became a way for the Jewish community to express commitment to God's election of Israel and remain in the land. With respect to this mentality, one scholar notes: "To the exiles, the Pentateuch's curses for disobedience to the covenant must have appeared to be a breathtakingly accurate prediction of the Babylonian invasion and subsequent exile (Lev 26:14–46; Deut 28:43–52, 64–67; 29:22–28; 31:14–29). Thus when the Persians overran the Babylonians and subsequently allowed expatriate Israelites to return to their native land the leaders of the return understandably resolved to adhere strictly to the law and so to avoid future punishment for disobedience. Their Achilles heel prior to the exile, they believed, was their seduction into idolatry by foreign influences. The road to a restored covenant relationship with God, they reasoned, was a renewed determination to fence themselves off from harmful foreign influences by strictly obeying the Law" (F. Theilman, "Law," in *Dictionary of Paul and His Letters* [ed. Gerald F. Hawthorne, Ralph P. Martin, and Daniel G. Reid; Downers Grove, IL: InterVarsity Press, 1993], 533).

3. Recall that the New Testament language for divine beings is less hierarchically precise than the Old Testament. As we'll see in chapter 37, while Paul uses terms for divine beings that reflect geographical authority (e.g., principalities and powers), most New Testament vocabulary is simplified. Good divine beings are predominantly referred to with *angelos* ("angel"), whereas the terms of choice for evil ones are *daimōn* and *daimonion*. All three of these terms are actually neutral (neither good nor evil) in wider Greek usage. They refer to, respectively, "messengers" and "spirit beings." The idea of a divine messenger presumes a being sent by God for good purposes, and so *angelos* became the common term for benevolent spirits. This is not to suggest, however, that Jewish theology in the Hellenistic era was trying to rid itself of terms like Hebrew (plural) *elohim* or *elim* ("gods") or Greek theoi. Jewish texts in both Hebrew and Greek before and during the first century utilize this vocabulary as well. In addition to the resources in chapter 37, see Michael S. Heiser, "Monotheism and the Language of Divine Plurality in the Hebrew Bible and the Dead Sea Scrolls," *Tyndale Bulletin* 65:1 (2014): 85–100; R. B. Salters, "Psalm 82, 1 and the Septuagint," *Zeitschrift für die alttestamentliche Wissenschaft* 103.2 (1991): 225–39.

dered where the New Testament writers were getting it. It's actually a prickly problem. There are passages that describe angels at Sinai, but none of them specifically reference the law.

For example, Psalm 68:15–18 reads:

> [15] A mountain of God is the mountain of Bashan;
>> a mountain of many peaks is the mountain of Bashan.
>
> [16] Why do you look with hostility, O many-peaked mountains?
>> This mountain God desires for his dwelling.
>> Yes, Yahweh will abide in it forever.
>
> [17] The chariots of God[4]
>> are twice ten thousand, with thousands doubled.
>> The Lord is among them at Sinai, distinctive in victory.
>
> [18] You have ascended on high; you have led away captives.[5]
>> You have received gifts from among humankind,
>> and even from the rebellious, so that Yah[6] God may dwell there.

Without direct reference to the law, the New Testament idea in Acts 7 and Hebrews 2 seems completely contrived—unless you're using as your Old Testament the Septuagint, the Greek translation of the Old Testament that was the Bible of the early church.

A second Sinai passage that is a key text for connecting the law and the heavenly host is Deuteronomy 33:1–4. The Septuagint version has a multitude of divine beings at Sinai whereas the traditional Hebrew text does not. That isn't the only divergence, either. Take a look at the passage in both versions, especially the bold words:[7]

Traditional (Masoretic) Hebrew Text	Septuagint
Now this is the blessing with which Moses, the man of God, blessed the Israelites before his death. Then he said,	And this is the blessing with which Moses, the man of God, blessed the Israelites before his death. He said:
"Yahweh came from Sinai, and he dawned upon them from Seir; he shone forth from Mount Paran, and **he came with myriads of holy ones, at his right hand a fiery law for them**. Moreover, he loves his people, all the holy ones were in your hand, and they bowed down to your feet, each one accepted directions from you. A law Moses instructed for us, as a possession for the assembly of Jacob.	The Lord has come from Sinai, and he appeared to us from Seir; **he made haste from Mount Paran with ten thousands of Kadesh, at his right, his angels with him**. And he had pity on his people, and all the holy ones were under your hands; even these were under you; and it [the people] received his words, the law which Moses commanded us, an inheritance for the assemblies of Jacob.

---

4. See 2 Kgs 6:17.

5. Readers may recognize that this is the passage quoted in the New Testament by Paul (Eph 4:8). See chapter 33 for comments on this quotation.

6. The Hebrew text uses the shortened form of YHWH (YH).

7. The translations are mine.

The fundamental difference is that the Septuagint version has angels at Sinai (v. 2) and the traditional text doesn't. In verse 3 the traditional Hebrew text seems to suggest that "the holy ones" are the Israelites who will receive the law. The Septuagint has angels at God's right hand—the position of authority —witnessing the giving of the law to Israel.[8]

Since the New Testament writers most often used the Septuagint when referencing the Old Testament, we can understand the point being made in Acts 7:52–53 and Hebrews 2:1–2.

However, Galatians 3:19 (ESV) adds a tantalizing detail that makes the connection more dramatic:

> Why then the law? It was added because of transgressions, until the offspring should come to whom the promise had been made, and it was put in place through angels by an intermediary.

Galatians 3:19 informs us that there was an intermediary between God, the angels, and Israel. Most scholars assume this is a reference to Moses. Other scholars have noted that, in light of the very next verse, this is problematic ("Now an intermediary implies more than one, but God is one"). Why would Paul feel the need to clarify that God's uniqueness wasn't disturbed by this intermediary if it was just Moses?[9]

There is another solution, one that explains Paul's ensuing comment: The intermediary is Yahweh in human form.[10]

Deuteronomy 33 uses language requiring the appearance of Yahweh in human form ("appeared"; "his right"). In this light, Deuteronomy 9:9–10 takes on new significance.[11] Moses says:

> [9] When I went up the mountain to receive the stone tablets, the tablets of the covenant that Yahweh made with you, and remained on the mountain forty

---

8. For a survey of ancient Jewish texts (before and after the New Testament) relating to the connection of the law and angels, see Terrance Callan, "Pauline Midrash: The Exegetical Background of Gal. 3:19b," *Journal of Biblical Literature* 99.4 (December 1980): 549–67.

9. This verse has been called one of the most confusing in the New Testament. See F. F. Bruce's discussion of Gal 3:19–20 in the New International Greek Testament Commentary series, *The Epistle to the Galatians: A Commentary on the Greek Text* (Grand Rapids, MI: Eerdmans, 1982), 175–80.

10. This approach, specifically with respect to the Angel of Yahweh, is found in Second Temple texts such as *Jubilees* 1:27–29. Amazingly, in that text God dictates the law to the Angel, who then delivers it to Moses. See Hindy Najman, "Angels at Sinai: Exegesis, Theology and Interpretive Authority," *Dead Sea Discoveries* 7.3 (2000): 313–33. A disputed passage in the writings of Josephus (*Antiquities* 15:136) is also relevant to the discussion. The passage clearly links angels and the law, though some scholars seek to translate Greek *angeloi* as "prophets" (W. D. Davies, "A Note on Josephus, Antiquities 15:136," *Harvard Theological Review* 47.03 [1954]: 135–40). This idea is ably refuted in Andrew J. Bandstra, "The Law and Angels: *Antiquities* 15.136 and Galatians 3: 19," *Calvin Theological Journal* 24 (1989): 223–40. However, Bandstra applies the angelic reference in Josephus to a different context than Sinai.

11. See also Exod 24:12; 31:18; 32:15–16; Deut 4:13; 5:22.

days and forty nights, I did not eat food and I did not drink water. [10]And Yahweh gave me the two tablets of stone written with the finger of God, and on them was writing according to all the words that Yahweh spoke with you at the mountain, from the midst of the fire on the day of the assembly.

This language is by now very familiar—the language of human physicality ("finger") applied to Yahweh. This is the stock description of the second Yahweh, the Angel. It shouldn't be a surprise that the New Testament speaks of angelic mediation for the law—it was written by the Angel who is God in the presence of council members ("the holy ones") and then dispensed to Israel through Moses.

THE SINAI LAW COVENANT AND ITS WITNESSES

The core idea of the law being "delivered" and "declared" by angels is depicted in Deuteronomy 33:1–4. The divine beings of Yahweh's council witness the agreement.[12] This information is provided somewhat cryptically, at least to our eye. We need to read closely and, to some degree, in Hebrew to catch the clues.

Scholars agree that the events of Sinai after the exodus established a covenant between Yahweh and his people Israel. Covenants were basically agreements or enactments of a relationship. Yahweh's deliverance of the Israelites from Egypt was prompted by the earlier covenant promises he had made to Abraham, Isaac, and Jacob (Gen 12:1–3; 15:1–6; 22:18; 26:4; 27:29; 28:14). The events leading up to the miraculous deliverance from Egypt alluded to the earlier promises (Exod 3:7–8, 16–22; 6:4–6; 13:5, 11). Abraham's offspring had become a multitude in Egypt (Exod 1:6–10) and, as God had told Abraham centuries earlier, had become strangers in a foreign land (Gen 15:13). God had rescued them and now, at Sinai, was setting the terms of the relationship.

The covenant between Yahweh and Israel enacted at Sinai follows the conventions of a type of covenant known from ancient Near Eastern sources. Scholars refer to it as a vassal treaty.[13] This type of covenant was, in essence,

---

12. The idea put forth in this chapter is that the language of those passages (in both testaments) that involve divine beings of the council with the law is not that God's law had to be approved by angels ("signed off"), or that select angels took the tablets, as it were, to the Israelites. Rather, it is that the divine council served as witnesses to the dispensing of the law, not in terms of them merely seeing the event, but as official participants in the context of the way covenants were enacted. This view not only is consistent with ancient Near Eastern treaty concepts but accounts for the various ways the idea is expressed in New Testament verses.

13. This type of treaty had discernible components which are present in the flow of the book of Exodus. These are described in detail, along with their evidence in Exodus for the Sinai covenant, in P. R. Williamson, "Covenant," in *Dictionary of the Old Testament: Pentateuch* (Downers Grove, IL: InterVarsity Press, 2003), 139–55 (esp. 149–55). See also George E. Mendenhall and Gary A. Herion, "Covenant," in *The Anchor Yale Bible Dictionary* (ed. David Noel Freedman; New York: Doubleday, 1992), 1179–1202 (esp. 1180–87).

an oath of loyalty by an inferior (the vassal, here Israel) to a superior (Yahweh, the initiator of the agreement).

The basic stipulations of the covenant relationship were what we know as the Ten Commandments (Exod 20), though there are other laws in Exodus 20-23. As with the earlier, Abrahamic covenant (Gen 15:9–10), a sacrificial ritual was performed to ratify the covenant (Exod 24:3–8). After the ritual there was a sacrificial meal *between the parties involved.* This was the divine council scene in Exodus 24:9–11 that we've already briefly noted.

A formal vassal treaty in the ancient Near East regularly listed "third party" witnesses to its enactment. As one scholar notes, "the witnesses were exclusively deities or deified elements of the natural world. … All gods relevant to *both* parties were called upon as witnesses, so that there was no god left that the vassal could appeal to for protection if he wanted to violate his solemn oath."[14] The gods were "covenant enforcers" in this worldview.

Israelites of course would not have recognized foreign gods in such a treaty. Consequently most scholars consider this element absent in the Sinai treaty account. But the *elohim* of Yahweh's council were not foreign gods. They were Yahweh's host and witness to the giving of the law, at least according to the Hebrew text behind the Septuagint and the New Testament writers. They were also, as the account of Ahab in 1 Kings 22 indicates, Yahweh's means of punishing covenant apostates.

It is at precisely this point that many scholars have failed to notice some relevant wordplay in the biblical text that also suggests this connection.

The tablets of the law are referred to frequently in Exodus by the term *'edūt.*[15] It is usually translated "testimony" in English Bibles. The term is used in parallel with *torah* ("law") in Psalms 19:7 and 78:5, so at the very least it speaks of the written text of the law. Exodus 25:16 informs us that Yahweh commanded Moses to place the *'edūt* in the ark of the covenant. In fact, the ark was made for the *'edūt.* This explains why the ark is also called the "ark of the *'edūt*" (e.g., Exod 25:22; 30:6, 26; 39:35; 40:3, 5, 21). Since the ark traveled inside the tabernacle, that mobile tent structure was also called "the tabernacle of the *'edūt*" (Exod 38:21; Num 1:50, 53; 10:11) or the "tent of the *'edūt*" (Num 9:15; 17:22–23; 18:2; 2 Chr 24:6).

What makes this interesting is that the term *'edūt* can also mean "witnesses."[16] In fact, this plural's equivalent in Akkadian, the language of the vassal

---

14. Mendenhall and Herion, "Covenant," 1181.

15. The Hebrew consonantal spelling is *'-d-w-t* (עדות). An excellent but technical discussion of this term can be found in Ernst Jenni and Claus Westermann, *Theological Lexicon of the Old Testament* (Peabody, MA: Hendrickson, 1997), 838–46 (esp. 844–46).

16. Ibid., 844–46.

treaties that serve as the model for the Sinai treaty in Exodus, is a technical term used exclusively of witnesses to such treaties.[17]

This is not to suggest that the term doesn't refer to the laws on the tablets. Rather, since the tablets themselves occupy sacred space reserved only for Yahweh's presence (inside the ark within the holy of holies), the term appears to signify that the tablets of the law were also a sort of proxy for the divine council members who witnessed the event. In other words, the tablets of law were tokens of the event at Sinai itself. They were stone reminders of a divine encounter with Yahweh and his council, in much the same way that altars and standing stones built by the patriarchs would have reminded passersby that they marked a divine encounter (Gen 12:7; 13:18; Exod 17:15; 24:4).

Again, Yahweh's presence *in his home* (Eden, Sinai, tabernacle, and eventually the temple) implies by definition his throne room along with his attending council. The tablets not only contained the covenant terms but were a reminder of the event as it occurred, with the divine council present on Sinai.

THE LAW AND SALVATION

In simplest terms, the Sinai covenant conveyed Yahweh's will for what he intended Israel to be—in relation both to him and to the disinherited nations. Israel was to be theologically and ethically distinct. These distinctions were obligations, not suggestions. Israel was to be holy (Lev 19:2) and fulfill God's original Edenic purpose of spreading his influence (his kingdom rule) throughout all the nations.

Israel's status as Yahweh's own portion was not an end in itself, but the means by which Israel would draw all nations back to Yahweh (Deut 4:6–8; 28:9–10). This is the idea behind Israel being a "kingdom of priests" (Exod 19:6) and "a light to the nations" (Isa 42:6; 49:6; 51:4; 60:3). It's no wonder that the book of Revelation uses the same language of believers in Revelation 5:10, a divine council scene, in connection with ruling over all the earth. The entire nation inherited the status and duty of Abraham, that through him—and now them—all nations would be blessed (Gen 12:3).

But did this salvation come by obeying rules? To ask the question is to miss the point. Salvation in the Old Testament meant love for Yahweh alone. One had to *believe* that Yahweh was the God of all gods, trusting that this Most High God had chosen covenant relationship with Israel to the detriment of all other nations. The law was how one demonstrated that love—that *loyalty*.

---

17. Ibid., 845.

Salvation was not merited. Yahweh alone had initiated the relationship. Yahweh's choice and covenant promise had to be *believed*. An Israelite's *believing loyalty* was shown by faithfulness to the law.

The core of the law was fidelity to Yahweh alone, above all gods. To worship other gods was to demonstrate the absence of belief, love, and loyalty. Doing the works of the law without having the heart aligned only to Yahweh was inadequate. This is why the promise of the possession of the promised land is repeatedly and inextricably linked in the Torah to the first two commandments (i.e., staying clear of idolatry and apostasy).[18]

The history of Israel's kings illustrates the point. King David was guilty of the worst of crimes against humanity in the incident with Bathsheba and Uriah the Hittite (2 Sam 11). He was clearly in violation of the law and deserving of death. Nevertheless, his belief in who Yahweh was among all gods never wavered. God was merciful to him, sparing him from death, though his sin had consequences the rest of his life. But there was no doubt that David was ever a believer in Yahweh and never worshiped another. Yet other kings of Israel and Judah were tossed aside and both kingdoms sent into exile—because they worshiped other gods. Personal failure, even of the worst kind, did not send the nation into exile. Choosing other gods did.

The same is true in the New Testament. Believing the gospel means believing that Yahweh, the God of Israel, came to earth incarnated as a man, voluntarily died on the cross as a sacrifice for our sin, and rose again on the third day. That is the content of our faith this side of the cross. Our believing loyalty is demonstrated by our obedience to "the law of Christ" (1 Cor 9:21; Gal 6:2). We cannot worship another. Salvation means believing loyalty to Christ, who was and is the visible Yahweh. There is no salvation in any other name (Acts 4:12), and faith must remain intact (Rom 11:17–24; Heb 3:19; 10:22, 38–39). Personal failure is not the same as trading Jesus for another god—and God knows that.

Believing loyalty was therefore not just academic. By definition it must be conscious and active. Israel knew that her God had fought for her and loved her, but the relationship came with expectations. As she embarked for the promised land, Israel would have daily, visible reminders not only of Yahweh's presence but of his total *otherness*. Having the divine presence with you could be both fantastic and frightening.

---

18. Lev 26; Deut 4:15–16; 5:7; 6:14; 7:4, 16; 8:19; 11:16, 28; 13:2, 6, 13; 17:3; 28:14, 36, 64; 29:18; 30:17–18.

CHAPTER 22

Realm Distinction

We've been tracking the story of Yahweh and his portion, Abraham's descendants. Yahweh chose to disinherit the nations at Babel. He chose to appear to Abraham in visible, human form to initiate a covenant relationship. He chose to reiterate that covenant with Isaac and Jacob, whom he renamed Israel. And he chose to deliver Israel from Egypt.

These choices telegraphed theological messages. Israel existed because Yahweh had supernaturally enabled the birth of Isaac. They continued to exist because Yahweh wanted a people on earth by his own plan and by his own power. The lesser *elohim* he had placed over the disinherited nations—particularly those in Egypt at this point of the story—cannot prevent his will. *There is no god like Yahweh.* His goal of making the earth a new Eden will not be overturned.

Before the plagues and the exodus from Egypt, the descendants of Jacob knew Yahweh only by reputation and oral storytelling. Now they were at his mountain, ready to journey to the land he had taken for himself, and for them. They had the tablets of the law, but that was just a starting point. Egypt and her gods had been defeated, but the conflict with the gods and their nations was just beginning. Israel needed to understand that being Yahweh's portion meant separation from the gods and the nations who stood ready to oppose them. The concept of realm distinction was fundamental to the supernatural worldview of ancient Israel.

HOLINESS AND SACRED SPACE

Yahweh is an *elohim*, not a mortal man. Appearing as a human being was a condescension that enabled the lesser minds of mortals to comprehend his presence—and live to tell about it. Yahweh is so *other* as to be incomprehensible without the façade of something familiar. And yet for Israel, his otherness would need to remain an ever-present reality, sensed at all times.

The concept of *otherness* was at the core of Israelite identity. Otherness is the core of holiness. The Hebrew vocabulary for holiness means to be set apart or to be distinct. While the idea has a moral dimension related to conduct, it is not intrinsically about morality. It is about *distinction*. Israel's identification with Yahweh by virtue of his covenant with Abraham and the terms of the covenant at Sinai meant that, as Leviticus 19:2 concisely summarizes, Israelites were to be set apart ("holy") as Yahweh was set apart ("holy").[1]

Yahweh's complete otherness was reinforced in the minds of Israelites through worship and sacrifice. Yahweh was not only the source of Israel's life—he *was* life. Yahweh was complete in his perfections. Yahweh was not of earth, a place where there is death, disease, and imperfection. His realm is supernatural; ours is terrestrial. The space he occupies is sacred and made otherworldly by his presence. The space we occupy is "profane" or ordinary. Yahweh is the antithesis of ordinary. Humans must be invited and purified to occupy the same space.

Many laws in the Torah illustrate this worldview and its messaging. Whether priest or not, male or female, people could be disqualified from sacred space by a variety of activities and conditions. Examples include sexual activity, bodily emissions, physical handicaps, contact with a dead body, and childbirth.[2]

The logic of such exclusions is simple, yet foreign to our modern clinical minds. Sexual intercourse, emission of sexual fluids, uterine discharges, and menstruation were not considered unclean out of prudishness. Rather, the concept was that the body had lost the fluids that contain, create, and sustain life.[3] That which is not whole and is associated with loss of life cannot enter Yahweh's presence until ritual restoration rectified that status. The same reasoning is behind the ritually unclean status of those with physical handicaps, infected with a disease, and who have touched a corpse, animal or human.[4] Yahweh's presence meant life and perfection, not death and defectiveness. These laws kept the community conscious of Yahweh's *otherness*.

---

1. The Hebrew word is *qadōsh*. I mean "set apart" in the sense described in various lexicons: "withheld from ordinary use, treated with special care, belonging to the sanctuary ... dedicate[d] for use by God" (see Willem VanGemeren, ed., *New International Dictionary of Old Testament Theology & Exegesis* [Grand Rapids, MI: Zondervan, 1997], 877).

2. Space forbids a discussion of how the logic of realm distinction informs laws about intermarriage and clean and unclean foods. See the companion website.

3. See Lev 12; 15:1–30; 18:19; 20:18; 22:4–6; Deut 23:10–15.

4. See Lev 11:24–25, 39; 21:16–24; Num 19:11, 16, 19; 31:19, 24.

Regulations governing the sanctity of Yahweh's dwelling provided concrete object lessons about realm distinction. The ground that that dwelling encompassed was sacred space in relationship to the people of Israel. The separateness of the divine realm was reinforced by the laws that allowed or disallowed proximity to Yahweh. These permissions or prohibitions even extended to inanimate objects associated with Yahweh and his service.[5]

Even within sacred space there were gradations of holiness or sanctity.[6] The closer one got to Yahweh's presence, the more holy the ground or the object in his proximity. The terms that describe the layout of the structure are evidence of this progression. From the entrance inward there was the court, the holy place, and the "most holy place" ("holy of holies"). The sacred space of the tabernacle got progressively more holy from the entrance to the innermost room.

The progressive "holiness zones" were also distinguished by the priestly clothing associated with them (Exod 28–29).[7] For example, the high priest, the person with permitted access to the holiest place, wore a unique ephod, breastplate, and headdress inscribed with "holy to Yahweh." The holier the zone, the more costly the animal sacrificed to sanctify the priests when they entered into the presence of Yahweh for rituals (Lev 8).

THE TABERNACLE: Heaven on Earth

That Yahweh dwelled in a tent before the construction of the temple (much later, during the time of Solomon) is important for marking sacred space. The tabernacle (Hebrew: *mishkan*—"dwelling") was the place where Yahweh would cause his name—his presence—to dwell.[8]

---

5. For example, the ark of the covenant, vessels and furniture used inside the tabernacle. See Exod 28–31. As with the tent structure itself, which receives some focus in the ensuing discussion, the furniture in Israelite sacred spaces also has ancient Near Eastern parallels. See W. F. Albright, "The Furniture of El in Canaanite Mythology," *Bulletin of the American Schools of Oriental Research* 91 (1943): 39–44.

6. See Menahem Haran, *Temples and Temple-Service in Ancient Israel: An Inquiry into the Character of Cult Phenomena and the Historical Setting of the Priestly School* (Oxford: Clarendon Press, 1978), 158–88, 205–21, 226–27.

7. On Israelite sacrifices and offerings and their meaning, I recommend the excellent articles by Richard Averbeck: "Sacrifices and Offerings," in *Dictionary of the Old Testament: Pentateuch* (Downers Grove, IL: InterVarsity Press, 2003), 721–33; "כָּפַר (kāpar II)," in *New International Dictionary of Old Testament Theology & Exegesis*, 689–709.

8. See chapter 18 for the "name theology" of the Old Testament. The whole subject of the tabernacle is not without problems. Before the tabernacle was constructed (Exod 35–40), Moses would meet with Yahweh in a small tent called "the tent of meeting." Though some scholars take the tent of meeting and the tabernacle as the same structure, Exod 33:7–11 has the tent of meeting in existence prior to the tabernacle. The issue is actually complicated, as the phrase "tent of meeting" is at times clearly used with respect to the tabernacle (e.g., Exod 27:21; 28:43; 30:26) and at other times clearly not. Passages such as Exod 33:7–11

As the divine abode, the tabernacle was also analogous to Eden. Like Eden, the tabernacle was cosmic in conception, the place where heaven and earth met, a veritable microcosm of the Edenic creation where God first dwelt on earth.[9]

There are many subtle connections between Eden and the tabernacle,[10] some of them discernible only in the Hebrew text. For our purposes, several of the more obvious are worth noting.

To begin, the description of the tabernacle as a tent dwelling is significant. Elsewhere in the biblical world, deities and their councils were considered to live in tents—atop their cosmic mountains and in their lush gardens.[11] The tent of the god or gods was, as with mountains or lush gardens, the place where

---

provide several indications that the tent of meeting was distinct from the tabernacle: (1) The passage itself appears in Exodus before the construction of the tabernacle; (2) one man (Moses) could construct the tent, unlike the much larger tabernacle, which took scores of workers to tear down, erect, and transport; (3) the tent of meeting was outside the camp, unlike the tabernacle, which was in the middle of the camp; (4) the tent of meeting was guarded and maintained by a single person; (5) there is no indication that the tent of meeting was a place of sacrifice, or that the ark of the covenant was kept in it. The solution is apparently that, prior to the tabernacle, there was a "tent of meeting" where Yahweh "lived" and would meet Moses. Either that tent structure was moved inside the tabernacle as the holy of holies or (more coherently) the tented holy of holies became a new "tent of meeting" after the tabernacle's construction. However, certain passages in the historical books inform us that there was a "tent of meeting" after the tabernacle was in existence (1 Sam 2:22; 2 Chr 1:3; 1 Kgs 8:4). Whether these passages describe a still-extant "original" tent of meeting or a tent structure that housed holy objects during the chaos of the period of the judges and the separation of the ark of the covenant from the tabernacle is a matter of debate.

9. The literature of Second Temple Judaism, particularly the works of Philo and Josephus, makes this connection frequently and clearly. See James Palmer, "Exodus and the Biblical Theology of the Tabernacle," in *Heaven on Earth* (ed. T. Desmond Alexander and Simon Gathercole; Carlisle, England: Paternoster Press, 2004), 11–22; Gregory Beale, "The Final Vision of the Apocalypse and Its Implications for a Biblical Theology of the Temple," in Alexander and Gathercole, *Heaven on Earth*, 191–210.

10. As with Second Temple Jewish writers, modern scholars also argue for symbolic and textual connections between Eden and the tabernacle. See Jon D. Levenson, *Creation and the Persistence of Evil: The Jewish Drama of Divine Omnipotence* (Princeton: Princeton University Press, 1988), especially chapter 7; Eric E. Elnes, "Creation and Tabernacle: The Priestly Writer's 'Environmentalism,'" *Horizons in Biblical Theology* 16.1 (1994): 144–55; Gordon J. Wenham, "Sanctuary Symbolism in the Garden of Eden Story," in *Proceedings of the Ninth World Congress of Jewish Studies* (ed. M. Goshen-Göttstein and D. Assaf; Jerusalem: World Union of Jewish Studies, 1986), 19–24; T. Stordalen, *Genesis 2–3 and Symbolism of the Eden Garden in Biblical Hebrew Literature*, Contributions to Biblical Exegesis and Theology 25 (Leuven: Peeters, 2000); A. M. Rodriguez, "Sanctuary Theology in the Book of Exodus," *Andrews University Seminary Studies* 29 (1991): 213–24; Shimon Bakon, "Creation, Tabernacle, and Sabbath," *Jewish Bible Quarterly* 25.2 (1997): 79–85; Daniel C. Timmer, *Creation, Tabernacle, and Sabbath: The Sabbath Frame of Exodus 31:12–17; 35:1–3 in Exegetical and Theological Perspective*, Forschungen zur Religion und Literatur des Alten und Neuen Testaments 227 (Göttingen: Vandenhoeck & Ruprecht, 2009).

11. See chapter 6 for the garden and mountain vocabulary associated with Yahweh and his divine council. The major scholarly discussions of Yahweh's tent sanctuary are found in works already cited in that chapter: Richard J. Clifford, *The Cosmic Mountain in Canaan and the Old Testament*, Harvard Semitic Monographs 4 (Cambridge: Harvard University Press, 1972; repr., Eugene, OR: Wipf & Stock, 2010), and E. Theodore Mullen Jr., *The Divine Council in Canaanite and Early Hebrew Literature*, Harvard Semitic Monographs 24 (Chico, CA: Scholars Press, 1980), 128–74. See also Richard J. Clifford, "The Tent of El and the Israelite Tent of Meeting," *Catholic Biblical Quarterly* 33.2 (1971): 221–27.

heaven and earth intersected and where divine decrees were issued. This was a common cultural idea, perhaps akin to how many people think of church—church is a place you'd expect to meet God, or where God can be found.

Moses was told to construct the tabernacle and its equipment according to the pattern shown to him by Yahweh on the holy mountain (Exod 25:9, 40; 26:30).[12] The implication is that the tabernacle on earth was to be a copy of the heavenly tent in accord with the religious principle of "as in heaven, so on earth."

The heavenly tent prototype was the heavens themselves, as Isaiah 40:22 tells us ("It is he who sits above the circle of the earth, and its inhabitants are like grasshoppers; who stretches out the heavens like a curtain, and spreads them like a tent to dwell in" [ESV]). This kind of language is also why the earth is referred to as God's footstool (Isa 66:1). Yahweh sits above the circle of the earth, in his heavenly tent, on his throne above the waters which are above "the firmament," and rests his feet on the earth, which is his footstool (Job 9:8; Psa 104:2).

As Eden was the place where humanity experienced the presence of God, so too was the tabernacle. This was particularly true for the priests, but God's presence occasionally met Israel's leaders outside the holy of holies (Lev 9:23; Num 12:5–19; 20:6; Deut 31:15), the most obvious instance being the glory cloud (Exod 40:34–35).

The menorah ("lampstand") in the tabernacle is a striking analogy with the tree of life in Eden.[13] The lampstand was fashioned in the appearance of a tree (Exod 25:31–36) and was stationed directly outside the holy of holies.

The cherubim inside the holy of holies are also a clear connection to Eden.[14] The Edenic cherubim stood guard at the dwelling place of God in Eden. Their position atop the lid to the ark of the covenant is not coincidental. The innermost sanctum of the tabernacle was the place from which God would govern Israel. The cherubim form a throne for the invisible Yahweh. Later, when the tent of the most holy place was moved into the temple, two giant cherubim were installed within for Yahweh's throne, making the ark his footstool.[15]

---

12. It is noteworthy that the same wording appears in regard to the design of the temple (1 Chr 28:19). See chapter 26.

13. Carol L. Myers, "Lampstand," in *Anchor Yale Bible Dictionary (ed. David Noel Freedman; New York: Doubleday, 1992),* 4:143. See also Carol L. Meyers, *The Tabernacle Menorah: A Synthetic Study of a Symbol from the Biblical Cult* (Piscataway, NJ: Gorgias Press, 2003).

14. Menahem Haran, "The Ark and the Cherubim: Their Symbolic Significance in Biblical Ritual," *Israel Exploration Journal* 9.1 (1959): 30–38.

15. See chapter 26.

Lastly, as Beale notes, "The entrance to Eden was from the east (Gen 3:24), which was also the direction from which one entered the tabernacle and later the temples of Israel. Genesis 2:12 says that 'good gold' and 'bdellium and onyx stone' were in 'the land of Havilah,' apparently where Eden was. Of course, various items of tabernacle furniture were made of gold, as were the walls, ceiling, and floor of the holy of holies in Solomon's Temple (1 Kgs 6:20–22)."[16]

SACRIFICE AND ISRAEL'S COSMIC GEOGRAPHY

One Israelite ritual in particular illustrates realm distinction. In the context of the Deuteronomy 32 worldview, which has the nations under the dominion of lesser gods, the entire Israelite camp was cosmic geography and sacred space. Israel was identified with Yahweh. Both the people and the land that Yahweh had determined would belong to the descendants of Abraham were Yahweh's "portion" (Deut 4:19–20; 32:8–9).

The Day of Atonement ritual (Lev 16) provides a fascinating convergence of these ideas. Part of that ritual's description goes like this:

> [7]And [Aaron] shall take the two goats, and he shall present them before Yahweh at the tent of assembly's entrance. [8]Then Aaron shall cast lots for the two goats: one lot for Yahweh and one for Azazel. [9]And Aaron shall present the goat on which the lot for Yahweh fell, and he shall sacrifice it as a sin offering. [10]But he must present alive before Yahweh the goat on which the lot for Azazel fell to make atonement for himself, to send it away into the desert to Azazel.

Why is one of the goats "for Azazel"? Who or what is "Azazel"? The passage is inexplicable unless you're acquainted with the cosmic geographical ideas we've been talking about.

The word "Azazel" in the Hebrew text can be translated "the goat that goes away." This is the justification for the common "scapegoat" translation in some English versions (NIV, NASB, KJV). The scapegoat, so the translator has it, symbolically carries the sins of the people away from the camp of Israel into the wilderness. Seems simple enough.

However, "Azazel" is really a proper name. In Lev 16:8 one goat is "*for* Yahweh," while the other goat is "*for* Azazel." Since Yahweh is a proper name and the goats are described in the same way, Hebrew parallelism informs us that Azazel is also a proper name. What needs resolution is what it means.

---

16. Beale, "Final Vision of the Apocalypse," 199.

Azazel is regarded as the name of a demon in the Dead Sea Scrolls and other ancient Jewish books.[17] In fact, in one scroll (4Q 180, 1:8) Azazel is the leader of the angels that sinned in Genesis 6:1–4. The same description appears in the book of 1 Enoch (8:1; 9:6; 10:4–8; 13:1; 54:5–6; 55:4; 69:2).

Recall that in intertestamental Judaism, the offending sons of God from Genesis 6 were believed to have been imprisoned in a pit or abyss in the netherworld. Azazel's realm was somewhere out in the desert, outside the confines of holy ground. It was a place associated with supernatural evil.

The Old Testament itself does not state that Azazel was a demon. Scholars have, however, connected the name to Mot, the god of death.[18] The identification of the term with a demon may also derive from cosmic geography and an association of the wilderness with the forces of chaos, which are hostile to God.[19] This would make sense on several levels, as the desert would not only be a place forbidding to life but, as ground outside the camp of Israel and Yahweh, the source of life, would have a clear association with chaos.

Leviticus 17:7 suggests that Israelites saw the desert as spiritually sinister: "So they shall no more sacrifice their sacrifices to goat demons, after whom they whore" (ESV). We are not told why they did this, but the placement of this problem in proximity to the ritual goat to Azazel suggests a conceptual connection. Jews of later periods certainly made such connections.[20]

In the Day of Atonement ritual, the goat for Yahweh—the goat that was sacrificed—purges the impurities caused by the people of Israel and purifies the sanctuary. The goat for Azazel was sent away after the sins of the Israelites were symbolically placed on it.

The point of the goat for Azazel was not that something was owed to the

---

17. See B. Janowski, "Azazel," in *Dictionary of Deities and Demons in the Bible,* 2nd ed. (ed. Karel van der Toorn, Bob Becking, and Pieter W. van der Horst; Leiden; Boston; Cologne; Grand Rapids, MI; Cambridge: Brill; Eerdmans, 1999), 128.

18. Hayim Tawil, "Azazel, the Prince of the Steepe: A Comparative Study," *Zeitschrift für die alttestamentliche Wissenschaft* 92.1 (1980): 43–59.

19. On this possibility see Dominic Rudman, "A Note on the Azazel Goat Ritual," *Zeitschrift für die alttestamentliche Wissenschaft* 116.3 (2004): 396–401.

20. J. B. Lightfoot notes how Jewish practice came to involve pushing the goat for Azazel over a cliff to ensure the sins of the nation never found their way back to holy ground: "When they sent forth the goat Azazel on the day of expiation … [the person attending the goat] snapped the scarlet thread into two parts, of which he bound one to the horns of the goat, and the other to the rock: and thrust the goat down; which, hardly coming to the middle of the precipice, was dashed and broke into pieces" (John Lightfoot, *A Commentary on the New Testament from the Talmud and Hebraica, Matthew–1 Corinthians, Place Names in the Gospels,* [Bellingham, WA: Logos Bible Software, 2010], 1:110–11). The fifth tractate of the Talmud and the Mishnah (*Seder Moed,* "Order of Festivals") describes the goat's fate in *Yoma* 6.6. See also Robert Helm, "Azazel in Early Jewish Tradition," *Andrews University Seminary Studies* 32.3 (Autumn 1994): 217–26.

demonic realm, as though a ransom was being paid.[21] The goat for Azazel banished the sins of the Israelites to the realm *outside* Israel. Why? Because the ground on which Yahweh had his dwelling was holy. Sin had to be "transported" to where evil belonged—the territory outside Israel, under the control of gods set over the pagan nations. The high priest was not sacrificing *to Azazel*. Rather, Azazel was getting what belonged to him: sin.

The concept of realm distinction and cosmic geography go hand in hand. Every day ancient Israel's journey to the promised land reiterated some point in regard to who they were and their purpose on earth. The invisible Yahweh and the visible Yahweh were present as cloud and Angel, leading his people through the domain of hostile gods and their people to Israel's own divinely allotted home. When they were camped, the glow of Yahweh's fire over the tabernacle, Eden returned to earth, illumined the camp. They were Yahweh's portion. The forces of chaos, seen and unseen, were on every border. One would think the living object lessons would have ensured faith when it came time to confront those forces. But that wasn't to be.

---

21. Some theologians use Azazel in Lev 16 to support what is called the "Ransom Theory" of the atonement. This theory argues that the Day of Atonement ought to be viewed as an offering of a ransom *to Satan* and not as a substitutionary atonement that satisfies the wrath *of God*. Since the Day of Atonement prefigures the atoning sacrifice of Christ, it is argued that Jesus' life was a ransom paid to Satan. The "Ransom Theory" is implicitly put forth in C. S. Lewis's classic, *The Lion, the Witch, and the Wardrobe*, where the death of Aslan is a payment owed to the White Witch.

Section Summary

The judgment at Babel made the world a very different place. Before Yahweh's disinheritance of the nations, he had been in covenant relationship with all the descendants of Noah. God had told Noah's sons to be fruitful and multiply and overspread the earth (Gen 9:1). It's no accident that these were also the words given to Adam and Eve (Gen 1:22, 28). The sons of Noah were to expand God's human family and carry on the original goal of an Edenic world. Babel undermined all that.

In response, Yahweh made the nations outsiders. If his will was too burdensome, then they could serve other gods. Yahweh would transfer the Edenic dream to someone else—a people who didn't yet exist, but soon would.

Yahweh came to Abraham in human form, just as he had with Adam and Eve (Gen 3:8). The contact was personal because the interest was personal. Yahweh's kingdom rule would be built on covenant loyalty. He would remain faithful, and beginning with Abraham, all who wished to participate could do so, if they, like Abraham, believed the covenant promises and turned away from the other gods.

The promises would pass from Abraham to Isaac and then to Jacob (Israel). Yahweh's family would be preserved through Joseph, and delivered through Moses. The deliverance, of course, was a means to an end. Yahweh wanted what he had wanted from the beginning: a mingling of his heavenly and earthly families on the earth he had called into existence. To that end he brought Israel home to Sinai. One element of the original pact with Abraham had come to pass. Israel was numerous. But as yet Yahweh's people had no land and had yet to fulfill the role of blessing the nations, drawing them back to the One who had cast them aside.

One task therefore remained. Yahweh would bring Israel to Canaan, where these two covenantal promises would be fulfilled. He would also live among them in that land. To those ends, the covenant for living in the presence of God, remaining in the land, and being a kingdom of priests was enacted in the presence of witnesses, Yahweh's divine council.

When his people were threatened, whether by gods or men, Yahweh would intervene visibly as the Angel in a burning bush, the embodied Name leading Israel through the wilderness, and the Commander of Yahweh's forces on the field of battle. In a conflict between gods and men, Israel was hopelessly outnumbered, but had the God who mattered. All that was needed was believing loyalty—trust and obey.

What could go wrong?

PART 5

CONQUEST AND FAILURE

CHAPTER 23

Giant Problems

Rᴇᴠɪᴇᴡɪɴɢ ᴡʜᴀᴛ ᴡᴇ ʜᴀᴅ ᴅɪsᴄᴜssᴇᴅ ɪɴ ᴀɴ ᴇᴀʀʟɪᴇʀ ᴄʜᴀᴘᴛᴇʀ, Gᴏᴅ ʜᴀᴅ told Eve that her offspring would be locked in conflict with those of the serpent (Gen 3:15). The serpent was actually a divine being, not a mere member of the animal kingdom. While the flexibility of the meaning of the term *nachash* forces us to consider double (and even triple) entendre, one thing is quite clear: The divine being in the garden who rebelled against Yahweh's desire to have humans rule an Edenic world is never cast in human form.[1] Unlike the sons of God in Genesis 6:1–4 who are cast as assuming human flesh and capable of cohabitation, the divine rebel of Eden does not appear to Eve that way.[2]

Consequently, the idea of a "seed" or offspring extending from the *nachash* would not have been literal for the biblical writer. Instead, the notion is metaphorical or spiritual. And this is precisely what we see when the phrase occurs elsewhere in the Bible. The metaphor is perhaps most clear in the New Testament, when Jesus himself referred to the Pharisees as serpents (Matt 23:33) who were "of [their] father the devil" (John 8:44; cf. Rev 12:6).[3]

---

1. Recall that the *saṭan* of Job 1–2 was not the enemy of Eden. The *nachash* is never called *saṭan* in the Hebrew Bible, and no passage in the Old Testament where the word *saṭan* is used to describe a divine being ever uses *nachash* as part of that description. It is also not clear from the language of Job 1–2 whether the *saṭan* is one of the sons of God or just makes an appearance among the sons of God.

2. As we saw earlier (ch. 10), the creaturely portrayal is consistent with the use of the term *cherub* to describe the Edenic enemy. Cherubim were *divine* creaturely guardians of the God's throne. A human portrayal of the divine beings ("sons of God") in Genesis 6 is also required because of the parallel to and polemic against the Mesopotamian *apkallus* (see ch. 13). The discussion in this and the next two chapters will introduce readers to a second interpretive approach to Genesis 6:1–4 that does not require literal divine-human cohabitation, but nevertheless does require a supernatural view of the sons of God. This alternative perspective is consistent with understanding the human offspring as the focus of Gen 6:1–4 while understanding offspring of the creaturely *nachash* metaphorically.

3. The Old Testament uses the metaphor as well. The oracle against the Philistines, for example, threatens that rogue nation with "the root of the snake [*nachash*]" (Isa 14:29). The word translated "root" (*shoresh*) is used in the very next verse to describe the Philistine people who will be the victims of this

Despite the metaphorical nature of the language in the Eden story, the idea of divine beings producing human spawn who would oppose Yahweh's desires does appear in Genesis 6:1–4. That passage in turn becomes grist for the biblical writers and their descriptions of the conquest of Canaan. In this and the next two chapters, we'll recapture their thinking on that part of biblical Israel's history.

The expulsion of Adam and Eve was followed by a series of episodes that pitted the descendants of Eve against the spiritual children of the original enemy. The opposition to God's plan came in both human and divine form. Cain was referenced specifically in this light (1 John 3:12—"Cain, who was of the evil one and violently murdered his brother"). Genesis 6:1–4 explicitly described a transgression of the domain boundary between heaven and earth that God wanted observed. Then there was the rebellion at Babel (Gen 11:1–9).

More review: Israel was reborn as a nation in the exodus from Egypt. After receiving the law, building the tabernacle, and establishing the priesthood, they departed for the promised land.[4] They soon arrived at the border of Canaan, where Moses sent twelve spies to reconnoiter the territory (Num 13). The spies returned with confirmation of the abundance and desirability of the land. Nevertheless, most of them were in despair. The land was occupied by people in walled cities—some of whom were giants descended from the Nephilim:

> [32] So they brought to the people of Israel a bad report of the land that they had spied out, saying, "The land, through which we have gone to spy it out, is a land that devours its inhabitants, and all the people that we saw in it are of great height. [33] And there we saw the Nephilim (the sons of Anak, who come from the Nephilim), and we seemed to ourselves like grasshoppers, and so we seemed to them" (Num 13:32–33 ESV).

Understanding the trauma of Israel in Numbers 13 is essential to understanding the subsequent conquest accounts. Any Israelite or Jew living after the time of the completion of the Hebrew Bible would have processed the wars for the promised land in terms of this passage, since it connected Israel's survival as the people of Yahweh with the defeat of the Nephilim descendants.

---

judgment. God's executing judgment on the Philistines by means of another human enemy is expressed metaphorically with serpent language. That the word *shoresh* ("root") speaks of human offspring is perhaps best known from the phrase "root of Jesse" to refer to the messiah (Isa 11:10; cf. Isa 11:1; Hos 9:16).

4. This series of events occupies a large portion of the Torah. From the Israelites' arrival at Sinai to their departure (Exod 19:1–Num 10:10) over thirteen months went by. Their departure from Sinai to begin the journey to Canaan therefore puts us in the book of Numbers.

NEPHILIM BEFORE THE FLOOD

In our earlier discussions about Genesis 6:1–4 we left some questions unaddressed.[5] How do we understand the note in Genesis 6:4, that the Nephilim were upon the earth at the time of the flood "and also afterward." How do we process their original presence?

As our earlier discussion made clear, viewpoints that strip the account of its supernatural flavor must be discarded. The events described in Genesis 6:1–4 were part of Israel's supernatural worldview. We cannot pretend they saw things as most modern readers would. Since the Nephilim were part of Israel's supernatural worldview and their descendants turn out to be Israel's primary obstacle for conquering the promised land, the conquest itself must also be understood in supernatural terms.

There are two possible approaches to the origin of the Nephilim in Genesis 6:1–4 that are consistent with the supernatural understanding of the sons of God in the Israelite worldview. The first and most transparent is that divine beings came to earth, assumed human flesh, cohabited with human women, and spawned unusual offspring known as Nephilim. Naturally, this view requires seeing the giant clans encountered in the conquest as physical descendants of the Nephilim (Num 13:32–33).[6]

The primary objection to this approach is the sexual component.[7] The modern enlightened mind simply can't tolerate it. Appeal is usually made to Matthew 22:23–33 in this regard, under the assumption that verse 30 teaches that angels cannot engage in sexual intercourse:

> [23] On that day Sadducees—who say there is no resurrection—came up to him and asked him, [24] saying, "Teacher, Moses said if someone dies without having children, his brother is to marry his wife and father descendants for his brother. [25] Now there were seven brothers with us. And the first died after getting married, and because he did not have descendants, he left his wife to his brother. [26] So also the second and the third, up to the seventh. [27] And last of all

5. The issues related to Gen 6:1–4 and the conquest accounts are complex. Several issues are discussed in the ensuing material and the next two chapters. However, see the companion website for greater detail, especially with regard to matters of grammar and syntax.

6. It is important to note that this view also must conclude that the Nephilim were *human* despite their unusual size. See the discussion in the notes in chapter 25.

7. The result of the cohabitation (or some other form of divine intervention per the ensuing discussion) is also something that causes hesitation. The information obtainable from the text of Scripture and archaeology leads to the conclusion that neither the Nephilim nor their descendants were freakishly tall. The evidence points to the same range for unusually tall people today (the upper six-foot range to eight feet; see chapter 25). The size of Og's bed (Deut 3:11) cannot be taken as a precise indication of Og's own dimensions. See the discussion in chapter 24.

the woman died. **28** In the resurrection, therefore, whose wife of the seven will she be? For they all had her as wife." **29** But Jesus answered and said to them, "You are mistaken, because you do not know the scriptures or the power of God! **30** For in the resurrection they neither marry nor are given in marriage, but are like angels of God in heaven. **31** Now concerning the resurrection of the dead, have you not read what was spoken to you by God, who said, **32** 'I am the God of Abraham and the God of Isaac and the God of Jacob'? He is not the God of the dead, but of the living!" **33** And when the crowds heard this, they were amazed at his teaching (Matt 22:23–33).

The text does not say angels *cannot* have sexual intercourse; it says they *don't*. The reason ought to be obvious. The context for the statement is the resurrection, which refers either broadly to the afterlife or, more precisely, to the final, renewed global Eden. The point is clear in either option. In the spiritual world, the realm of divine beings, there is no need for procreation. Procreation is part of the embodied world and is necessary to maintain the physical population. In like manner, life in the perfected Edenic world also does not require maintaining the human species by having children—*everyone has an immortal resurrection body.* Consequently, there is no need for sex in the resurrection, just as there is no need for it in the nonhuman spiritual realm.

But Genesis 6 doesn't have the spiritual realm or the final Edenic world as its context. The analogy breaks down completely. The passage in Matthew is therefore useless as a commentary on Genesis 6:1–4.

Despite the flawed use of this gospel passage, Christians still balk at this interpretive option for Genesis 6:1–4. The ancient reader would have had no problem with it. But for moderns, it seems impossible that a divine being could assume human flesh and do what this passage describes.

The objection is odd, since this interpretation is *less* dramatic than the incarnation of Yahweh as Jesus Christ. How is the virgin birth of God as a man *more* acceptable? What *isn't* mind-blowing about Jesus having both a divine and human nature fused together? For that matter, what doesn't offend the modern scientific mind about God going through a woman's birth canal and enduring life as a human, having to learn how to talk, walk, eat with a spoon, be potty trained, and go through puberty? All these things are far more shocking than Genesis 6:1–4, and yet this is what Scripture explicitly affirms when it informs us that the second person of the Godhead became a man. *God became a man from conception onward.*

The truth is that Christians affirm the incarnation because they have to—it defines Christianity. Genesis 6:1–4 is set aside as peripheral. But belief in a personal God as the Bible describes means embracing the supernatural. For the Christian, the high point of the supernatural story of Scripture—its most dramatic and unthinkable expression—is the incarnation of God in Christ. The notion that the sons of God came to earth in fleshly form ought to be *more* palatable than the incarnation, since it is *less* supernaturally spectacular. There is no suggestion that any corporeal appearance of a divine being was accomplished through incarnation—becoming an actual human. All such instances are lesser than the incarnation. This particular supernatural approach to Genesis 6:1–4 derives from other passages that plainly have divine beings (angels) in embodied human form.

For example, Genesis 18–19 is quite clear that Yahweh himself and two other divine beings met with Abraham in physical flesh. They ate a meal together (Gen 18:1–8). Genesis 19:10 informs us that the two angels had to physically grab Lot and pull him back into his house to avoid harm in Sodom, something that would be hard to do if the two beings were not truly physical.

Another example we looked at earlier is Genesis 32:22–31, where we read that Jacob wrestled with a "man" (32:24), whom the text also describes as *elohim* twice (32:30–31). Hosea 12:3–4 refers to this incident and describes the being who wrestled with Jacob as *elohim* and *mal'ak* ("angel"). This was a physical struggle, and one that left Jacob injured (32:31–32).

While *visual* appearances in human form are more common,[8] the New Testament also describes episodes where angels are best understood as corporeal. In Matthew 4:11, angels came to Jesus after he was tempted by the devil and "ministered" to him (cf. Mark 1:13). Surely this means more than floating around before Jesus' face. Angels appear and speak (Matt 28:5; Luke 1:11–21, 30–38), instances that presume actual sound waves being created. If a merely auditory experience was meant, one would expect the communication to be described as a dream-vision (Acts 10:3). Angels open doors (Acts 5:19) and hit disciples to wake them up (Acts 12:7). This particular episode is especially interesting, because the text has Peter *mistakenly* thinking the angel was only a vision.

There is a second supernaturalist approach to Genesis 6:1–4 that takes the sexual language as euphemistic, not literal. In this perspective, the language of cohabitation is used to convey the idea that divine beings who are rivals to Yahweh are responsible for producing the Nephilim, and therefore are responsible for the later giant clans.

This approach uses Yahweh's relationship to Abraham and Sarah as an

---

8. For example, Matt 2:19; Acts 10:3; 11:13.

analogy.[9] While there is no suggestion of a sexual relationship between an embodied Yahweh and Sarah to produce Isaac and, therefore, the Israelites, it is nonetheless true that the Israelites came about through supernatural intervention.[10] In that sense, Yahweh "fathered" Israel. The means God used to enable Abraham and Sarah to have a child are never described in the Bible, but Scripture is clear that divine intervention of some sort was necessary. The Bible's silence on the nature of the supernatural intervention opens the door to the idea that other rival gods produced offspring to oppose Yahweh's children.

As we'll see in the following chapter, this belief on the part of the biblical writers (with respect to either approach) became the rationale for the extermination of certain people groups in Canaan. Either the giant clans are the result of literal cohabitation, or the sexual language is merely a vehicle to communicate the idea that, as Yahweh was responsible for the Israelites' existence, so the giant clans existed because of some sort of supernatural intervention of rival gods.[11]

---

9. Sarah would have been well past the age of producing an egg for fertilization and the physical demands of bringing a child to term.

10. One scholar has recently put forth the idea that Yahweh is perceived as a "sexual deity" in the Old Testament: David E. Bokovoy, "Did Eve Acquire, Create, or Procreate with Yahweh? A Grammatical and Contextual Reassessment of קנה in Genesis 4:1," *Vetus Testamentum* 63 (2013): 19–35. I do not believe a phrase like "sexual deity" captures the semantic point of Gen 4:1. Bokovoy argues that the verb in question in Gen 4:1 (*qanah*) means to create or procreate. I would agree that the verb can certainly have this meaning. Bokovoy's argument is that the biblical writer believed God participated in the mystery of procreation. Although he doesn't state it, his assumption appears to be that the biblical writers attributed conception to the deity because, unlike us, they didn't know scientifically how human fertilization and what happens in the womb worked. I would also agree with that point. However, Bokovoy's conclusion, that Yahweh "actively participated" in Cain's procreation, needs qualifications that he does not include in his work. One can say that, in the perception of the biblical writer, and even Eve herself, God caused Eve's pregnancy. But what does that mean? The biblical writer wasn't ignorant of the man's (Adam's) involvement. The text of the first half of Gen 4:1 says explicitly that Adam "knew Eve his wife, and she [subsequently] conceived." In other words, the biblical writer understood that sexual intercourse between a man and a woman led to pregnancy. There is no prerequisite for modern scientific understanding for grasping that point. In the second half of the verse Eve says (ESV), "I have gotten [lemma: *qanah*; form: *qaniti*] a man with the LORD." But note that Eve is the grammatical subject of this "sexual" verb, *not* the object. Bokovoy's writing sounds as though Yahweh is the subject here, and that Yahweh is participating *sexually* with Eve. That isn't what the grammar of the text says. The author's wording lacks precision and is therefore misleading. Nevertheless, following Bokovoy for the sake of discussion, one could translate Eve's statement this way: "I have procreated a man with YHWH." What would this mean since the writer clearly has Adam as the one having sexual relations with Eve? The answer is simple. This passage is akin to others in the Old Testament where the author narrates the fact that couples have sexual intercourse and then attributes the pregnancy (e.g., "opening of the womb") to Yahweh—i.e., God gets credit for the mystery of procreation (Gen 18:9–14; 21:1–2; 25:21; 29:32–35; 30:16–24; 1 Sam 1:19–20; Pss 17:14; 127:3; Isa 44:2, 24). This is neither complicated nor shocking, and it isn't proof that Yahweh was thought to participate sexually with anyone. The mystery of procreation and the act of intercourse are *distinguished* in Gen 4:1 and other passages.

11. Reconciling the first view with what 2 Pet 2:4–10 and Jude 6–7 say about "the angels who sinned" is straightforward, especially given the sexual nature of the events of Sodom and Gomorrah, which both writers use as analogous situations. The second approach doesn't question the sexual language; it considers

Both approaches therefore presume that the Nephilim and the subsequent giant clans had a supernatural origin, but they disagree on the means.

NEPHILIM AFTER THE FLOOD

Genesis 6:4 pointedly informs readers that the Nephilim were on earth before the flood "and also afterward." The phrase looks forward to Numbers 13:33, which says with equal clarity that the oversized descendants of Anak "came from the Nephilim."[12] The sons of Anak, the Anakim, were one of the giant clans described in the conquest narratives (e.g., Deut 2:10–11, 21; Josh 11:21–22; 14:12, 15). The text clearly links them to the Nephilim, but how is this possible given the account of the flood?[13]

The problem is one that has puzzled interpreters since antiquity. As I noted in chapter 13, some Jewish writers presumed the answer was that Noah himself had been fathered by one of the sons of God and was a Nephilim giant. Genesis 6:9 clearly wants to distance Noah from the unrighteousness that precipitated the flood, so this explanation doesn't work.

There are two alternatives for explaining the presence of giants after the flood who descended from the giant Nephilim: (1) the flood of Genesis 6–8 was a regional, not global, catastrophe; (2) the same kind of behavior described in Genesis 6:1–4 happened again (or continued to happen) *after* the flood, producing other Nephilim, from whom the giant clans descended.

The first option, a localized flood, naturally depends on the coherence of the arguments in defense of a local flood, especially those arguments dealing with the wording in the biblical text that seems to suggest the flood was worldwide. Many biblical scholars, scientists, and other researchers have marshaled

---

it euphemistic. Peter and Jude's inclusion of sexual language is no surprise—it is present in the Old Testament. This approach would argue that there is no reason to insist that Peter and Jude did not also consider it euphemistic. In any respect, what cannot be coherently denied is that Peter and Jude have divine beings as the offenders, not mere humans.

12. Both phrases are regarded as late editorial glosses by many evangelical and nonconfessional scholars. See, for example, Brian Doak, *The Last of the Rephaim: Conquest and Cataclysm in the Heroic Ages of Ancient Israel*, Ilex Series 7 [(Cambridge: Harvard University Press, 2013), 78; Claus Westermann, *Genesis 1–11: A Continental Commentary* (Minneapolis: Fortress, 1994), 378. That they are part of the final form of the biblical text means they must be included in the canonical material that was the product of the process of inspiration.

13. The Hebrew of the phrase in Num 13:33 literally reads that the sons of (*beney*) Anak were "from" (*min*) the Nephilim. The meaning is either that the Anakim were lineal (biological) descendants or were viewed as part of a group that descended from the Nephilim. Some have argued that the preposition *min* suggests the Anaqim were only "like" the Nephilim, but there is no clear instance in the Hebrew Bible for this semantic nuance. As Doak notes in his discussion of the phrase, "Whatever the case, the Anaqim here are most certainly thought to be the physical (and thus "moral" or "spiritual") descendants of the Nephilim" (*Last of the Rephaim*, 79).

the evidence in favor of this reading.[14] For our purposes, this option would allow human survival somewhere in the regions known to the biblical authors (Gen 10), specifically the ancient Near East, the Mediterranean Sea, and the Aegean Sea.[15]

The second option is a possibility deriving from Hebrew grammar. Genesis 6:4 tells us there were Nephilim on earth before the flood "and also afterward, when the sons of God went into the daughters of humankind." The "when" in the verse could be translated "whenever," thereby suggesting a repetition of these preflood events after the flood.[16] In other words, since Genesis 6:4 points forward to the later giant clans, the phrasing could suggest that other

---

14. The argument for a local flood proceeds along several trajectories aside from scientific arguments. For scientific discussion, see David F. Siemens Jr., "Some Relatively Non-Technical Problems with Flood Geology," *Perspectives on Science and the Christian Faith* 44.3 (1992): 169–74; Davis Young and Ralph Searley, *The Bible, Rocks and Time: Geological Evidence for the Age of the Earth* (Downers Grove, IL: IVP Academic, 2008), 224–40. Our concern is with the biblical text and its own evidence for a local flood. First, the phrases in the flood narrative that suggest a global event occur a number of times in the Hebrew Bible where their context cannot be global or include all people on the planet. For example, the phrase "the whole earth" (*kol 'erets*) occurs in passages that clearly speak of localized geography (e.g., Gen 13:9; 41:57; Lev 25:9, 24; Judg 6:37; 1 Sam 13:3; 2 Sam 24:8). In such cases, "whole land" or "all the people in the area" are better understandings. Those options produce a regional flood event if used in Gen 6–8 where the phrase occurs. Second, the Gen 9:19 clearly informs us that "the whole earth" was populated by the sons of Noah. Gen 10 (see 10:1) gives us the list of the nations spawned by the sons of Noah—all of which are located in the regions of the ancient Near East, the Mediterranean, and the Aegean. The biblical writers knew nothing of nations in another hemisphere (the Americas) or places like India, China, or Australia. The language of Gen 10 therefore allows Gen 7:21 to be restricted to only (or even some) of the people groups listed in the Table of Nations. That interpretation is consistent with a localized flood. Third, the phrase "all humankind" (*kol 'adam*) used in Gen 7:21 also appears in contexts that cannot speak to all humans everywhere (e.g., Jer 32:20; Psa 64:9 can only refer to people who had seen what God had done, not people on the other side of the world). Lastly, Psa 104:9 appears to forbid a global flood, since it has God promising to never cover the earth with water *as had been the case at creation*.

15. Both supernatural approaches to Gen 6:1–4 can accommodate a local flood. Both posit flood survivors (by whatever means) somewhere in the Mediterranean or Aegean, the known biblical world. Those survivors (at least some of them) would have had to eventually migrate to Canaan. At least one of the giant lineages can be traced to the Aegean (see ch. 25). In like manner, positing a postflood origin for more Nephilim would require more divine intervention of the same (undescribed) type.

16. A translation of "when" takes the *'asher* clause as temporal. According to Westermann, this is the view espoused by most commentators. He is, however, apathetic as to whether a temporal understanding or another possibility is more coherent: "It does not really matter whether אשר is understood as temporal (with most interpreters) or iterative (so E. König, W. H. Schmidt and others) or as causal (e.g., B. S. Childs; against, and correctly, W. H. Schmidt); אשר is an afterthought, its function being in fact only to link and so to subordinate" (Westermann, *Genesis 1–11*, 377). Wenham notes that some Hebrew scholars consider the use of the Hebrew imperfect in this clause to allow for repetition: " 'Whenever the sons of the gods went into the daughters of men, they bore them children.' Though it is not impossible to translate this as a simple past event—'When they went in …'—it is more natural (with Skinner, König, Gispen) to take the imperfect 'went' and perfect preceded by *waw* ('bore … children') as frequentative. To 'go in to' is a frequent euphemism for sexual intercourse (cf. Gen 30:16; 38:16)" (Gordon J. Wenham, *Genesis 1–15*, Word Biblical Commentary 1 (Dallas: Word, 1998], 143. See also Friedrich Wilhelm Gesenius, *Gesenius' Hebrew Grammar*, 2nd English ed. (ed. E. Kautzsch and Sir Arthur Ernest Cowley; Oxford: Clarendon Press, 1910), 315 (sec. 107e). Gesenius includes Gen 6:4 as an instance of this interpretive nuance.

sons of God fathered more Nephilim after the flood.[17] As a result, there would be no survival of *original* Nephilim, and so the postflood dilemma would be resolved. A later appearance of other Nephilim occurred by the same means as before the flood.

All of this sets the stage for Numbers 13. Fear of the giant clans results in a spiritual failure that means wandering in the desert outside the land of promise for forty years. The generation who came out of Egypt is sentenced to die off outside of holy ground. The new generation under Joshua will wind up facing the same threat.

17. I say "other" since all ancient Jewish traditions, including 2 Peter and Jude in the New Testament, have the offending sons of God (also called Watchers) imprisoned in the underworld for what they did until the end of days. Both supernaturalist approaches are also workable with this possible translation, as it would suggest a repetition of whatever intervention event one envisions for producing the Nephilim of Gen 6:1–4.

CHAPTER 24

The Place of the Serpent

IN NUMBERS 13, THE ISRAELITES HAD ARRIVED AT THE BORDER OF CANAAN. Moses sent twelve spies into Canaan to report on the land and its inhabitants. They came back with the news that what God had said was true—the land was "flowing with milk and honey" (Num 13:27)—but then added, "there we saw the Nephilim (the sons of Anak, who come from the Nephilim), and we seemed to ourselves like grasshoppers, and so we seemed to them" (ESV).

The very next chapter of the book of Numbers tells us that, despite the miracles of their deliverance from Egypt, the people refused to believe that God would help them defeat the Anakim ("sons of Anak"). Because they rebelled, God sentenced them to wander in the desert for forty years until all who did not believe had died off. Only then would God bring them back to the promised land (Num 14:33–35).[1]

Who were the Anakim? Were these giants the kind of monstrous beings we read about in Greek mythology? How many of them lived in the land? The text clearly connects them to the Nephilim, but how exactly were they connected?

Answers to these questions can only be understood when framed by the original ancient context of the biblical writers who put the Old Testament account of Israel's history in its final form. It is no accident that, by all accounts, this work was finished in exile in Babylon. The biblical writers deliberately connect the giant clan enemies Israel would face in the conquest back to the ancient apostasies that had Babylon at their root: the sons of God and the Nephilim, and the disinheritance of the nations at the Tower of Babel.

---

1. Some try to argue that the report of the spies was a lie or deliberate exaggeration motivated by fear. This is a poorly conceived idea, since it requires either ignoring all the other biblical references to giants (Anakim or otherwise) or considering them to be lies as well. It also requires removing the term *nephilim* from its context and ignoring the morphology of the word (see chapters 12–13). There is no sound exegetical support for this idea.

These incidents inform the Israelite supernatural worldview. They are at the heart of what's at stake in the war for the promised land. Israel will encounter two deadly forces: the descendants of the Nephilim and the people of nations under the dominion of hostile gods. The two are at times conflated in the narrative. Both must be defeated, but one in particular must be annihilated.

THE GIANTS OF THE TRANSJORDAN

As the forty years of wandering neared completion, God directed Moses to lead the new generation of Israelites (and the few members of the old generation whose faith had not failed) back toward Canaan. But instead of heading into Canaan from the south as before, God brought them alongside Canaan through territory to the east (the "Transjordan"). (See map on next page.)

This was no accident. Deuteronomy 2 (ESV) picks up the story.

[8]"So we went on, away from our brothers, the people of Esau, who live in Seir, away from the Arabah road from Elath and Ezion-geber.

[9]"And we turned and went in the direction of the wilderness of Moab. [10]And the LORD said to me, 'Do not harass Moab or contend with them in battle, for I will not give you any of their land for a possession, because I have given Ar to the people of Lot for a possession.' [10](The Emim formerly lived there, a people great and many, and tall as the Anakim. [11]Like the Anakim they are also counted as Rephaim, but the Moabites call them Emim. [12]The Horites also lived in Seir formerly, but the people of Esau dispossessed them and destroyed them from before them and settled in their place, as Israel did to the land of their possession, which the LORD gave to them.) ...

[17]"The LORD said to me, [18]'Today you are to cross the border of Moab at Ar. [19]And when you approach the territory of the people of Ammon, do not harass them or contend with them, for I will not give you any of the land of the people of Ammon as a possession, because I have given it to the sons of Lot for a possession.' [20](It is also counted as a land of Rephaim. Rephaim formerly lived there—but the Ammonites call them Zamzummim—[21]a people great and many, and tall as the Anakim; but the LORD destroyed them before the Ammonites, and they dispossessed them and settled in their place, [22]as he did for the people of Esau, who live in Seir, when he destroyed the Horites before them and they dispossessed them and settled in their place even to this day. [23]As for the Avvim, who lived in villages as far as Gaza, the Caphtorim, who came from Caphtor, destroyed them and settled in their place)" (Deut 2:8–23).

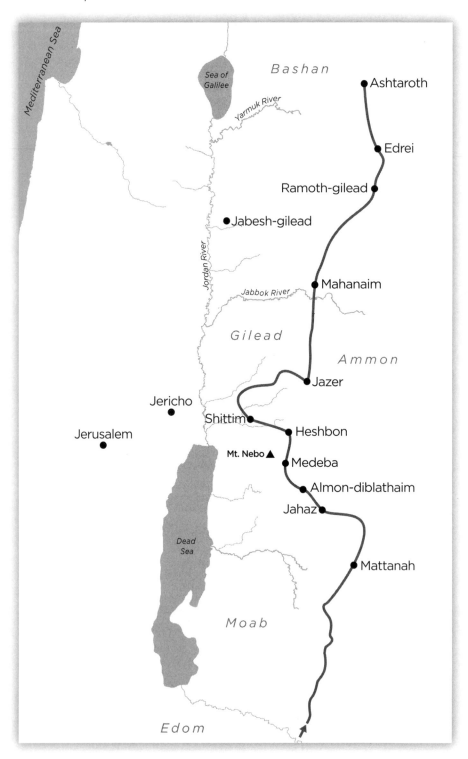

We learn several things of significance in this passage and its geography. Proceeding from south to north, the Edomites, Moabites, and Ammonites were to be left unmolested by the Israelites because God had long ago allotted that land to Abraham's nephew Lot and his grandson, Esau, Jacob's brother. It is fascinating to note (vv. 10–11, 19–20) that giants had once lived in those territories prior to the arrival of Moses, Joshua, and the Israelites. These giant clans were known among the Moabites and Ammonites as the Emim and the Zamzummim. Other inhabitants had also been driven out: the Horites, the Avvim, and the Caphtorim. These tribal groups are never themselves referred to as being unusually tall, though they surface in connection with giant clans in a number of other passages.[2] The thing to observe here is that these giant clans *had already been removed from the land promised to Abraham's descendants by the descendants of Esau and Lot, who were also descended from Abraham, like Israel* (vv. 12, 21).

These giant clans were related to the Anakim (vv. 10–11), who were, of course, "from the Nephilim" (Num 13:32–33). We aren't told specifically how the bloodline lineages worked, but we are told a relationship existed. Additionally, all of these groups seem to also have been referred to as Rephaim (vv. 11, 20), a term that will take on more importance as we proceed.[3]

MARCHING TO SIHON … AND BASHAN

God told Moses to ask travel permission of the sons of Lot and Esau as the Israelites journeyed northward through the Transjordan. They received that permission (Deut 2:27–29) and passed through. They were on their way at God's leading to what was actually the last area under the dominion of the Nephilim bloodline in the Transjordan. Moses is seemingly unaware of God's aim in this leg of the journey. Deuteronomy 2 (ESV) continues as Moses sends word to the enemy in God's crosshairs:

> [26] "So I sent messengers from the wilderness of Kedemoth to Sihon the king of Heshbon, with words of peace, saying, [27] 'Let me pass through your land. I will go only by the road; I will turn aside neither to the right nor to the left. [28] You shall sell me food for money, that I may eat, and give me water for money, that

---

2. Note that the Caphtorim "lived in villages as far as Gaza" (v. 23). Gaza would become known as a Philistine city. Caphtor is an island in the Aegean, likely Crete. In David's era, Goliath would be numbered among the Philistines.

3. On the Rephaim, see Michael S. Heiser, "Rephaim," in *Lexham Bible Dictionary* (Bellingham, WA: Lexham Press, 2015). On the geographical area under the control of Og, see Doak, *Last of the Rephaim*, 81–83.

I may drink. Only let me pass through on foot, [29] as the sons of Esau who live in Seir and the Moabites who live in Ar did for me, until I go over the Jordan into the land that the LORD our God is giving to us.' [30] But Sihon the king of Heshbon would not let us pass by him, for the LORD your God hardened his spirit and made his heart obstinate, that he might give him into your hand, as he is this day (Deut 2:26–30 ESV).

Did you catch the last line? God hardened the heart of Sihon. The wording is designed to make us think of God's battle with Pharaoh, the presumed god of Egypt. It was time for Sihon to go. But why target him? The answer to that question requires a look back into biblical history, and then a look forward into the next chapter of Deuteronomy. Let's look back first—to Abraham.

In Genesis 15, one of the passages where Yahweh appeared to Abraham to form a covenant relationship with him, God told Abraham the following in a dream:

[13] Know for certain that your offspring will be sojourners in a land that is not theirs and will be servants there, and they will be afflicted for four hundred years. [14] But I will bring judgment on the nation that they serve, and afterward they shall come out with great possessions. [15] As for you, you shall go to your fathers in peace; you shall be buried in a good old age. [16] And they shall come back here in the fourth generation, for the iniquity of the Amorites is not yet complete (Gen 15:13–16 ESV).

God told Abraham that his descendants (the people of Edom, Ammon, Moab, and, of course, Israel) would live in bondage but would one day return to the land of promise—at a time when the iniquity of the *Amorites* had reached the point when God was ready to judge it. Why Sihon? He was an Amorite king (Deut 3:2). But why the Amorites?

The historical material on the Amorites is sparse. Broadly speaking, the Amorite culture was *Mesopotamian*. The term and the people are known from Sumerian and Akkadian material centuries older than the Old Testament and the time of Moses and the Israelites. The word for "Amorite" actually comes from a Sumerian word ("MAR.TU") which vaguely referred to the area and population west of Sumer and *Babylon*.

The use of "Amorite" in the Old Testament is indiscriminate.[4] In some passages it's a label for the entire population of Canaan (Josh 7:7).[5] In that sense,

---

4. In Gen 14:13 an Amorite is said to have been an ally to Abraham. This is not much of a surprise since the term could simply denote Mesopotamian ethnicity. But in the broad strokes of the conquest narratives, the Amorites are enemies, and their Babylonian heritage becomes a link back to the Nephilim.

5. The "Amorites" in that passage are clearly not those of the Transjordan—they are, in effect, "Canaanites."

"Amorites" and "Canaanites" are interchangeable, both denoting non-Israelite in the land of Canaan.[6] In other passages its use is more specific to one people group among several within Canaan (Gen 15:19–21).[7]

"Canaanites" and "Amorites" were therefore generic terms used to describe the enemies of Israel. Of the two, "Amorites" takes on a more sinister tone in the context of the Babylonian polemic that precedes this point in Israel's story. Tarring and feathering the inhabitants of Canaan with a label that would take an Israelite reader back to supernatural disasters of Genesis 6 and 11 would have a profound theological effect.

But the connection is actually more direct than rhetoric. One passage in Scripture specifically connects the Amorites (Canaanites) to the giants that were derivative of the Nephilim.[8] God says through the prophet Amos:

> [9] Yet it was I who destroyed the Amorite before them,
>   whose height was like the height of the cedars
>   and who was as strong as the oaks;
> I destroyed his fruit above
>   and his roots beneath.
> [10] Also it was I who brought you up out of the land of Egypt
>   and led you forty years in the wilderness,
>   to possess the land of the Amorite (Amos 2:9–10 ESV).

Note that the context for this statement is the exodus and the conquest. That at least some Amorites were unusually tall would have been proof to the Israelites they had descended from the Nephilim—and that case, of course, was made in Num 13:32–33. For an Israelite, all this meant that the native population of Canaan had a supernaturally sinister point of origin. This wouldn't be just a battle for land. It was a battle between Yahweh and the other gods— gods who had raised up competing human bloodlines that were opposed to Yahweh's plan and people.

---

6. On "Canaanites" as an umbrella term, see Gen 12:6; 28:1, 6. Some scholars consider the two to be synonymous terms used in different Pentateuchal sources ("Canaan, Canaanites," in *Harper's Bible Dictionary* [ed. Paul J. Achtemeier; San Francisco: Harper & Row, 1985], 152–53).

7. It is interesting that both the comprehensive (Gen 15:16) and subset usage (Gen 15:19–21) can be found in Gen 15.

8. The wording of Amos 2:9 cannot be conclusively isolated to reference only the individual Sihon or Og. The phrase "the Amorite" (*ha-ʾemoriy*) can refer to a single person (e.g., Gen 14:13) or a collective (e.g., Gen 10:16). "Whose" is the simple relative pronoun *ʾasher*. The third person singular suffix pronoun ("his" [fruit]) can be used with respect to a collective as well, precisely because its grammatical agreement will align with the noun it represents. Since "Amorite" is *morphologically* singular, the suffix pronoun is singular. But the singular noun, as noted above, can be *semantically* plural. Consequently, the suffix pronoun would contextually be understood the same way.

Something else about Sihon factors into this interpretation. He was allied to a fellow named Og, another king of the Amorites who ruled in the region of Bashan. *Og was a giant.* Deuteronomy 3 (ESV) tells us what happened after Israel's battle with Sihon:

> Then we turned and went up the way to Bashan. And Og the king of Bashan came out against us, he and all his people, to battle at Edrei. ²But the LORD said to me, 'Do not fear him, for I have given him and all his people and his land into your hand. And you shall do to him as you did to Sihon the king of the Amorites, who lived at Heshbon.' ³So the LORD our God gave into our hand Og also, the king of Bashan, and all his people, and we struck him down until he had no survivor left.... ⁶And we devoted them to destruction, as we did to Sihon the king of Heshbon, devoting to destruction every city, men, women, and children. ⁷But all the livestock and the spoil of the cities we took as our plunder. ⁸So we took the land at that time out of the hand of the two kings of the Amorites who were beyond the Jordan, from the Valley of the Arnon to Mount Hermon ⁹(the Sidonians call Hermon Sirion, while the Amorites call it Senir), ¹⁰all the cities of the tableland and all Gilead and all Bashan, as far as Salecah and Edrei, cities of the kingdom of Og in Bashan. ¹¹(For only Og the king of Bashan was left of the remnant of the Rephaim. Behold, his bed was a bed of iron. Is it not in Rabbah of the Ammonites? Nine cubits was its length, and four cubits its breadth, according to the common cubit) (Deut 3:1–11 ESV).

For an ancient Israelite reader with a command of Hebrew and a worldview that included the idea that supernatural opposition to Israel had something to do with preflood events in Mesopotamia, several things in this short passage would have jumped out immediately. None of them are obvious in English translation.

First, the most immediate link back to the Babylonian polemic is Og's bed (Hebrew: *ʿeres*).[9] Its dimensions (9 x 4 cubits) are precisely those of the cultic bed in the ziggurat called Etemenanki—which is the ziggurat most archaeologists identify as the Tower of Babel referred to in the Bible.[10] Ziggurats functioned as temples and divine abodes. The unusually large bed at Etemenanki

---

9. The dimensions were roughly six by thirteen feet.

10. Etemenanki = Esagil (Sumerian) (Brian Doak, *The Last of the Rephaim: Conquest and Cataclysm in the Heroic Ages of Ancient Israel*, Ilex Series 7 [Cambridge: Harvard University Press, 2013], 92). Doak goes on to note that scholars who have detected this connection conclude that the point of matching the dimensions was that the biblical writer wanted to compare Og with a cultic prostitute. This not only is an awkward referent, but fails to consider the wider Babylonian polemic connected back to Gen 6. See also Andrew R. George, "The Tower of Babel: Archaeology, History, and Cuneiform Texts," *Archiv für Orientforschung* 51 (2005/2006): 75–95; John H. Walton, "The Mesopotamian Background of the Tower of Babel Account and Its Implications," *Bulletin for Biblical Research* 5 (1995): 155–75.

was housed in "the house of the bed" (*bit erši*). It was the place where the god Marduk and his divine wife, Zarpanitu, met annually for ritual lovemaking, the purpose of which was divine blessing upon the land.[11]

Scholars have been struck by the precise correlation. It's hard not to conclude that, as with Genesis 6:1–4, so with Deuteronomy 3, those who put the finishing touches on the Old Testament during the exile in Babylon were connecting Marduk and Og in some way. The most transparent path is in fact giant stature. Og is said to have been the last of the Rephaim—a term connected to the giant Anakim and other ancient giant clans in the Transjordan (Deut 2:11, 20). Marduk, like other deities in antiquity, was portrayed as superhuman in size.[12] However, the real matrix of ideas in the mind of the biblical author may be derived from wordplay based on Babylonian mythology.[13]

---

11. Sacred marriage rituals included the blessing of fertility for both the land and its inhabitants. See Martti Nissinen, "Akkadian Rituals and Poetry of Divine Love," in *Mythology and Mythologies: Methodological Approaches to Intercultural Influences; Proceedings of the Second Annual Symposium of the Assyrian and Babylonian Intellectual Heritage Project Held in Paris, France, October 4–7, 1999*, Melammu Symposia 2 (ed. R. M. Whiting; Helsinki: Neo-Assyrian Text Corpus Project, 2001), 93–136. The ritual was also concerned with maintaining the cosmic order instituted by the gods. Consequently, in addition to the giantism element, a link between Og and Marduk via the matching bed dimensions may also have telegraphed the idea that Og was the inheritor and perpetuator of the Babylonian knowledge and cosmic order from before the flood. This would of course tie him back to Gen 6:1–4 and its *apkallu* polemic. See Beate Pongratz-Leisten, "Sacred Marriage and the Transfer of Divine Knowledge: Alliances between the Gods and the King in Ancient Mesopotamia," in *Sacred Marriages: The Divine-Human Sexual Metaphor from Sumer to Early Christianity* (ed. Martti Nissinen and Risto Uro; Winona Lake, IN: Eisenbrauns, 2008), 43–72. In any event, the size of Og's bed cannot be taken as a precise indication of Og's own dimensions. There is much more at play here.

12. See *Enûma Elish* 1.99–100: "He was the loftiest of the gods, surpassing was his stature; his members were enormous, he was exceedingly tall." One scholar notes in this regard, "The huge images of Marduk at Babylon could have served as the basis for the description of Marduk and other Babylonian gods as giants. Herodotus, *Histories* 1.183 said the golden image of Bel in the temple at Babylon stood twelve cubits; Ktesias (Diodorus Siculus, *Library* 2.9.5) claimed the statue had a height of forty feet" (Russell E. Gmirkin, *Berossus and Genesis, Manetho and Exodus: Hellenistic Histories and the Date of the Pentateuch*, Library of Hebrew Bible/Old Testament Studies 433 [London: T&T Clark, 2006], 128).

13. Marduk was a minor deity prior to the Babylonian era, when he was elevated to be king of the gods and the patron deity of the city of Babylon. His main temple was, as we have noted, Etemenanki, the ziggurat at Babylon (see Jeremy A. Black, "Marduk," in *Dictionary of the Ancient Near East* [ed. Piotr Bienkowski and Alan Millard; London: British Museum Press, 2000], 188–89). Marduk was therefore the chief theological rival to Yahweh in the exilic period. In biblical literature, Marduk is referred to as Merodach or Bel. Second Temple period Jewish texts contain a tradition about a giant who survived the flood named Belus, who was credited with building a tower in Babylon (the Tower of Babel), in which he lived. The train of thought conceptually links Marduk and Belus the giant. The same tradition identifies Belus with the biblical Nimrod, and suggests Nimrod might also be identified with Noah. Biblical editors during the exile may have taken note of the same Bel/Belus wordplay and used the dimensions of Og's bed to identify him with Marduk, though we cannot of course know that with any certainty. What we can know is that this sort of thinking did surface in Second Temple period Jewish writings. Van der Toorn summarizes: "The opinion that Nimrod goes back to a Mesopotamian deity is not new. As early as 1871, J. Grivel suggested that Nimrod is to be identified with Marduk (biblical Merodach or Bel). Unwittingly, he thus revived an ancient haggadic speculation in which Nimrod is identified with Belus.... In one of

Second, Deuteronomy 3 mentions Og's reign over the city of Edrei (v. 10). Joshua 12:4–5, which looks back on the battle with Og, refers to him as the king of Bashan and living at Ashtaroth and Edrei.[14] These terms—Ashtaroth, Edrei, and Bashan—were theologically loaded terms for an Israelite, and even for their neighbors who worshiped other gods.

Ashtaroth, Edrei, and the Rephaim are mentioned by name in Ugaritic texts.[15] The Rephaim of Ugarit are not described as giants. Rather, they are quasi-divine dead warrior kings who inhabit the underworld. In the Ugaritic language, the location of Ashtaroth and Edrei was not spelled Bashan, but was pronounced and spelled *Bathan*. The linguistic note is intriguing since Bashan/Bathan both also mean "serpent," so that the region of Bashan was "the place of the serpent."[16] As we saw earlier, the divine serpent (*nachash*, another word so translated) became lord of the dead after his rebellion in

---

the fragments of Pseudo-Eupolemus ... we read the following: 'Abraham traced his family to the giants. While these giants were living in Babylonia, they were destroyed by the gods because of their wickedness. One of them, Belus, escaped death and came to dwell in Babylon. There he built a tower and lived in it. It was named Belus, after Belus who built it' (quoted from Alexander Polyhistor by Eusebius, *Praeparatio Evangelica* 9.18.2). Here is a medley of allusions to Gen 6 (both the motif of the giants and that of the flood) and Gen 11 (the building of the tower of Babel). As we shall see in other instances of linking Gen 6 to Gen 11, the intermediate link is Nimrod from Gen 10. The problem in this case, however, is that if Belus, one of the giants who built the tower, is identical with Nimrod, he also is said to have escaped the flood, which would imply an identification of Noah and Nimrod!" (K. van der Toorn, "Nimrod before and after the Bible," *Harvard Theological Review* 83.1 (January 1990): 8, 16. Lastly, though it is only speculation, it is interesting to note that Marduk's name in Sumerian name was AMAR.UTU ("calf of Utu"; i.e., "the young bull of the Sun god"). The Sumerian for "Amorite" is MAR.TU. One wonders if the biblical scribes heard a pun behind the description of Og the giant Amorite king and Marduk's name.

14. Josh 13:11–12, 30–31 describes Og's general kingdom as the region of Bashan, which encompassed sixty cities.

15. On the significance of Ugarit and its language and literature for Hebrew and Israelite religion, see chapter 6. The Ugaritic word that corresponds to Hebrew *rephaim* is *rapiuma*. See the companion website for more on these terms.

16. See G. del Olmo Lete, "Bashan," in *Dictionary of Deities and Demons in the Bible*, 2nd ed. (ed. Karel van der Toorn, Bob Becking, and Pieter W. van der Horst; Leiden; Boston; Cologne; Grand Rapids, MI; Cambridge: Brill; Eerdmans, 1999), 161–63. Charlesworth agrees that geographical Bashan should be identified with serpent language (James H. Charlesworth, "Bashan, Symbology, Haplography, and Theology in Psalm 68," in *David and Zion: Biblical Studies in Honor of J. J. M. Roberts* [ed. Bernard Frank Batto and Kathryn L. Roberts; Winona Lake, Ind.: Eisenbrauns, 2004], 351–372 [esp. 355–56]). As we saw earlier, the divine serpent (*nachash*, another word so translated) became lord of the dead after his rebellion in Eden. Therefore, the "serpentine" connection is conceptual, not philological/linguistic. In effect, Bashan was conceived of, to borrow a New Testament phrase, "the gates of hell." We'll return to both the imagery and this place in a later chapter. This is precisely the region where Jesus utters his famous "gates of hell" statement (Matt 16:18). The Old Testament also has Rephaim in the underworld (Sheol; see Isa 14:9; Ezek 32:27; Psa 88:10–12 [Hebrew, vv. 11–13]; Job 26:1–6). See the companion website for more discussion of Sheol in the Old Testament. Because of the Babylonian context of Gen 6:1–4 (a polemic against the divine *apkallus* and their quasi-divine giant offspring *apkallus*; see chs. 12–13), the subsequent connection by the biblical writers between the Nephilim and the Rephaim results in a departure from the tradition of Ugaritic literature, which did not have the Rephaim as giants.

Eden. In effect, Bashan was considered the location of (to borrow a New Testament phrase) "the gates of hell." Later Jewish writers understood these conceptual connections. Their intersection is at the heart of why books like 1 Enoch teach that demons are actually the spirits of dead Nephilim.[17]

Lastly, aside from Bashan being the gateway to the underworld, the region has another sinister feature identified in the Deuteronomy 3 passage: Mount Hermon. According to 1 Enoch 6:1–6, Mount Hermon was the place where the sons of God of Genesis 6 descended when they came to earth to cohabit with human women—the episode that produced the Nephilim.[18] Joshua 12:4–5 unites all the threads: "Og king of Bashan, one of the remnant of the Rephaim, who lived at Ashtaroth and at Edrei and ruled over Mount Hermon."

Just the name "Hermon" would have caught the attention of Israelite and Jewish readers. In Hebrew it's pronounced *khermon*. The noun has the same root as a verb that is of central importance in Deuteronomy 3 and the conquest narratives: *kharam*, "to devote to destruction." *This is the distinct verb of holy war*, the verb of extermination. It has deep theological meaning, a meaning explicitly connected to the giant clans God commanded Joshua and his armies to eradicate. It is to that phase of the war for the land that we now turn.

---

17. See the companion website for more development of this belief. The major scholarly study on this topic is Archie T. Wright, *The Origin of Evil Spirits: The Reception of Genesis 6:1–4 in Early Jewish Literature*, Wissenschaftliche Untersuchungen zum Neuen Testament 198, second series; Tübingen: Mohr Siebeck, 2013).

18. Recall that in 1 Enoch the term used for the divine "sons of God" was "Watchers" (see chs. 12–13).

CHAPTER 25

Holy War

THE LAST CHAPTER CLOSED WITH THE DEMISE OF THE GIANT OG, LAST OF the Rephaim (Deut 3:1–11). Israel's battles in the Transjordan bring us face-to-face with an issue that has troubled Bible students and scholars for centuries: the practice of extermination in Israel's war of conquest. Og's defeat is illustrative: "And we devoted them to destruction, as we did to Sihon the king of Heshbon, devoting to destruction every city, men, women, and children" (Deut 3:6 ESV).[1]

Og was lord of Bashan, the region that included Mount Hermon. We saw that the verb translated "devote to destruction" (*kharam*) shares the same root consonants (*kh-r-m*) as Mount Hermon (*khermon*).[2] The wars with Sihon and Og foreshadowed the logic of *kherem*,[3] the act of devoting something to destruction, a logic that, as we will see in this chapter, has the Nephilim bloodlines as its focus.

---

1. Despite their unusual size, the biblical text is clear that the giant clan members were *human*. For example, the word *'adam* ("humankind"; cf. Gen 1:26–27) is used to describe the victims of the conquest in cities associated with giant clans (Josh 11:14). Arba is called "the greatest man (*'adam*) among the Anakim." The generic Hebrew word for people (*'am*; i.e., human populations) is also used of giant clans: Deut 2:10 (the Emim); Deut 2:20 (the Zamzummim); Deut 3:1–3 (Og's people); Deut 9:2 (the Anakim). This language raises the question of how both supernaturalist views of Gen 6:1–4 (see ch. 13) would understand this human description of the Anakim against the clear genealogical link back to the quasi-divine Nephilim (Num 13:33). For those favoring literal cohabitation in Gen 6:1–4, the point of the language ascribing humanity to Nephilim descendants would simply mean Anakim were mortal—not immortal gods. For those preferring the sort of divine parentage of which Yahweh's intervention to produce the Israelites is an analogy, human descriptions would not be unexpected, as Israelites were obviously human despite Yahweh's intervention.

2. *Theological Lexicon of the Old Testament* points out the correlation. See Ernst Jenni and Claus Westermann, *Theological Lexicon of the Old Testament* (Peabody, MA: Hendrickson, 1997), 474.

3. *Kherem* is the corresponding noun to the verb *kharam*.

KHEREM AND THE BIBLICAL
SUPERNATURAL WORLDVIEW

The idea of *kherem* is broader than warfare. Fundamental to the concept is a sanctioning of some person or thing because it is forbidden either due to an accursed status or due to Yahweh's exclusive ownership and use.[4] Persons or objects could be consecrated to Yahweh using this verb (Lev 27:28; Num 18:14; Josh 6:18; Mic 4:13). No other object or person could be substituted for that which was sanctified in this sense. The death sentence for worshiping another god was described with the verb *kharam* (Exod 22:20). Any person guilty of this crime was accursed. The sentence could not be revoked. Yahweh was the exclusive owner of that life or thing.

Joshua's *kherem* must be viewed against the backdrop of Genesis 6:1–4 and what I've called the "Deuteronomy 32 worldview": Yahweh had disinherited the nations, assigning them to the rule of lesser gods. Genesis 6:1–4 is evoked by Israel's initial contact with the occupants of the land in Numbers 13:32–33, where the giant Anakim are described as descendants of the Nephilim. As we'll see in the discussion that follows, this belief is behind the conquest passages that use the verb *kharam* ("devote to destruction") to describe Israel's warfare on certain occasions. Deuteronomy 32:8–9 is the basis for the general goal of the conquest. Israel is Yahweh's elect portion of humanity, and the land of Canaan is the geography that Yahweh, as owner, specifically allotted to his people.[5]

In the view of the biblical writers, Israel is at war with enemies spawned by rival divine beings. The Nephilim bloodlines were not like the peoples of the disinherited nations. Genesis 10 clearly casts the human inhabitants of those nations as owing their existence to Yahweh, as they descended from Noah's sons and, therefore, Noah—all the way back to Adam, Yahweh's first human son. The Nephilim bloodlines had a different pedigree. They were produced by other divine beings. They did not belong to Yahweh, and he therefore had no interest in claiming them. Coexistence was not possible with the spawn of other gods.

Viewed against this backdrop, Joshua's *kherem* is a holy war begun under Moses in the Transjordan, specifically against the Amorite giant kings Sihon

---

4. *Theological Lexicon of the Old Testament*, 474. See also Jackie A. Naudé, "חָרַם (I), חֵרֶם (I)," in *New International Dictionary of Old Testament Theology & Exegesis* (ed. Willem VanGemeren; Grand Rapids, MI: Zondervan, 1997), 276.

5. Several passages have Yahweh referring to Canaan/Israel as "my land" or "my inheritance" (e.g., 2 Chr 7:20; Isa 19:25; Jer 2:7; 16:18; Ezek 38:16; Joel 1:6; 3:2).

(Deut 2:34) and Og (Deut 3:6).[6] The lives of Israel's enemies were to be "devoted to destruction" as an act of sacrifice to Yahweh. But just who was in Yahweh's crosshairs to this extent?

THE RATIONALE OF JOSHUA'S KHEREM

How is Joshua's *kherem* presented to readers? As in other instances, we must return to Numbers 13:32–33 to begin. One specific line is of importance (in boldface type):

> [32] So they brought to the people of Israel a bad report of the land that they had spied out, saying, "The land, through which we have gone to spy it out, is a land that devours its inhabitants, and **all the people that we saw in it are of great height.** [33] And there we saw the Nephilim (the sons of Anak, who come from the Nephilim), and we seemed to ourselves like grasshoppers, and so we seemed to them" (ESV).

The first encounter of Israel with the inhabitants of the land involves the Anakim. The report of the spies contains the sweeping comment that everyone they saw in the land was unusually tall. There are good textual reasons for not taking this statement as a literally true assessment in terms of its comprehensive nature. We've already noted that the biblical writers at times use sweeping generalizations that are not intended to be precise. For instance, Genesis 15:16 and Joshua 7:7 referred to the occupants of the land as "Amorites" when it is abundantly clear that there were other ethnic groups in the land.[7] The term "Canaanite" is also used in the same imprecise way (Gen 12:6; 28:1, 6).

Consequently, it is much more coherent to read the statement as indicating that the Israelite spies saw unusually tall people groups everywhere they went in the land.[8] Numbers 13:28–29 supports this reading. Those verses tell us

---

6. There is one earlier instance of *kharam* in the context of warfare prior to the Transjordanian wars against the giants: Num 21:2–3. In this instance, Yahweh does not command the *kherem*. Rather, "Israel" (the speaker is not further identified) promises God that the king of Arad and his city will be put under *kherem* in retaliation for that king's kidnapping of some Israelites. Yahweh acquiesced and the name of the place of the destruction was called Hormah (*khormah*, which means "destruction"—again, the same consonants as *kherem*). While God did not command the *kherem*, the narrative notes that the "Canaanites" were "devoted to destruction." I noted the indiscriminate use of this term (along with "Amorite") in the previous chapter. See the ensuing discussion for how this relates to the giant clans as the specific targets of *kherem*.

7. For example, Perizzites, Hittites, Hivites, Girgashites, etc. (Exod 3:8; 23:23; Deut 7:1; 20:17; Josh 12:8).

8. This is not to say, however, that there were vast numbers of giant clan members. The account of Caleb is of interest in this regard. Caleb was one of the original twelve spies sent in by Moses (Num 13:6, 30). He

where the spies ventured: the Negeb, the hill country, the seacoast, and along the Jordan. Verse 29 has the spies noting that they saw Anakim in those locations among Amalekites, Hittites, Jebusites, Amorites, and Canaanites.

This point helps explain something that will become apparent as we proceed —that the lemma *kharam* in the conquest accounts is used only of assaults in cities or locales that overlap with giant clan population clusters. There is one exception, a lone indiscriminate use of *kharam* in Deuteronomy 7:1–2.[9] That passage calls for an indiscriminate *kherem* because of the indiscriminate generalization in Numbers 13:32–33. The words of Moses in Deuteronomy7:1–2 reflect the report Moses had received forty years earlier. Its meaning is not that all inhabitants of the land are put under *kherem* because everyone is a giant. Its meaning is that, wherever they are found, the bloodlines of the giant clans—descendants of the Nephilim—are to be eradicated. Once the conquest of Canaan actually begins, that is indeed how the term is used in the reports of Israelite victories. We must allow the more precise passages to inform the generalizations.

---

and Joshua were the only two who believed that Yahweh would give victory over the giant Anakim and were therefore allowed to enter the land forty years later (Num 14:30). Part of the original spying account in Num 13:22 notes that the spies encountered "Ahiman, Sheshai, and Talmai the descendants of Anak" in Hebron. The same three individuals are listed in Josh 15:14 as being driven out by the returning Caleb. Were these the only Anakim in Hebron? Were these three names representative of lineages? The latter seems likelier than the former, because the same three names surface again in Judg 1:10, where they are defeated by the tribe of Judah. Either the same three Anakim (or their families) escaped death at the hands of Caleb (note they were "driven out" in Josh 15:14) only to meet their demise later, or these names are emblematic of tribes (or clans) which were part of the Nephilim bloodline targeted by Israelites in both Joshua's wars and the efforts noted in the book of Judges after Joshua's death. If we presume the situation in Hebron is representative of the situation in Canaan, then various cities mentioned in the conquest narratives may have been home to various clans or family groups belonging to Anak. One certainly does not get the picture of huge numbers of Anakim, much less the entire population of Canaan being Anakim. Doak references Deut 9:1–2 and Josh 11:21–22 as evidence that the Anakim were conceived of as ubiquitous throughout the land (Brian Doak, *The Last of the Rephaim: Conquest and Cataclysm in the Heroic Ages of Ancient Israel*, Ilex Series 7 [Cambridge: Harvard University Press, 2013], 73–74). In my view, this is an overreading of these passages. Deut 9:1–2 can quite easily be read as first referencing the general population (v. 1—"nations greater and mightier than you"—note the plural) and then singling out the Anakim who live among those nations (v. 2). The statement in Josh 11:21–22 that "Joshua came at that time and cut off the Anakim from the hill country, from Hebron, from Debir, from Anab, and from all the hill country of Judah, and from all the hill country of Israel" does not require the conclusion that Anakim are to be equated with the entire population of Canaan. Rather, it could just as well mean that *wherever* Anakim were encountered within Canaan they were eliminated. In other words, the passages can speak to how the Anakim had permeated Canaan without making the term a virtual synonym for "the nations" within Canaan.

9. The term is also used in two passages in Deuteronomy whose context is actually *post*-conquest. Deut 13:12–18 presupposes Israelite occupation ("one of *your* cities") and is a command for *kherem* against anyone who would seek to make Israelites worship other gods. Deut 20:10–18 is concerned with rules for future wars when Israel is settled in the land. The passage has Israel in possession of chariots (a weapon they did not have coming out of Egypt) and allows Israel to offer peace to targeted cities. The *kherem* ensues when peace is rejected. The logic (threat of apostasy and idolatry) is the same.

THE WARS OF JOSHUA

Soon after the victories over Sihon and Og, Moses died without ever having stepped into the promised land. The leadership of the nation passed to Joshua (Num 27:18–23; Deut 34:9; Josh 1), who was directed by God to spy out the land (Josh 2), then cross the Jordan from the site of Shittim (Josh 3–4), and renew the covenant between God and Israel (Josh 5). The conquest began at Jericho, a central location in the land. A central military campaign would have the immediate effect of separating the cities of the north and south regions. It was a strategy of divide and conquer.

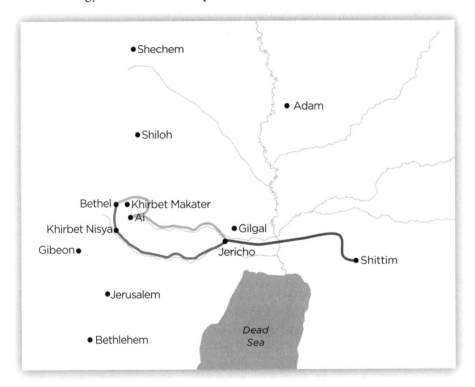

As with Jericho (Josh 6:18, 21), the city of Ai was "devoted to destruction" after the spiritual failure of the Israelite Achan (Josh 8:26).[10] Joshua then moved south into the hill country, part of the land that the spies had surveyed and where they had seen Anakim. The southern campaign is described in Joshua 10.

---

10. The conquest had begun at Jericho, a city in the Jordan River Valley, a few miles north of the Dead Sea, into which the Jordan enters. The city is thus in one of the locations spied out forty years earlier. Since these locations were put under *kherem* (when others were not), we have to conclude that some Anakim were known to live in these cities based on the wording of Num 13:28–29.

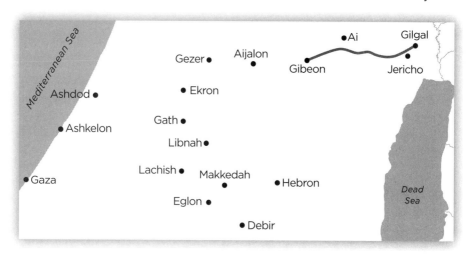

28 As for Makkedah, Joshua captured it on that day and struck it, and its king, with the edge of the sword. He devoted to destruction every person in it; he left none remaining. And he did to the king of Makkedah just as he had done to the king of Jericho.

29 Then Joshua and all Israel with him passed on from Makkedah to Libnah and fought against Libnah. **30** And the LORD gave it also and its king into the hand of Israel. And he struck it with the edge of the sword, and every person in it; he left none remaining in it. And he did to its king as he had done to the king of Jericho.

31 Then Joshua and all Israel with him passed on from Libnah to Lachish and laid siege to it and fought against it. **32** And the LORD gave Lachish into the hand of Israel, and he captured it on the second day and struck it with the edge of the sword, and every person in it, as he had done to Libnah.

33 Then Horam king of Gezer came up to help Lachish. And Joshua struck him and his people, until he left none remaining.

34 Then Joshua and all Israel with him passed on from Lachish to Eglon. And they laid siege to it and fought against it. **35** And they captured it on that day, and struck it with the edge of the sword. And he devoted every person in it to destruction that day, as he had done to Lachish.

36 Then Joshua and all Israel with him went up from Eglon to Hebron. And they fought against it **37** and captured it and struck it with the edge of the sword, and its king and its towns, and every person in it. He left none remaining, as he had done to Eglon, and devoted it to destruction and every person in it.

38 Then Joshua and all Israel with him turned back to Debir and fought against it **39** and he captured it with its king and all its towns. And they struck them with the edge of the sword and devoted to destruction every person in it; he left none remaining. Just as he had done to Hebron and to Libnah and its king, so he did to Debir and to its king.

⁴⁰So Joshua struck the whole land, the hill country and the Negeb and the lowland and the slopes, and all their kings. He left none remaining, but devoted to destruction all that breathed, just as the LORD God of Israel commanded. ⁴¹And Joshua struck them from Kadesh-barnea as far as Gaza, and all the country of Goshen, as far as Gibeon. ⁴²And Joshua captured all these kings and their land at one time, because the LORD God of Israel fought for Israel. ⁴³Then Joshua returned, and all Israel with him, to the camp at Gilgal (Josh 10:28–43 ESV).

This passage tells us on five occasions that the inhabitants of these hill country cities were "devoted to destruction," along with six editorial comments that Joshua "left none remaining." The strategy of the Israelites is apparent at this point. Israel's *kherem* focused on those regions where Anakim were known to live in the land (the Num 13:28–29 report) and, therefore, certain cities in

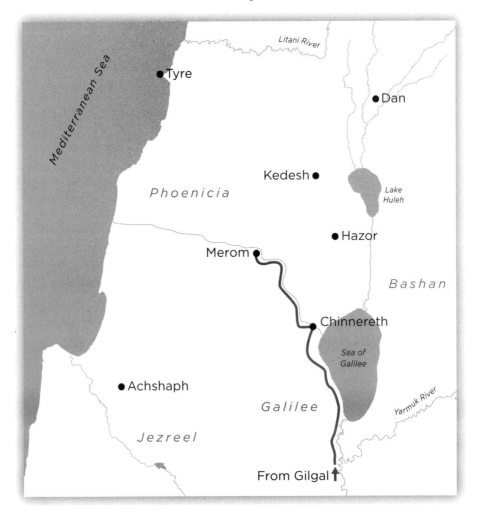

those regions. Other people living in those regions and towns were naturally also under threat—they were in the wrong place at the wrong time. Joshua and his army didn't check identification, so to speak, or interview the occupants to weed out non-Anakim. When they arrived at a place under *kherem*, the intent was to leave no Anakim alive.

After the invasion of the southern hill country, Joshua went north and carried out the same plan.

The northern campaign is described in Joshua 11. Various people groups are named in the descriptions there who also appear in Num 13:28–29, where it is explained that the twelve Israelite spies had seen Anakim (Hittites, Jebusites, and Amorites; v. 3). Interestingly, Joshua ran into warriors from nearby Mount Hermon in the region of Bashan as well (v. 4). Once again, we are told that Joshua's armies "left none remaining" (v. 8) and devoted the cities of the region to destruction (v. 12).

The destruction seems wanton, but it isn't. The logic of the *kherem* emerges in Joshua 11:21–23 (ESV).

> 21 And Joshua came at that time and cut off the Anakim from the hill country, from Hebron, from Debir, from Anab, and from all the hill country of Judah, and from all the hill country of Israel. Joshua devoted them to destruction with their cities. 22 There was none of the Anakim left in the land of the people of Israel. Only in Gaza, in Gath, and in Ashdod did some remain. 23 So Joshua took the whole land, according to all that the LORD had spoken to Moses. And Joshua gave it for an inheritance to Israel according to their tribal allotments. And the land had rest from war.

This passage makes it evident that the target of *kherem* was the Anakim. It is crucial to notice that this passage refers to the "hill country of Judah" and the "hill country of Israel." That is language that would only make sense *after* the tribal allotments under Joshua—which had not yet taken place—and *after* the country of Israel split into two under Rehoboam, an event centuries yet *future*. The book of Joshua very obviously was written long after the events it describes. The anachronistic language is important. The "hill country of Judah" refers to the southern campaign (Judah was the southern kingdom in the divided monarchy after Rehoboam). The "hill country of Israel" speaks to the northern campaign (Israel was the northern kingdom in the divided monarchy). Joshua 11:21–23 tells us that *in both campaigns the object was the Anakim*.[11]

---

11. This passage therefore adds another clarification to the generalized description of Num 13:28–29. As discussed earlier, the spies had made the blanket statement that they had seen Anakim *wherever* they had gone. One of those locations was the "hill country" where the Hittites, Jebusites, and Amorites dwelled. These

As if this were not enough of an indication to draw the reader's attention to the Nephilim bloodlines, the writer adds in verse 22, "Only in Gaza, in Gath, and in Ashdod" did some of the Anakim remain. Why add that note? Gaza, Gath, and Ashdod were Philistine cities. One needs only to recall Goliath of Gath and his brothers to understand that the writer of Joshua is setting the stage for the fact that annihilation of these bloodlines would continue into David's era.[12]

SUPERNATURAL, NOT BIZARRE, ORIENTATION

The point of this brief reconstruction is not that Israelites took only the lives of the remnant of the giant clans. Others were certainly slain. The point is that the rationale for *kherem* annihilation was the specific elimination of the

---

people groups are noted in Joshua 11's description of the northern campaign. Deut 9:1–2 seems to support this approach, as the Anakim of verse 2 appear to be cast as a subset of the population described in verse 1. Deut 9:1–2 is important in this regard as it is included in those passages that provide the rationale for the conquest. Not only were the Israelites outnumbered by an entrenched population (Deut 9:1), but the giant Anakim they had feared back in Num 13:33 had to be dealt with (Deut 9:2). Hendel makes a similar point about the giant clans: "The function of the Nephilim-Rephaim in all of these [biblical] traditions is constant—they exist in order to be wiped out: by the flood, by Moses, by David, and others.... Note that the giant aboriginal inhabitants of Seir, Ammon, and Gaza are also utterly annihilated, generally by Yahweh (Deut 2:12, 20–23); see also Deut 9:1–3; Amos 2:9" (Ronald S. Hendel, "Of Demigods and the Deluge: Toward and Interpretation of Genesis 6:1–4," *Journal of Biblical Literature* 106.1 [March 1987]: 21 and note 40).

12. See Josh 13:2–3; 1 Sam 17:4, 23; 2 Sam 21:15–22; 1 Chr 20:4–8. It is interesting to note that the Philistines are known from ancient texts outside the Bible to have been one of the Sea Peoples. The Sea Peoples were seafaring people from the Aegean who tried to invade (with varying degrees of success) the coast of Canaan and Egypt in roughly 1200–1150 BC. One of their points of origin was Caphtor, an island in the Aegean. Jeremiah 47:4 and Amos 9:7 explicitly connect the Philistines with Caphtor. The Caphtorim are among the peoples discussed in Deut 2:20–23 in connection with the Anakim. Goliath was from Gath, a Philistine city. The Old Testament has other giants from Gath (2 Sam 21:16, 18, 20, 22; 1 Chr 20:4, 6, 8), descendants of Rapha, a name that many scholars connect to the Rephaim (see B. Becking, "Rapha," in *Dictionary of Deities and Demons in the Bible*, 2nd ed. [ed. Karel van der Toorn, Bob Becking, and Pieter W. van der Horst; Leiden; Boston; Cologne; Grand Rapids, MI; Cambridge: Brill; Eerdmans, 1999], 687). The name "Goliath" is either Luwian or Lydian, that is, deriving from one of the cultures that are connected to the Aegean region (see Aharon Kempinski, "Some Philistine Names from the Kingdom of Gaza," *Israel Exploration Journal* 37:1 [1987]: 20–24). An inscription from Gath has surfaced with what appears to be the name "Goliath" on it (see Aren M. Maeir, Stefan J. Wimmer, Alexander Zukerman, and Aaron Demsky, "A Late Iron Age I/Early Iron Age II Old Canaanite Inscription from Tell eṣ-Ṣâfî /Gath, Israel: Palaeography, Dating, and Historical-Cultural Significance," *Bulletin of the American Schools of Oriental Research* 351 [2008]: 39–71 [esp. 48–50]). Lastly, fifty years ago E. C. B. MacLaurin put forth the interesting thesis that biblical ʾanaqim (ענקים) might be equitable to Greek (digamma) *anx*, a title used of gods and mythic heroes in Greek literature (MacLaurin, "Anak/ʾανξ," *Vetus Testamentum* 15:4 [1965]: 468–74). MacLaurin further argues for a correlation of ʾanaqim and *seranim*, a biblical term used of Philistine military governors (e.g., Judg 3:3; 16:5). Given the apparent relationship of the Anakim with the Philistines in several biblical passages, and the classification of the Philistines with the Sea Peoples from the Aegean, these correlations, though speculative, deserve consideration. See the companion website for more detail. It seems certain that some relationship existed between these people groups, though what precisely that isn't clear. It also seems fair to suggest that in the context of a local flood perspective, these connections provide a possible historical trajectory for giants after the flood.

descendants of the Nephilim. Ridding the land of these bloodlines was the motivation.[13] If Numbers 13:28–29 is to be believed, the Anakim were scattered throughout the land of Canaan. Joshua 11:21–23 makes it clear that these were the peoples targeted for complete elimination, not every last Canaanite.

In point of fact, the conquest narratives utilize other verbs besides *kharam* that are not necessarily words for taking life.[14] This indicates that *kherem* was not the goal of every engagement. The picture that emerges when all the descriptions are woven together was that, when Israelite soldiers encountered a member of the giant clans or others known to be descended from those clans, they were under *kherem*. Others might be killed in warfare, but their lives were not required by the supernatural-theological orientation that is telegraphed in Num 13:26–33, Deut 2–3, and Josh 11:21–23.

The unusual size of these people groups was attributed to divine origin, something a belief in the supernatural must allow. It is not, however, an excuse for a reading of the text that is cartoonish or bizarre.[15]

How tall were the biblical giants? The only measurement for a giant that exists in the biblical text is that of Goliath.[16] The traditional (Masoretic) Hebrew text has him at "six cubits and a span" (1 Sam 17:4), roughly 9 feet, 9 inches. The Dead Sea Scroll reading of 1 Sam 17:4 disagrees and has Goliath at four cubits and a span, or 6 feet 6 inches. Virtually all scholars consider the Dead Sea Scrolls reading superior and authentic.[17]

---

13. The idea of *kherem* is that of devoting something wholly to God. As Naudé notes, the verb "involves consecration of something or someone as a permanent and definitive offering for the sanctuary; or in war, the consecration of a city and its inhabitants to destruction and the carrying out of this destruction" ("חָרַם (I), חֵרֶם (I)," 276). The logic is that the elimination of these targeted bloodlines, perceived as the spawn of hostile gods, was a gesture of burnt offering back to Yahweh. Not only had other gods encroached on Yahweh's portion (Deut 32:9), violating the boundaries of their own allotment, but they had raised up warriors to prevent Yahweh's children from inheriting his land. The only way to ensure occupation of the land was to eliminate the giant-warrior clans raised up to prevent that occupation. *Kherem* was a fierce judgment on any lethal threat by other gods against Yahweh's own children in Yahweh's own land.

14. That is, they lack the specificity of *kharam* in that regard. When the biblical text in certain instances says that "no one remained" in a city or region, it cannot be assumed that this means everyone died (i.e., was a victim of *kherem*) unless that clarification is added. They may have been driven away or fled, since the commands of conquest utilize other vocabulary: *garash* ("to drive out": Exod 23:28, 29, 30, 31; 33:2; Deut 33:27; Josh 24:12, 18); *yarash* ("to dispossess, drive out": Exod 34:24; Num 21:32; 33:52, 53, 55; Josh 3:10; 12:1; 13:6; 17:12, 13; 23:5, 9).

15. I speak here of discussions (usually online, and never under peer review) that have the biblical giants tens or even hundreds of feet tall. There is no justification for these sorts of ideas in the biblical text.

16. Recall from chapter 23 that the dimensions for Og's bed are not a reliable indicator of his own size. The dimensions are an overt link back to the sacred marriage bed of Marduk, a deity whose own size is of mythological proportions. While there is no doubt that Deut 3:11 has Og as a Rephaim giant, we cannot know how tall he was from his bed.

17. The smaller size is also the reading of the Septuagint. See the comments in P. Kyle McCarter Jr., *I Samuel: A New Translation with Introduction, Notes and Commentary*, Anchor Yale Bible 8 (New Haven: Yale University Press, 2008), 286; Generally, the Dead Sea Scroll readings for Samuel are regarded as superior

Archaeological work across the ancient Near East confirms that six and one-half feet tall was, by the standards of the day, a giant.[18] One scholar of Israelite culture notes that the average height of an ancient Israelite in the patriarchal period was around five feet.[19] Famed biblical archaeologist G. Ernest Wright notes, "At Gezer were found at least one hundred skeletons from about 3000 B.C. And from various graves and deposits there are many other remains of the third and second millennia, especially from Megiddo, Jericho, and Gezer.... There are no remains of any aborigines of abnormal size."[20] This last comment is noteworthy since these are areas where one would expect giant clan settlements. To date, there is no human skeletal evidence from Syria-Palestine (Canaan) that shows extraordinary height.[21] The same is true of the Mediterranean world of the biblical time period.[22]

---

to the Masoretic text when the two disagree, especially when the scrolls also coincide with the Septuagint. Bergen's thoughts are representative: "Serious concerns—and, frequently, highly negative evaluations—have arisen concerning the quality of text transmitted to us in the MT.... The majority of modern researchers who have studied this issue conclude that in most cases where there is disagreement in the wording of a passage, the LXX's reading is superior to that of the MT" (Robert D. Bergen, *1, 2 Samuel*, New American Commentary 7 [Nashville: Broadman & Holman, 1996], 26).

18. See Daniel J. Hays, "The Height of Goliath: A Response to Clyde Billington," *Journal of the Evangelical Theological Society* 50.3 (2007): 509–16. See the companion website for my own interaction with Billington.

19. Victor Matthews, *Manners and Customs in the Bible*, rev. ed. (Peabody, MA: Hendrickson, 1991), 3.

20. G. Ernest Wright, "Troglodytes and Giants in Palestine," *Journal of Biblical Literature* 57.3 (September 1938): 305–09 (esp. 307). For the archaeological reports, see A. Macalister, "Report on the Human Remains Found at Gezer, 1902–3," *Palestine Exploration Quarterly* 35.4 (1903): 322–26. See also Yossi Nagar, "Human Osteological Database at the Israel Antiquities Authority: Overview and Some Samples of Use," *Bioarchaeology of the Near East* 5 (2011): 1–18, http://anthropology.uw.edu.pl/05/bne-05-01.pdf; Baruch Arensburg, "The Peoples in the Land of Israel from the Epipaleolithic to Present Times: A Study Based on Their Skeletal Remains" (PhD diss., Tel-Aviv University, 1973); B. Arensburg and Y. Rak, "Jewish Skeletal Remains from the Period of the Kings of Judaea," *Palestine Exploration Quarterly* 117.1 (1985): 30–34.

21. A number of amateur researchers and websites have asserted that two seven-foot female skeletons were found in a twelfth-century-BC cemetery at Tell es-Sa'idiyeh on the east bank of the Jordan. This assertion comes from a commentary on Deuteronomy written by Jeffrey Tigay of the University of Pennsylvania (J. Tigay, *Deuteronomy*, JPS Torah Commentary [Philadelphia: Jewish Publication Society, 1996], 17). Tigay gave the following footnote information after mentioning this alleged discovery: "The discovery in Jordan was reported by Jonathan Tubb of the British Museum in a lecture at the University of Pennsylvania in 1995; see the British Museum's forthcoming *Excavations at Tell es-Sa'idiyeh* III/2." As it turns out, this is not true. I wrote professor Tubb at the British Museum to ask if he had published a report on these two skeletons, and I mentioned Tigay's footnote. He replied (April 29, 2014): "I'm sorry to disappoint, but I'm afraid the footnote resulted from a misunderstood comment I made at a lecture on Sa'idiyeh I gave at Penn some time ago. We don't, in fact, have any unusually large skeletons from the Sa'idiyeh cemetery. We are in the last stages of preparing the final report on the graves, and all of the metrics will be contained in the volume." Readers can visit the companion website for a screenshot of the original email. To date, there are no human skeletons from Canaan that show bizarre height.

22. Readers are urged to read the pioneering research of Adrienne Mayor in this regard (*The First Fossil Hunters: Paleontology in Greek and Roman Times* (Princeton: Princeton University Press, 2001). Mayor surveys all the reports in classical Greek and Roman texts about sighting of skeletal remains of human giants and then correlates the location with paleontological discoveries of the bones of dinosaurs and large

This is no surprise. The ancient Israelites, like other peoples of Canaan at the time, did not embalm their dead. Consequently, human skeletal remains from the first two millennia BC are not common. Of the millions of people that lived in ancient Syria-Palestine during that two-thousand-year span, a few thousand skeletons have survived. The situation in ancient Egypt is proportionally better due to embalming. Moreover, people who were embalmed tended to be among the elite class, which meant their diets were better, which in turn meant better health and optimal growth. Based on examination of mummies, the average height of an Egyptian male was between 5 and 5.5 feet.[23]

This is not to say that there is no evidence external to the Bible for unusually tall people in Canaan during the biblical period. One Egyptian text from the period of Ramesses II, described by Pritchard in a chapter entitled "Problems of Asiatic Geography," specifically makes that point. The text reads at one point:

> The narrow valley is dangerous with Bedouin, hidden under the bushes. Some of them are of four or five cubits [*from*] *their noses to the heel*, and fierce of face. Their hearts are not mild, and they do not listen to wheedling.[24]

The picture that emerges from the biblical text and archaeology is that vestiges of the Nephilim bloodline were scattered throughout Canaan among a number of other people groups. The aim of the conquest was to drive out all the inhabitants and eliminate these bloodlines in the process. The thinking is foreign to us, but it was part of the supernatural worldview of the biblical writers.

---

prehistoric mammals (e.g., mastodons) to demonstrate that these ancient reports were misidentifications of animal remains unknown to people in the classical period. Mayor conducts the same sort of research for North American reports of giant bones in a follow-up volume, *Fossil Legends of the First Americans* (Princeton: Princeton University Press, 2005). Paleontologists have done similar research as well. See James L. Hayward, "Fossil Proboscidians and Myths of Giant Men," *Transactions of the Nebraska Academy of Sciences and Affiliated Societies* 12 (1984): 95–102. The same sort of mistakes in identification occurred in modern times in centuries before paleontological science achieved the level of expertise it now enjoys. In 1643 what were thought to be the skeletal remains of a giant man were discovered in Belgium. Years later the bones were identified as thigh bones from a mammoth (Taika Helola Dahlbom, "A Mammoth History: The Extraordinary Journey of Two Thighbones," *Endeavour* 31.3 (2007): 110–14.

23. Sonia R. Zakrewski, "Variation in Ancient Egyptian Stature and Body Proportions," *American Journal of Physical Anthropology* 121.3 (2003): 219–29; P. H. K. Gray, "The Radiography of Mummies of Ancient Egyptians," *Journal of Human Evolution* 2.1 (1973): 51–53; Michelle H. Raxter, Christopher B. Ruff, Ayman Azab, Moushira Erfan, Muhammad Soliman, and Aly El-Sawaf, "Stature Estimation in Ancient Egyptians: A New Technique Based on Anatomical Reconstruction of Stature," *American Journal of Physical Anthropology* 136.2 (2008): 147–55.

24. James Bennett Pritchard, ed., *The Ancient Near East: An Anthology of Texts and Pictures*, 3rd ed., with supplement (Princeton: Princeton University Press, 1969), 477. "Four to five cubits" would be between 7 and 9 feet, the known range for unusually tall humans in modern experience. This Egyptian text is interesting since Ramesses II is the pharaoh most biblical scholars presume was the pharaoh of the exodus.

Israel failed, of course. It would be centuries before the sort of kingdom envisioned by Moses and Joshua would arise. And that was mostly a mess. We tend to process the Old Testament after Joshua as just a bunch of genealogies with some murder, sex, and scandal thrown in to keep our attention. There's more to it than that—a lot more.

Section Summary

The wars of conquest under Moses and Joshua were supposed to cleanse the land of a competing divine bloodline and install Yahweh's own children, his inheritance, into the place he had allotted for them. Yahweh's rule on earth was to be reconstituted in Canaan.

Frankly, it didn't seem much like Eden.

In contrast to the idyllic beginnings in Eden, the installation of Israel into the land had been violent. Those means were necessary to revive Yahweh's original vision in a fallen world, a world full of divine and human conflict, of free imagers seeking their own will, not the will of the creator. Yahweh could have just spoken Israel into existence in the land. He could have acted unilaterally as high sovereign to resuscitate his rule on earth. But Yahweh's decisions in the original Eden meant that he would not overturn human (or divine) freedom in his imagers. Yahweh had chosen to accomplish his ends through imagers loyal to him against imagers who weren't. This commitment to humanity, his original imagers on earth, is one often-missed reason why, when humanity (Israel) failed to restore God's rule, God took matters into his own hands *by becoming human* in Jesus Christ.

Consequently, in a world governed by other gods who had become hostile rivals in the wake of Yahweh's judgment at Babel, Yahweh's presence was unwelcome. There would be war. There would be death. The land had to be repossessed and made holy. Canaan would be Yahweh's beachhead of cosmic geography from which Israel could fulfill its mission. Israel would be a kingdom of priests, a conduit through which the disinherited nations of the earth would see Israel's prosperity. The surrounding peoples would hear of Israel's God, see his unmatched power, and seek his covenantal love. The nations would be reclaimed, not by force, but by free imagers choosing to turn toward the true God—the creator and Lord of all.

At least that was the plan.

We know that Israel ultimately failed. The seeds of that failure were sown in the events of the conquest. For whatever reasons—lack of faith or lack of effort, or both—Israel failed to drive out their enemies. They allowed vestiges of the targeted bloodlines to remain in the land in the Philistine cities. They chose to coexist (Judg 1:27–36). The visible Yahweh, the Angel, asks the rhetorical question, "Why would you do such a thing?" and then announces the consequence: "Now I say, I will not drive them out from before you; they will become as thorns for you, and their gods will be a trap for you" (Judg 2:2–3). The name of the place where he uttered these words was thereafter appropriately remembered as Bochim, a Hebrew word that means "weeping" (Judg 2:5).

Not surprisingly, the rest of Israel's history is a sordid roller-coaster ride. Loyalty to Yahweh—refusing to worship any other god—was of course at the heart of salvation in the Old Testament. Possession of the land is linked to this loyalty as far back as the Abrahamic covenant (Gen 17:1–2, 8–10; 22:15–18). The covenant at Sinai reinforced that connection (Lev 26; Deut 4:25–27, 39–40; 11:18–24). It would be due to failure in this loyalty that Israel was sent into exile—expelled from the land of promise.

But Yahweh wouldn't give up entirely on Israel. The book of Judges makes it clear that he would respond to both repentance and apostasy with equal consistency. The visible Yahweh did show up from time to time, as in the cases of Gideon (Judg 6) and Samson (Judg 13). But it was only with Israel's last judge, the faithful Samuel, that Yahweh's appearances became less rare.

Israel's monarchy would suffer through Saul and eventually flourish under David and his son Solomon. But the monarchy thereafter crumbled, dragging God's intended kingdom into centuries of apostasy and civil war before ending in divine judgment.

The terrible end would produce theological lessons: Eden cannot come and survive without Yahweh's constant presence—as had been the case in the original Eden. The kingdom of God cannot be built with human hands. As Israel reached the final stages of failure, God announced through the prophets that plans had changed. Restoring Eden would require God's enduring presence in the hearts of his children, and an ideal king who would remain loyal to Yahweh. God himself would supply the second Adam, the son of David, the perfect ruling servant.

Old Testament history after the conquest is the story of what might have been. But the Old Testament after the book of Joshua shouldn't be read like a protracted obituary. The spiritual war doesn't end. The biblical writers have messages to communicate against the backdrop of their supernatural worldview. The stories of prophets and kings aren't just a biblical soap opera. There's an unseen reality show going on at the same time. What's playing on that channel will occupy us the rest of the way through the Old Testament.

PART 6

THUS SAYS THE LORD

CHAPTER 26

Mountains and Valleys

Penetrating into Canaan and establishing itself as an independent state didn't solve the problem of cosmic geography for Israel.[1] If anything, it sharpened the conflict. Not only was Israel surrounded by hostile nations and their gods, but there were also pockets of divine resistance from within.

The period of the judges and the monarchy form a tale of military and spiritual struggle. On the ground, the Israelites were still hamstrung by the presence of the vestiges of the Rephaim/Nephilim who had escaped annihilation in the conquest and by incursions from enemies on the peripheries. Toward the end of the last chapter I briefly noted Joshua 11:21–23, which informed us that the eradication of the Anakim had not been total. The writer of Joshua noted in that passage that some Anakim were known to live in cities that would later become cities of the Philistines—Israel's chief enemy during the united monarchy. Spiritually, these conflicts had high stakes, as they signaled the infiltration of other gods siphoning off Israelite worshipers into their own cults. Since believing loyalty to Yahweh was foundational to Yahweh's protection and remaining in the land, the spiritual battle was just as much a threat as the physical one.

The books of Judges, Samuel, and Kings clearly describe the military conflict. That's the one that's easy to see through modern eyes and with a modern worldview. But beneath the surface there's a war of a different nature raging. We'll cover a few examples in this chapter.

---

1. Earlier, in chapter 15, we briefly discussed cosmic geographical thinking in passages from the historical books and the period of the monarchy (e.g., 1 Sam 26:17–19; 2 Kgs 5:15–19).

HOLY GROUND

When Moses was told to construct the tabernacle and its equipment, the Bible tells us that God revealed a pattern for doing so ("And you will erect the tabernacle according to its plan, which you have been shown on the mountain"—Exod 26:30). Earlier, in chapter 22, we discussed how the tabernacle description aligned with divine abodes of other gods, namely from Ugarit. We need to revisit the tabernacle here, since its history prepares us for the more permanent temple—the place where the Name would dwell.

The implication of God having Moses follow a divine pattern is that the tabernacle tent structure on earth was to be a copy of the heavenly tent—as in heaven, so on earth. The heavenly tent prototype was the heavens themselves, as Isaiah 40:22 tells us ("He is the one who sits above the circle of the earth, and its inhabitants are like grasshoppers; the one who stretches out the heavens like a veil and spreads them out like a tent to live in"). In other words, the heavens and earth were conceived of as Yahweh's true tabernacle or temple. The earthly dwelling place erected by the Israelites mimicked the grand habitation of the cosmos.[2]

The tabernacle was not only the abode of Yahweh; it was also his throne room. Yahweh sits above the circle of the earth, in his heavenly tent, on his throne above the waters that are above "the firmament," and rests his feet on the earth ("Thus says the LORD: 'Heaven is my throne, and the earth is my footstool'"—Isaiah 66:1 ESV).[3] The ark of the covenant was there, the sacred object associated with Yahweh's presence—his Name.[4]

---

2. A number of scholars have devoted attention to the way the cosmos, tabernacle, and temple are described in similar terms in the Old Testament. See, for example, Moshe Weinfeld, "Sabbath, Temple and the Enthronement of the Lord," *Mélanges bibliques et orientaux en l'honneur de M. Henri Cazelles* (ed. A. Caquot, and M. Delcor; Alter Orient und Altes Testament 212; Kevelaer and Neukirchen-Vluyn, 1981), 501–12; Daniel T. Lioy, "The Garden of Eden as a Primordial Temple or Sacred Space for Humankind," *Conspectus: The Journal of the South African Theological Seminary* 10 (2010): 25–57; Gordon Wenham, "Sanctuary Symbolism in the Garden of Eden Story," in *Cult and Cosmos: Tilting toward a Temple-Centered Biblical Theology*, Biblical Tools and Studies 18 (ed. L. Michael Morales; Leuven: Peeters, 2014), 161–66.

3. For example, see Job 9:8; Psa 104:2. See the companion website for more on Israelite cosmology.

4. In 2 Sam 6:1–2 (cf. 1 Sam 4:4; Jer 7:12) we read: "David again gathered all the chosen men in Israel, thirty thousand. David got up and went and all the people who were with him, from Baale-judah to bring up from there the ark of God which is called the name, the name of Yahweh of hosts [אֲשֶׁר־נִקְרָא שֵׁם שֵׁם יְהוָה צְבָאוֹת], upon which the cherubim sit."

The word *shem* (שֵׁם) appears twice in this verse—the ark is called the name, the name of Yahweh of hosts. The point is that the ark is identified with the Name, who is Yahweh, since Yahweh is the one seated on the cherubim. Many English translations obscure the Hebrew text here, rendering something like "which is called by the name of the LORD of hosts," which omits one of the occurrences of *shem*. The reason is that many scholars consider the dual occurrence of *shem* to be an accidental repetition by a scribe, what textual critics call dittography (see for example, P. Kyle McCarter Jr., *II Samuel: A New Translation with Introduction, Notes, and Commentary*, Anchor Yale Bible Commentary 9 [New Haven: Yale University Press, 1964,

The tabernacle traveled with Israel during the entire journey to the promised land. Once Israel penetrated the land, the ark of the covenant (and therefore the tabernacle structure) was situated at Bethel (Judg 20:27), a name that means "house of God." You know Bethel by now. It was the place where Jacob had his encounter with Yahweh and the angels of his council atop the "ladder" (i.e., a ziggurat; Gen 28:10–22). It was the place where the "angels of God" appeared to him again when he was fleeing from Esau, his brother (32:1–5). It was the place where Jacob built an altar and a pillar to commemorate the appearance of the visible Yahweh (31:13; cf. 35:1–7).[5]

Sometime later the tabernacle moved from Bethel to Shiloh. Once that move occurred, it was said that the "house of God" was Shiloh (Judg 18:31; 1 Sam 1:24; Jer 7:12). The Old Testament indicates that Shiloh became the place of sacrifice (Judg 21:19; 1 Sam 1:3). At Shiloh we see the boy Samuel encounter the physicalized Yahweh, the Word (1 Sam 3).

Eli the priest later foolishly sent the ark of the covenant out to battle, and it fell into the hands of the Philistines, who took it to Ashdod and installed it in the temple of their god, Dagon. In a fascinating (and funny) incident of cosmic geography, Yahweh's presence destroyed the statue of Dagon. First Samuel 5:5 describes the reaction of the Philistine priests: "Therefore the priests of Dagon and all who come into the house of Dagon do not tread on the threshold of Dagon in Ashdod until this very day." This threshold was now Yahweh's geography—they dared not walk on it.[6]

Eventually the ark was brought to Jerusalem. At first, David placed it in

---

2008], 163). While this is possible, there is no inherent interpretive problem with the Masoretic Text as it stands in view of the evidence for divine co-regency (the two Yahwehs) already noted. That the ark would be called the name is understandable, since the ark was a placeholder for the very presence of Yahweh, who is the name. The same association (note the anthropomorphic language) is conveyed in 2 Sam 7:2, where the *ark* is said to *dwell* in a tent.

5. Bethel was also the place where Deborah the prophetess, who sat under the terebinth tree, lived (Judg 4:5). I have omitted subjects like divination from much of the book. See the companion website for how that subject is informed by the divine council and Israel's supernatural worldview.

6. In light of the supernatural-theological connections between the biblical text and Mesopotamia, which we've discussed elsewhere, it is worth noting that Dagon had Mesopotamian roots as well. Healey writes: "Dagan is one of the most persistent deities of the world of Semitic religion. His worship is well attested from the third millennium BCE in the Ebla texts and he appears in Sargonic personal names, but neither source gives any hint of the precise nature of this deity…. Sargon attributed his conquest of Upper/Western Mesopotamia to Dagan and worshipped him in Tuttul. This confirms Dagan's regional authority, leaving southern Mesopotamia to other deities, including Enlil. He is well attested in the Mari texts as one of the principal deities of the Amorites of Old Babylonian Upper Mesopotamia" (see J. F. Healey, "Dagon," in *Dictionary of Deities and Demons in the Bible*, 2nd ed. [ed. Karel van der Toorn, Bob Becking, and Pieter W. van der Horst; Leiden; Boston; Cologne; Grand Rapids, MI; Cambridge: Brill; Eerdmans, 1999], 216–17).

a temporary tent he had made for it (2 Sam 6:17; 2 Chr 1:3–4), under the assumption that he was going to build a temple for it.[7]

Like the tabernacle, the temple contains striking imagery associated with Eden. Eden was a lush garden and a holy mountain.[8] The tabernacle's tent enclosure contained furnishings and decorations that evoked Edenic imagery.[9] All of these motifs—tent, mountain, garden—come together in the temple, the fixed place where Yahweh was considered to dwell and order the earth and the heavens with his council.

THE TEMPLE AS COSMIC TENT DWELLING

Many Bible readers assume that once the temple was built the tabernacle was forgotten or perhaps permanently dismantled. In reality, *the tabernacle tent, with its holy of holies, was moved into the temple with the ark.*

Recall that within the tabernacle was another building, completely covered with curtains, called the holy place. This room was divided in two by a veil, behind which was the holy of holies, the room that contained the ark (Exod 26).

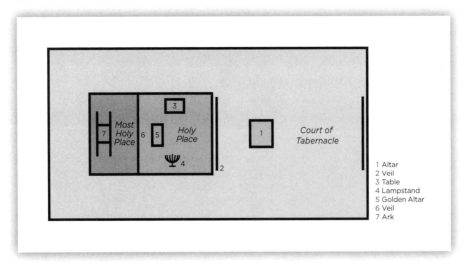

---

7. David later removed it during the time of civil unrest caused by his son Absalom (2 Sam 15:24–25). In the meantime, the place of sacrifice had become Gibeon (1 Kgs 3:4), where, we are told, an ancient "tent of meeting" of Moses had been moved (2 Chr 1:3 ESV). In Solomon's day, Gibeon was the high place of worship. The "tent of meeting" at Gibeon was actually the Mosaic tabernacle, since sacrifices were offered there (something that was not true of *the* tent of meeting in Moses' day). This separation of the ark at Jerusalem and the tabernacle tent at Gibeon was the situation during the time of Solomon as well, prior to Solomon's construction of the temple.

8. See chapter 6.

9. See chapter 22.

The inside of the temple also had this same type of inner room arrangement.

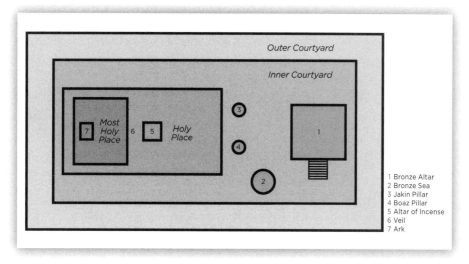

There was one major difference, though, between the inner sanctum of the temple and that of the tabernacle. The inner area of the temple had two giant cherubim in it, standing side by side, the tips of their wings stretching across to touch each other, like so:

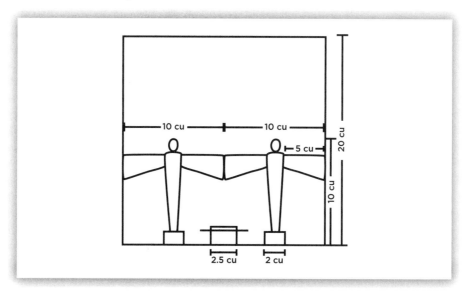

The effect of this was that the cherubim wings formed the seat of a throne for Yahweh, and the ark was his footstool. The width and height dimensions between the cherubim can accommodate the size of the tented holy of holies. This has led some scholars to theorize that the tented holy of holies was moved inside the temple, erected under and between the cherubim.[10] In the temple, the imagery of Yahweh on his throne and "living" in the ancient tent were both preserved.[11]

THE TEMPLE AS COSMIC MOUNTAIN AND GARDEN

The Temple of Yahweh in Israel was naturally associated with a cosmic mountain dwelling like Sinai because it was situated in Jerusalem on Mount Zion, the new Sinai.[12] Psalm 48 makes this quite clear:

> [1] Great is the LORD and greatly to be praised
> in the city of our God!

---

10. See R. E. Friedman, "Tabernacle," in *Anchor Bible Dictionary* (ed. *David Noel Freedman; New York: Doubleday, 1992),* 6:292–300; Friedman, "The Tabernacle in the Temple," *Biblical Archaeologist* 43 (1980): 241–48. Friedman seeks to incorporate more of the tabernacle structure within the temple than the holy of holies, an idea that has drawn sharp criticism (see Victor Avigdor Hurowitz, "The Form and Fate of the Tabernacle: Reflections on a Recent Proposal," *Jewish Quarterly Review* 86.1–2 [July–October 1995], 127–51). My position is only that it is coherent to see the tented holy of holies from the tabernacle within the holy of holies in Solomon's temple. According to Exod 38–39, the tented area of the tabernacle (holy place and holy of holies) measured ten cubits wide and thirty cubits long (15 feet by 45 feet). The holy of holies was a ten-cubit cube area. The corresponding spaces in Solomon's temple were larger: sixty cubits long, twenty cubits wide, and thirty cubits high (1 Kgs 6:2), with the holy of holies a twenty-cubit cube. In terms of spacing, there is no obstacle to having the tented holy of holies from the desert tabernacle within the innermost sanctum of the temple. In my view, this explains some of the "tent" language associated with the temple (see the following note). The cherubim throne graphic is from Martin Metzger, *Königsthron und Gottesthron: Thronformen und Throndarstellungen in Ägypten und im Vorderen Orient im dritten und zweiten Jahrtausend vor Christus und deren Bedeutung für das Verständis von Aussagen über den Thron im Alten Testament* (Kevelaer: Butzon and Bercker, 1985).

11. We know the tabernacle tent structure (*mishkan*) was moved inside the temple from several other considerations. 1 Kgs 8:4–8 tells us that it wasn't only the ark that was brought to the finished temple, but also the tabernacle and its accoutrements. Although the passage does not explicitly say the tent was moved inside the temple sanctum, other passages suggest that the tent and the temple were somehow co-identified. Well after the days of Solomon, 2 Chr 24:6 reports that when King Joash ordered repairs for the temple, he angrily asked, "Why have you not required the Levites to bring from Judah and Jerusalem the tax of Moses, the servant of Yahweh, and of the assembly of Israel **for the tent of the testimony**?" (emphasis added). In 2 Chr 29:3–7 (ESV, emphasis added), Hezekiah laments the disrepair of the temple. His complaint contains both temple and tabernacle tent wordings: "In the first year of his reign, in the first month, [Hezekiah] **opened the doors of the house of the LORD** and repaired them. He brought in the priests and the Levites and assembled them in the square on the east and said to them, "Hear me, Levites! Now consecrate yourselves, and consecrate the house of the LORD, the God of your fathers, and carry out the filth from the Holy Place. For our fathers have been unfaithful and have done what was evil in the sight of the LORD our God. They have forsaken him and have turned away their faces **from the tabernacle [*mishkan*] of the LORD** and turned their backs. They also shut the doors of the vestibule and put out the lamps and have not burned incense or offered burnt offerings in the Holy Place to the God of Israel." It is interesting that in Hurowitz's lengthy rejection of Friedman's proposal, none of these passages from 1 Kings and 2 Chronicles are to be found.

12. See Ronald E. Clements, "Sacred Mountains, Temples, and the Presence of God," in *Cult and Cosmos: Tilting toward a Temple-Centered Biblical Theology*, Biblical Tools and Studies 18 (ed. L. Michael Morales; Leuven: Peeters, 2014), 69–85; Richard J. Clifford, "The Temple and the Holy Mountain," in Morales, *Cult and Cosmos*, 85–98.

His holy mountain, [2]beautiful in elevation,
  is the joy of all the earth,
Mount Zion, in the far north [Lit.: heights of the north],
  the city of the great King (Psa 48:1–2 ESV).

Zechariah 8:3 (ESV) echoes the same notion: "Thus says the LORD: I have returned to Zion and will dwell [literally, "will tabernacle"; *shakan*] in the midst of Jerusalem, and Jerusalem shall be called the faithful city, and the mountain of the LORD of hosts, the holy mountain."

As anyone who has been to Jerusalem knows, Mount Zion isn't much of a mountain. It certainly isn't located in the geographical north—it's actually in the southern part of the country. So what's meant by "the heights of the north"?

This description would be a familiar one to Israel's pagan neighbors, particularly at Ugarit. It's actually taken out of their literature. The "heights of the north" (Ugaritic: "the heights of *tsaphon*") is the place where Baal lived and, supposedly, ran the cosmos at the behest of the high god El and the divine council.[13] The psalmist is stealing glory from Baal, restoring it to the One to whom it rightfully belongs—Yahweh. It's a theological and literary slap in the face, another polemic.

This explains why the description sounds odd in terms of Jerusalem's actual geography. This is why Isaiah and Micah used phrases like "the mountain of the house of Yahweh" (Isa 2:2; Mic 4:1). The description is designed to make a theological point, not a geographical one. Zion is the center of the cosmos, and Yahweh and *his* council are its king and administrators, not Baal.

The temple is also the Edenic garden, full of lush vegetation and animals. The description of the temple's construction in 1 Kings 6–7 is explicit in this regard.[14] Flowers, palm trees, gourds, cypress trees, cherubim, lions, and pomegranates all adorn the temple via its carved architectural features.

In Ezekiel's vision of the new temple (Ezek 40–48), he saw a temple built

---

13. The word for "north" in Hebrew is *tsaphon*. At Ugarit it is *tsapanu*. In both languages the term refers to geographical location and the cosmic mountain to the far north, the dwelling place of the divine council. See H. Niehr, "Zaphon," in *Dictionary of Deities and Demons in the Bible*, 2nd ed. (ed. Karel van der Toorn, Bob Becking, and Pieter W. van der Horst; Leiden; Boston; Cologne; Grand Rapids, MI; Cambridge: Brill; Eerdmans, 1999), 927–29; Richard J. Clifford, *The Cosmic Mountain in Canaan and the Old Testament*, Harvard Semitic Monographs 4 (Cambridge: Harvard University Press, 1972) 57–79, 131–60; C. Grave, "The Etymology of Northwest Semitic *ṣapānu, Ugarit Forschungen* 12 (1980): 221–29; E. Lipinski, "El's Abode," *Orientalia Lovaniensia Periodica* 2 (1971): 13–68.

14. See Lawrence E. Stager, "Jerusalem and the Garden of Eden," in Morales, *Cult and Cosmos*, 99–118; Victor A. Hurowitz, "Yhwh's Exalted House—Aspects of the Design and Symbolism of Solomon's Temple," in *Temple and Worship in Biblical Israel*, Proceedings of the Oxford Old Testament Seminar, rev. ed.; (ed. John Day; London: Bloomsbury/T & T Clark, 2007), 63–110 (esp. 87–90).

on a high mountain (40:2), whose courts were decorated with palm trees (40:31–34). The interior was decorated with more palm trees and cherubim (41:17–20.). Ezekiel's temple-garden was well watered, like Eden, since a river flowed from it that supernaturally gave life to everything else (47:1–12).

In Israel's theology, Eden, the tabernacle, Sinai, and the temple were equally the abode of Yahweh and his council. The Israelites who had the tabernacle and the temple were constantly reminded of the fact that they had the God of the cosmic mountain and the cosmic garden living in their midst, and if they obeyed him, Zion would become the kingdom domain of Yahweh, which would serve as the place to which he would regather the disinherited nations cast aside at Babel to himself. Micah 4 puts it well:

> ¹ It shall come to pass in the latter days
>> that the mountain of the house of the LORD
> shall be established as the highest of the mountains,
>> and it shall be lifted up above the hills;
> and peoples shall flow to it,
> ²   and many nations shall come, and say:
> "Come, let us go up to the mountain of the LORD,
>> to the house of the God of Jacob,
> that he may teach us his ways
>> and that we may walk in his paths."
> For out of Zion shall go forth the law,
>> and the word of the LORD from Jerusalem (Mic 4:1–2 ESV).

UNHOLY GROUND

In stark contrast to the temple, the place in Israel's cosmic-geographical thinking where heaven and earth intersected, there were sinister places within Canaan that became associated with the powers of darkness, specifically the vestiges of the Rephaim/Nephilim bloodlines.

In our earlier discussion of the conquest we came across the Rephaim. The Rephaim were giants. Deuteronomy informed us that the Anakim were considered Rephaim (Deut 2:11), as were the Zamzummim (Deut 2:20). Og of Bashan "was left from the remnant of the Rephaim" (Deut 3:11), so that "Bashan was called the land of the Rephaim" (Deut 3:13).

Joshua 11:22 tells us that the conquest had failed to eliminate all the Anakim, that some remained in the Philistine cities of Gaza, Gath, and Ashdod. The Rephaim presence persisted in the land until the time of David. The giant Goliath, who came from Gath (1 Sam 17:4, 23), was a descendant of the refugee Anakim/Rephaim. He had brothers, too, as we learn in 1 Chronicles 20:

> [4]And after this there arose a war in Gezer with the Philistines. Then Sibbecai the Hushathite struck down Sippai, one of the descendants of the Rephaim. And they were subdued. [5]And again there was war with the Philistines. And Elhanan son of Jair struck down Lahmi, the brother of Goliath the Gittite, the shaft of whose spear was like a weaver's beam. [6]And again there was war in Gath. And there was a very tall man there, and he had six fingers on each hand and six toes on each foot, twenty-four in all. He himself was also a descendant of the Rephaim. [7]And he taunted Israel, but Jehonathan son of Shimea, brother of David, struck him down. [8]These were born to the giants in Gath, and they fell by the hand of David and by the hand of his servants (vv. 4–8).

The Rephaim of the Transjordan in the days of Moses were associated not only with Bashan but also Ashtaroth and Edrei, two cities that, in the literature of Ugarit, were considered as marking the gateway to the underworld. In David's time, the Rephaim were also associated with death in a more peripheral, but conceptually similar, way.

There are nearly ten references in the Old Testament to a place known as the Valley of the Rephaim. On several occasions the Philistines are described as camped there (2 Sam 5:18, 22; 23:13).[15] Joshua 15:8 and 18:16 tell us that the Valley of the Rephaim adjoined another valley—the Valley of Hinnom, also known as the Valley of the Son of Hinnom.[16] In Hebrew "Valley of Hinnom" is *ge hinnom*, a phrase from which the name gehenna derives.

In New Testament times, gehenna had become a designation for the fiery realm of the dead—hell or Hades. The history of the Valley of Hinnom no doubt was part of the reason for this conception. The translated meaning of *ge hinnom* in Hebrew is most likely "valley of wailing," an understandable description given the child sacrifice that took place there. The Valley of

---

15. This is not to suggest that the valley was named after Rephaim within the Philistine camp. Scripture doesn't indicate the origin of the name, though it's obvious it had some association with the Rephaim. Edelstein notes: "In the LXX, the valley is called (1) 'Valley of the Rephaim (Gk *Raphaim*)' (2 Sam 23:13); (2) 'Valley of the *Titans* (Gk *Titanōn*)' (2 Sam 5:18); (3) 'Valley of the Giants (Gk *gigantōn*)' (1 Chr 11:15; 14:9). This reflects a tradition in which 'Rephaim' is the equivalent of 'Giants.' It may have been a matter of deliberate choice that the text has the descendants of giants (cf. Hesiod *Theog.* 132–60, 207–10), the Philistines (2 Samuel 15–22), outwitted by the mighty three (2 Sam 23:13–17 = 1 Chr 11:15–19) and ultimately defeated by David's army in the 'Valley of the Giants' (2 Sam 5:17–25 = 1 Chr 14:8–17)"—see Gershon Edelstein, "Rephaim, Valley of (Place)," in *Anchor Yale Bible Dictionary*, vol. 5 (ed. David Noel Freedman; New York: Doubleday, 1992), 676.

16. See Duane F. Watson, "Hinnom Valley (Place)," *Anchor Bible Dictionary*, 3:202. Josh 18:16 (ESV) refers to "the Valley of the Son of Hinnom, which is at the north end of the Valley of Rephaim."

Hinnom was the place where King Ahaz and King Manasseh sacrificed their own sons as burnt offerings to Molech (2 Chr 28:3; 33:6). These sacrifices took place at ritual centers called *topheth* ("burning place"), and later the Valley of Hinnom became referred to by the place name Tophet (Jer 7:32; 19:6).

The meaning and identity of Molech (Hebrew consonants, m-l-k) is hotly debated by scholars.[17] It is hard to see one clear association, however, as coincidental. Molech's name appears in two snake charms from Ugarit in connection with the city of Ashtaroth (Ugaritic: *ʿttrt*), the place known from the biblical accounts about Og (Deut 1:4; 9:10; 12:4).[18] Another Ugaritic text puts the god Rpu, the patron deity of the Rephaim, in Ashtaroth as well. These texts at the very least inform us that there was a close religious association between Molech and the Rephaim. This makes sense in light of the geographical relationship between the Valley of the Rephaim and the Valley of Hinnom in the Old Testament.

What's particularly fascinating—or disturbing—is that the location of these valleys is directly adjacent to the southern side of Jerusalem, Mount Zion, the place of Yahweh's presence in his temple.

THE SPIRITUAL VALLEY

These examples are just a sampling of the cosmic-geographical worldview of the biblical writers and their times. Spiritual conflict lurks behind a wide range of Old Testament episodes and practices. The conflict between the powers of darkness and the presence of Yahweh was an ever-present part of life for the ancient Israelite. Unfortunately, the biblical record is riddled with examples of Israelites being seduced by or embracing those powers.

Israel enjoyed a united monarchy—meaning that all twelve tribes were united under one king—through the reigns of Saul, David, and Solomon. The enterprise began poorly. The Israelites' demand for a king (1 Sam 8) was not a call for someone who would administer righteousness within the country and bring stability. Rather, it was a rejection of Yahweh's ability to fight for his obedient people (1 Sam 8:20). The divine warrior of the exodus and wars against the Anakim had been cast aside for—ironically—the tallest person on

---

17. See G. C. Heider, "Molech," in *Dictionary of Deities and Demons in the Bible*, 2nd ed. (ed. Karel van der Toorn, Bob Becking, and Pieter W. van der Horst; Leiden; Boston; Cologne; Grand Rapids, MI; Cambridge: Brill; Eerdmans, 1999), 581–85.

18. Ibid. Heider notes: "… the Ugaritic 'address' for Mlk, *ʿttrt*, is likely to be identified with the city Ashtaroth in Bashan, just north of Ammon. In sum, the Semitic comparative evidence yields the portrait of an ancient god of the netherworld, involved in the cult of the dead ancestors (and perhaps their king, given the meaning of the root *mlk*, at least in West Semitic)."

the Israelite side (1 Sam 9:2). "Make us a king like the other nations!" God gave them what they asked for, and they paid the price.

Eventually the kingdom solidified under David, the man after God's own heart. In fact, God had picked him out specifically for the task (1 Sam 16) and validated his status with a victory over a Rephaim giant (Goliath) in single combat. God went so far as to initiate a covenant with David, declaring that only David's descendants would be legitimate heirs of his kingship (2 Sam 7).

That succession lasted one generation, through the kingship of Solomon. Once Solomon was gone, the kingdom split into two kingdoms: Israel (ten tribes) to the north and Judah (two tribes), with its capital in Jerusalem. It was only a matter of time before each of them succumbed to idolatrous disloyalty to Yahweh. In the northern kingdom, it happened immediately. Jeroboam, Israel's first rebel king, made a rebuilt Shechem his first capital city (1 Kgs 12:25). Shechem had been the place where Joshua had gathered Israel before his death to dedicate the nation to finishing the conquest and remaining pure before Yahweh (Josh 24). Jeroboam set up cult centers (1 Kgs 12:26–33) for Baal worship in two places to mark the extent of his realm: Dan (which was in the region of Bashan, close to Mount Hermon) and Bethel (the place where Yahweh had appeared to the patriarchs).[19] The symbolism of spiritual warfare in these decisions was palpable. No one faithful to Yahweh would have missed their intended contempt. Ten of Israel's tribes were now under the dominion of other gods. Yahweh would destroy Israel in 722 via the Assyrian Empire.

Judah, the southern kingdom, ostensibly loyal to David and Yahweh, would also fail. They too would have kings who turned from Yahweh. The Davidic dynasty eventually collapsed and Judah's people were sent into exile in—of all places—Babylon.

We mustn't conclude that God didn't try to turn the hearts of his people back to himself. That's precisely why he raised up prophets—after they had met with him and his council.

---

19. See Donald J. Wiseman, *1 and 2 Kings: An Introduction and Commentary*, Tyndale Old Testament Commentaries 9 (Downers Grove, IL: InterVarsity Press, 1993), 154–55.

CHAPTER 27

Standing in the Council

Let's face it. Few Bible readers know much about the prophets, who after the conquest take a backseat to David, Solomon, and maybe a couple of the judges. The average Christian reads the prophetic material only when the pastor needs a good sermon on sin or judgment. The prophets are just a bunch of wild-eyed doom-and-gloom fanatics.

The caricature is not completely without foundation, but it fails to accurately communicate who the prophets were, why God raised them up, and what their mission was. There is a distinct pattern to Yahweh's sovereign choice of human leaders, a pattern that includes the divine council.

JUST WHAT WAS A PROPHET?

To discern the full implications of this pattern, it is vital to first understand what is meant by the term "prophet." Forecasting future events was only a small part of what prophetic figures did and what they were about. Prophets were simply people who spoke for God—men and women who, at God's direction, looked their fellow Israelites in the eye and told them they were being disloyal to the God to whom they owed their existence and who had chosen a relationship with them over everyone else on earth. Prophets told people the unvarnished truth and often paid dearly for it.

The "classical prophets" (e.g., Isaiah, Jeremiah, and Ezekiel) preached during the days of the monarchy (from the time of Saul onward). But God had been appointing people to speak on his behalf for much longer than that. For example, Samuel, the last of the judges, is called a prophet (1 Sam 3:20). Since Samuel is a transitional figure from the time of the judges to the establishment of the first king in Israel, Samuel is thought of as the first prophet.

That isn't actually the case. If we define prophets simply as spokespeople for God, prophets go all the way back to the beginning.[1]

THE FIRST PROPHET

Eden was the dwelling place of Yahweh, the place from which he ruled with his council. Humanity was created to be part of God's family and his ruling council. That's not difficult to discern when approaching Genesis in its original ancient context, but seeing Adam as a prophetic figure requires moving outside Genesis. In Job 15:7–8 (ESV), Eliphaz, one of Job's friends, asks Job some intriguing questions: "Are you the first man who was born? Or were you brought forth before the hills? Have you listened in the council of God? And do you limit wisdom to yourself?"

The questions are obviously rhetorical. By using contrast, they each anticipate an answer of no. Of course Job was not the first man—Adam was. Job had not listened in the council of God (Hebrew: *sod eloah*), but the rhetorical contrast implies that Adam *had* listened in the council of God. This would make sense, given that Adam lived in Eden, the meeting place of the council, and that it had been God's intent for human beings to be his earthly children and human members of his council.

Think back to Genesis 3:8, a passage I've alluded to before, in which Yahweh approaches humans as a man. When Adam and Eve violated God's command, they suddenly heard "the sound of the LORD God walking in the garden in the cool of the day." This "walking" terminology suggests that God appeared to them in human form (spirits don't "walk"). The text says that Adam and Eve knew it was God—there was no surprise or shock. This was an experience they'd had before. Adam and Eve were familiar with being in God's presence. We don't think of that in prophetic terms because there were no other people. But once there were, Adam and Eve would have been the mediators between God and other humans, their own children.

---

1. Jesus affirmed that perspective. He accused the Pharisees of spilling the blood of all the prophets sent by God to his people, beginning with Abel, the righteous son of Adam (Luke 11:49–51). Why would Jesus reference Abel this way as among the prophets? Because he represented God—of Adam and Eve's two children, he was the godly son. We might say prophets speak for God, but even more broadly than that, a prophet is someone God views or calls as his chief representative among the population of his human imagers. Adam, of course, was the original imager of God, and Abel stood in the stead of his father as one who walked with God, imaging his Maker on earth. Cain killed Abel, and Abel was replaced by Seth, who we are told was in the "likeness" and "image" of his father, Adam. Not coincidentally, that terminology comes from Gen 1:26. All humans are divine imagers, but in our fallen condition we often don't image God as we are able and as he intended. If the Bible teaches anything it's that people need divine intervention and divinely appointed leadership to avoid abusing our free will by following our own inclination to be our own master instead of remaining loyal to God.

The description of Yahweh "walking" is also used of God's active presence *inside Israel's tabernacle*, creating another link between Eden, the cosmic mountain, and the tabernacle sanctuary.[2] One can read the Old Testament in vain for any instance where Yahweh walked around the camp of Israel, as opposed to appearing in a cloud over the holy of holies, and so the description here isn't describing God literally glad-handing with the Israelites. Rather, the language is another way of saying that Yahweh's abode was among the Israelites—and where Yahweh's house was, his council was. On the other side of the veil was where Yahweh and his council could be found.

ENOCH AND NOAH

The idea that "walking" was language that expressed presence shouldn't be foreign to us. We use it, too, when we talk about "walking with God." Our conception is one of communion or relationship. Scripture uses the phrase for at least that much, but it could also mean more direct contact with the divine presence. And understanding the notion of "meeting with God" is crucial to understanding what being God's spokesperson meant. When God chose someone to speak for him—to represent him to the rest of humanity or to his own people, they had to meet first. This is the idea behind the biblical "call" to service.

In the Old Testament, two men "walked with God" (the same Hebrew verb used to describe God's "walking" above). They were both prophetic figures: Enoch and Noah. It is certain that these two men directly encountered God, though few details are given.

Enoch is remembered in Genesis 5:22, 24 as never seeing death. These passages note that he walked with God, and God took him. Jewish writings from the time period between the Old and New Testaments do in fact connect these few words with the divine council. In the book of 1 Enoch (12:1ff.) the events of Genesis 5:22, 24 serve as the springboard to Enoch's visions of heaven and God's throne room. Enoch was considered God's mouthpiece by Jewish readers primarily because he was the person who delivered God's words of judgment to the fallen sons of God after the Genesis 6:1–4 incident (1 Enoch 13–16). The New Testament also reports that Enoch "prophesied":

> It was also about these that Enoch, the seventh from Adam, prophesied, saying, "Behold, the Lord comes with ten thousands of his holy ones, to execute judgment on all and to convict all the ungodly of all their deeds of ungodliness

---

2. See Lev 26:12; Deut 23:14 (Hebrew: 15); 2 Sam 7:6–7.

that they have committed in such an ungodly way, and of all the harsh things that ungodly sinners have spoken against him"[3] (Jude 14–15 ESV).

Noah also walked with God, according to Genesis 6:9. God spoke directly to Noah, as he had done to Adam before him and many prophets after him. Noah was God's mouthpiece, prophesying the coming flood to his contemporaries, warning them of the coming judgment (2 Pet 2:5).

THE PATRIARCHS[4]

The pattern of an encounter with God or with divine council members as validation of one's prophetic status gets even clearer with the patriarchs. Since we've covered this ground in previous chapters, though not with an eye to understanding the pattern behind these events, we'll take an abbreviated tour here.

The reader will surely recall that Yahweh *appeared* to Abraham on several occasions (Gen 12:1–7; 15:1–6; cf. Acts 7:2–4). There's a detail in these encounters that I've not mentioned before. In Gen 12:6–7, we're told that Yahweh appeared to Abraham at the Oak of Moreh, which was near Shechem. Yahweh's subsequent visitation with Abraham just before the destruction of Sodom and Gomorrah occurred at a place called the Oaks of Mamre (Gen 18:1).

The Oak of Moreh and the Oaks of Mamre are each what scholars call a terebinth—a sacred tree that got its sacred reputation because it marked a spot where divine beings appeared. In fact, "Oak of Moreh" literally means "Oak of the Teacher." The point behind the name would be that some divine figure teaches people or dispenses information at this location—what we commonly think of as an oracle. Because they were thought to be holy ground, places where God was present,[5] such places were considered good places to bury loved ones. The dispensing of divine knowledge and divine decrees is of course something the biblical writers associated with the divine council (Job 15:7–8; 1 Kgs 22:13–23). This connection will be especially transparent when we get to the classical prophets.

While Abraham was still a pagan, God had chosen him to be the father of Yahweh's new earthly inheritance after the debacle at Babel, where the nations

---

3. The source of the quotation is 1 Enoch 1:9. See chapter 38 for more New Testament connections to Enoch's role (in 1 Enoch) in delivering the sentence of doom to the fallen sons of God.

4. Joseph is omitted from this discussion, since God's activity in his life is described in providential terms. However, his meeting with "a man" (Gen 37:12–17, esp. 15) is often taken by interpreters as an encounter with an embodied angel. The text isn't clear that this supposition is accurate. However, this incident happened at Shechem, the location of the Oak of Moreh (see the discussion on sacred trees and the Angel of Yahweh).

5. See 1 Chr 10:12; Gen 35:8.

were given over to lesser *elohim* (Deut 32:8–9). Abraham became the conduit for God's truth to the disinherited nations. Abraham's son, Isaac, enjoyed the same status, and Yahweh appeared to him also when confirming the covenant (Gen 26:1–5). Jacob had a number of direct divine encounters (Gen 28:10–22; 31:11–13; 32:22–32). He inherited the covenantal prophetic status of his father and grandfather.

The pattern that emerges from the patriarchal sagas is that when God chooses someone to represent him, that person must first meet with God. By necessity, that meeting is with the visible Yahweh, who can be discerned by human senses. In many cases, the divine job interview occurs in a place that is described as God's home or headquarters, the place where the divine council meets.

MOSES, JOSHUA, AND THE JUDGES

It should be obvious that the pattern for divine approval of prophetic status holds true for Moses. Deuteronomy 34:10 makes it clear that Moses was a prophet, and his numerous divine encounters validated that status (Exod 3:1–3; 24:15–18; 33:7–11). For the Israelites, divine encounter was what convinced people that Moses was God's man. Exodus 19:9 makes the connection explicit: "And Yahweh said to Moses, 'Look, I am going to come to you in a thick cloud in order that the people will hear when I speak with you and will also trust in you forever.'"

The implication is clear—the people need to listen and will listen to the person who is validated by an encounter with the presence of God.

Divine encounter was also what initially validated Joshua as a prophet. In Exodus 24:13, just before the description of how Moses and the elders of Israel shared a meal with Yahweh on Sinai, we read, "So Moses rose with his assistant Joshua, and Moses went up into the mountain of God" (ESV). The verse implies that Joshua went along with Moses to see God. Exodus 33:9–11 makes Joshua's contact with Yahweh a bit clearer:

> [9] When Moses entered the tent, the pillar of cloud would descend and stand at the entrance of the tent, and the LORD would speak with Moses. [10] And when all the people saw the pillar of cloud standing at the entrance of the tent, all the people would rise up and worship, each at his tent door. [11] Thus the LORD used to speak to Moses face to face, as a man speaks to his friend. When Moses turned again into the camp, his assistant Joshua the son of Nun, a young man, would not depart from the tent (Exod 33:9–11 ESV).

In Deuteronomy 31:14–23 Yahweh specifically commands Moses to bring Joshua to the tent of meeting, where God himself commissioned Joshua to replace Moses.

THE CLASSICAL PROPHETS

Perhaps the most familiar initiation of a prophet into Yahweh's presence—and his divine council throne room—is the case of Isaiah. Isaiah 6:1–2 (ESV) reads:

> [1] In the year that King Uzziah died **I saw the Lord sitting upon a throne**, high and lifted up; and the train of **his robe filled the temple.** [2] **Above him stood the seraphim.** Each had six wings: with two he covered his face, and with two he covered his feet, and with two he flew.

Verse 8 (ESV) makes it clear why Isaiah has been summoned:

> "And I heard the voice of the Lord saying, '**Whom shall I send, and who will go for us?**' Then I said, '**Here I am! Send me.**'"

It is important not to miss the wording of Isaiah 6:8—whom shall *I* send, and who will go *for us?* As we saw in an earlier chapter about the divine council, the participatory nature of God's rule with his council is again evident.[6] God is the commissioner, but the commission extends from his divine council as well.

The same divine rite of passage was experienced by Ezekiel in an even more dramatic call to ministry. Instead of transporting Ezekiel to Yahweh's throne room, Yahweh and members of his entourage come to Ezekiel (1:1–28), who is then commissioned as Yahweh's spokesman (2:1–3). Ezekiel begins his book:

> [1] In the thirtieth year, in the fourth month, on the fifth day of the month, as I was among the exiles by the Chebar canal, the heavens were opened, and I saw visions of God....

> [4] As I looked, behold, a stormy wind came out of the north, and a great cloud, with brightness around it, and fire flashing forth continually, and in the midst of the fire, as it were gleaming metal. [5] And from the midst of it came the likeness of four living creatures....

> [26] And above the expanse over their heads there was the likeness of a throne, in appearance like sapphire; and seated above the likeness of a throne was a likeness with a human appearance....

---

6. See chapter 3.

²⁸ Such was the appearance of the likeness of the glory of the Lord. And when I saw it, I fell on my face, and I heard the voice of one speaking.

²:¹ And he said to me, "Son of man, stand on your feet, and I will speak with you." ² And as he spoke to me, the Spirit entered into me and set me on my feet, and I heard him speaking to me. ³ And he said to me, "Son of man, I send you to the people of Israel, to nations of rebels, who have rebelled against me. They and their fathers have transgressed against me to this very day (esv).

The prophet Jeremiah fits the pattern as well. We saw in an earlier chapter that the embodied Word appeared to Jeremiah to commission him for duty:

> ⁷ "To all to whom I send you, you shall go,
>   and whatever I command you, you shall speak.
> ⁸ Do not be afraid of them,
>   for I am with you to deliver you,
>   declares the Lord."
>
> ⁹ Then the Lord put out his hand and touched my mouth. And the Lord said to me,
>
> "Behold, I have put my words in your mouth" (Jer 1:7–9 esv).

Jeremiah's dramatic call by the embodied Yahweh is quite important in the book of Jeremiah, for *it serves as the basis of true prophet status*. What began in the days of Moses as public validation of his call and the call of those who served with him became fixated in the minds of Israelites as a litmus test to apply to any who claimed to be God's vessel. In Jeremiah 23 we read God's own words about false prophets:

> ¹⁶ Thus says the Lord of hosts: "Do not listen to the words of the prophets who prophesy to you, filling you with vain hopes. They speak visions of their own minds, not from the mouth of the Lord. ¹⁷ They say continually to those who despise the word of the Lord, 'It shall be well with you'; and to everyone who stubbornly follows his own heart, they say, 'No disaster shall come upon you.'"
>
> ¹⁸ For who among them has stood in the council of the Lord
>   to see and to hear his word,
>   or who has paid attention to his word and listened? …
>
> ²¹ "I did not send the prophets,
>   yet they ran;
>   I did not speak to them,
>   yet they prophesied.

^{22}But if they had stood in my council,
    then they would have proclaimed my words to my people,
  and they would have turned them from their evil way,
    and from the evil of their deeds" (Jer 23:16–18, 21–22 ESV).

The implications are clear: true prophets have stood and listened in Yahweh's divine council; false prophets have not.

The litmus test of direct divine encounter for validating one who claimed to speak for God never went away in Israel. It was alive and well in New Testament times. The next three chapters—the final ones devoted to the Old Testament—will ready our minds for Yahweh's ultimate human voice. The prophets would fail in their ministry, in the sense that they were not able to preserve and revive Israel's loyalty to Yahweh. Israel's failure meant a change in Yahweh's approach to reviving his kingdom rule. The prophetic message would change to judgment and redemption—but the means was deliberately veiled. Even God's loyal angels couldn't quite figure out exactly what God was plotting (1 Pet 1:12).

You and I have the advantage of hindsight—but we still need to know what we're looking at.

CHAPTER 28

Divine Misdirection

We're at a significant stage in the epic saga of God's goal for humanity, his desire to have a human family with whom he and his divine family could rule in a new Eden. Ever since the disruption of Eden, God has been at work to use men and women to restore the original vision. The most visible manifestation of that effort was the creation of a new family through Abraham and Sarah: Israel. But Israel failed miserably in its mission, from the incomplete conquest to the splintering of the unity of its twelve tribes to the collapse of the Davidic dynasty into exile in *Babylon*, the very place at which Yahweh had decided to disinherit the nations and create his own people millennia earlier.

The apostasy of his people and their subsequent exile prompted a change in Yahweh's approach to restoring his rule on earth. He could not depend on humans, though he had pledged himself to humanity's preservation. He would no more forgo the role of his human imagers than he would destroy them. Because his original creation of humanity as his image had meant free-will agency, his kingdom must of necessity include humanity in its recovery and in rulership, else the Edenic vision would be undermined. There could be only one solution, though it would have two strategic deployments. God understood that only *he* could be trusted with perfectly accomplishing his own will. He would therefore have to become man and, in addition, he would have to inhabit the hearts of his children.[1] Residing in a tabernacle or temple was not enough. He had to indwell those who chose to follow him.

The second of these strategies is the most transparent. Through the prophet Jeremiah, God announced in the days before the southern kingdom of Judah fell to Babylon that, though the kingdom of Judah would be destroyed, he was making a new covenant with his people (Jer 31:33): "I will put my law in their

---

1. This is not the only trajectory in biblical theology necessitating the incarnation, but it is an essential one.

inward parts and on their hearts I will write it, and I will be to them God, and they themselves will be to me people." Yahweh would send his Spirit to indwell his people. They could not be trusted with their freedom, but he would not eradicate it, nor would he leave them without enablement.[2]

The first strategy, however, is much more cryptic. It will occupy our attention the rest of the chapter.

THIS IS NOT THE MESSIAH YOU'RE LOOKING FOR

Readers will instinctively realize that by this "first strategy" of God becoming a man I'm ultimately referring to Old Testament prophecies about messiah. Thoughts of Jesus naturally flow through your mind. But that's because we have the New Testament. We have 20–20 hindsight. Israelites and Jews in exile had no such thing. But the disconnection is much deeper than that.

By God's design, the Scripture presents the messiah in terms of a mosaic *profile* that can only be discerned *after* the pieces are assembled. Paul tells us why in 1 Corinthians 2:6–8. If the plan of God for the messiah's mission had been clear, the powers of darkness would never have killed Jesus—they would have known that his death and resurrection were the key to reclaiming the nations forever.[3]

Chances are good that you've heard the New Testament mistakenly read back into the Old hundreds of times. Therefore you might be surprised to hear me say that the Old Testament profile of the messiah was deliberately veiled. Let me illustrate.

The word translated "messiah" (*mashiach*) is fairly common in the Old Testament. It occurs over three dozen times. It simply means "anointed." Lots of people were anointed in the Old Testament, particularly kings, but many of those were unscrupulous or incompetent or both. *Mashiach* occurs with reference to a deliverer whose appearance would be future to the Old Testament era in only a handful of places, and some of those aren't clear as to whether the anointed is even a follower of Yahweh.[4] *And there is no Old Testament*

---

2. I'll pick up some of the threads regarding the Spirit and his coming in later chapters focused on the New Testament.

3. See chapter 37 for more about Paul's vocabulary for the powers of darkness.

4. For example, Psa 2:2, due to the mention of the "kings of the earth," would likely have been taken by a Jew living in the Old Testament era as referring to a time in the distant future. How far into the future Dan 9:25–26 may have been placed by a Jewish reader depends on when it was written. As anyone knows who has studied eschatology in depth, a good case can be made for the passage being fulfilled in the Second Temple period, as well as a time yet future. It also isn't clear whether the passage refers to one "anointed" (*mashiach*) prince or two, and whether one or the other is good or evil. The fact that Cyrus the Persian, a pagan, could be called *mashiach* by God (Isa 45:1) illustrates the flexibility and ambiguity of the concept.

verse that has a dying and rising mashiach. If you're thinking Isaiah 53 is the exception, it isn't. The word *mashiach* does not appear in that passage. That doesn't mean Isaiah 53 isn't part of the messianic profile—it means that the content of Isaiah 53 is just *one* piece of a much larger whole.[5] The pieces were kept separate to obscure the big picture.

This sheds light on certain episodes in the New Testament, such as why Peter couldn't grasp the notion of Jesus going up to Jerusalem to die. Peter believed Jesus was the messiah (the word for "anointed one" in Greek is *christos*, "christ"). When Jesus announced he was going to die in Jerusalem, Peter didn't say, "I know—I read that in my Bible." He *couldn't* read it in his Bible because *there was no single verse for the idea.* Rather, the concept of a dying and rising messiah must be pieced together from a scattering of disparate fragments in the Old Testament that, each taken alone, don't seem to have anything like a messiah in mind. None of the fragments reveal the final assemblage.

Even *after* the resurrection the disciples had to have their minds supernaturally opened to see a suffering messiah. The risen Jesus says that explicitly in Luke 24:

> [44] "These are my words that I spoke to you while I was still with you, that everything that is written about me in the law of Moses and the prophets and psalms must be fulfilled." [45] Then he opened their minds to understand the scriptures.

The point is straightforward: *Only someone who knew the outcome of the puzzle, who knew how all the elements of the messianic mosaic would come together, could make sense of the pieces.* Jesus had to enable the disciples to understand what the Old Testament was simultaneously *hiding* and *revealing*. It wasn't a matter of reading a verse here and there.

Unfortunately, most Christians today don't understand the complexity that Luke 24:44–45 reveals. Instead, they repeatedly hear the New Testament read back into the Old. That's unfortunate, since this makes Old Testament passages say things that no New Testament writer ever quoted them as saying.

Genesis 3:15 is a good example. This is the passage where God told the serpent (*nachash*) that one of his offspring would bruise the heel of one of Eve's offspring, and that Eve's offspring would bruise his (the serpent's) head. This is often taken as evidence for a suffering and dying messiah and the messiah's victory over the forces of evil through the resurrection. *But that isn't how the*

There is no single verse in the Old Testament that contains the word *mashiach* that one could point to and discern the scope of what Jesus did in the New Testament.

5. For a recent technical treatment of Isaiah 53 as being a legitimate part of a dying and rising messiah theology, see John D. Barry, *The Resurrected Servant in Isaiah* (Downers Grove, IL: InterVarsity Press, 2012). Barry's work focuses on one piece of the messianic profile, the servant motif in Isaiah.

New Testament cites the passage. The verse is indeed alluded to by Paul in Romans 16:20, where he mentions the prospect of the serpent being crushed (not just his head, and not just bruised). But the crushing isn't performed by Jesus, the son of Eve and risen messiah. Rather, Paul has *God* crushing the serpent under the feet of *believers*![6]

The account of Abraham's near offering of Isaac (Gen 22) is another example. Not only does no New Testament author ever cite the story as a picture of either the crucifixion or resurrection, but *Isaac didn't die in the incident.* Some see an allusion to this passage at Jesus' baptism, when a voice from heaven announced, "This is my beloved son, in whom I am well pleased," but that *isn't* what the voice said in Genesis 22 (see Matt 3:17; Mark 1:11; Luke 3:22).[7]

These Old Testament passages and others have been made by modern commentators to speak about the messiah and his work in ways the New Testament authors *don't* claim. We shouldn't create connections where the biblical text doesn't. Instead, we need to think more carefully about what we *do* find in the text.

God's plan to redeem humanity, reclaim the nations, and revive Eden depended on the incarnation of the second Yahweh figure and his subsequent death and resurrection. The story of the cross is the biblical-theological catalyst to God's plan for regaining all that was lost in Eden. It couldn't be emblazoned across the Old Testament in transparent statements. *It had to be expressed in sophisticated and cryptic ways to ensure that the powers of darkness would be misled.* And it was. Even the angels didn't know the plan (1 Pet 1:12).[8]

HIDDEN IN PLAIN SIGHT

I want now to give you a glimpse of God's secret plan for the hope of Israel and the disinherited nations—in biblical theology, all humanity. We'll focus on

---

6. Note that Rom 16:20 identifies the serpent as Satan. As I noted in chapter 8 when discussing the Hebrew word *saṭan*, the Old Testament never uses that term of the divine Edenic rebel. Since the term's meaning ("adversary") was conceptually appropriate, though, it became used as a label for God's original opposer after the Old Testament period.

7. There are other alternatives for an allusion here, but there may in fact be no allusion at all. The gospel writers don't say "this happened in fulfillment" of any particular verse with respect to the heavenly voice.

8. In chapter 37 I briefly discuss two related items: (1) Paul's comments in 1 Cor 2:8 that, had "the rulers of this age" known what God's plan of redemption was—that the messiah must die to accomplish salvation—they "would not have crucified the Lord of glory"; and (2) the meaning of Jas 2:19 ("You believe that God is one; you do well. Even the demons believe—and shudder!" [ESV]). In regard to the first item, the gospel accounts of demons recognizing Jesus make it clear that the powers of darkness knew that the messiah had arrived. Only demons address Jesus as "son of the Most High" in Scripture (Mark 5:7; Luke 8:28). However, they did not know God's means for accomplishing salvation and the restoration of the Edenic kingdom—hence Paul's statement. The complete messianic profile and plan of salvation was cryptically scattered and veiled throughout the Old Testament.

simple but fundamental pieces of the messianic mosaic that form meaningful patterns of thought.[9]

Let's begin with Adam. The obvious description of his role and identity is "the first man." But look at Adam a bit more closely. If I ask, "How is Adam cast in the biblical story?" some other ways of thinking about Adam present themselves. Adam was the son of God. As son of the king (God), he was royalty.[10] He was his father's designated ruler in Eden. He was also put in the garden to "work" the land (Gen 2:15). One Hebrew lemma for his activity is 'abad (consonants: 'bd).

Once expelled from the garden, he was displaced from God's kingdom to suffer—working the garden became a difficult drudgery. But that isn't all. Adam lost his earthly immortality. He died, but Scripture is careful to note, via the genealogies, that his lineage lived on, most precariously through Noah, all the way to Abraham and then Israel, and finally to Jesus.[11] His eternal life is guaranteed by God's power, but his bodily return to the new Eden depends on the resurrection of Christ, "the firstborn from the dead" (Col 1:18; Rev 1:5).

We could summarize Adam's profile this way:

Adam
son of God
ruler-king (governs in God's place)
servant ('bd)
suffers (effect of sin)
exile and death (ceases to exist on earth)
lives on through descendants (resurrection contingent)

---

9. The messianic mosaic has many pieces and complex patterns. See the companion website for more examples and detail.

10. Second Temple Jewish literature has much to say about the kingship of Adam and (see following) Moses. This theology is an important part of Jewish messianic expectations prior to the time of Jesus. Major studies in this regard include D. E. Callender, *Adam in Myth and History: Ancient Israelite Perspectives on the Primal Human,* Harvard Semitic Studies 48 (Winona Lake, IN: Eisenbrauns, 2000), 21–65; Crispin H. T. Fletcher-Louis, *All the Glory of Adam: Liturgical Anthropology in the Dead Sea Scrolls,* Studies of the Texts of the Desert of Judah 42 (Leiden: Brill, 2002); Charles Gieschen, *Angelomorphic Christology: Antecedents and Early Evidence,* Arbeiten zur Geschichte des antiken Judentums und des Urchristentums 42 (Leiden: Brill, 1998), 153–55; 163–67; John R. Levison, *Portraits of Adam in Early Judaism: from Sirach to 2 Baruch,* Journal for the Study of the Pseudepigrapha Supplement Series 1 (Sheffield: JSOT Press, 1988); Wayne Meeks, *The Prophet-King: Moses Traditions and the Johannine Christology,* Supplements to Novum Testamentum 14 (Leiden: Brill, 1965); M. E. Stone, *A History of the Literature of Adam and Eve* (Early Judaism and Its Literature 3 (Atlanta: Society of Biblical Literature, 1992).

11. See Luke 3:23–38.

Now let's think about Israel. In terms of descent, Israelites trace their heritage back to Adam. But a closer examination of the story of the nation produces remarkable similarities to Adam's profile. God calls the nation his son (Exod 4:23; Hos 11:1).[12] Israel is not only the light to the nations (Isa 42:6; 49:6), but God intended Israel to rule over the nations (Deut 15:6; 26:19; 28:1; Rom 4:13). This only makes sense given that God is ruler of the nations (Psa 22:28) and Israel is his son. This vision, of course, will be tied to the messianic heir of David (Zech 9:9–10; Psa 89:27).

Israel (corporately) is referred to as God's servant (*'ebed*; lemma: *'bd*; Isa 41:8–9; 44:1–2, 21; 45:4; 49:3). Like Adam, Israel's transgressions lead to exile from the place where the divine presence resided (Isa 2:6–8; Ezek 7–9; Jer 13:10).[13] The result is suffering—many times over—under foreign powers and wicked kings. Eventually, Israel is exiled and ceases to exist as a nation. But the prophets foretold Israel's resurrection, most vividly through the vision of the dry bones (Ezek 37). The nation is reborn after the exile in the form of the returning inhabitants of Judah from Babylon. Israel's profile looks familiar:

Adam	Israel
son of God	son of God
ruler-king (governs in God's place)	highest among nations (Israel's king is most high)
servant ('bd)	servant ('bd)
suffers (effect of sin)	suffers (effect of sin)
exile and death (ceases to exist on earth)	exile and death (ceases to exist on earth)
lives on with God and through descendants (resurrection contingent)	lives on through Judah (resurrection contingent)

Next, Moses. As a believing Israelite, Moses was a son of Abraham and therefore of God (Rom 4:11–12, 16; Gal 3:7, 23–29). His status in that regard was special since he was God's appointed deliverer-ruler of the nation. Curiously, Yahweh tells him that he will be "as God/a god [*elohim*] to Pharaoh" and to Moses' brother Aaron (Exod 4:16; 7:1). It would be through Moses, of course, that God's signs and wonders would be wielded against Egypt. As a leader

---

12. For more on this concept, see John J. Schmitt, "Israel as Son of God in Torah," *Biblical Theology Bulletin: A Journal of Bible and Theology* 34.2 (2004): 69–79.

13. It is possible, though uncertain, that Israel is compared to Adam in Hosea 6:7. The term *'adam* in that verse could refer to a city or be a generic reference to humankind.

through whom flowed divine power, he would naturally come to be seen by the Israelites as a quasi-divine figure, though he was just a man.[14]

Moses is called the servant of God (*'ebed*; lemma: *'bd*; Exod 14:31; Num 12:7; Deut 34:5; Josh 8:31). He suffers for his sin and is prohibited from entering the promised land (Num 20:1–12; Deut 1:37; 34:4–6), though God permits him to see it from a distance before his death (34:4–6). The transfiguration (Matt 17:1–4) informs us that Moses lived on with God but, as with everyone, his resurrection in a new Eden was contingent on one who was to come. We can now add Moses to our table:

Adam	Israel	Moses
son of God	son of God	son of God
ruler-king (governs in God's place)	highest among nations (Israel's king is most high)	ruler-king (over God's people)
servant ('bd)	servant ('bd)	servant ('bd)
suffers (effect of sin)	suffers (effect of sin)	suffers (effect of sin)
exile and death (ceases to exist on earth)	exile and death (ceases to exist on earth)	exile and death (ceases to exist on earth)
lives on with God and through descendants (resurrection contingent)	lives on through Judah (resurrection contingent)	lives on with God (resurrection contingent)

We now come to Israel's king. Recall that God had promised David an everlasting dynastic succession in what we now call the Davidic covenant (2 Sam 7; Psa 89). The fulfillment of this promise would fail in the Old Testament era due to the death of Israel in exile. But Israel's resurrection through Judah—the tribe of David—would keep the promise alive. As we'll see in more detail later, the fulfillment of the promise would be inaugurated at the first coming of Jesus, Yahweh incarnate. The consummation of the promise is yet future. For our purposes here, how do the patterns emerge in Israelite (Davidic) kingship and the messianic son of David?

Like Moses and all believing Israelites, David was an earthly son of Yahweh. But we learn from certain psalms that the kings of David's line were also called "son of God" in an act of anointed adoption specific to the enthroned king (Psa 2:7). The king was Yahweh's anointed (*mashiach*) descendant of Judah (Gen 49:10), his ruling representative among all his earthly children (Psa 2:2). As with Moses, the kingship, by virtue of this adoptive language, carried with it a

---

14. Second Temple Jewish writers adopted this perspective, both in terms of Moses' role as Yahweh's instrument against Pharaoh and the effect that God's glory had on his physical appearance (Exod 34:29–30). See Wayne Meeks, "Moses as God and King," *Religions in Antiquity* 69 (1968): 361–65.

quasi-divine aspect (Psa 45:6–7).[15] Psalm 89:27 casts the throne of David as the "most high" (*elyon*) among all the nations. The ultimate son of David, it was presumed, would be "a prophet like unto Moses" (Deut 18:15; cf. Acts 3:22; 7:37).

Not only were Adam, Moses, and Israel (corporately) God's servant, but King David was Yahweh's servant (*ebed*; lemma: *bd*; 2 Sam 3:18; 7:5, 8; Psa 89:3), as were other godly kings (1 Kgs 3:7; 2 Chr 32:16). One particular "branch" or offshoot from the tribe of Judah and David's line would be the individual servant God would use to bring salvation to Israel (Isa 11:1; 49:5 [cf. 49:3]; Jer 23:5; 33:15; Zech 3:8; 6:12). Like the corporate servant Israel, this individual servant would suffer and die (Isa 53:1–9), but yet live to see his offspring (Isa 53:10), a multitude made righteous by his service (Isa 53:11).[16]

The picture of messiah begins to appear:

Adam	Israel	Moses	King/Messiah
son of God	son of God	son of God	son of God
ruler-king (governs in God's place)	highest among nations (Israel's king is most high)	ruler-king (over God's people)	ruler-king (represents David and Israel; ruler over God's people and all nations)
servant ('bd)	servant ('bd)	servant ('bd)	servant ('bd) (represents Israel; redeems Israel, the failed servant)
suffers (effect of sin)	suffers (effect of sin)	suffers (effect of sin)	suffers (effect of sin of others—Israel's and all nations')
exile and death (ceases to exist on earth)	exile and death (ceases to exist on earth)	exile and death (ceases to exist on earth)	exile and death (ceases to exist on earth)
lives on with God and through descendants (resurrection contingent)	lives on through Judah (resurrection contingent)	lives on with God (resurrection contingent)	(resurrected by the power and plan of God; all who are his—from Israel and all nations—will rise and rule with him)

15. For information on Israelite divine kingship in its ancient Near Eastern context, see Adela Y. Collins and John Joseph Collins eds., *King and Messiah as Son of God: Divine, Human, and Angelic Messianic Figures in Biblical and Related Literature* (Grand Rapids: Eerdmans, 2008); Arthur E. Cundall, "Sacral Kingship—Old Testament Background," *Vox Evangelica* 6 (1969): 31–41; K. M. Heim, "Kings and Kingship," *Dictionary of the Old Testament: Historical Books* (Downers Grove, IL: InterVarsity Press, 2005), 610–22; Tryggve N. D. Mettinger, *King and Messiah: The Civil and Sacral Legitimation of the Israelite Kings* (Lund: CWK Gleerup, 1976); Aubrey R. Johnson, *Sacral Kingship in Ancient Israel* (Wales: University of Wales Press, 1967); J. J. M. Roberts, "The Enthronement of YHWH and David: The Abiding Theological Significance of the Kingship Language of the Psalms," *Catholic Biblical Quarterly* 64.4 (2002): 675–86.

16. On the interplay between the corporate and individual servant and its relationship to Mosaic servant motifs, see G. P. Hugenberger, "The Servant of the Lord in the Servant Songs of Isaiah: A Second Moses Figure," *Irish Biblical Studies* 1 (1979): 3–18.

The identity and purpose of the messiah are unknowable from a Bible verse—and even many Bible verses. The profile proceeds along conceptual trajectories that eventually merge into a portrait. And so Jesus' question (Luke 24:26) to the two men on the road to Emmaus makes eminent sense: "Was it not necessary *that* the Christ suffer these *things* and enter into his glory?" Yes, of course it was. *It's just hard to see that unless you know what you're looking for.* The messianic portrait can only be discerned by assembling a hundred terms, phrases, metaphors, and symbols, which themselves take on meaning only when their patterns and convergences are detected.

There are a few other pieces to show you. They deserve a chapter all their own.

CHAPTER 29

The Rider of the Clouds

Our last chapter focused on a few of the fundamental elements of the Old Testament's messianic mosaic. One of those elements was kingship. I noted that Israelite kingship possessed a quasi-divine flavor. This was common throughout the ancient Near East—civilizations believed that kingship was instituted by the gods, and therefore the king was a descendant of the gods. What that meant and how it worked varied. In Israel's case, the human king was chosen or adopted into the role of the "son of God" to carry out Yahweh's rule. This official status was legitimized to only one dynasty in Israel—the line of David.

Although it's clear how that would be important to a messianic claim, it leaves us with an important question: Would the messiah be truly divine—Yahweh incarnate—or would he be merely a man *thought* to be divine, by adoption?[1] By the time of Jesus' birth—as God incarnate—Jews were intellectually acclimated to the idea of Yahweh being (at least) in human form, including being embodied. The incarnation takes that notion another step. There is indeed a clear indication from the Old Testament that Israel's final Davidic ruler would be God become man—an idea reinforced by the New Testament, particularly in one telling scene.

THE DIVINE COUNCIL MEETING OF DANIEL 7

All roads seem to intersect somewhere with the divine council. The divine nature of the messiah is no exception. The idea derives from a divine council scene in Daniel 7. The scene begins (Dan 7:1–8) with an odd vision. Daniel

---

1. This question is core to the heretical idea of "adoptionist Christology," the idea that God chose the human man, Jesus, to be messiah. That notion does not require that Jesus was actually Yahweh incarnate—in fact, it denies it.

sees four beasts coming out of the sea.[2] The fourth beast is the most terrifying and imposing. We learn that the four beasts represent four empires, as had been the case with Nebuchadnezzar's dream in Daniel 2.

What's described next is significant.

> [9]I continued watching until thrones were placed and an Ancient of Days sat; his clothing was like white snow and the hair of his head was like pure wool and his throne was a flame of fire and its wheels were burning fire. [10]A stream of fire issued forth and flowed from his presence; thousands upon thousands served him and ten thousand upon ten thousand stood before him. The judge sat, and the books were opened (Dan 7:9–10).

Several things jump out at us right away. First, we know that the Ancient of Days is the God of Israel because the description of his throne as fiery and having wheels matches that of the vision of Ezekiel 1. Ezekiel's vision also included a human figure on the throne of God (Ezek 1:26–27). Second, there are *many* thrones in heaven, not just one ("thrones were set up"). These thrones mark the presence of the divine council.[3] Third, the council is called to session to decide the fate of the beasts—national empires. The decision of the council to slay the fourth beast and remove the dominion of all the beasts (vv. 11–12) is important for eschatology, but that's peripheral to our focus here.[4] Daniel 7:13–14 moves us forward in our pursuit of a truly divine messiah. Daniel says:

> [13]I continued watching in the visions of the night, and look, with the clouds of heaven one like a son of man was coming, and he came to the Ancient of Days, and was presented before him. [14]And to him was given dominion and glory and kingship that all the peoples, the nations, and languages would serve him; his dominion is a dominion without end that will not cease, and his kingdom is one that will not be destroyed.

---

2. Dan 7 is in Aramaic. The Hebrew and Aramaic lemma translated "sea" is *yam*.

3. As we'll see, Dan 7 was a crucial passage for the ancient doctrine of two (good) powers in heaven in ancient *Judaism* prior to Christianity. Judaism eventually declared the two powers doctrine heretical as it was a useful apologetic for the Christian belief in Jesus as God. For scholarly discussion of the two powers and the theological struggle it caused within Judaism, see Alan F. Segal, *Two Powers in Heaven: Early Rabbinic Reports about Christianity and Gnosticism* (repr., Waco, TX: Baylor University Press, 2012); Daniel Boyarin, "The Gospel of the Memra: Jewish Binitarianism and the Prologue to John," *Harvard Theological Review* 94.3 (July 2001), 243–84. Further, some sects of Judaism after the exile were resistant to any sort of divine plurality, including the divine council of their own Bible. Consequently, rabbis tried to argue that there were only two thrones in Dan 7, one for God and one for King David. This idea fails for a number of reasons, not the least of which is that the second figure that is specifically named in the scene (the "son of man") takes no seat. Dan 7 actually follows (literally) a divine council scene in the Ugaritic Baal Cycle.

4. See chapter 30 for more on the eschatological implications of this divine council meeting.

There's a lot to unpack here. It's clear from the text that the Ancient of Days (the God of Israel) and the "one like a son of man" are different characters in the scene. "Son of man" is a fairly frequent phrase in the Old Testament. Ezekiel, for example, is called "son of man" dozens of times in the book of Ezekiel (e.g., Ezek 2:1–8). The phrase simply means "human one," and so Daniel 7:13 describes someone who appeared human *coming on or with the clouds* to the Ancient of Days. It is *that* description that points in the direction of a *second* deity figure in the scene. We are back to the concept of two Yahweh figures we saw earlier in the Old Testament.

THE CLOUD RIDER

The first thing we need to understand is the wider ancient context for this description. We've talked a good bit about the ancient literature of Ugarit, Israel's close neighbor to the north. In the Ugaritic texts, the god Baal is called "the one who rides the clouds."[5] The description became an official title of Baal, whom the entire ancient Near Eastern world considered a deity of rank. To ancient people all over the Mediterranean, Israelite or not, the "one who rides the clouds" was a deity—his status as a god was unquestioned. Consequently, any figure to whom the title was attributed was a god.

Old Testament writers were quite familiar with Baal. Baal was the main source of consternation about Israel's propensity toward idolatry. In an effort to make the point that Yahweh, the God of Israel, deserved worship instead of Baal, the biblical writers occasionally pilfered this stock description of Baal as "cloud rider" and assigned it to Yahweh (emphasis in the following passages is added).

> There is no one like God, O, Jeshurun, **who rides through the heavens** to your help, and with his majesty through the skies (Deut 33:26).

> O kingdoms of the earth, sing to God; sing praise to the Lord, Selah, to the one **who rides in the highest heavens** of old. See, he gives forth his voice, a mighty voice (Psa 68:32–33).

> Bless Yahweh, O my soul. O Yahweh my God, you are very great. You clothe yourself with splendor and majesty, you who cover yourself with light as with

---

5. On this title for Baal, see W. Hermann, "Rider upon the Clouds," in *Dictionary of Deities and Demons in the Bible*, 2nd ed. (ed. Karel van der Toorn, Bob Becking, and Pieter W. van der Horst; Leiden; Boston; Cologne; Grand Rapids, MI; Cambridge: Brill; Eerdmans, 1999), 703–05. Daniel 7 actually follows (literarily) a scene in the Ugaritic Baal Cycle. See the companion website for my paper, drawn from my dissertation: "The Baal Cycle as Backdrop to Daniel 7: An Old Testament Rationale for Jewish Binitarianism" (paper presented at the Annual Meeting of the Evangelical Theological Society, Atlanta, GA, November 2003).

a garment, who stretch out the heavens like a tent curtain, the one who sets beams in the waters for his upper chambers, **who makes clouds his chariot**, who rides on the wings of the wind (Psa 104:1–4).

An oracle of Egypt: Look! Yahweh is **riding on a swift cloud** and is coming to Egypt. And the idols of Egypt will tremble in front of him, and the heart of Egypt melts in his inner parts (Isa 19:1).

The literary tactic made a theological statement. The effect was to "displace" or snub Baal and hold up Yahweh as the deity who legitimately rode through the heavens surveying and governing the world.

The lone exception to the pattern of using this unambiguous deity title of the God of Israel is Daniel 7:13. There a second figure—a human figure—receives this description. The description was known across the ancient world as Baal's. No one questioned Baal's deity status. Daniel 7 therefore describes two powers in heaven—two Yahweh figures, since, in all other places in the Old Testament, Yahweh is the cloud rider.

Just as importantly, the one who rides the clouds in Daniel 7:13 receives everlasting kingship from the Ancient of Days. As we saw in the previous chapter, everlasting kingship belonged only to the son of David. We've just filled in more of the messianic mosaic: The ultimate son of David, the messianic king, will be both human ("son of man") and deity ("the rider of the clouds").

That's precisely what we get in the New Testament.

JESUS AS DANIEL'S SON OF MAN, THE CLOUD RIDER

With respect to New Testament studies, the descriptive phrase "son of man" is intensely debated. Since it means "human one" and was a title used of prophets in the Old Testament, many scholars see no divine status attached to it. That's likely the case in most of the description's occurrences of Jesus. But when the New Testament writer quotes Daniel 7:13, it's a different story. The backdrop of Daniel 7 and the divine nature of the phrase must be willfully ignored to avoid a statement of deity.

Two verses in Luke make a transparent connection between the profile of the suffering messiah ("anointed one"; Greek: *christos*) and the "son of man" phrase (emphasis added):

For just as the lightning shines forth, flashing from one place under heaven to another place under heaven, so **the Son of Man** will be in his day. But first **it**

is necessary for him to suffer many things, and to be rejected by this generation (Luke 17:24–25).

Was it not necessary that **the Christ suffer these things** and enter into his glory? (Luke 24:26).

But the most dramatic passage in regard to Jesus as the *divine* son of man is Matthew 26. The scene has Jesus standing before Caiaphas prior to his condemnation and crucifixion:

> **⁵⁷** Now those who had arrested Jesus led him away to Caiaphas the high priest, where the scribes and the elders had gathered. **⁵⁸** But Peter was following him from a distance, as far as the courtyard of the high priest. And he went inside and was sitting with the officers to see the outcome. **⁵⁹** Now the chief priests and the whole Sanhedrin were looking for false testimony against Jesus in order that they could put him to death. **⁶⁰** And they did not find it, although many false witnesses came forward. And finally two came forward **⁶¹** and said, "This man said, 'I am able to destroy the temple of God and rebuild it within three days.'" **⁶²** And the high priest stood up and said to him, "Do you reply nothing? What are these people testifying against you?" **⁶³** But Jesus was silent. And the high priest said to him, "I put you under oath by the living God, that you tell us if you are the Christ, the Son of God!" **⁶⁴** Jesus said to him, "You have said it. But I tell you, from now on **you will see the Son of Man sitting at the right hand of the Power and coming on the clouds of heaven.**" **⁶⁵** Then the high priest **tore his robes**, saying, "He has **blasphemed**! What further need do we have of witnesses? Behold, you have just now heard the **blasphemy**! **⁶⁶** What do you think?" And they answered and said, "He deserves death!" (Matt 26:57–66).

In what seems like a cryptic answer to a very clear question, Jesus quotes Daniel 7:13 to answer Caiaphas. The reaction is swift and unyielding. Caiaphas understood that Jesus was claiming to be the second Yahweh figure of Daniel 7:13—and that was an intolerable blasphemy. Jesus' answer provides the high priest with the accusation he needs for a death sentence, but also gives us a clear testimony of Jesus as the final son of David, Yahweh incarnate, through whom Yahweh will reclaim the nations disinherited at Babel.

As with the ancient conquest under Joshua, that dominion isn't going to come without conflict. But this time, there will be no failure at the end of the campaign. Yahweh's message of the messianic mosaic to the hostile gods opposing his global Edenic vision was, "You'll never know what hit you." But he has one more thing to say to them before the kingdom is launched under Jesus: "You can try and stop my plans, but you're all going to die like men."

CHAPTER 30

Prepare to Die

The close of the Old Testament period was a dark, desperate time. By the end, the vestige of Yahweh's portion, the family he had raised up through Abraham after forsaking the nations at Babel, consisted of only two tribes (Judah and Benjamin), collectively referred to as the kingdom of Judah. But even as the hordes of Babylon, the army of Nebuchadnezzar, descended on Jerusalem for the last time, the prophets offered a glimmer of hope. Yes, Yahweh would punish his children for turning to other gods, but a remnant would survive. Yahweh's plan had not been overturned. He would send a servant who would ensure its survival. There *would* be an Edenic kingdom, but in the future, not in the Old Testament era.

I've sketched the encrypted signals concerning the coming king and his kingdom in the last two chapters. Daniel 7, our stopping point in the previous chapter about the divine nature of the deliverer, linked his appearance with this message of hope in the wake of the exile: The kingdom of God had failed in the Old Testament, but it would rise from the ashes when the divine king made his appearance. That messianic king would inaugurate a kingdom that would spread throughout the earth and eventually succeed in restoring Eden.

These ideas are familiar. Less apparent, however, is the way the Old Testament characterizes the launching of God's kingdom as a war between gods and men. In this chapter I want to briefly overview this vision. The Deuteronomy 32 worldview we've looked at many times looms large. The kingdom will come. The divine holy ones loyal to Yahweh and Yahweh's people are his agents to expand that kingdom. But the nations and the gods who rule them ("princes" in Daniel's description) will stand opposed. As the kingdom of God grows, the dominions of the dark powers will shrink and their gods will ultimately perish.

THE KINGDOM WILL COME

In the divine council scene of Daniel 7, the son of man, a second Yahweh figure, received an everlasting kingdom. But it is crucial to note that this kingdom came only in the wake of the council's decision to judge the four beasts (four empires) reported in the vision of Daniel with which the chapter began. Daniel reported:

> [11] I continued watching until the beast was slain and its body was destroyed, and it was given over to burning with fire. [12] And as for the remainder of the beasts, their dominion was taken away, but a prolongation of their life was given to them for a season and a time.

> [13] I continued watching in the visions of the night, and look, with the clouds of heaven one like a son of man was coming, and he came to the Ancient of Days, and was presented before him. [14] And to him was given dominion and glory and kingship that all the peoples, the nations, and languages would serve him; his dominion is a dominion without end that will not cease, and his kingdom is one that will not be destroyed (Dan 7:11–14).

A more precise description of this kingdom follows in verses 15–28. We need to look carefully at certain statements in this passage.

> As for me, Daniel, my spirit was troubled within me, and the visions of my head terrified me. [16] So I approached one of the attendants and I asked him about the truth concerning all this; and he told me that he would make known to me the explanation of the matter. [17] "These great beasts which are four in number are four kings who will arise from the earth. [18] But the holy ones of the Most High will receive the kingdom, and they will take possession of the kingdom forever, forever and ever. (Dan 7:15–18).

In his vision, Daniel asks one of the standing divine attendants at the council meeting (Dan 7:16) about the meaning of what he has seen. He learns that the beasts are kings, but "the kingdom" will be given to the "holy ones of the Most High," who will never lose possession of it.

Two items are noteworthy. First, the interpretation is interesting in that, in verses 13–14, it was the divine son of man who received an everlasting kingdom from the Most High. We therefore have two recipients of this everlasting kingdom: the son of man and the holy ones of the Most High. We have to keep reading to discern who the holy ones are. Second, verses 13–14 didn't describe any conflict before the son of man received the kingdom, only that the four beasts had been judged before the kingdom was given. We can agree with Daniel that more information is needed. He asks the attendant:

> [19] Then I desired to make certain concerning the fourth beast that was different from all the others—exceedingly terrifying, with its iron teeth and its claws of bronze; it devoured and crushed and stamped the remainder with its feet—[20] and concerning the horns that were on its head, and concerning the other horn that came up and before which three horns fell, and this horn had eyes and a mouth speaking boastfully, and its appearance was larger than its companions. [21] I continued watching, and this horn made war with the holy ones and it prevailed over them, [22] until the Ancient of Days came and gave judgment to the holy ones of the Most High; and the time arrived and the holy ones took possession of the kingdom (Dan 7:19–22).

The chronology of events gets some clarification here. The fourth beast—obviously prior to its death in verse 11—makes war with the holy ones and defeats them. This causes the Most High to act on their behalf, and so they take possession of the kingdom, something that must follow the demise of the fourth beast. The interpretation and the chronology are reiterated in what follows:

> [23] And he said, "The fourth beast is the fourth kingdom that will be on the earth that will be different from all the other kingdoms, and it will devour the whole earth and it will trample it and it will crush it. [24] And as for the ten horns coming from it, from this kingdom ten kings will arise, and another will arise after them. And he will be different from the earlier ones, and he will subdue three kings. [25] And he will speak words against the Most High, and he will wear out the holy ones of the Most High, and he will attempt to change times and law, and they will be given into his hand for a time and two times and half a time. [26] Then the court will sit, and his dominion will be removed, to be eradicated and to be destroyed totally. [27] And the kingdom and the dominion and the greatness of the kingdoms under the whole heaven will be given to the nation [Hebrew: 'am, "people"] of the holy ones of the Most High; his kingdom is an everlasting kingdom, and all the dominions will serve and obey him."
>
> [28] This is the end of the account. As for me, Daniel—my thoughts terrified me greatly and my face changed over me, but I kept the matter in my heart (Dan 7:23–28).

The reference to the fourth beast "[wearing] out the holy ones of the Most High" (v. 25) harks back to his victory over the holy ones in verse 21. The enemy (this "little horn") defeats the holy ones. In response, the divine council ("court") holds session—the assembly Daniel is witnessing—to deal with (destroy) the fourth beast. The result of that meeting in verse 27 is that the kingdom is given to "the nation of the holy ones of the Most High." Interestingly, earlier the kingdom had been given to "the holy ones of the Most High" (vv. 18, 22) and before that (v. 14) to the divine son of man.

The passage is clear in one respect—before the everlasting kingdom is received, the fourth beast is destroyed. It is less clear in terms of who inherits the kingdom. There are three candidates: the son of man, the holy ones of the Most High, and the nation of the holy ones of the Most High.

THE HOLY ONES OF THE MOST HIGH

In the previous chapter, I briefly noted the parallel nature of the vision of Daniel 2 to this vision in Daniel 7. The kingdom received by these three parties is the kingdom from Daniel 2:44–45 "not made by human hands" that will never be destroyed—the kingdom of God.

Bible readers and scholars of course argue about how best to identify the fourth kingdom. Daniel 2:44 makes identification with Rome obvious enough, in that the kingdom of God appears at the time of the fourth kingdom.[1] The New Testament, of course, has the kingdom of God inaugurated at the coming of Jesus during the Roman Empire, and yet still in the process of coming.[2]

The description of this kingdom has both divine and earthly aspects. This is just what we would expect, since God's goal of reviving a global Eden involves people but is a supernatural rule. Considering the identity of the "holy ones" helps us see this anew.

The phrase "holy ones" is a translation of Hebrew *qedoshim* (or *qedoshin* in the case of the Aramaic in Dan 7). The term can refer to the members of the divine council in heaven (e.g., Psa 89:5–7).[3] However, the term can also refer to people. Several times in Leviticus the people are referred to collectively as *qedoshim*. This again is not unexpected, since the imagery of the priesthood, tabernacle, and temple creates an analogy to the sacred space of God's throne room and those who have access to Yahweh in heaven—his divine family, the divine council.[4]

---

1. Since the fourth beast/kingdom subsumes the others, the wording in Dan 2:44 is "in the days of those kings."

2. See, for example, Matt 12:28; Mark 1:15; Luke 8:1, 10; 16:16; 21:31; Rom 14:17; Col 1:13; cf. 1 Cor 15:24, 50; 2 Tim 4:1, 18.

3. The Hebrew term *qedoshim* occurs twice in these verses. Some English translations have "saints," but this is misleading.

4. See Lev 11:44–45; 19:2; 20:7, 26; 21:6; Psa 16:3; 34:9. Psa 16:3 refers to the *qedoshim* that are in the land, making it certain that the term can refer to people.

The range of usage for *qedoshim* helps us parse the "holy ones" of Daniel 7. The phrase refers to both human followers of Yahweh and the members of his divine council. Both families rule together in Yahweh's everlasting kingdom, along with the Yahweh in human form, the son of man, the risen Christ. We'll see more of how this works in upcoming chapters, but here's a preview:

The kingdom of God is reborn at the *first* coming of Jesus. His arrival marks the beginning of the end of the rule of darkness and the initiation of Yahweh's reclamation of the nations ruled by the other gods. Jesus is the son of man, and the kingdom is his. Ruling with him will be the holy ones of Yahweh's (and his) council.

Note in Daniel 7:27 that the kingdom is given to *the nation* of the holy ones of the Most High but it is still referred to as God's kingdom ("*his*" kingdom"). This is a subtle reference to joint rulership in God's kingdom. The nation of the holy ones refers to the human followers of Yahweh aligned with him and his council. As we'll see in later chapters, in New Testament theology, all believers—Jew or Gentile—are the people of God, having inherited the promises of the covenant with Abraham (Gal 3:7–9, 23–29). The kingdom language of Daniel 7 informs us that all the nations once disinherited and ruled by corrupt gods will be made subject both to *God* and to *his people*.[5] This is why the book of Revelation says of believers, "The one who conquers and who keeps my works until the end, I will give him authority **over the nations**.... I will grant to him to sit down with me on my throne, as I also have conquered and have sat down with my Father on his throne" (Rev 2:26; 3:21).

A COMING WAR OF GODS AND MEN

The triumph of the kingdom of God will not come before the final conflict known in Scripture as the day of the Lord. The words of Zechariah 14 are telling:

> [1] Look! A day is coming for Yahweh, when your plunder will be divided in your midst. [2] I will gather all the nations against Jerusalem to battle, and the city will be captured, and they will loot the houses, and the women will be raped; half of the city will go into exile, but the remainder of the people will not be cut off from the city. [3] Then Yahweh will go forth and fight against those nations, like when he fights on a day of battle. [4] On that day his feet will stand

---

5. Some translations have "their kingdom" in Dan 7:27. This requires viewing the referent of the Aramaic suffix pronoun to be the people. The pronoun is singular, though. It is possible to have a singular pronoun refer to a collective group, but usually the pronoun refers back to its nearest antecedent, in this case the singular entity referred to as "Most High."

on the Mount of Olives, which faces Jerusalem on the east; and the Mount of Olives will be split in half, from east to west, by a very great valley; and half of the mountain will withdraw toward the north, and the other half toward the south. ⁵And you will flee by the valley of my mountains, because the valley of the mountains will reach to Azal, and you will flee like you fled from the earthquake in the days of King Uzziah of Judah. And **Yahweh my God will come, and all the holy ones with him** (Zech 14:1–5).

Yahweh comes with his heavenly army at the day of the Lord to disarm and defeat the hostile supernatural powers. Isaiah said the same thing:

> ²¹And this shall happen on that day:
>
> Yahweh will punish the host of heaven in heaven,
>   and the kings of the earth on the earth.
> ²² And they will be gathered in a gathering, like a prisoner in a pit.
> And they will be shut in a prison and be punished after many days.
> ²³ And the full moon will be ashamed
>   and the sun will be ashamed,
> for Yahweh of hosts will rule on Mount Zion and in Jerusalem,
>   and before his elders in glory (Isa 24:21–23).

Yahweh will rule before his council—here called elders—having punished both his human foes ("kings of the earth") and his supernatural enemies ("the host of heaven in heaven"),[6] in order to re-establish his rule in his earthly abode, Mount Zion.

What does the punishment of the gods entail? For that we return to Psalm 82, where we got our first exposure to Yahweh's council in this book. In the first few verses of that psalm, Yahweh was standing in the council to accuse his divine sons of corruption. Instead of governing the nations in righteousness, the gods who had received the disinherited nations after the Babel incident had led the people astray, away from the Most High. Their time comes at the climax of the kingdom when Yahweh reclaims the nations from them. The final verses portend their fate. The God of Israel speaks:

> ⁶I have said, "You are gods,
>   and sons of the Most High, all of you.
> ⁷However, you will die like men,
>   and you will fall like one of the princes" (Psa 82:6–7).

---

6. More literally, "the host of heaven in the heavens." The phrase refers to nonhuman beings, i.e., beings that are divine and supernatural.

The psalmist then exclaims:

> ⁸ Rise up, O God, judge the earth,
> because you shall inherit all the nations (Psa 82:8).

The rule of the gods will be ended when the Most High reclaims the nations he once disinherited. Daniel 7 makes clear that Yahweh's loyal divine and human families will share that rule.

THE FUTURE RE-INHERITANCE OF THE NATIONS

The Day of the Lord is a time of judgment, but it is also cast in Scripture as a time of rejoicing for Yahweh's people. When the rule of the gods begins to crumble, Yahweh will call his own from among the nations. Isaiah 66, a passage that plays a crucial role in explaining the explosion of the gospel after the resurrection, describes the judgment and hope looming in a time future to the Old Testament period:

> ¹⁶ For Yahweh enters into judgment on all flesh with fire and his sword,
> and those slain by Yahweh shall be many.
> ¹⁷ Those who sanctify themselves
> and those who cleanse themselves to go into the gardens after
> the one in the middle,
> eating the flesh of swine
> and detestable things and rodents together
> shall come to an end!" declares Yahweh.
> ¹⁸ "And I—their works and thoughts!—am about to come to gather
> all nations and tongues,
> and they shall come and see my glory.
> ¹⁹ And I will set a sign among them,
> and I will send survivors from them to the nations:
> Tarshish, Pul, and Lud, who draw the bow;
> Tubal and Javan, the faraway coastlands
> that have not heard of my fame,
> and have not seen my glory.

And they shall declare my glory among the nations, ²⁰ and bring all your countrymen from all the nations as an offering to Yahweh on horses and chariots and in litters and on mules and camels, to my holy mountain, Jerusalem," says Yahweh, "just as the sons of Israel bring an offering in a clean vessel to the house of Yahweh. ²¹ And indeed, I will take some of them as priests and the

Levites," says Yahweh. [22] "For just as the new heavens and earth that I am about to make shall stand before me," declares Yahweh, "so shall your descendants and your name stand (Isa 66:16–22).

Incredible as it sounds, people from the disinherited nations will return to Yahweh, out from under the dominion of their gods. Where Israel failed in that mission as a kingdom of priests (Exod 19:6) Yahweh himself will succeed. He will be the agent for his own mission. This is the story of how Eden will be reborn—a story told by the New Testament.

I'll have more to say about the final conflict. There are other startling connections to the divine council worldview in eschatology. But we don't have to wait until the end times for New Testament connections to the supernatural worldview of the Old Testament. In that regard, the New Testament hits the ground running.

Section Summary

The story of Israel's monarchy is about more than David's battle with Goliath, his guerrilla war with Saul, the impulsive affair with Bathsheba, and his son Solomon's accumulation of wisdom and wives. We tend to be fixated on Saul, David, and Solomon because that's normally the exposure we get to the books from Samuel through Malachi. But there's more to these Old Testament books—almost half the Bible—than stories about kings.

As intriguing as Israel's kings were, the men who wrote the monarchy's history weren't aiming at producing biographies. Their messaging was primarily theological. They had a story to tell—about the spiritual cause and effect of Israel's failure, the wrath of God, and Yahweh's plan to prevent his original Edenic goal from being a legacy of ashes.

The historical books and the writings of the prophets operate within the scope of the supernatural worldview of the biblical writers. The nations were still under the domain of hostile foreign gods. Israel was in constant conflict with enemy nations. In the time of the judges, spiritual and moral apostasy prevailed. Everyone did what was right in his own eyes. The failure of the conquest produced, instead of the Edenic rule of God reborn, something akin to the lawless American West.

The anarchy culminated in the demand for a king. The choice came too early and with a misguided motive. But Yahweh had begun planning for David's rise even before he was born, via the ministry of Samuel—the last judge, as well as a priest, prophet, and anointer of kings. David eventually rose to prominence, but the fraternal conflict between Saul (chosen by rebellious Israelites for his height) and David (chosen by Yahweh for his heart) was emblematic of the unseen spiritual war for the land and the people. The vestiges of the Rephaim persisted, and the ark of the covenant and the tabernacle were at separate locations, dividing the priesthood.

The crisis points were eventually resolved. David's men eliminated

Goliath's brothers. Solomon reunited the ark and the tabernacle after the construction of the temple (2 Chr 5:1–14). The land promised to Abraham came under Solomon's rule and jurisdiction (1 Kgs 4:21; cf. Gen 15:18). Then everything fell apart in the wake of Solomon's death.

Two things happened during the dual death spirals of the two kingdoms of Israel and Judah. Yahweh called prophets, assured them of his presence and power through divine encounter, and decreed a new covenant, a new solution to the re-establishment of Edenic rule. In the bitterest of ironies, Babylon would swallow up Yahweh's inheritance. The tables seemed completely turned. But appearances can be deceiving.

The real irony, as prophets like Jeremiah, Ezekiel, and Habakkuk informed anyone who would listen, was that Babylon was Yahweh's tool. Even as Judah was taking its last gasp, Yahweh was engineering the circumstances of an everlasting kingdom that could not be contained by geography. It would be ruled by a man who was also God, whose identity must be concealed long enough for him to die and rise again, so that the curse of sin would be overturned, the lord of the dead would lose his authority, and the eternal life of Eden would encircle the earth.

All of that would play out in New Testament theology. Scholars have long thought of that narrative in two phases: the kingdom *already*, and the kingdom *not yet*.

PART 7

THE KINGDOM ALREADY

CHAPTER 31

Who Will Go for Us?

THE ARRIVAL OF JESUS, THE MESSIAH OF ISRAEL, IS THE FULCRUM UPON which God's plan for the restoration of Eden tilts toward realization. He is the center of the biblical epic. Even though someone reading the Bible straight through has to wade three-quarters into it before encountering him, he's been in the shadows the whole time. No, Jesus wasn't an earthly man before he was born. Rather, Yahweh—the visible, second Yahweh—has been part of the biblical story in the form of a man since Eden.

It is this second personage who would, four hundred years after the close of the Old Testament period, be born of the Virgin Mary as the human man we know as Jesus of Nazareth. He had to become a man to ensure that humanity, God's imager, is not erased from the Edenic vision due to his mortal weakness and invariable propensity to use his free will to attempt to gain autonomy from God.

An Edenic realization without human participation would mean that the *nachash* would then have won a victory—the abolition of humankind as God's image. God need not change his plan in response to human weakness or the self-willed rebellion of a divine council member. He need not remove humanity or human freedom—and with it, his image—to accomplish what he wants. An omniscient, all-powerful being doesn't need to cheat. He knows how best to win—and how best to misdirect his opponents.

We've already included Jesus in certain aspects of the supernaturalist Old Testament worldview and theology. We've seen that he ranks as unique among the divine sons of God of Yahweh's council.[1] We've talked about the Old Testament backdrop to Jesus as the Word and the One who comes on the clouds.[2] But those items barely scratch the surface.

---

1. See the discussion of *monogenes* in chapter 4.
2. See chapters 16 and 29, respectively.

In this chapter, our goal is to accomplish two things. We'll fill in a few more pieces of the messianic mosaic by noting more connections between Jesus and the second Yahweh figure, and then take a brief look at the divine council backdrop to the beginning of Jesus' public ministry.[3]

JESUS AS THE NAME

In an earlier chapter, we learned about the Angel of Yahweh, in whom was the Name, another term for the essence or presence of Yahweh (Exod 23:20–23).[4] The New Testament applies that concept to Jesus in several passages. For example in John 17, the famous prayer of Jesus in the garden of Gethsemane, Jesus prays:

[5]And now, Father, you glorify me at your side with the glory that I had at your side before the world existed.

[6]I have revealed your name to the men whom you gave me out of the world. They were yours, and you have given them to me, and they have kept your word…. [11]And I am no longer in the world, and they are in the world, and I am coming to you. Holy Father, keep them in your name, which you have given to me, so that they may be one, just as we are. [12]When I was with them, I kept them in your name, which you have given to me, and guarded them, and none of them has perished except the son of destruction, in order that the scripture would be fulfilled….

[25]Righteous Father, although the world does not know you, yet I have known you, and these men have come to know that you sent me. [26]And I made known to them your name, and will make it known, in order that the love with which

---

3. Due to space constraints I have excluded discussion of John 10:34–35, where John has Jesus citing Psa 82:6 in defense of his deity. Nearly all modern commentators fail to take the verse in light of the original context of Psa 82, which has the divine council as its focus. They strangely have the *elohim* of Psa 82:6 as mere humans, which reduces Jesus' self-defense to saying that he is allowed to call himself the son of God because every other Jew could as well. This undermines Jesus' claim to deity in the passage and ignores how the quotation is bookended with two suggestions of his deity: (1) identification with the Father (John 10:30)—who is Lord of the council; and (2) the assertion that the Father is *in* Jesus (John 10:38). Interpretation of the quotation of Psa 82:6 in John 10 must not ignore the original divine—not human—context of the psalm. That context is part of the power of the quotation—that the Jewish Scriptures bore witness to *nonhuman* sons of God. This reminder is the gist of Psa 82:6. Juxtaposed as its quotation is in John 10, between two statements that identify Jesus with the Father, the point of the theology produced by the quotation in context is that Jesus is not only a divine son of God, but superior to all divine sons of God in his identification with the Father, the Lord of the divine council. I have addressed this issue in an academic paper available on the companion website: Michael S. Heiser, "Jesus' Quotation of Psalm 82:6 in John 10:34: A Different View of John's Theological Strategy" (presented at the Pacific Northwest Regional Meeting of the Society of Biblical Literature, Gonzaga University, Spokane, WA, May 13–15, 2011).

4. See chapter 18.

you loved me may be in them, and I may be in them (John 17:5–6, 11–12, 25–26).

When Jesus tells God the Father that he has revealed God's name to the disciples (John 17:6), he isn't talking about telling the disciples what God's name was. They could read their Old Testament and see that in thousands of places (e.g., Exod 3:1–14). Revealing God's name to them meant showing them who God was and what he was like. He did that by living among them as a man. Jesus was God among them. He was the incarnation of God's essence (Heb 1:3).[5]

The notion of making God known by revealing his name also takes us back to Yahweh's Angel in the Old Testament. Recall that Yahweh's Angel was Yahweh in human form—Yahweh's "name" or presence resided in that Angel (Exod 23:20–23). John draws on that language in his presentation of Jesus as God.[6] When Jesus says he has "kept them in your name," he means he has kept those followers the Father gave to him *by means of* God's own power and presence—the Name, now incarnated in Jesus.

In this regard it is worth noting that, just as "the Name" was another expression for Yahweh, so "the Name" was used to refer to Jesus.[7] For example, in Romans 10 we read:

[9]If you **confess with your mouth "Jesus is Lord"** and believe in your heart that God raised him from the dead, you will be saved. [10]For with the heart one believes, resulting in righteousness, and with the mouth one confesses, resulting in salvation. [11]For the scripture says, "Everyone who believes in him will not be put to shame." [12]For there is no distinction between Jew and Greek, for the same Lord is Lord of all, who is rich to all who call upon him. [13]For "**everyone who calls upon the name of the Lord**" will be saved" (Rom 10:9–13).

---

5. The citation of Heb 1:3 draws attention to the Greek word *hypostasis*, often translated as "nature." The term refers to "essence, actual being, reality" (see William F. Arndt, F. W. Gingrich, Frederick W. Danker, and Walter Bauer, *A Greek-English Lexicon of the New Testament and Other Early Christian Literature* [Chicago: University of Chicago Press, 2000], 1040). Hereafter abbreviated as BDAG.

6. As we'll discuss in a later chapter, the New Testament also says that the presence of God dwells in each believer. The indwelling presence (the Name) with respect to Jesus goes beyond mere indwelling, as the language of John 17 makes clear. John 17 has Jesus with the Father before the world existed (17:5; cf. John 1:1–14). The language also goes beyond the idea that Jesus "became" God or received God at his baptism. That cannot be the point because of John 17:24, where Jesus says that the Father loved him "before the foundation of the world."

7. As C. K. Barrett notes on Acts 5:40–42, "The Jews used שם [*shem*; "the name"] to avoid saying *God*; the Christians took this up for Jesus; therefore they thought of Jesus as God" (C. K. Barrett, *A Critical and Exegetical Commentary on the Acts of the Apostles; The Acts of the Apostles, vol. 1* [Edinburgh: T&T Clark International, 2004], 301).

The important thing to note here is that the quotation of verse 13 comes from Joel 2:32. In that Old Testament text we read: "everyone who calls on the name of the Yahweh shall be saved." The apostle Paul deftly links "confessing Jesus is Lord" in verse 9 with the statement of the Old Testament prophet. This happens many times, especially in Paul's writings.[8] The Name and Yahweh were interchanged in Israelite theology, so that trusting in "the Name of Yahweh" meant trusting in Yahweh. Likewise, trusting in the name of the Lord, who is Yahweh in the Old Testament quotation, is the same as confessing Jesus as Lord.

JESUS AS THE ANGEL OF YAHWEH

The identification of Jesus and the Angel who is the visible Yahweh by virtue of embodying the Name is made explicit in Jude 5:

> Now I want to remind you, although you know everything once and for all, that Jesus, having saved the people out of the land of Egypt, the second time destroyed those who did not believe.

This short verse credits Jesus with delivering the Israelites from Egypt.[9] The reference is to Exodus 23:20–23 (cf. Judg 2:1–2), where the Angel of the Lord, in whom is the Name, goes before Israel in the procession out of Egypt. The reference to destruction could be to the death of the Egyptians, but it is more likely post-Sinai, where judgments of enemies of Yahweh during the wilderness wanderings and the conquest (cf. Josh 5:13–15) resulted in destruction of unbelievers.

---

8. The major scholarly work on how Jesus is "swapped for Yahweh" in Old Testament quotations is David C. Capes, *Old Testament Yahweh Texts in Paul's Christology* (Tübingen: Mohr Siebeck, 1992).

9. The wording of this verse is not the same in every manuscript of the Greek New Testament. It occurs in some of the oldest manuscripts of Jude (e.g., Alexandrinus and Vaticanus). Some New Testament scholars prefer the variant reading *kurios* ("Lord," likely pointing to Yahweh himself) on the grounds that it is ambiguous and that Jude probably didn't have the incarnation in view, which would have prompted a reading of "Jesus" (see Richard J. Bauckham, *2 Peter, Jude*, Word Biblical Commentary 50 (Dallas: Word, 1998], 42–43). This view of course must presume Jude was ignorant of the Old Testament motif of Yahweh in human form applied to Jesus by other New Testament writers. In other words, there is a clear conceptual relationship between Yahweh in human form (the Angel, who is said to have delivered Israel from Egypt in Judg 2:1–2) and the incarnation, though they are not precisely the same in nature. Jude didn't need to have the incarnation in view to write "Jesus" in verse 5. He only had to identify Jesus with the visible Yahweh tradition of the Old Testament, something that is hardly odd in the New Testament. And since the visible Yahweh is Yahweh, the note about punishing the angels is no objection to a connection with the incarnate Jesus. See the discussion in this regard in Thomas R. Schreiner, *1, 2 Peter, Jude*, New American Commentary 37 (Nashville: Broadman & Holman, 2003), 444.

THE COUNCIL IS IN SESSION

We often think of the commencement of the ministry and mission of Jesus as something quiet and mundane. Not so. A day in the ministry of the incarnate Yahweh was a spiritual assault on the forces of darkness to reclaim what rightfully belonged to him, his Father the invisible Yahweh, and those human beings who were part of the divine council family. The Gospels are far more than a boring point-to-point travelogue.

We've all read about Jesus' baptism before, perhaps dozens of times—but we have likely missed the context for it. John's gospel (John 1:19–23, 29–31) sets it up this way:

> ¹⁹And this is the testimony of John, when the Jews sent priests and Levites from Jerusalem so that they could ask him, "Who are you?" ²⁰And he confessed—and he did not deny, and confessed—"I am not the Christ!" ²¹And they asked him, "Then who *are* you? Are you Elijah?" And he said, "I am not!" "Are you the Prophet?" And he answered, "No!" ²²Then they said to him, "Who are you, so that we can give an answer to those who sent us? What do you say about yourself?"
>
> ²³He said,
>
> > "I *am* 'the voice of one crying out in the wilderness,
> >   "Make straight the way of the Lord," '
>
> just as Isaiah the prophet said." …
>
> ²⁹On the next day he saw Jesus coming to him and said, "Look! The Lamb of God who takes away the sin of the world! ³⁰This one is the one about whom I said, 'After me is coming a man who is ahead of me, because he existed before me.' ³¹And I did not know him, but in order that he could be revealed to Israel, because of this I came baptizing with water" (John 1:19–23, 29–31).

What's startling is the passage cited by John the Baptist. He identifies himself with the anonymous voice of Isaiah 40:3 that heralded the coming of Yahweh. The significance is obscured in English translations:

> ¹   **"Comfort; comfort** my people," says your God.
>
> ²**"Speak** to the heart of Jerusalem, and **call** to her,
>
> >   that her compulsory labor is fulfilled, that her sin is paid for,
> >   that she has received from the hand of Yahweh double for all her sins."
>
> ³   A voice is calling in the wilderness, "Clear the way of Yahweh!
> >   Make a highway smooth in the desert for our God!

4   Every valley shall be lifted up,
          and every mountain and hill shall become low,
      And the rough ground shall be like a plain,
          and the rugged ground like a valley-plain.
5   And the glory of Yahweh shall be revealed,
          and all humankind together shall see it" (Isa 40:1–5).

In Isaiah 40:1 we learn that God is the speaker. He issues four commands, which I've put in boldfacing. *All four commands are grammatically plural in Hebrew.* That means that Yahweh is commanding a *group.* The group cannot be Israelites or a collective Israel, since it is Israel that Yahweh is commanding the group to comfort, speak to, and call. You should know the identity of the group by now: the divine council.[10]

The context of Isaiah 40 is a new beginning for Israel. Judah, the remaining two tribes, had spent seventy years in captivity in Babylon. God brought them out of exile and back to the land. However—and this is frequently overlooked—the other ten tribes never emerged from exile. They were lost, scattered among the disinherited nations. But the coming of the messiah will result in redemption for *all* the tribes. Yahweh will draw his children from every tribe and nation, whether Abraham's literal descendants or not.[11]

In response to the commands in Isaiah 40:1–2, a lone response comes:

A voice is calling in the wilderness, "Clear the way of Yahweh!
Make a highway smooth in the desert for our God!" (Isa 40:3).

It is this verse that constitutes John the Baptist's answer to the priests and the Levites. In Isaiah 40:3, the council member who responds is not identified. Earlier, in Isaiah 6:8, when Yahweh asks, "Whom shall I send, and who will go *for us?*" Isaiah the prophet answers, "I am here! Send me!" But that was centuries earlier. The exchange in Isaiah 40 also brings to mind the divine council scene of 1 Kings 22, where a council member steps forward with a plan to finish Ahab.

---

10. Hebrew scholars of course have long noticed the grammatical forms in the initial verses of Isaiah and identified them with the assembled divine council. See Frank Moore Cross, "The Council of Yahweh in Second Isaiah," *Journal of Near Eastern Studies* 12 (1953): 274–77; Christopher R. Seitz, "The Divine Council: Temporal Transition and New Prophecy in the Book of Isaiah," *Journal of Biblical Literature* 109.2 (1990): 229–47.

11. Jeremiah has all the tribes in view when he declares the Lord says, "I myself will gather together the remnant of my flock *from all the lands* where I have driven them" (Jer 23:3; italics mine). Jer 29:14 ("all the lands"; "all the places") presents the same vision. Ezekiel prophesies the same sort of comprehensive return (Ezek 36:22–36). See also Isa 49:6; Ezek 37:19; 47:13, 21–22; 48:1–31.

With the arrival of the messiah, the apostle John casts John the Baptist in Isaiah's role. Like the prophet of old, John the Baptist has "stood in the council" (Jer 23:16–22) and answered the call. To a Jew familiar with the Old Testament, the pattern would not be lost. As had been the case at the time of Isaiah, Yahweh's council had met in regard to the fate of an apostate Israel. Isaiah had been sent to a spiritually blind and deaf nation. The calling of John the Baptist tells the reader that Yahweh's divine council is in session again, only this time the aim is to launch the kingdom of God with the second Yahweh, now incarnate, as its point man.

THE INCARNATE YAHWEH LEADING A NEW EXODUS

The description of the baptism of Jesus added to the unfolding drama—for those who knew what they were reading. Mark's account of the baptism (Mark 1:9–11) provides some key insights that connect to the Old Testament worldview we've been tracking:

> [9]And it happened that in those days Jesus came from Nazareth in Galilee and was baptized in the Jordan by John. [10]And immediately as he was coming up out of the water, he saw the heavens being split apart and the Spirit descending like a dove on him. [11]And a voice came from heaven, "You are my beloved Son; with you I am well pleased."

There are two items in this passage whose importance is not conveyed in English translation.

First, Mark's note that the heavens were "split apart" is significant. The Greek lemma is *schizo*. Mark's choice of the term in connection with the water baptism of Jesus has drawn the attention of scholars because of the use of *schizo* in the Septuagint, the Greek translation of the Old Testament used by Jesus and the apostles. Not coincidentally, *schizo* is the verb used in Exodus 14:21 to describe the miraculous parting of the sea.[12]

Think back to our discussion of the exodus event.[13] The deliverance from Egypt was a victory over hostile gods. In Exodus 15:11 Moses asked the rhetorical question, "Who is like Yahweh among the gods?" The answer was obvious: no one. The exodus event was a release from exile. Yahweh brought

---

12. One of the better scholarly works on Mark's use of the Old Testament to portray the events of Jesus' life and ministry as a new exodus is Rikki E. Watts, *Isaiah's New Exodus and Mark* (Tübingen: Mohr Siebeck, 1997; rev. and repr., Grand Rapids, MI: Baker Academic, 2001).

13. See chapter 19.

his people out of Egypt to reconstitute them as a nation and re-establish his Edenic kingdom rule on earth.

Mark wants readers to see that a new exodus event is happening. The kingdom of God is back, and this time it will not fail because it's being led by the visible Yahweh, now incarnate as Jesus of Nazareth.[14] The imagery is even more startling when we factor in Jude 5, a passage we looked at earlier in this chapter. Jude has Jesus *leading a people out of Egypt.* The reference was to the visible Angel, who was Yahweh in human form, who brought Israel out of Egypt into the promised land (Judg 2:1–2; cf. Exod 23:20–23).

Second, Mark 1:11 has God's voice from heaven pronouncing, "You are my beloved Son; with you I am well pleased."[15] We tend to think of this declaration as a sentimental one, or perhaps some verbal token of affection. It is far more than that. When God refers to Jesus as his "beloved" he is affirming the kingship of Jesus—his legitimate status as the heir to David's throne.

The key term is "beloved." Scholars have noticed that the term was used of Solomon, the original heir to David's throne. It's difficult to discern that in English translation, though, since the Hebrew term gets translated as a proper name: Jedidiah. Solomon is referred to as "Jedidiah" in 2 Samuel 12:24–25:

> [24] David consoled Bathsheba his wife, and he went to her and slept with her. She bore a son, and he called him Solomon, and Yahweh loved him. [25] He sent word by the hand of Nathan the prophet, so he called him Jedidiah because of Yahweh.

Notice the wording. "Jedidiah" is a name or term that Nathan told David the Lord wanted assigned to Solomon. The name in Hebrew is *yediydyahu* and is related to *dawid/dawiyd,* the proper name "David," which also means "beloved."[16] Used of Solomon, the term amounts to a title that marked Solomon as the legitimate heir to the Davidic covenantal throne.[17] The same message is telegraphed with respect to Jesus. God's own voice announces, *This is the king, the legitimate heir to David's throne.*

The New Testament story, then, begins with a dramatic revisitation of Yahweh's call to the divine council to send someone to announce the appearance

---

14. For other exodus motifs in Mark, see Watts, *Isaiah's New Exodus and Mark.*

15. See also Matt 3:17; Luke 3:22.

16. "David" is spelled two ways in the Hebrew Bible. See Ludwig Koehler et al., *The Hebrew and Aramaic Lexicon of the Old Testament* (Leiden; New York: Brill, 1999), 215.

17. See Tryggve N. D. Mettinger, *King and Messiah: The Civil and Sacral Legitimation of the Israelite Kings* (Lund: C. W. K. Gleerup, 1976), 30–31; Nicolas Wyatt, " 'Jedidiah' and Cognate Forms as a Title of Royal Legitimization," *Biblica* 66 (1985): 112–25 (republished in *"There's Such Divinity Doth Hedge a King": Selected Essays of Nicolas Wyatt on Royal Ideology in Ugaritic and Old Testament Literature,* Society for Old Testament Study Monographs; [Farnham, Surrey: Ashgate, 2005], 13–22).

of Yahweh in the man Jesus of Nazareth. That much will become evident to friend and foe, human and divine. The strategy behind the appearance of the king, however, is cloaked.[18] It had been over five hundred years since the return of Judah from exile. The emergence of Jesus, born and raised in obscurity, from the water launches a battle of wits that entangles both the divine and the human realms.

18. See chapter 28.

CHAPTER 32

Preeminent Domain

In the previous chapter we saw that the arrival of John the Baptist and Jesus the messiah played out against the backdrop of a divine council passage found in Isaiah 40. While the episodes of John's appearance and Jesus' baptism are familiar, the theological framework provided by Isaiah is easy to miss.

The supernatural context of Jesus' actions and statements also frequently goes unnoticed. We have space to share only a few examples. The cosmic backdrop of the divine council worldview of the Old Testament to which you're now acclimated will make them quite discernible. Even though they are too often taught that way, the Gospels are far more than a boring point-to-point travelogue. Consider this chapter a cure.

THIS IS MY FATHER'S WORLD

In the last chapter we saw how the Gospels portrayed the baptism of Jesus as a new exodus. The exodus, of course, was the precursor to reviving the kingdom of God in the land of promise. Israel danced while Moses sang out, "Who is like Yahweh among the gods?" As Moses led Israel through the watery chaos and the unholy ground of other gods, so Jesus, "the prophet like Moses" (Acts 3:22; 7:37), first came through the waters (his baptism) before launching the kingdom.

This mission was not only about the single land and people of Israel, whom Yahweh had created after consigning the existing nations to the dominion of lesser gods at Babel. The coming of the incarnate Yahweh *was the beginning of reclaiming those nations as well.* But the gods of darkness were not going to surrender their domains without a fight—and the battle began so quickly that Jesus barely had time to dry off.

The gospel writers tell us the event that immediately followed Jesus' baptism was his journey into the wilderness to be tempted by the devil at the direction of the Holy Spirit (Matt 4:1; Mark 1:12; Luke 4:1–13). Think about the location: the *wilderness.* The term obviously refers to a literal place, most likely the wilderness of Judea (Matt 3:1), but it's also a metaphor for unholy ground.

We've seen this in one particular instance. Conceptually, the wilderness was where Israelites believed "desert demons," including Azazel, lived. The Azazel material is especially telling, since, as I noted in our earlier discussion, Jewish practice of the Day of Atonement ritual in Jesus' day included driving the goat "for Azazel" into the desert outside Jerusalem and pushing it over a cliff so it could not return.[1] The wilderness was a place associated with the demonic, so it's no surprise that this is where Jesus meets the devil.

But why would the Spirit compel Jesus to go into the desert to face the devil? The answer takes us back to the previous chapter and the Gospels' presentation of Jesus' baptism and revival of God's kingdom as a new exodus event. In the Old Testament, Israel, the son of God (Exod 4:23), passed through the sea (Exod 14–15) and then ventured out into the wilderness on the way to Canaan to re-establish Yahweh's kingdom. But Israel's faith and loyalty to Yahweh faltered (Judg 2:11–15). They were eventually seduced by the hostile divine powers ("demons") whose domain was the wilderness (Deut 32:15–20). Jesus, the messianic son of God and royal representative of the nation, would succeed where Israel failed. As R. T. France notes:

> The most significant key to the understanding of this story is to be found in Jesus' three scriptural quotations. All come from Deut 6–8, the part of Moses' address to the Israelites before their entry into Canaan in which he reminds them of their forty years of wilderness experiences. It has been a time of preparation and of proving the faithfulness of their God. He has deliberately put them through a time of privation as an educative process. They have been learning, or should have been learning, what it means to live in trusting obedience to God.... Now another "Son of God" is in the wilderness, this time for forty days rather than forty years, as a preparation for entering into his divine calling. There in the wilderness he too faces those same tests, and he has learned the lessons which Israel had so imperfectly grasped. His Father is testing him in the school of privation, and his triumphant rebuttal of the devil's suggestions will ensure that the filial bond can survive in spite of the conflict that lies ahead. Israel's occupation of the promised land was at best a flawed fulfillment of the hopes with which they came to the Jordan, but this

---

1. See chapter 22.

new "Son of God" will not fail and the new Exodus (to which we have seen a number of allusions in ch. 2) will succeed. "Where Israel of old stumbled and fell, Christ the new Israel stood firm.... The story of the testing in the wilderness is thus an elaborate typological presentation of Jesus as himself the true Israel, the 'Son of God' through whom God's redemptive purpose for his people is now at last to reach its fulfillment."[2]

In the first temptation of Jesus, Satan tried to entice him into satisfying his hunger by turning stones to bread. The problem of hunger was, of course, an issue in Israel's wanderings in the wilderness on the way to Canaan. Jesus responds by quoting Deuteronomy 8:3, which reads in context, "And [Yahweh] humbled you and let you go hungry, and *then* he fed you with that which you did not know nor did your ancestors know, in order to make you know that not by bread alone but by all *that* goes out of the mouth of Yahweh humankind shall live." Jesus' point was that his loyalty was to the invisible Yahweh alone; he would obey no other.

The second temptation was like the first. Satan dared Jesus to jump from the top of the temple to prove he was the son of God, whom God's angels would protect. Jesus quotes Deuteronomy 6:16, which again is in the context of obedience to Yahweh alone: [16]"You shall not put Yahweh your God to the test, as you tested him at Massah. [17]You shall diligently keep the commandments of Yahweh your God and his legal provisions and his rules that he has commanded you" (Deut 6:16–17).

The ultimate temptation comes last, and hits directly at Jesus' ultimate mission—to reclaim the nations that are rightfully Yahweh's:

> [8]Again the devil took him to a very high mountain and showed him all the kingdoms of the world and their glory, [9]and he said to him, "I will give to you all these things, if you will fall down and worship me" (Matt 4:8–9).

Satan offered Jesus the nations that had been disinherited by Yahweh at Babel. Coming from the "ruler of this world" (John 12:31), the offer was not a hollow one. As the original rebel, the *nachash* of Genesis 3 (cf. Rev 12:9) had, by New Testament times, achieved the status of the lead opposition to Yahweh.[3] This was part of the logic of attributing the term *satan* to him as a proper

---

2. R. T. France, *The Gospel of Matthew*, New International Commentary on the New Testament (Grand Rapids, MI: Eerdmans, 2007), 128. France's quotation includes an excerpt from M. D. Goulder, *Midrash and Lection in Matthew* (London: SPCK, 1974), 245.

3. Recall that in the Old Testament, the Hebrew word *satan* ("adversary, challenger") was not a proper name (see chapter 8). The theology of spiritual war and the perceived hierarchy of the unseen forces hostile to God evolved in the progress of revelation. See G. H. Twelftree, "Demon, Devil, Satan," in *Dictionary of Jesus and the Gospels* (ed. Joel B. Green and Scot McKnight; Downers Grove, IL: InterVarsity Press, 1992);

personal name. Recall as well that the *nachash* has been cast down to the *'erets*, a term that referred not only to "earth" but also the realm of the dead, Sheol.[4] The "original rebel," whose domain became earth/Sheol, *nachash*/Satan was perceived by Second Temple and New Testament theology as primary authority over all other rebels and their domains. Consequently, his lordship over the gods who ruled the nations in the Deuteronomy 32 worldview of the Old Testament was presumed.

Had Jesus given in, it would have been an acknowledgment that Satan's permission was *needed* to possess the nations. It wasn't. Satan presumed power and ownership of something that, ultimately, was not his but God's. The messaging behind Jesus' answer is clear: Yahweh will *take* the nations back by his own means in his own time. He doesn't need them to be given away in a bargain. Jesus was loyal to his Father. Since reclaiming the nations was connected with salvation and redemption from the effects of the fall in Eden, accepting Satan's offer would have undermined the necessity of the atonement of the cross.[5]

GAME ON

Immediately following this confrontation, Jesus "returned in the power of the Spirit to Galilee," where he preached in the region's synagogues and was rejected by those in his home town of Nazareth (Luke 4:14–15). Matthew and Mark tell us that Jesus moved out of Nazareth and went to live in Capernaum (Matt 4:12–16). At Capernaum he began his ministry with a simple but appropriate message: "Repent, because the kingdom of heaven is near" (Matt 4:17). Jesus then did two things: called his first disciples (Peter, Andrew, James, and John) and healed a demon-possessed man (Mark 1:16–28; Luke 4:31–5:11). Let the holy war begin.[6]

T. Elgvin, "Belial, Beliar, Devil, Satan," in *Dictionary of New Testament Background: A Compendium of Contemporary Biblical Scholarship* (ed. Craig A. Evans and Stanley E. Porter; Downers Grove, IL: InterVarsity Press, 2000); Philip S. Alexander, "The Demonology of the Dead Sea Scrolls," in *The Dead Sea Scrolls after Fifty Years: A Comprehensive Assessment* (Leiden: Brill, 1998–99), 2:351–53.

4. See chapters 10–11, along with footnote 9 on page 281.

5. As I noted in chapter 28 and briefly discuss in chapter 37, the powers of darkness were not aware of God's plan of salvation. They, like Satan in the wilderness, knew that Yahweh's messiah had come and that at least one purpose was the repatriation of the nations of the world under Yahweh's dominion. But they did not discern that the death of the messiah was the lynchpin to the plan. The death, burial, and resurrection of the messiah would result in the reconstitution of God's family as one body united to Christ, the Church, which was "circumcision neutral" and not tied to physical descent from Abraham.

6. Other scholars have noted how the announcement of the kingdom coincides with the expulsion of demons. See Craig A. Evans, "Inaugurating the Kingdom of God and Defeating the Kingdom of Satan," *Bulletin for Biblical Research* 15.1 (2005): 49–75.

It might sound hard to believe, but this event is the first time in the entire Bible we read about a demon being cast out of a person. No such event is ever recorded in the Old Testament. The defeat of demons, falling on the heels of Jesus' victory over Satan's temptations, marks the beginning of the re-establishment of the kingdom of God on earth. Jesus himself made this connection absolutely explicit: "If it is by the finger of God that I cast out demons, then the kingdom of God has come upon you" (Luke 11:20 ESV). And since the lesser *elohim* over the nations are cast as demons in the Old Testament, the implications for our study are clear: The ministry of Jesus marked the beginning of repossession of the nations and defeat of their *elohim*.[7]

In Luke's account, Jesus preaches, heals, and casts out more demons after this initial exorcism. He also gathers more disciples. In Luke 9, Jesus gathers his twelve disciples together and gives them power and authority over the demons, sending them out to proclaim the kingdom of God (9:1–6). The symbolic telegraphing of choosing *twelve* disciples (one to correspond to each of the tribes of *Israel*, Yahweh's domain) is evident.

As if the intention wasn't clear enough, in the next chapter Jesus does something dramatic to announce to all who understood the cosmic geography of Babel what was really happening:

> After this the Lord appointed seventy others and sent them on ahead of him in pairs to every town and place where He Himself was going to come (Luke 10:1 NRSV).

Jesus sent out *seventy* disciples. The number is not accidental.[8] Seventy is the

---

7. The connection of the gods of the nations installed in Deut 32:8–9 with the demons (Hebrew: *shedim*) of Deut 32:17 can be traced by comparing Deut 32:8–9 with Deut 4:19–20; 17:3; 29:25–26; 32:17. The interconnections of these passages is why Deuteronomy 32:17 refers to the *shedim* ("demons") as *elohim* ("gods"). Many English translations obscure all this, sometimes in very awkward ways that require ignoring grammar and syntax. See Michael S. Heiser, "Does Deuteronomy 32:17 Assume or Deny the Reality of Other Gods?" *Bible Translator* 59.3 (July 2008): 137–45. As noted in earlier chapters, the term *shedim* comes from Akkadian *shadu*, which describes a guardian spirit. The word choice is appropriate in Deut 32:17 given the context of Deut 32:8–9 and cosmic geography: the nations are the domains of other gods who are, in turn, their guardians. Instead of administering Yahweh's just rule in these nations under his authority, preparing them for their return to Yahweh via Israel and the terms of the Abrahamic covenant (Gen 12:3), these divine beings lured Yahweh's children to worship them and abused their charge (Psa 82).

8. Some translations read seventy-two instead of seventy. Greek New Testament manuscript evidence for both readings is divided among very ancient manuscript traditions. The difference arose on account of the Septuagint, which has "seventy-two" for the number nations in Gen 10. The traditional Hebrew (Masoretic) text has the number of nations as seventy. Consequently, *either number points to a correlation back to the nations divided at Babel and the cosmic-geographical worldview of Deut 32:8–9.* The number seventy of the traditional Hebrew text is best on external grounds, given the witness to seventy "sons of El" in the divine council at Ugarit. As Fitzymer, noting Deut 32:8, writes: the number "has often been thought to reflect the nations of the world in the table of Gen 10:2–31 and would symbolize the coming evangelization of the Gentiles and diaspora Jews by the disciples, whereas the Twelve would have been sent to Israel

number of nations listed in Genesis 10 that were dispossessed at Babel. The seventy "return with joy" (Luke 10:17) and announce to Jesus, "Lord, even the demons are subject to us in your name!" Jesus' response is telling: "I saw Satan fall like lightning from heaven" (10:18). The implications are clear: Jesus' ministry is the beginning of the end for Satan and the gods of the nations. The great reversal is underway.[9]

GROUND ZERO: The Gates of Hell

The spiritual skirmishes against the powers of darkness are evident throughout Jesus' ministry. One of the more dramatic is described in Matthew 16:13–20. Jesus goes with his disciples to the district of Caesarea Philippi. On the way he asks the famous question, "Who do people say that I am?" Peter answers, "You are the Christ, the Son of the living God." Jesus commends Peter:

> Blessed are you, Simon Bar-Jonah! For flesh and blood has not revealed this to you, but my Father who is in heaven. [18]And I tell you, you are Peter, and on this rock I will build my church, and the gates of hell shall not prevail against it (Matt 16:17–18 ESV).

This passage is among the most controversial in the Bible, as it is a focal point of debate between Roman Catholics, who reference it to argue that the passage makes Peter the leader of the original church (and thus the first pope), and those who oppose that idea. There's actually something much more cosmic

---

itself" (Joseph A. Fitzmyer, S.J., *The Gospel according to Luke X–XXIV: Introduction, Translation, and Notes,* Anchor Yale Bible 28A [New Haven: Yale University Press, 2008], 846).

9. Given the connection made in the New Testament between the *nachash* (serpent) figure and the Hebrew word *saṭan* ("adversary") in Rev 12:9, the judicial role of the *satan* described in the Hebrew Bible (Job 1–2) becomes noteworthy. The role of the *satan* in Job involved roaming through the earth. In the context of the divine courtroom scene of Job 1–2, the ostensible purpose was to see, among humanity, who was (or wasn't) obedient to God. This precipitates God's words about Job. The *satan* issues a challenge to God's assessment, and perhaps to the justness of God's ordering of the world. Job becomes the focus of that challenge, as his integrity (and, by implication, God's) is questioned. Presuming this accusatorial role, when the New Testament writers have Satan expelled from heaven in Luke 10:17–18, the theological message would be that, with the commencement of the kingdom of God, Satan's role as "accuser of the brethren" is finished. God is no longer listening to challenges as to whom he deems righteous. That this phrase ("accuser of the brethren") occurs uniquely in Rev 12:10, right after the only verse in the New Testament that connects the terms Satan, devil, and dragon (cf. the serpent) cannot be coincidental. The inauguration of the kingdom of God by the messiah means that Satan, the lord of the dead, has no "legal" authority in God's court (council) by which to condemn any member of that kingdom. On Job 1–2 and the accuser, see Peggy Day, *An Adversary in Heaven: śāṭān in the Hebrew Bible,* Harvard Semitic Monographs 43 (Atlanta: Scholars Press, 1988), 79–83. For a scholarly treatment of the divine courtroom, tracing its constituent ideas from the Hebrew Bible through the Second Temple period on into the New Testament, see Meira Z. Kensky, *Trying Man, Trying God,* Wissenschaftliche Untersuchungen zum Neuen Testament 289, second series (Tübingen: Mohr-Siebeck, 2010).

going on here. The location of the incident—Caesarea Philippi—and the reference to the "gates of hell" provide the context for the "rock" of which Jesus is speaking.

The location of Caesarea Philippi should be familiar from our earlier discussions about the wars against the giant clans.

Caesarea Philippi is adjacent to the Pharpar River. Noting this geography, we can see exactly where Jesus was when he uttered the famous words about "this rock" and the "gates of hell" to Peter.

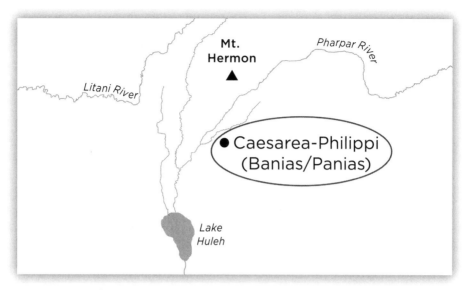

Caesarea Philippi was located in the northern part of the Old Testament region of Bashan, the "place of the serpent," at the foot of Mount Hermon.[10]

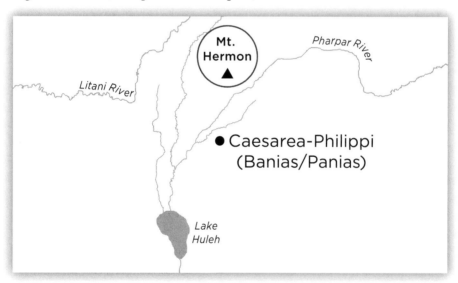

---

10. See chapter 24. As one scholar of the Bible's historical geography notes: "The northern frontier of Canaan is drawn from the Mediterranean Sea to Mount Hor, north of Gebal (Byblos). It extends to Apheka ('Afqa) on the Nahr 'Ibrahim then to Lebo-hamath (Labweh) in the Valley of Lebanon, and further encompasses the land of Damascus and northern Transjordan, the Bashan, to the southern end of Lake Chinnereth.... Extra Canaanite Transjordan is extended to encompass the Bashan as well.... Hence, the land of Israel includes Mount Hermon and the northern and central part of Transjordan, comprising the Bashan, Gilead and the Plain (Mishor) up to the river Arnon" (Zecharia Kallai, "The Patriarchal Boundaries, Canaan, and the Land of Israel: Patterns and Application for Biblical Historiography," *Israel Exploration Journal* 47.1–2 [1997]: 71–73).

Things hadn't changed much by Jesus' day, at least in terms of spiritual control. You may have noticed on these maps that Caesarea Philippi was also called "Panias." The early church historian Eusebius notes: "Until today the mount in front of Panias and Lebanon is known as Hermon and it is respected by nations as a sanctuary."[11]

The site was famous in the ancient world as a center of the worship of Pan and for a temple to the high god Zeus, considered in Jesus' day to be incarnate in Augustus Caesar.[12] As one authority notes:

> More than twenty temples have been surveyed on Mt. Hermon and its environs. This is an unprecedented number in comparison with other regions of the Phoenician coast. They appear to be the ancient cult sites of the Mt. Hermon population and represent the Canaanite/Phoenician concept of open-air cult centers dedicated, evidently, to the celestial gods.[13]

The reference in the quotation to "celestial gods" takes our minds back to the "host of heaven," the sons of God who were put in authority over the nations at Babel (Deut 32:8–9) who were not to be worshiped by Israelites (Deut 4:19–20; 17:3; 29:25).

The basis for Catholicism's contention that the Church is built on Peter's leadership is that his name means "stone."[14] For sure there is wordplay going on in Peter's confession, but I would suggest there is also an important double entendre: the "rock" refers to the mountain *location* where Jesus makes the statement. When viewed from this perspective, Peter confesses Jesus as the Christ, the Son of the living God, at "this rock" (this *mountain*—Mount Hermon). Why? This place was considered the "gates of hell," the gateway to the realm of the dead, in Old Testament times.[15]

The theological messaging couldn't be more dramatic. Jesus says he will build his church—and the "gates of hell" will not prevail against it. We often

---

11. As quoted in Rami Arav, "Hermon, Mount (Place)," in *The Anchor Yale Bible Dictionary* (ed. David Noel Freedman; New York: Doubleday, 1992), 159. Panias is the Arabic pronunciation for the Greek Banias.

12. See "Archaeological Sites in Israel-Banyas: Cult Center of the God Pan," at the website for the Israel Ministry of Foreign Affairs: http://www.mfa.gov.il/MFA/IsraelExperience/History/Pages/default.aspx. For a thorough scholarly treatment of Banias/Panias and its religious history, including connections to biblical Bashan and Hermon, see Judd H. Burton, "Religion, Society, and Sacred Space at Banias: A Religious History of Banias/Caesarea Philippi, 21 BC–AD 1635" (PhD diss., Texas Tech University, 2010).

13. Arav, "Hermon, Mount (Place)," 159.

14. The name "Peter" is Greek *petros*, a word that refers broadly to stone. The word translated "rock" in Matt 16:18 is *petra* ("bedrock, massive rock formation"), a word closely related to *petros*. SeeBDAG, 809. Peter was also called Cephas (John 1:42; Gal 2:11), which is a transliteration of *kephas*, deriving from Aramaic *kepha'*, which means "rock" as well. On the wordplay, see Gerald L. Borchert, *John 1–11*, New American Commentary 25A (Nashville: Broadman & Holman, 1996), 143–44.

15. See chapter 24.

think of this phrase as though God's people are in a posture of having to bravely fend off Satan and his demons. This simply isn't correct. Gates are defensive structures, not offensive weapons. The kingdom of God is the aggressor.[16] Jesus begins at ground zero in the cosmic geography of both testaments to announce the great reversal. *It is the gates of hell that are under assault*—and they will *not* hold up against the Church. Hell will one day be *Satan's tomb*.

BAITING THE ENEMY

It's hard to imagine, but the conflict ratchets up one more notch after Peter's confession.

Mount Hermon, as readers will recall, was the place where, in Jewish literature such as the book of 1 Enoch, the sons of God of Genesis 6:1–4 chose to launch their rebellion against Yahweh. Jesus had one more statement to make to his unseen enemies.

Matthew, Mark, and Luke all agree that the next event in the ministry of Jesus after Peter's confession was the transfiguration:

> [2]And after six days Jesus took with him Peter and James and John, and led them up a high mountain by themselves. And he was transfigured before them, [3]and his clothes became radiant, intensely white, as no one on earth could bleach them. [4]And there appeared to them Elijah with Moses, and they were talking with Jesus. [5]And Peter said to Jesus, "Rabbi, it is good that we are here. Let us make three tents, one for you and one for Moses and one for Elijah." [6]For he did not know what to say, for they were terrified. [7]And a cloud overshadowed them, and a voice came out of the cloud, "This is my beloved Son; listen to him." [8]And suddenly, looking around, they no longer saw anyone with them but Jesus only (Mark 9:2–8 ESV).

We've already learned the significance of "beloved" with respect to Jesus— that it is a divinely affixed title marking the rightful heir to David's throne and, therefore, the kingdom of God on earth.[17] Our focus here is on the event itself.

In early church tradition, the location of the mount of transfiguration was believed by many to be Mount Tabor.[18] The earliest witness to this tradition

---

16. See the discussion in John Nolland, *The Gospel of Matthew: A Commentary on the Greek Text,* New International Greek Testament Commentary (Grand Rapids, MI; Eerdmans, 2005), 675.

17. See chapter 31.

18. See G. Mussies, "Tabor," in *Dictionary of Deities and Demons in the Bible, 2nd ed.* (ed. Karel van der Toorn, Bob Becking, and Pieter W. van der Horst; Leiden; Boston; Cologne; Grand Rapids, MI; Cambridge: Brill; Eerdmans, 1999), 828.

is the fourth century AD.[19] The gospels themselves give no name, and so the tradition has no biblical precedent. Mount Hermon is also much higher than Tabor (8,500 feet vs. 1,843 feet), which would fit better with the description of a "high mountain" by Mark (and in Matt 17:1).[20] Some scholars still hold to the Tabor identification, but many have come to agree that the close proximity of Caesarea Philippi to Mount Hermon and the symbolic-religious associations that relationship entails make Mount Hermon the logical choice for the transfiguration.[21]

The imagery is striking. We've seen already that the Jewish tradition about the descent of the Watchers, the sons of God of Genesis 6:1–4, informed the writings of Peter and Jude. Now we see that the transfiguration of Jesus takes place on the same location identified by that tradition. Jesus picks Mount Hermon to reveal to Peter, James, and John exactly who he is—the embodied glory-essence of God, the divine Name made visible by incarnation. The meaning is just as transparent: *I'm putting the hostile powers of the unseen world on notice. I've come to earth to take back what is mine. The kingdom of God is at hand.*

The account of Peter's confession at the foot of Mount Hermon and the revelation of the transfiguration on its unholy slopes marked a key transition point in Jesus' life, particularly as the Gospel of Mark presents it. After he throws down the gauntlet at the transfiguration, he begins to move toward Jerusalem to his death. One scholar puts it this way:

> Mark not only presents a consistent and historically probable account of the movements of Jesus during the last weeks or months of his life … indeed there is good reason for accepting the account as historically accurate. How long the period was cannot be determined. But it begins with Peter's Confession near Caesarea Philippi and a practically simultaneous conviction or announcement on Jesus' part that he could not expect such recognition from the multitudes or the authorities, but that he must appear in Jerusalem and there in some

---

19. Mussies writes, "This tradition can be traced back to Cyril of Jerusalem (348–c. 386 CE), who speaks of it in passing: 'They (Moses and Elijah) were with Him when He was transfigured on Mt. Thabor and told the disciples about the end which He was to fulfil in Jerusalem' (*Catech.* 12, 16). His contemporary Jerome (348–420 CE) likewise mentions it only casually when describing to Eustochium the journeys made in the Near East by her mother Paula: 'She climbed Mt. Thabor on which the Lord was transfigurated' (*Epistle* 108, 13)" (Mussies, "Tabor," in *Dictionary of Deities and Demons in the Bible*, 828).

20. Avraham Negev, *The Archaeological Encyclopedia of the Holy Land,* 3rd ed. (New York: Prentice Hall Press, 1990); "Tabor, Mount (Place)," in *Anchor Yale Bible Dictionary*, vol. 6 *(ed. David Noel Freedman; New York: Doubleday, 1992)*, 305.

21. See John J. Rousseau and Rami Arav, *Jesus and His World: An Archaeological and Cultural Dictionary* (Minneapolis: Fortress, 1995), 209–10. Mount Hermon also makes good sense in light of Psa 68:15. See chapters 33–34 for more on Bashan.

way or measure suffer the woes of the last days before the kingdom of God could come.[22]

The enemy knows who Jesus is, but, as noted earlier, the forces of darkness do not know the plan.[23] Jesus has baited them into action, and act they will. He has given them the rope, and they will eagerly hang themselves with it. Jesus will go to Jerusalem to drink from the cup that the Father has planned for him. But the instrument of death will be the catalyst that launches the kingdom of God in its full force.

---

22. See Chester Charlton McCown, "The Geography of Jesus' Last Journey to Jerusalem," *Journal of Biblical Literature* 51:2 (1932): 107–29. McCown, along with most scholars, does not see the gospel accounts as presenting a reliable chronology of Jesus' ministry. Rather, each had his own literary-theological agenda, which accounts for differences in the geographical presentation in the Gospels of Jesus' ministry. McCown sees Mark as the most succinct record and, consequently for him, the most historically reliable accounting.

23. See footnote 5 on page 279.

CHAPTER 33

A Beneficial Death

By the time of the events in the region known in Old Testament days as Bashan—Peter's confession at Caesarea Philippi and the transfiguration on Mount Hermon—Jesus knew that the hour of his death was fast approaching. He had provoked a confrontation with intelligent evil in many ways over the years of his ministry, but what he did and said in those two places was especially defiant. The move was calculated.

THE BULLS OF BASHAN

All four gospels describe the crucifixion of Jesus in varying degrees of detail. One of the more thorough descriptions is that of Matthew:

> [35]And when they had crucified him, they divided his clothes among themselves by casting lots. [36]And they sat down and were watching over him there. [37]And they put above his head the charge against him in writing: "This is Jesus, the king of the Jews." [38]Then two robbers were crucified with him, one on his right and one on his left. [39]And those who passed by reviled him, shaking their heads [40]and saying, "The one who would destroy the temple and rebuild it in three days, save yourself! If you are the Son of God, come down from the cross!" [41]In the same way also the chief priests, along with the scribes and elders, were mocking him, saying, [42]"He saved others; he is not able to save himself! He is the king of Israel! Let him come down now from the cross, and we will believe in him! [43]He trusts in God; let him deliver him now if he wants to, because he said, 'I am the Son of God'!" [44]And in the same way even the robbers who were crucified with him were reviling him.
>
> [45]Now from the sixth hour, darkness came over all the land until the ninth hour. [46]And about the ninth hour Jesus cried out with a loud voice, saying, "*Eli, Eli, lema sabachthani?*" (that is, "My God, my God, why have you forsaken me?") (Matt 27:35–46).

Many readers will know that Matthew tracks on Psalm 22 in this description. The parallels are impossible to miss:

Matthew 27	Psalm 22
They divided his clothes among themselves by casting lots (v. 35).	"They divide my garments among them, and for my clothing they cast lots" (v. 18).
"Those who passed by reviled him, shaking their heads.... In the same way also the chief priests, along with the scribes and elders, were mocking him" (vv. 39, 41).	"All who see me mock me. They open wide their lips; they shake the head ... they gaze, they look at me" (vv. 7, 17).
"Jesus cried out with a loud voice, saying, 'Eli, Eli, lema sabachthani?' (that is, 'My God, my God, why have you forsaken me?')" (v. 46).	"My God, my God why have you forsaken me?" (v. 1).

In addition to the clear textual links between Matthew and Psalm 22, scholars have long noticed that elements of Psalm 22 appear to describe injuries and conditions congruent with crucifixion:

- I am poured out like water, and all my bones are out of joint (v. 14).
- My strength is dry like a potsherd, and my tongue is sticking to my jaws (v. 15).[1]

Less apparent are some under-the-surface connections to the divine council worldview and its cosmic holy war context. If you were to read all of Psalm 22 at this point in our journey, verse 12 would no doubt jump off the page: "Many bulls encompass me; strong bulls of Bashan surround me."

STRONG BULLS OF *BASHAN*?

We know by now that Bashan carries a lot of theological baggage.[2] It was the Old Testament version of the gates of hell, the gateway to the underworld realm of the dead. It was known as "the place of the serpent" outside the Bible.

---

1. Readers may presume I've missed verse 16 (v. 17 in the Hebrew text): "They have pierced my hands and feet." (That rendering is the ESV translation.) I have not. Most Hebrew manuscripts of this verse do not have a reference to piercing the hands and feet, but read something to the effect: "Like the lion *they are at* my hands and feet" (LEB) or "my hands and feet have shriveled" (NRSV). The verse is arguably one of the most textually difficult in the Old Testament. With respect to our ensuing discussion, the lion imagery is interesting, since that imagery is applied to the devil in the New Testament (1 Pet 5:8). For piercing, see Zech 12:10. The scholarly literature on this verse is copious. A sampling illustrates the interpretive quandary: John Kaltner, "Psalm 22:17b: Second Guessing 'The Old Guess,'" *Journal of Biblical Literature* 117:3 (1998): 503–06; Brent A. Strawn, "Psalm 22:17b: More Guessing," *Journal of Biblical Literature* 119:3 (2000): 439–51; Kristin M. Swenson, "Psalm 22:17: Circling around the Problem Again," *Journal of Biblical Literature* 123:4 (2004): 637–48.

2. See chapter 24.

It's associated with Mount Hermon, the place where Jews believed the rebellious sons of God from Genesis 6:1–4 descended.

Simply put, if you wanted to conjure up images of the demonic and death, you'd refer to Bashan. If it's true that elements of Psalm 22 prefigure the crucifixion, it makes sense that a reference to Bashan would be part of that. But we still need a bit more context for understanding it.

In earlier discussion of Bashan, I briefly noted the presence of the cult site at Dan located within its northern region. The site was infamous with respect to the idolatrous worship of Samaria, the renegade northern kingdom of the ten tribes of Israel who forsook David's dynasty after Solomon died. This confederacy and rival kingdom was set up by Jeroboam (1 Kgs 12:25–33). So the worship of other gods—gods besides Yahweh who were called demons (*shedim*)—was part of the identity of Bashan.

That helps us process Amos 4, where the "bovines of Bashan" also appear:

> [1] Hear this word, you cows of Bashan who live on the mountain of Samaria, who oppress the powerless, who crush the poor, who say to their husbands, "Bring something so that we may drink!" [2] My Lord Yahweh has sworn by his holiness that, "Behold, the days are coming upon you when they will take you away with hooks, even the last of you with fishing hooks (Amos 4:1–2).

Since the "cows of Bashan" are said to speak to their "husbands," scholars are universally agreed that Amos is specifically addressing upper-class women of northern Israel who were idolaters of the golden calves of Bashan. I wouldn't disagree with that necessarily, but there's more to the wording than that.

Amos could be targeting temple priestesses who served the gods along with male priests. It is also quite possible that the cows of Bashan are the deities themselves in the form of the idols. This possibility is strengthened by noticing their crimes: "oppressing the poor [*dallim*]" and "crushing the needy [*ebyonim*]." These same two Hebrew words are used in Psalm 82, where the corrupt *elohim* are accused of exactly these same crimes (Psa 82:3–4).[3]

For our purposes, what we know for sure about Bashan is that it has secure associations with demonic powers. Although Psalm 22 wasn't originally mes-

---

3. The association is even stronger if the word "Harmon" in verse 3 is changed to "Hermon." The reference to being "dragged off to Harmon" has puzzled scholars, since there is no such place known. Some choose to change the text so that it reads "garbage dump," but most scholars think the original text should read "Hermon." The Hebrew letter that produces the "h" in "Harmon" (ה) is nearly identical to the one that produces "Khermon" / "Hermon" (ח), and so most scholars think the puzzle is the result of a simple scribal error. See Elmer H. Dyck, "Harmon (Place)," in *The Anchor Yale Bible Dictionary* (ed. David Noel Freedman; New York: Doubleday, 1992), 60–61.

sianic in focus, Matthew's use of it fixes that association.[4] The implication is that Jesus, at the moment of agony and death, was surrounded by the "bulls of Bashan"—demonic *elohim* who had been the foes of Yahweh and his children for millennia.[5]

THE FALL OF BASHAN

Bashan was ground zero for Old Testament demonic geography. But for all the darkness conjured up by the term, references to "Bashan" in the Old Testament aren't all sinister. Psalm 68:15–23 describes a time when Yahweh takes ownership of Bashan.

> [15] A mountain of God is the mountain of Bashan;
>   a mountain of many peaks is the mountain of Bashan.
> [16] Why do you look with hostility, O many-peaked mountains?
>   This mountain God desires for his dwelling.
>   Yes, Yahweh will abide in it forever.
> [17] The chariots of God
>   are twice ten thousand, with thousands doubled.
>   The Lord is among them at Sinai, distinctive in victory.
> [18] You have ascended on high; you have led away captives.
>   You have received gifts from among humankind,
>   and even from the rebellious, so that Yah God may dwell there.

The first thing that sticks out in this passage is that the infamous Mount Bashan is called the "mountain of God" (68:15). The phrase "mountain of God" is actually "mountain of *elohim*" (*har elohim*) in Hebrew. That means it can be translated as either "mountain of God" or "mountain of the gods."

The latter makes more sense than the former in context for the very observable reason that the two mountains in the passage—Bashan and Sinai—are rivals at the beginning of the psalm. The mountain of the gods (Bashan) "looks with hatred" at Yahweh's mountain, Mount Sinai. God desired Sinai for his abode, and the psalmist asks Bashan, "Why the envy?" This would make little sense if Bashan was already under Yahweh's authority.

The psalmist intends a contrast of association. In the Old Testament, Sinai

---

4. The word for "messiah" (*mashiach*) appears nowhere in Psa 22. See chapter 28 for the cryptic nature of messianic prophecy.

5. Although it's doubtful that he was thinking of Bashan, C. S. Lewis's scene in *The Lion, the Witch and the Wardrobe* depicting the voluntary death of Aslan on the stone table, surrounded by a horde of ghastly creatures under the command of the White Witch, is a vivid analogy to the point of Psa 22:12.

is firmly associated with Yahweh and Israel. Bashan is the polar opposite of Sinai. It symbolizes unholy ground.

The rest of the psalm describes an assault on Bashan by Yahweh and his holy army. We know the description refers to spiritual warfare since there was no such engagement of the Israelites in the Old Testament, and also because verse 17 clearly speaks of a divine army. Yahweh, the divine warrior, will one day tear down the strongholds of Bashan. He will lead a train of captives down from the mountain (v. 18).

TAKING PRISONERS

Psalm 68:18, where Yahweh leads a host of captives, may sound familiar. Paul cites the verse in Ephesians 4:

Psalm 68:18	Ephesians 4:8
You have ascended on high; you have led away captives. You have received gifts from among humankind.	Therefore it says, "When he ascended on high he led a host of captives, and he gave gifts to men" (ESV).

If you look closely, there is a problem in the quotation. For Paul, Psalm 68:18 was about Jesus ascending on high and *giving* gifts to humanity. Jesus is somehow the fulfillment of Psalm 68. But the Old Testament text has God ascending and *receiving* gifts.

Reconciling this conflict of ideas requires getting some context first.

Psalm 68 gives us a standard description of conquest, known from other ancient texts and even from ancient sculpture and iconography. The victorious captain of the army leads the enemy captives behind him; they are the human booty of war.

When Paul quotes Psalm 68:18 in Ephesians 4:8, he does so thinking of Jesus. Part of the confusion over how to interpret what Paul is saying is that so many commentators have assumed that captives are being *liberated* in Ephesians 4. That isn't the case. That idea would flatly contradict the well-understood Old Testament imagery. There is no liberation; there is *conquest*.

Paul's words identify Jesus with Yahweh. In Psalm 68:18 it was Yahweh who is described as the conqueror of the demonic stronghold. For Paul it is Jesus, the incarnate second Yahweh, surrounded by the demonic *elohim*, "bulls of Bashan," fulfilling the imagery of Psalm 68. Jesus puts the evil gods "to an open shame" (ESV) by "triumphing over them by [the cross]" (LEB) (Col 2:15). Psalm 68:18 and Ephesians 4:8 are in agreement if one sees conquest, not liberation.

What about the "receiving" and "giving" problem? Paul's wording doesn't deny there was conquest. What it does is point to the *result* of the conquest.

In the ancient world the conqueror would parade the captives and demand tribute for himself. Jesus is the conqueror of Psalm 68, and the booty does indeed rightfully belong to him. But booty was also distributed after a conquest. Paul knows that. He quotes Psalm 68:18 to make the point that after Jesus conquered his demonic enemies, he distributed the benefits of the conquest to his people, believers. Specifically, those benefits are apostles, prophets, evangelists, pastors, and teachers (Eph 4:11).

But how is Paul getting that idea? He explains himself in Ephesians 4:9–10.

Psalm 68:18	Ephesians 4:8
You have ascended on high; you have led away captives. You have received gifts from among humankind.	Therefore it says, "When he ascended on high he led a host of captives, and he gave gifts to men." (In saying, "He ascended," what does it mean but that he had also descended into the lower regions, the earth? He who descended is the one who also ascended far above all the heavens, that he might fill all things.) (ESV).

Christ's conquest results in the dispensing of gifts to his people after ascending (in conquest) in verse 8. But that ascent was accompanied by a descent ("into the lower regions").

Paul's logic is not at all clear, at least at first. What ascent and descent is he talking about? The text does not make clear the order of events, or even whether there *was* an intended order.

The key to understanding Paul's thinking is the descent. There are two possible explanations. The most common view is that, upon his death, Jesus descended into the lower regions *of the earth*. This is the way Ephesians 4:9 is worded in many translations. In this case, the language speaks both of the grave and of cosmic Sheol, the underworld. This is possible since elsewhere in the New Testament we read that Jesus descended into the underworld to confront the "spirits in prison"—the original transgressing sons of God from Genesis 6 (1 Pet 3:18–22).[6] But that visitation may not be Paul's point of reference here.

The second view is reflected in the ESV, which is the translation I used for Ephesians 4. Note that instead of "lower parts of the earth" the ESV inserts a comma: "the lower regions, the earth." The effect of the comma is that Jesus descended to "the lower regions, [in other words] *the earth*." This option fits

---

6. See chapter 12.

the context better (the gifts are given to people who are of course on earth) and has some other literary advantages. If this option is correct, then the descent of verses 9–10 does not refer to Jesus' time in the grave, but rather to the Holy Spirit's coming to earth after Jesus' conquering ascension on the day of Pentecost.

JESUS AND THE SPIRIT

This view makes sense in that the ascent (victory) would refer to the resurrection, and the descent would speak of the ensuing coming of the Spirit at Pentecost. *They are both triumphs*. But it raises an obvious question: Is Paul confusing Jesus with the Spirit?

Perhaps we should instead ask, is the Spirit Jesus in some way? The question sounds odd, but it's akin to asking if the man Jesus is God in some way. The answer, as we've seen in previous chapters, is that Jesus is the second Yahweh, the embodied Yahweh of the Old Testament. But Jesus is not the "Father" Yahweh. He therefore *is but isn't* Yahweh. It's the same with the Spirit. The Spirit is Yahweh, and so he is Jesus as well, but not incarnate or embodied. The Spirit *is but isn't* Jesus, just as Jesus *is but isn't* Yahweh the Father. The same sort of "two Yahwehs" idea from the Old Testament is found in the New Testament with respect to Jesus and the Spirit. *That* is the source of Trinitarian theology.[7]

Viewed against this backdrop, the idea that Jesus and the Spirit might be identified with each other isn't so strange. In fact, it helps us make sense of some things certain New Testament writers said about the Spirit.

It is clear that Jesus and the Spirit are different persons. That's clear from passages about Jesus' baptism (Matt 3:16), his temptation (Matt 4:1), and other passages (Matt 28:18–20; Acts 7:55). Jesus also said he and the Father would

---

7. There are seeds of this in the Old Testament as well, where the distinction between the Spirit and God is blurred just as the distinction between the Angel and God is blurred. For example, in Isa 63:7–11, an account of the wilderness wanderings, Yahweh is mentioned (v. 7) along with the Angel of his presence (v. 9). Yahweh was the savior of Israel (v. 8), but so was the Angel (v. 9); thus the writer interchanges the two. In verse 10 the Israelites are said to have "rebelled against" (Hebrew: *marah*) and "grieved" (Hebrew: *atsab*) the Holy Spirit. Psa 78:40–41 is a parallel passage to Isa 63:7–11, but that passage has the rebellion and grieving (the Hebrew words are the same) directed against "the Holy One of Israel," a well-known title for God. Taken together, the two passages interchange Yahweh, the Angel, and the Spirit. In Ezek 8 the prophet sees a divine being in the form of a man (v. 2). The being is embodied, since he extends his hand to Ezekiel (v. 3) and grabs him by a lock of the hair to lift him up. But it is *the Spirit* who is said to lift him up (v. 3). Later (vv. 5–6), the entity speaks to Ezekiel and refers to the temple as "my sanctuary." Is the entity the Spirit, who is identified as Yahweh by virtue of his reference to "my sanctuary," or is he the embodied Yahweh, who seems to have been the Spirit as well? The point is that the language of the passage blurs the distinctions between three figures: Yahweh, the second (embodied) Yahweh, and the Spirit.

send the Spirit (John 14:26; 15:26; cf. Luke 24:49). The Spirit was to come and indwell and empower believers. The events on Pentecost in Acts 2 mark the coming of the Spirit.

But the New Testament also identifies the Spirit with Jesus:[8]

> **6**And they traveled through the Phrygian and Galatian region, having been prevented by the Holy Spirit from speaking the message in Asia. **7**And when they came to Mysia, they attempted to go into Bithynia, and **the Spirit of Jesus** did not permit them (Acts 16:6–7).

> **9**But you are not in the flesh but in the Spirit, if indeed the Spirit of God lives in you. But if anyone does not have **the Spirit of Christ**, this person does not belong to him. **10**But if Christ is in you, the body is dead because of sin, but the Spirit is life because of righteousness (Rom 8:9–10).

> For I know that this will turn out to me for deliverance through your prayer and the support of **the Spirit of Jesus Christ** (Phil 1:19).

> **4**But when the fullness of time came, God sent out his Son, born of a woman, born under the law, **5**in order that he might redeem those under the law, in order that we might receive the adoption. **6**And because you are sons, God sent out **the Spirit of his Son** into our hearts, crying out, "Abba! (Father!)" (Gal 4:4–6).

> **10**Concerning this salvation, the prophets who prophesied about the grace meant for you sought and made careful inquiry, **11**investigating for what person or which time **the Spirit of Christ** in them was indicating when he testified beforehand to the sufferings with reference to Christ and the glories after these things (1 Pet 1:10–11).

Paul's quotation directs our attention in two important ways. First, not only did the sacrifice of Jesus on the cross mean the fall of Bashan, emblematic of the cosmic powers of evil, but it also triggered the empowerment of the Church by the gifts of the Spirit. Second, that victory and empowerment also had something to do with Pentecost.

Paul's thought about Pentecost in Ephesians 4 is quite the understatement. As it turned out, what happened at Pentecost cannot be understood without cosmic geography—the Deuteronomy 32 worldview. Like the gospel accounts, there's much more behind Acts 2 than we might have presumed.

---

8. Note that the effect of these verses is to make Jesus and God transposable as well (i.e., the Spirit of God and the Spirit of Jesus is the same Spirit, and so Jesus and God are interchangeable).

CHAPTER 34

Infiltration

THE DAY OF PENTECOST IS AN EVENT REMEMBERED BY MILLIONS OF CHRIStians each year. Although Acts 2 is one of the more familiar passages in the New Testament outside the Gospels, what the passage describes as happening that day definitely sounds strange.

> ¹And when the day of Pentecost had come, they were all together in the same place. ²And suddenly a sound like a violent rushing wind came from heaven and filled the whole house where they were sitting. ³And divided tongues like fire appeared to them and rested on each one of them. ⁴And they were all filled with the Holy Spirit and began to speak in other languages as the Spirit gave them ability to speak out.
>
> ⁵Now there were Jews residing in Jerusalem, devout men from every nation under heaven. ⁶And when this sound occurred, the crowd gathered and was in confusion, because each one was hearing them speaking in his own language. ⁷And they were astounded and astonished, saying, "Behold, are not all these who are speaking Galileans? ⁸And how do we hear, each one of us, in our own native language? ⁹Parthians and Medes and Elamites and those residing in Mesopotamia, Judea and Cappadocia, Pontus and Asia, ¹⁰Phrygia and Pamphylia, Egypt and the parts of Libya toward Cyrene, and the Romans who were in town, ¹¹both Jews and proselytes, Cretans and Arabs—we hear them speaking in our own languages the great deeds of God!" ¹²And all were amazed and greatly perplexed, saying to one another, "What can this mean?" ¹³But others jeered and said, "They are full of sweet new wine!" (Acts 2:1–13).

This description of the events of Pentecost is sprinkled with divine council imagery and has secure connections to the supernatural Deuteronomy 32 worldview we've talked about at length. Revealing those features is central to understanding what's happening in Acts 2 and the role it plays in Yahweh's plan to reclaim the nations and restore Eden.

DIVINE COMMISSIONING

The first two points of the description that deserve attention are the "violent rushing wind" and the "divided tongues like fire." Both are images in the Old Testament associated with God's presence—the disciples are being commissioned by God in his council like the prophets of old.

The whirlwind is familiar from divine encounters of Elijah (2 Kgs 2:1, 11) and Job (Job 38:1; 40:6). Ezekiel's divine commissioning likewise has the enthroned Yahweh coming with great wind (Ezek 1:4). The whirlwind motif is often accompanied by storm imagery, which can also include fire (Isa 30:30).[1] Having "wind" as an element in describing God's presence makes sense given that the Hebrew word translated "wind" can also be rendered "spirit/Spirit" (*ruach*).

Ezekiel's commissioning is particularly instructive since not only does Yahweh come to him with a wind, but with the wind there is "fire flashing" (Ezek 1:4). Burning fire is a familiar element of divine-council throne-room scenes (e.g., Isa 6:4, 6; Dan 7:9). It is especially prominent in the appearances at Sinai (Exod 3:2; 19:18; 20:18; Isa 4:5).[2] Fire in the Old Testament was an identifier of the presence of God, a visible manifestation of Yahweh's glory and essence.[3] It was also a way of describing divine beings in God's service (Judg 13:20; Psa 104:4).[4]

The wind and fire in Acts 2 signified to readers informed by divine council scenes that the gathered followers of Jesus were being commissioned by divine encounter. They were being chosen to preach the good news of Jesus' work. The fire connects them to the throne room. The tongues are emblematic of their speaking ministry.[5]

---

1. See E. J. Mabie, "Chaos," in *Dictionary of the Old Testament: Wisdom, Poetry & Writings* (ed. Tremper Longman III and Peter Enns; Downers Grove, IL: InterVarsity Press, 2008), 41–54 (esp. 46–47).

2. See also 2 Sam 22:9–13.

3. See also Gen 15:17 and Patrick D. Miller, "Fire in the Mythology of Canaan and Israel," *Catholic Biblical Quarterly* 27 (1965): 256–61.

4. The flame of Gen 3:24 may actually describe an individual divine being (see Ronald Hendel, " 'The Flame of the Whirling Sword': A Note on Genesis 3:24," *Journal of Biblical Literature* 104:4 [1985]: 671–74). The *seraphim* of Isa 6:2, 6 that attend Yahweh's throne may also have been fiery beings if the noun derives from the verb *saraph* ("to burn"). It is more likely that *seraphim* derives from the Hebrew noun *saraph* ("serpent"), which in turn is drawn from Egyptian throne guardian terminology and conceptions. If that is the case, Egyptian imagery relating to the divine throne guardians includes fire as well. See Philippe Provençal, "Regarding the Noun *saraph* in the Hebrew Bible," *Journal for the Study of the Old Testament* 29.3 (2005): 371–79.

5. What happened on the day of Pentecost shouldn't have been completely unexpected. It might certainly be the case that none of the gathered disciples were around on the day of Jesus' baptism when John the Baptist said that Jesus would baptize people "with the Holy Spirit and with fire" (Matt 3:11; Luke 3:16). But we know from Acts 1:1–5 that Jesus had indeed told the disciples he would send the Spirit after his resur-

BACK TO BABEL

At first glance there doesn't seem to be much in the Pentecost description that relates to the incident at Babel which had such cosmic-geographical and theological importance in the Old Testament. That first glance would be mistaken.

There are two key terms in the passage that connect it back to Babel in an unmistakable way. The flaming tongues are described as "divided" (Greek: *diamerizo*), and the crowd, composed of Jews from all the nations, is said to have been "confused" (Greek: *suncheo*).[6]

The second term, *suncheo* (v. 6), is the same word used in the Septuagint version of the Babel story in Genesis 11:7: "Come, let us go down and **confuse** [Septuagint: *suncheo*] their language there."[7] The multiplicity of nations represented at Pentecost is another link to Babel. Each nation had a national language. More importantly, all those nations referred to in Acts 2:9–11 had been disinherited by Yahweh when they were divided.

The other word of importance (*diamerizo*; v. 3) is also used in the Septuagint, but not in Genesis 11. It is found exactly where one would expect it if one were thinking in cosmic-geographical terms—Deuteronomy 32:8 (Septuagint: "When the Most High **divided** [*diamerizo*] the nations, when he scattered humankind, he fixed the boundaries of the nations").[8] This is a strong indication that Luke is drawing on the Septuagint, and specifically the Tower of Babel story in Genesis 11 and Deuteronomy 32:8–9, to describe the events on Pentecost. What happened there has some relationship to what happened at Babel—but what is it?

---

rection and therefore gave them orders to wait for that event (see John 14:26; 15:26; Luke 24:49; John 7:39). Additionally, although baptism "with the Holy Spirit and with fire" sounds like people would be baptized with two separate things (the Holy Spirit; fire), the grammar and syntax of these passages allow an equation or identification of these two elements. That is, they speak of the same thing, which would make good sense since fire symbolized the divine presence. See David L. Turner, *Matthew,* Baker Exegetical Commentary on the New Testament (Grand Rapids, MI: Baker Academic, 2008), 115–16.

6. The more technical, correct transliteration for the latter term is *sygcheo.* The one in the running text is to facilitate pronunciation.

7. A handful of New Testament commentators have noticed this but were at a loss as to what to make of it since they lack the divine council worldview backdrop with which Old Testament scholars are familiar. For example, C. K. Barrett says, "The use of the word suggests an intended allusion to the story of Babel, but the word, or words (συγχεῖν, συγχύννειν), are not uncommon (in the NT Acts only: 2:6; 9:22; 19:32; 21:27, 31) and it would be unwise to press too strongly the thought of a reversal of the dispersion of mankind as a result of diversity of speech" (*A Critical and Exegetical Commentary on the Acts of the Apostles; The Acts of the Apostles, 2 vols.* [Edinburgh: T&T Clark International, 2004], 119). Barrett is correct that the reversal of the dispersion has nothing *directly* to do *with diversity of speech.* But it has everything to do with regathering the disinherited nations given up in Deut 32:8–9, the event of Babel.

8. The Septuagint renders the Hebrew *beney elohim* ("sons of God") as "angels." For full discussion, see Michael S. Heiser, "Deuteronomy 32:8 and the Sons of God," *Bibliotheca Sacra* 158 (January–March 2001): 52–74.

At Pentecost the tongues are "divided" (*diamerizo*) or, perhaps more coherently, "distributed" among the disciples as they are commissioned to preach the good news to the throngs at Pentecost. As Jews gathered in Jerusalem for the celebration heard and embraced the news of Jesus and his resurrection, Jews who embraced Jesus as messiah would carry that message back to their home countries—the nations. Babel's disinheritance was going to be rectified by the message of Jesus, the second Yahweh incarnate, and his Spirit. The nations would again be his.

GO INTO ALL THE EARTH

The really amazing thing about Acts 2 is the part people skip: the list of nations. To understand what Luke's list telegraphs, we have to go back to Genesis 11 again. Here's a map of the nations listed in Genesis 10 that were divided in Genesis 11:[9]

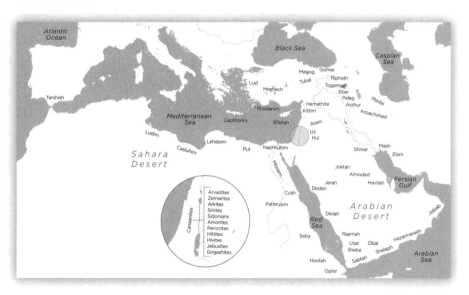

---

9. Some Bible maps have "Gether" near India, but this is hardly correct. As David Baker notes in the *Anchor Bible Dictionary*, "According to the Table of Nations (Gen 10:23), Gether is the son of Aram, the forefather of the Arameans or Syrians, who himself was the son of Shem, son of Noah. He and his descendants are thus Semitic. The corresponding genealogy in 1 Chr 1:17 places Gether as a son of Shem and brother of Aram. This is probably due to a simple copying error by an early scribe. His eye slipped from the first to the second of two lines which ended with the same word, 'Aram,' leading to the loss of the original line 'the sons of Aram (are)' which is still found in Genesis. Little else is known about the identity or geographical location of Gether, although the association with Aram would suggest an Aramean city" (see David W. Baker, "Gether [Person]," in *The Anchor Yale Bible Dictionary* [ed. David Noel Freedman; New York: Doubleday, 1992], 997).

What are we looking at? The key idea to grasp is that the "Table of Nations" in Genesis *represents the known world at the time it was written.* The Old Testament is a product of the ancient Near Eastern environment in which the biblical writers lived. There are no references in it (or anywhere else in the Bible) to locations like China, South America, North America, or Australia. What this means is that the Old Testament description of the disinheriting of the nations in Genesis 11 and Deuteronomy 32:8–9 is based on the nations known in biblical times. The Table of Nations lists known nations east to west, from eastern Mesopotamia to Tarshish (Gen 10:4), the most remote western point. What lay beyond Tarshish, through what we now call the Straits of Gibraltar, was a complete mystery to the biblical writers.

The list of nations in Acts 2 is not merely a rehashing of all the names in Genesis 10. Many names are different. A few observations about the list, however, reveal that it nevertheless correlates with the Table of Nations and its significance for cosmic geography.

First, the book of Acts is about the spread of the gospel *to the known world at the time.* The book begins with the statement in Acts 1:8 that the disciples who will encounter the Spirit are to be Jesus' witnesses to the known world: "But you will receive power when the Holy Spirit has come upon you, and you will be my witnesses in Jerusalem and in all Judea and Samaria, and to the end of the earth" (ESV). The "end of the earth" in the days of Luke, and of course the apostle Paul, was the extent of the Roman Empire.

This brings us to a second important observation: In terms of geographical coverage, *the reach of the gospel chronicled in the book of Acts constitutes an*

east-to-west sweep through the known world. Establishing that requires a closer inspection of the nations listed in Acts 2:9–11 at the Pentecost event:

⁹ Parthians and Medes and Elamites and those residing *in* Mesopotamia, Judea and Cappadocia, Pontus and Asia, ¹⁰ Phrygia and Pamphylia, Egypt and the parts of Libya toward Cyrene, and the Romans who were in town, ¹¹ both Jews and proselytes, Cretans and Arabs (Acts 2:9–11).

There is significant patterning to the list of nations in Acts 2 connected with the coming of the Spirit and the commissioning of the disciples.

The list begins with "Parthians and Medes and Elamites and those residing in Mesopotamia" (2:9). Jewish literature from the intertestamental period tells us that there was a Jewish population in Parthia (=Persia) at this time (1 Macc 15:15–22).[10] These were Jews who had migrated to Persia after choosing not to return to Jerusalem after the end of the exile. The Medes are known from the Old Testament in connection with where the ten northern tribes of Israel had been deported by the Assyrians (2 Kgs 17:6; 18:11). Persians (Parthians) and Medes are mentioned together in the Old Testament (Esth 1:19; Dan 5:28; 6:8, 12, 15), and the kings of Media are mentioned with the Elamites as well (Jer 25:25). *The list in Acts, then, begins at the farthest points east where there were Jewish populations, then progresses westward.*

After moving westward through Mesopotamia, the list naturally splits into southern and northern directions, following the land as it forks at the

---

10. This passage in 1 Maccabees is about Rome's support of Jewish populations in various parts of its empire. The reference to Arsaces in v. 22 is of significance for our discussion here, as Arsaces (also spelled Arsakes) was king in Parthia (Persia). On a Jewish population in Parthia, see also Josephus, *Antiquities* 15.2.2 par. 14.

Mediterranean Sea. The southern fork extends through Judea and Arabia.[11] The island of Crete is also mentioned. Paul took the gospel to both places (Titus 1:5; Gal 1:15–17). For the most part, Paul's missionary journeys followed the north fork through Asia Minor and Greece. But there were people at Pentecost from the nations of the south fork. We know the gospel followed the Nile down into Ethiopia (Acts 8:26–40) and bore fruit in Cyrene (Acts 11:20; 13:1).

The list keeps moving westward to Rome. By starting in the east, where there were Jewish populations because of the exile, and moving west, the Pentecost list confirms God's evangelism strategy articulated by Paul, who said that the gospel was for the Jew first, and then the Gentile (Rom 1:16). Three thousand Jews came to believe in Jesus as a result of the events at Pentecost (Acts 2:41), and those three thousand Jewish converts went back to their homelands after the Pentecost pilgrimage. These new disciples were the seeds of the gospel, Yahweh's plan to reclaim the nations.

The book of Acts ends with Rome, the destination of the imprisoned Paul on his way to appeal to Caesar. Luke's account therefore has Rome as its westernmost progression. But reversing the disinheritance of the nations required going farther than Rome. The most westerly point in the Table of Nations was Tarshish. Does the pattern of reversal initiated at Pentecost include Tarshish? Amazingly, it does.

I MUST GET TO SPAIN

The New Testament and early church tradition suggest that Paul was released from his bondage and went *farther* west before being taken into custody by the Romans for a second and final time.[12] In fact, Paul told people that he fully

---

11. Scholars have pondered why Judea is in the list, since the rest of the list consists of people groups speaking foreign languages. Some early church fathers thought that there might be a textual problem here and proposed alternative place names. The most natural solution would be that "Judea" refers to the parameters of the Old Testament's Davidic Empire, which extended from the Euphrates to Egypt. After the mention of Mesopotamia, David's empire covered most of the Fertile Crescent (Syria and Damascus; cf. Gal 1:15–21). *These areas included foreigners and foreign languages.*

12. The most thorough study on Paul's imprisonment and martyrdom is Harry W. Tajra, *The Martyrdom of St. Paul: Historical and Judicial Context, Traditions, and Legends*, vol. 3 (Tübingen: Mohr Siebeck, 1994). Tajra argues that Paul's appeal lapsed due to prosecutorial failure to successfully prosecute the case within the required time period and that Paul was released, at least for a couple of years, during which he visited Spain. Paul was later arrested again during the reign of Nero and executed for treason to the empire. There is also evidence for the belief in Paul's visit to Spain in early church writings such as Eusebius (260–339 AD; *Hist. eccl.* 2.22), the Muratorian Canon (ca. 170 AD), the *Acts of Peter* (late 2nd century AD), and Clement of Rome (ca. 96 AD, First Epistle to the Corinthians, V). Clement has Paul reaching "the farthest bounds of the West" after his release. As one scholar notes, "For a Roman, the 'farthest bounds of the West,' a phrase

expected to go to Spain after the Roman imprisonment mentioned in Acts. In his letter to the Romans, Paul told them twice that he intended to go to Spain (Rom 15:24, 28):

> [22] For this reason also I was hindered many times from coming to you, [23] and now, no longer having a place in these regions, but having a desire for many years to come to you [24] whenever I travel to Spain. For I hope while I am passing through to see you and to be sent on my way by you, whenever I have first enjoyed your company for a while. [25] But now I am traveling to Jerusalem, serving the saints. [26] For Macedonia and Achaia were pleased to make some contribution for the poor among the saints in Jerusalem. [27] For they were pleased to do so, and they are obligated to them. For if the Gentiles have shared in their spiritual things, they ought also to serve them in material things. [28] Therefore, after I have accomplished this and sealed this fruit for delivery to them, I will depart by way of you for Spain (Rom 15:22–28).

Why is Spain of any concern to us, and why did Paul want so badly to go there? *In Paul's day, Spain was where Tarshish was.* Tarshish was a Phoenician colony in what was later Spain.

The point is profound: Paul was convinced that his life's mission as apostle to the Gentiles—the disinherited nations—would only be finished when he got to Spain.[13] As incredible as it sounds, Paul was conscious that his mission for Jesus actually involved spreading the gospel to the westernmost part of the known world—Tarshish—so that the disinheritance at Babel would be reversed.

THE FULLNESS OF THE GENTILES

Paul telegraphed that belief in Romans 11—even before he told his readers he wanted to go to Spain (Rom 15:24, 28). Discerning that requires observing how Paul is tracking on certain Old Testament passages about the reclamation of the nations—the Gentiles.

> [25] For I do not want you to be ignorant, brothers, of this mystery, so that you will not be wise in your own sight, that a partial hardening has happened to

---

often used by Roman writers to refer to Spain, could only mean the Iberian peninsula" (Otto F. A. Meinardus, "Paul's Missionary Journey to Spain: Tradition and Folklore." *The Biblical Archaeologist* [1978]: 61–63).

13. Paul's language indicates he expected to get to Spain. See the discussion of ὡς ἄν with the subjunctive as equivalent to ὅταν with the subjunctive in Friedrich Blass, Albert Debrunner, and Robert Walter Funk, *A Greek Grammar of the New Testament and Other Early Christian Literature* (Chicago: University of Chicago Press, 1961), 237. On the Old Testament context for Paul's urgency to get to Spain, see Roger Aus, "Paul's Travel Plans to Spain and the 'Full Number of the Gentiles' of Rom XI 25," *Novum Testamentum* 21:3 (July, 1979): 232–262.

Israel, until the full number of the Gentiles has come in, [26] and so all Israel will be saved, just as it is written,

> "The deliverer will come out of Zion;
> he will turn away ungodliness from Jacob.
> [27] And this is the covenant from me with them
> when I take away their sins" (Rom 11:25–27).

Paul says, "I want you to understand this mystery." What mystery? That God's own portion and son, Israel, hardened their heart. For how long? "Until the full number of the Gentiles has come in." Why is it important that this inclusion of the Gentiles happen? "And so *all Israel* will be saved." Paul includes people from the disinherited nations in Israel, Yahweh's family. This family reunion will only happen when "the deliverer comes out of Zion."

But why would Paul link the "the full number of the Gentiles" with Spain (Tarshish)? Why did he believe that his life and ministry would not be over until he got there? Because he knew Isaiah 66:15–23. The passage has a number of correlations with the events of Pentecost, not only with respect to Acts 2 but other passages as well. (Recall that in the last chapter, we saw how Psalm 68, including the conquest of Bashan, was quoted by Paul in Ephesians 4 about the victory of Jesus and the coming of the Spirit at Pentecost.) I've listed those correlations in the table below and inserted footnotes to guide our reading.

Isaiah 66:15–23	Other Passages and Notes
For look! Yahweh will come **in fire**, and his **chariots** like the **storm wind**, to give back his anger in wrath, and his rebuke in **flames of fire**. For Yahweh enters into judgment on all flesh with fire and his sword, and those slain by Yahweh shall be many (vv. 15–16).	A **violent rushing wind** came from heaven.... And divided tongues like **fire** appeared to them (Acts 2:2–3). A mountain of God is the mountain of Bashan ... This mountain God desires for his dwelling.... The chariots of God are twice ten thousand, with thousands doubled.... You have ascended on high; you have led away captives. You have received gifts from among humankind (Psa 68:15–18).
"And I ... am about to come to **gather** all **nations** and **tongues,** and they shall come and see my glory[1] (v. 18).	Now there were Jews residing in **Jerusalem**, devout men from **every nation** under heaven. And when this sound occurred, the crowd **gathered** and was in confusion, because each one was hearing them speaking in **his own language** (Acts 2:5).
I will set a sign among them. And I will send survivors[2] from them to the nations: **Tarshish, Pul, and Lud,**[3] who draw the bow; **Tubal and Javan,** the faraway coastlands that have not heard of my fame, and have not seen my glory.[4] And they shall declare my glory among the nations, (v. 19)	Cappadocia, Pontus and Asia, Phrygia and Pamphylia,[5] **Egypt** and the parts of **Libya** toward Cyrene[6] (Acts 2:9–10).

Isaiah 66:15–23	Other Passages and Notes
and bring all your countrymen[7] **from all the nations** as an offering to Yahweh on horses and chariots and in litters and on mules and camels, **to my holy mountain, Jerusalem**," says Yahweh, "just as the sons of Israel bring an offering in a clean vessel to the house of Yahweh. And indeed, I will take some of them as priests and for Levites," says Yahweh (vv. 20–21). "For just as the new heavens and earth that I *am* about to make shall stand before me," declares Yahweh, "so shall your descendants and your name stand. And this shall happen: From new moon to new moon and from Sabbath to Sabbath **all flesh shall come to bow in worship before me**," says Yahweh (vv. 22–23).	See Paul's mission as apostle to the Gentiles.

1. Jerusalem is the place where the glory of God resided in Israel.

2. The "survivors" are those Jews who survived the exile. Isaiah prophesies that God's punishment of exile has served to send Israelites/Judeans into the nations to spread the knowledge of Yahweh in them ("declare his glory"). Paul sees Isa 66:19 as fulfilled at Pentecost—Jews that embrace Jesus go back to their nations to "declare God's glory" in those nations. See verse 20.

3. Some English translations, like the LEB, read "Pul" here. The reading should be "Put" (from LXX) because there is no nation or people known as Pul in ancient history (see ESV). The Septuagint reading of "Put" makes good sense, as Put is a nation regularly mentioned with Lud elsewhere in the Old Testament (e.g., Jer 46:9; Ezek 27:10; 30:5; 38:5). See Shalom M. Paul, *Isaiah 40–66: Translation and Commentary* (Eerdmans Critical Commentary; Grand Rapids, MI; Cambridge, UK: William B. Eerdmans Publishing Company, 2012), 627.

4. Put, Lud, Tarshish, Tubal, and Javan all appear in the Table of Nations in Gen 10. Put and Lud are associated with Libya, North Africa (western Egypt), and Cush (Ethiopia). Tubal and Javan correspond to Asia Minor and (Ionian) Greece. See Shalom M. Paul, *Isaiah 40–66*, Eerdmans Critical Commentary (Grand Rapids, MI: Eerdmans, 2012), 627–28; David W. Baker, "Lud (Person)," in *The Anchor Yale Bible Dictionary* (ed. David Noel Freedman; New York: Doubleday, 1992), 397.

5. These places are all found in Asia Minor (see the map for the Pentecost nations).

6. These places are all in North Africa (see the map for the Pentecost nations). Acts 8 has the gospel taken into Ethiopia.

7. In other words, the Jewish evangelists will bring more people—Gentiles, now called "brothers"—as an "offering to the Lord." This would fulfill the original covenant with Abraham, and all Israel as a kingdom of priests—to bless the nations (Gen 12:1–3).

Why did Paul want to get to Spain (Tarshish)? Paul saw his ministry as the fulfillment of the prophecy of Isaiah 66, where Yahweh would take people from all nations to be his children. Paul believed he was the instrument to bring in the "full number of the Gentiles" that would result in all true Israelites—those who believe in Jesus—being saved (Rom 11:25–27).[14] Tarshish is listed in Isaiah 66, but was not represented in the names at Pentecost. The farthest point west in the Pentecost list is Rome (Acts 2:10). Paul knew that Spain (Tarshish) was part of the mission of Isaiah 66. He needed Spain so that

---

14. Compare what Paul wrote in Gal 3:7–9, 28–29: [7]"Understand that the ones who have faith, these are sons of Abraham. [8]And the scripture, foreseeing that God would justify the Gentiles by faith, proclaimed the good news in advance to Abraham: 'In you all the nations will be blessed.' [9]So then, the ones *who have* faith are blessed together with Abraham who believed.... [28]There is neither Jew nor Greek, there is neither slave nor free, there is neither male and female, for you are all one in Christ Jesus. [29]And if you *are* Christ's, then you are descendants of Abraham, heirs according to the promise."

his "offering of the Gentiles may become acceptable, sanctified by the Holy Spirit" (Rom 15:16).

And so it was that a room full of Jews, commissioned directly by the Spirit, went out and began the process by which the disinherited nations would be brought back into Yahweh's family. Pentecost marked the beginning of an unstoppable march across the known world—and our world, a world they didn't know—that would culminate in a global Eden.

CHAPTER 35

Sons of God, Seed of Abraham

We've devoted a lot of space to describing God's plan to reclaim the disinherited nations and restore his rule. Let's review: Yahweh's original intention was that all humankind would be his earthly family, ruling in cooperation with him and his heavenly family. The Old Testament describes the ruin of Yahweh's desire through a series of primeval rebellions. But the original objective was not defeated, only delayed. After the rebellion at Babel, Yahweh set aside the nations and called Abraham to begin anew.

Even as Yahweh started his kingdom plan with this one man and his wife, there were hints that the nations were not forgotten—in fact, God said that through Abraham all nations would be blessed (Gen 12:3). The focal point of that blessing was to be the ultimate son of Abraham, the messiah. After his resurrection, the Spirit promised by Jesus—and by the prophets of old—came at Pentecost and began the great reversal. The gospel was carried to all the nations of the known world, transforming men and women held hostage to other gods into sons and daughters of Yahweh.[1]

IF YOU ARE CHRIST'S, YOU ARE ABRAHAM'S SEED

We saw in the last chapter that Paul understood God's plan of infiltration in the wake of Pentecost and, once confronted by Jesus on the road to Damascus,

---

1. There have been several lengthy scholarly studies on divine sonship as it relates to Christians: Brendan Byrne, *"Sons of God"-"Seed of Abraham": A Study of the Idea of the Sonship of God of All Christians in Paul Against the Jewish Background* (Analecta Biblica 83; Rome: Pontifical Biblical Institute Press, 1979); James M. Scott, *Adoption as Sons of God: An Exegetical Investigation Into the Background of Yiothesia in the Pauline Corpus* (*Wissenschaftliche Untersuchungen zum Neuen Testament* 48; Tübingen: Mohr Siebeck, 1992); Matthew Vellanichal, *The Divine Sonship of Christians in the Johannine Writings* (Analecta Biblica 72; Rome: Pontifical Biblical Institute Press, 1977). Shorter articles include: Michael Peppard, "Adopted and Begotten Sons of God: Paul and John on Divine Sonship," *Catholic Biblical Quarterly* 73:1 (Jan 2011):92–110; James Tabor, "Firstborn of Many Brothers: A Pauline Notion of Apotheosis," (Society of Biblical Literature Seminar Papers 21; Chico: Calif.: Scholars Press, 1984), 295–303.

his own role in that plan. In his letters he referred to it as a mystery—how God could make the Gentile, a member of the disinherited nations, a full member in the family that he'd begun with Abraham. Instead of being *disinherited* by Yahweh, Gentiles were now joint heirs of the true God. Paul's letter to the predominantly Gentile church at Ephesus is one example:

> [1]On account of this I, Paul, the prisoner of Christ Jesus for the sake of you Gentiles [2]—if indeed you have heard about the stewardship of God's grace given to me for you. [3]According to revelation the **mystery** was made known to me, just as I wrote beforehand in brief, [4]so that you may be able when you read to understand my insight into the **mystery** of Christ [5](which in other generations was not made known to the sons of men as it has now been revealed to his holy apostles and prophets by the Spirit): [6]**that the Gentiles are fellow heirs**, and fellow members of the body, and fellow sharers of the promise in Christ Jesus through the gospel (Eph 3:1–6).

Paul's message to the church at Galatia was just as dramatic:

> [6]Just as Abraham believed God, and it was credited to him for righteousness, [7]then understand that the ones who have faith, these are sons of Abraham. [8]And the scripture, foreseeing that God would justify the Gentiles by faith, proclaimed the good news in advance to Abraham: "In you all the nations will be blessed." [9]So then, the ones who have faith are blessed together with Abraham who believed…. [26]For you are all sons of God through faith in Christ Jesus, [27]for as many of you as were baptized into Christ have put on Christ. [28]There is neither Jew nor Greek, there is neither slave nor free, there is neither male and female, for you are all one in Christ Jesus. [29]And **if you are Christ's, then you are descendants of Abraham, heirs according to the promise** (Gal 3:6–9, 26–29).

In Christ, believers are "the sons of God." The language of inheritance is crystal clear. It derives from and advances the Old Testament idea that humans were meant to be in the *family* of God all along. It's no coincidence that the New Testament writers repeatedly describe salvation into Yahweh's family with words like "adoption," "heir," and "inheritance" to describe what the Church really is—the reconstituted divine-human family of God. The believer's destiny is to become what Adam and Eve originally were: immortal, glorified imagers of God, living in God's presence as his children.[2] The theological mes-

---

2. Recent studies on angelic–human relationships in Second Temple Jewish angelology and New Testament angelology have focused on this "angelification" (divinization) of believers. For example, one scholar focusing on this material concludes that original humanity ought to be considered "both angelomorphic and divine" (Crispin Fletcher-Louis, "The Worship of Divine Humanity as God's Image and the Worship

saging is unmistakable in the context of the epic story we've tracked through the Old Testament:

> [11] He came to his own things, and his own people did not receive him. [12] But as many as received him—to those who believe in his name—he gave to them authority to become children of God, [13] who were born not of blood, nor of the will of the flesh, nor of the will of a husband, but of God (John 1:11–13).

> [1] See what sort of love the Father has given to us: that we should be called children of God, and we are! Because of this the world does not know us: because it did not know him. [2] Dear friends, now we are children of God, and what we will be has not yet been revealed. We know that whenever he is revealed we will be like him, because we will see him just as he is (1 John 3:1–2).

> [4] But when the fullness of time came, God sent out his Son, born of a woman, born under the law, [5] in order that he might redeem those under the law, in order that we might receive the adoption. [6] And because you are sons, God sent out the Spirit of his Son into our hearts, crying out, "Abba! (Father!)," [7] so that you are no longer a slave but a son, and if a son, also an heir through God (Gal 4:4–7).

> [15] For you have not received a spirit of slavery leading to fear again, but you have received the Spirit of adoption, by whom we cry out, "Abba! Father!" [16] The Spirit himself confirms to our spirit that we are children of God, [17] and if children, also heirs—heirs of God and fellow heirs with Christ, if indeed we suffer together with him so that we may also be glorified together with him (Rom 8:15–17).

> [4] Just as he chose us in him before the foundation of the world, that we should be holy and blameless before him in love, [5] having predestined us to adoption through Jesus Christ to himself according to the good pleasure of his will (Eph 1:4–5).

We are accustomed, of course, to thinking of the Church as the "body of Christ." It is certainly that as well. But this term points us to the family metaphor. The idea of the Church being "the body of Christ" reflects the truth that it is through Christ's *physical* incarnation, *physical* death, and *physical*

---

of Jesus," in *The Jewish Roots of Christological Monotheism: Papers from the St. Andrews Conference on the Historical Origins of the Worship of Jesus* (ed. Carey C. Newman, James R. Davila, Gladys S. Lewis; Leiden: E. J. Brill, 1999), 112–128 (esp. 113–120). Another notes: "Comparing and relating humans to angels was in the time of Paul an important feature of Jewish religious life" (Guy Williams, *The Spirit World in the Letters of Paul the Apostle: A Critical Examination of the Role of Spiritual Beings in the Authentic Pauline Epistles*, Forschungen zur Religion und Literatur des Alten und Neuen Testaments 231 [Göttingen: Vandenhoeck & Ruprecht, 2009], 113–14).

resurrection that believers—Jew or Gentile—become members of God's family. Quoting Paul once again: "The Gentiles are fellow heirs, and fellow members of the body, and fellow sharers of the promise in Christ Jesus through the gospel" (Eph 3:6).

It is Christ who fuses the chosen sons of God from Abraham's line to the sons of God called from the nations. His work on the cross is where the exiled and the disinherited meet, forming one new entity. But that's only one aspect of who we are.

INHERITED AUTHORITY: A Stake in the Family Business

Believers are more than God's family. Being "the sons of God" also means being members of God's governing rule—his council. Believers have a divinely appointed purpose. Adam and Eve were supposed to make all the world Eden—to spread the kingdom rule of God so that we could enjoy the love of God, our Father. That hasn't changed.

Recall that, in ancient Israelite thinking, God's home was not only where his family lived, but also where the council met. The place was one and the same, and the members were one and the same. So it is in the New Testament. While New Testament writers employ family terms to describe the Church, it is also no coincidence that they use Old Testament terminology we would associate with the divine council. Ephesians 1:5, 11–19 is a good starting point:

> ⁵ having predestined us to adoption through Jesus Christ to himself according to the good pleasure of his will … ¹¹ in whom also we were chosen, having been predestined according to the purpose of the One who works all things according to the counsel of his will, ¹² that we who hoped beforehand in Christ should be for the praise of his glory, ¹³ in whom also you, when you heard the word of truth, the gospel of your salvation, in whom also when you believed you were sealed with the promised Holy Spirit, ¹⁴ who is the down payment of our **inheritance**, until the redemption of the possession, to the praise of his glory.
>
> ¹⁵ Because of this I also, hearing of your faith in the Lord Jesus and your love for all the saints, ¹⁶ do not cease giving thanks for you, making mention in my prayers, ¹⁷ that the God of our Lord Jesus Christ, the glorious Father, may give you a spirit of wisdom and revelation in the knowledge of him ¹⁸ (the eyes of your hearts having been enlightened), so that you may know what is the hope of his calling, what are the riches of the glory of his **inheritance** among the **saints**, ¹⁹ and what is the surpassing greatness of his power toward us who believe.

The English translation obscures an important Old Testament connection back to the divine council. The word for "saints" in verse 18 (and elsewhere in the New Testament) is *hagioi*, which means "holy ones." Paul tells the Ephesians that believers have a glorious inheritance *among the holy ones.*

We've discussed the term "holy ones" in the Old Testament before.[3] It is used of divine beings in Yahweh's divine council (e.g., Job 5:1; 15:15; Psa 89:5–7; Zech 14:5). The Hebrew term is *qedoshim.* The Septuagint, the Greek translation of the Old Testament used by New Testament writers, translates that term with *hagioi,* the same word as in Ephesians 1:18. We also saw earlier that the Old Testament uses *qedoshim* of people—specifically of believing Israelites—those not guilty of worshipping other gods and bringing the disaster of exile to pass (Psa 16:3; 34:9; cp. Lev 26:14–33).

We saw earlier, in chapter 30, that both uses come together in a crucial chapter—Daniel 7. That chapter had the second Yahweh figure in human form, the son of man, receiving an everlasting kingdom from the enthroned Ancient of Days. The kingdom was also given to the holy ones—both divine and human (Dan 7:22, 27). The passage conveyed the idea of joint rulership in God's kingdom.

Paul echoes that thought in his letter to the Ephesians when he says that we have an inheritance among the holy ones. We are not only heirs and children in God's divine family, but we inherit the right to rule and reign with Jesus. Paul described our kingdom inheritance in Col 1:11–13. He prays that his readers will be

> [11] enabled with all power, according to his glorious might, for all steadfastness and patience with joy, [12] giving thanks to the Father who has qualified you for a share of the **inheritance** of the saints [holy ones] in light, [13] who has rescued us from the domain of darkness and transferred us to the **kingdom** of the Son he loves.

Once the nations are restored to Yahweh through the gospel, believers will displace the divine beings who presently dominate the nations and rule in their place as Yahweh's children and corulers. As Paul wrote elsewhere, believers will "judge angels" (1 Cor 6:3).[4] The apostle John is just as direct in Revelation 2:

> [Jesus says]: [25] Nevertheless, hold fast to what you have until I come. [26] And the one who conquers and who keeps my works until the end, I will give him **authority over the nations,** [27] and "he will shepherd them with an iron rod; he

---

3. See chapter 30.

4. As noted earlier, other scholars refer to this teaching as the "angelification" of the believing community (see Williams, *Spirit World in the Letters of Paul the Apostle,* 117–18).

will break them in pieces like jars made of clay," [28] as I also have received from my Father, and I will give him the morning star (Rev 2:25–28).

The power of this passage is found in John's citation (in v. 27) of Psalm 2, which describes the messiah's reign. Before telling his messianic king, "You will break them with an iron rod," Yahweh says to him, "You are my son; today I have begotten you. Ask from me and I will make the nations your heritage, and your possession the end of the earth" (Psa 2:7–8). Jesus, the messiah, inherits the everlasting kingdom—and then shares it with his children, "those who overcome" until his return. John tells us directly in his next chapter (Rev 3:21) that those who overcome rule and reign with Jesus:

> [20] Behold, I stand at the door and knock! If anyone hears my voice and opens the door, indeed I will come in to him and dine with him, and he with me. [21] The one who conquers, I will grant to him to **sit down with me on my throne**, as I also have conquered and have sat down with my Father on his throne (Rev 3:20–21).

The destiny of the believer is not only a place in God's home, but dominion with Jesus "among the holy ones" (Eph 1:18).

THE MORNING STAR

Revelation 2:28, quoted just above, had an unusual phrase in it. To the one who overcomes, Jesus says, "I will give him the morning star." The odd wording reinforces the idea of our joint rule with Jesus over the nations.

The "morning star" phrase takes us back once more to the Old Testament, which at times uses astral terminology to describe divine beings. Job 38:7 is the best example ("the morning stars were singing together and all the sons of God shouted for joy").[5] Stars were bright and, in the worldview of the ancients, living divine beings since they moved in the sky and were beyond the human realm.

The morning star language in Revelation 2:28 is messianic—it refers to a divine being who would come from Judah. We know this by considering two other passages in tandem.

In Numbers 24:17, we read the prophecy that "a star will go out from Jacob, and a scepter will rise from Israel." Numbers 24:17 was considered messianic in Judaism, completely apart from the New Testament writers.[6] In other

---

5. See also Judg 5:20; Dan 8:10; 12:3; Rev 1:20; 12:4, 9.
6. See Testament of Levi 18:3; Testament of Judah 24:1; 1QM 11:6–7; 4QTestim 9–13; CD 7:18–20.

words, literate readers of John's writing would have known the morning star reference was not about literal brightness. It was about the dawning of the returned kingdom of God under its messiah. Later in the book of Revelation, Jesus himself refers to his messianic standing with the morning star language: "I am the root and the descendant of David, the bright morning star" (Rev 22:16).

The wording of Revelation 2 is especially powerful when read against this backdrop. Not only does Jesus *say* that he is the messianic morning star in Revelation 22:16, but when he says "I will give him [who overcomes] the morning star" (Rev 2:28), he grants us the authority to rule with him.

As dramatic as these thoughts are, we'll see one that trumps them all in the next chapter. We aren't just God's children and corulers with his Son. We're Jesus' *siblings*—and each of us will meet the council with him at our side.

CHAPTER 36

Lower Than the *Elohim*

THE LAST CHAPTER LEFT US WITH A LIFE-CHANGING THOUGHT: *WE ARE THE children of God, destined to displace the defeated, disloyal sons of God who now rule the nations.* Believing followers of Jesus Christ are the fulfillment of God's plan to have humanity join the divine family-council and restore Eden.

But that's still not the full story. We will be made like him (1 John 3:1–3). We will become divine. In this chapter I'll unpack that in more detail, explaining what it means and doesn't mean, beginning with our introduction to the divine council after death—or in life if we are alive when Jesus returns.

JESUS, ANGELS, AND US

No other passage in the New Testament is as powerful in its divine council theology as Hebrews 1–2. Once you grasp the divine council worldview, these chapters explode. You'll recognize several terms and ideas we've covered to this point.

> [1]Although God spoke long ago in many parts and in many ways to the fathers by the prophets, [2]in these last days he has spoken to us by a Son, whom he appointed heir of all things, through whom also he made the world, [3]who is the radiance of his glory and the representation of his essence, sustaining all things by the word of power. When he had made purification for sins through him, he sat down at the right hand of the Majesty on high, [4]having become by so much better than the angels, by as much as he has inherited a more excellent name than theirs (Heb 1:1–4).

Jesus is heir to all things because he is Yahweh, made flesh to provide a secure way of restoring humanity's place and role in a global Eden. He is superior to angels (v. 4). The writer explains in verses 5 and 6:

⁵For to which of the angels did he ever say,

"You are my son,
today I have begotten you,"

and again,

"I will be his father,
and he will be my son"?

⁶And again, when he brings the firstborn into the world, he says,
"And let all the angels of God worship him" (Heb 1:5–6).

Jesus is superior to the angels since he was "begotten" as the son of God. The term is an antiquated one that is seldom used in modern English. It has a wide range of meanings, from procreation to a more ambiguous "bringing forth."[1] Used of Jesus, the term cannot refer to being created at some point in time. Jesus is Yahweh himself in human form, an idea that derives from the Old Testament.

It is best to understand the term as "brought forth" in the sense of *revealed in a unique way*—in this instance, the full incarnation of Yahweh. Jesus is the lone divine son who deserves worship, because he is the uncreated essence of Yahweh in a human body, now resurrected from death.

Because of the failure of Israel in the course of God's attempts to revive his Edenic rule and plan, we saw that he adopted a new strategy that would not fail. The Old Testament knows this as the new covenant (Jer 31:31–33), a covenant wherein the Spirit would instill God's rule in the hearts of believers. God could depend only on himself.

Because God's original plan included human participation, humanity could not be simply set aside. The solution was to become man and do what needed to be done in order to inaugurate the new Eden. And so he did. God himself became man in Jesus of Nazareth. His death and resurrection were the catalysts. This is why Jesus, at the Last Supper, referred to the new covenant in terms of his body and blood. The result of Jesus' obedience unto death, resurrection, and the coming of the Spirit is laid out by the writer of Hebrews, who uses God's plan to explain the distinction between Jesus and angels:

⁷And concerning the angels he says,

"The one who makes his angels winds,
and his servants a flame of fire,"

---

1. BDAG, 193–94.

8but concerning the Son,

> "Your throne, O God, is forever and ever,
> and the scepter of righteous is the scepter of your kingdom.
> **9**   You have loved righteousness and hated lawlessness;
> because of this God, your God, has anointed you
>   with the olive oil of joy more than your companions.

10And,

> "You, Lord, laid the foundation of the earth in the beginning,
> and the heavens are the works of your hands;
> **11**   they will perish, but you continue,
>   and they will all become old like a garment,
> **12**   and like a robe you will roll them up,
> and like a garment they will be changed;
> but you are the same, and your years will not run out."

13But to which of the angels has he ever said,

> "Sit down at my right hand,
> until I make your enemies a footstool for your feet."

14Are they not all spirits engaged in special service, sent on assignment for the sake of those who are going to inherit salvation? (Heb 1:7–14).

Did you catch the distinctions? Jesus inherits rulership and dominion, angels do not. Angels are "ministering spirits" who serve the human believers who inherit salvation and are adopted into Yahweh's family.

Cast against what we learned in the last chapter, this is a bombshell. *We* are the ones united to Christ, not angels. *We* are the ones given the morning star, the credential for rule, by Jesus himself. *We* are the ones who will be put over the nations. To echo Paul once more: *Don't you realize that you will judge angels?* (1 Cor 6:3).

The writer of Hebrews did.

JESUS, OUR BROTHER IN THE COUNCIL

Hebrews 2 builds on the superiority of Christ and its implications for believers.

1Because of this, it is all the more necessary that we pay attention to the things we have heard, lest we drift away. **2**For if the word spoken through angels was binding and every transgression and act of disobedience received a just penalty, **3**how will we escape if we neglect so great a salvation which had its beginning when it was spoken through the Lord and was confirmed to us by those who heard, [4]while God was testifying at the same time by signs and wonders and various miracles and distributions of the Holy Spirit according to his will (Heb 2:1–4).

The word spoken by angels that was "binding and every transgression and act of disobedience received a just penalty"? Of course—the divine council was there at Sinai witnessing the delivering of the law.[2] Signs, wonders, miracles, and distributions of the Holy Spirit? Remember Pentecost and the conquest of Bashan?[3] Paul saw the coming of the Spirit at Pentecost as the fulfillment of the defeat of Bashan—symbolic of the forces of darkness (Eph 4:8–10).

The coming of the Spirit at Pentecost was, of course, the launch of the reclaiming of the nations. Hebrews 2:5–8 tells us that the ultimate outcome of that re-inheritance is the rule of those nations by believers, to whom the preeminent Christ has given authority:

[5]For he [God] did not subject to angels the world to come, about which we are speaking. [6]But someone testified somewhere, saying,

> "What is man, that you remember him,
>   or the son of man, that you care for him?
> [7]You made him for a short time lower than the angels;
>   you crowned him with glory and honor;
> [8]   you subjected all things under his feet (Heb 2:5–8).

Note that Hebrews is clear—earth wasn't created to be subject to the members of God's divine family, but to his human family. The council was with God in Eden, and so heaven and earth were meant to be transposed, but the task of administrating God's good world was *ours*. This despite the fact that we were lesser beings compared to God's divine family-council.

The Old Testament text quoted in Hebrews 2:6–8 is Psalm 8:4–6. The Hebrew reads that humankind was created "a little lower than the *elohim*." And this is how it was in Eden. Humans were lesser than *elohim*—but God's plan was to elevate humanity to be included in his family, and take charge of God's new earthly domain.[4]

---

2. See chapter 21.

3. See chapter 33.

4. This is what led early Christian thinkers to speculate that it was envy that caused one member of the council, a trusted throne guardian, to plot against humanity. For example, the Apocalypse of Sedrach 5:1–2 reads: "Sedrach said to him, 'It was by your will that Adam was deceived, my Master. You commanded your angels to worship Adam, but he who was first among the angels disobeyed your order and did not worship him; and so you banished him, because he transgressed your commandment and did not come forth (to worship) the creation of your hands'" (James H. Charlesworth, ed., *The Old Testament Pseudepigrapha*

For in subjecting all things, he left nothing that was not subject to him. But now we do not yet see all things subjected to him, [9]but we see Jesus, for a short time made lower than the angels, because of the suffering of death crowned with glory and honor, so that apart from God he might taste death on behalf of everyone (Heb 2:8–9).

The second Yahweh of Hebrews 1, who is the essence of Yahweh, was incarnated as a man to taste death for everyone. And since he became man, we are his siblings. Someday, Jesus will introduce us to the council—unashamed at our humanity. He became as we are so that we might become as he is.

[10]For it was fitting for him for whom are all things and through whom are all things in bringing many sons to glory to perfect the originator of their salvation through sufferings. [11]For both the one who sanctifies and the ones who are sanctified are all from one, for which reason he [Jesus] is not ashamed to call them brothers, [12]saying,

"I will proclaim your name to my brothers;
in the midst of the assembly I will sing in praise of you."

[13]And again,

"I will trust in him."

And again,

"Behold, I and the children God has given me."

[14]Therefore, since the children share in blood and flesh, he also in like manner shared in these same things, in order that through death he could destroy the one who has the power of death, that is, the devil, [15]and could set free these who through fear of death were subject to slavery throughout all their lives (Heb 2:10–15).

This is an incredible text. Verse 10 speaks of Jesus as God's cocreator, yet he became human. This same Jesus brought many sons into the divine family. Far from being embarrassed before the *elohim* of his own council at becoming human—becoming lesser for a short time—Jesus revels in it. Standing in the council ("in the midst of the assembly") he presents us: *Behold—look at me,*

[New Haven: Yale University Press, 1983], 1:610). See also *Life of Adam and Eve* 16. Scholarly articles dealing with this subject include G. A. Anderson, "The Exultation of Adam and *the fall* of Satan," *Journal of Jewish Thought and Philosophy* 6:1 (1997): 105–134 (= G. Anderson, M. E. Stone, and J. Trump, eds., *Literature on Adam and Eve: Collected Essays*, Studia in Veteris Testamenti Pseudepigraphica 15 [Leiden: Brill, 2000], 83–110); C. L. Patton, "Adam as the Image of God: An Exploration of *the fall* of Satan in the Life of Adam and Eve," *Society of Biblical Literature Seminar Papers* 33 (ed. E. H. Lovering Jr.; Atlanta: Society of Biblical Literature, 1994), 294–300.

and the children Yahweh has given me. We are all together now—forever. And that was the plan from the beginning:

> [16] For surely he is not concerned with angels, but he is concerned with the descendants of Abraham. [17] Therefore he was obligated to be made like his brothers in all respects, in order that he could become a merciful and faithful high priest in the things relating to God, in order to make atonement for the sins of the people. [18] For in that which he himself suffered when he was tempted, he is able to help those who are tempted (Heb 2:16–18).

WE SHALL BE LIKE HIM

Joining God's divine family is inextricably linked to the New Testament concept of becoming like Jesus—becoming divine. The academic term describing this point of biblical theology is "*theosis.*"[5] As one evangelical theologian laments:

> The idea of divinization, of redeemed human nature somehow participating in the very life of God, is found to a surprising extent throughout Christian history, although it is practically unknown to the majority of Christians (and even many theologians) in the west.[6]

The concept of "*theosis*" has strong biblical roots, and extends from the divine council worldview, specifically the aspect of the original Edenic goal of having humans join the divine family.[7] In the beginning, God made humans to image

---

5. One will encounter various synonyms in the scholarly literature, such as divinization, glorification, and deification.

6. Robert Rakestraw, "Becoming like God: An Evangelical Doctrine of Theosis," *Journal of the Evangelical Theological Society* 40.2 (1997): 255. *Theosis* is a significant element of Christian Orthodox theology, though Catholicism and all the major reformers embraced some form of the idea. Naturally, theological articulations will differ. See John McClean, "'Perichoresis,' 'Theosis' and Union with Christ in the thought of John Calvin," *Reformed Theological Review* 68.2 (2009): 130–41; Vladimir Kharlamov, "Theosis in Patristic Thought," *Theology Today* 65.2 (2008): 158–68; S. T. Kimbrough Jr., "Theosis in the Writings of Charles Wesley," *St. Vladimir's Theological Seminary Quarterly* 52.2 (2008): 199–212; Daniel B. Clendenin, "Partakers of Divinity: The Orthodox Doctrine of Theosis," *Journal of the Evangelical Theological Society* 37 (1994): 365–379; Michael J. Christensen and Jeffery A. Wittung, eds., *Partakers of the Divine Nature: The History and Development of Deification in the Christian Traditions* (Grand Rapids, MI: Baker Academic, 2008). My own views on *theosis* are in line with Rakestraw's. We do not become God or Jesus, as though joining the Trinity. We do not become deities on ontological par with Yahweh, akin to Mormon thought. Rather, we are made like him, receiving a glorified body of, as Paul puts it, "celestial flesh" (1 Cor 15:42–54). On the nature of this body, see Litwa (*We Are Being Transformed*) below.

7. There have been a number of helpful studies of *theosis*. See for example: G. L. Bray, "Deification," *New Dictionary of Theology* (ed. S. B. Ferguson, D. F. Wright and J. I. Packer; Downers Grove: InterVarsity, 1988) 189; M. David Litwa, "2 Corinthians 3:18 and Its Implications for Theosis," *Journal of Theological Interpretation* 2 (2008): 117–34; idem, *We Are Being Transformed: Deification in Paul's Soteriology* (Beihefte zur Zeitschrift fur die Neutestamentliche Wissenschaft und die Kunde der Alteren Kirche 187; Berlin: Walter de Gruyter, 2012). Litwa's book has a thorough, up-to-date discussion on the nature of the celestial body (pp. 119–171).

him, to be like him, to dwell with him. He made us like his heavenly imagers and came to earth to unite his families, elevating humanity to share in divine life in a new world.

The message of "*theosis*" is that, in Christ, we are being transformed into his likeness—the perfect imager of God. The Spirit—who, as we saw earlier in our study, "is but isn't" Jesus—conforms us to Jesus' own image. Scripture is clear that immortality as a divinized human is the destiny of the believer, and that our present lives in Christ are a process of becoming what we are:

> Those whom he foreknew, he also predestined to be **conformed to the image of his Son**, so that he should be the firstborn among many brothers (Rom 8:29).

> Now **the Lord is the Spirit**, and where the Spirit of the Lord is, there is freedom. [18]And we all, with unveiled face, **reflecting the glory of the Lord, are being transformed into the same image** from glory into glory, just as from the Lord, the Spirit (2 Cor 3:17–18).

> We know that whenever he is revealed **we will be like him**, because we will see him just as he is (1 John 3:2).

> May grace and peace be multiplied to you in the knowledge of God and of Jesus our Lord, [3]because his divine power has bestowed on us all things that are necessary for life and godliness, through the knowledge of the one who called us by his own glory and excellence of character, [4]through which things he has bestowed on us his precious and very great promises, so that through these you may become **sharers of the divine nature** after escaping from the corruption that is in the world because of evil desire (2 Pet 1:2–4).

> If there is a natural body, there is also **a spiritual body**. [45]Thus also it is written, "The first man, Adam, became a living soul"; the last Adam became a life-giving spirit. [46]But the spiritual is not first, but the natural; then the spiritual. [47]The first man is from the earth, made of earth; the second man is from heaven. [48]As the one who is made of earth, so also are those who are made of earth, and as the heavenly, so also are those who are heavenly. [49]And just as we have borne the image of the one who is made of earth, **we will also bear the image of the heavenly**.

> [50]But I say this, brothers, that flesh and blood is not able to inherit the kingdom of God, nor can corruption inherit incorruptibility. [51]Behold, I tell you a mystery: we will not all fall asleep, but we will all be changed, [52]in a moment, in the blink of an eye, at the last trumpet. For the trumpet will sound, and the dead will be raised imperishable, and we will be changed. [53]For **it is necessary**

for this perishable body to put on incorruptibility, and this mortal body to put on immortality (1 Cor 15:44–54).

And so it is that when God's original plan was ruined by rebellion, God did not destroy humanity but promised that, one day, a human being would reverse the fall. When he had to disinherit humanity at Babel, he did not abandon the human race. Instead, he was so "concerned with the descendants of Abraham" (Heb 2:16) that he became a man.

CHAPTER 37

This Means War

In the last few chapters we've devoted attention to the inaugura-tion of the kingdom of God. Yahweh's plan to revive the Edenic program was launched as part of his new covenant plan to become man to ensure success where Israel had failed. Yahweh's good rule would overspread the globe as originally intended.

It would be a mistake, however, to presume that the gods of the nations would not resist—or that they saw such resistance as pointless. This is not the view of the spiritual world the New Testament presents to us.

Though originally given their dominions by Yahweh, the lesser *elohim* had governed corruptly and had not maintained loyalty to the Most High. Instead, they embraced the worship that should have gone only to Yahweh (Deut 17:3; 29:25).

Although Yahweh told these *elohim* that they would die like men (Psa 82:6–8)—that he would strip them of their immortality—there is no indi-cation that the threat tempered opposition to Yahweh. The New Testament makes it clear that, once the powers of darkness understood that they had been duped by the crucifixion and resurrection, there was a sense that the timetable of their judgment had been set in motion (Rev 12:12).

The judgment against the *elohim* in the divine council meeting of Psalm 82 had been linked to the repossession of the nations (Psa 82:8; "Rise up, O God, judge the earth, because you shall inherit all the nations"). So long as that could be forestalled and opposed, the struggle would continue. And since Yahweh had linked that repossession to human participation, the forces of darkness had good reason to suppose that they could drag on the long war against Yahweh. Yahweh had lived among his people in the days of Moses and the monarchy, and they had been lured away from him.

The New Testament describes a spiritual struggle in the unseen world in the wake of the inauguration of the kingdom of God. Understanding the portrayal of the conflict and its correlation with the Old Testament divine council worldview is the goal of this chapter.

THE UNSEEN COMBATANTS: General Terminology

We saw earlier that the Hebrew Bible uses the term *elohim* to speak of any inhabitant of the spiritual world. The word itself provides no differentiation among beings within that realm, though hierarchy is certainly present. Yahweh, for example, is an *elohim*, but no other *elohim* is Yahweh. Nevertheless, the term *elohim* tells us very little about how an ancient reader would have parsed the pecking order of the unseen realm. The same is true of certain Greek terms that are used in the New Testament.[1]

When the subject of spiritual warfare surfaces, most students of Scripture think of angels and demons. Those terms are very broad and don't shed a great deal of light on how New Testament writers thought of rank and power in the unseen world.

There are roughly 175 references to angels in the New Testament (*aggelos/angelos*). Like the Hebrew counterpart (*mal'ak*), the term means "messenger."

---

1. The angelology and demonology of the New Testament are the subjects of much scholarly controversy. Several phenomena work against a consensus on practically any issue: (1) New Testament terms may be used infrequently or rarely, and what usage exists is often ambiguous when it comes to addressing issues like how one type of spiritual entity relates to another; (2) Second Temple material that informs New Testament terminology and that provides parallels to certain statements at times conflicts and therefore fails to produce a coherent picture of the unseen world of Judaism after the Old Testament period; (3) it is at times difficult to know whether a New Testament writer makes a statement from the stance of a Hellenistic Jewish worldview, a more ancient framework, or a Greco-Roman perspective. Consequently, this chapter provides only a basic overview of the material. See the companion website for more discussion of some of the issues presented here. Important scholarly works relating to the angelology and demonology of first-century Judaism and Christianity include Bennie H. Reynolds, "Understanding the Demonologies of the Dead Sea Scrolls: Accomplishments and Directions for the Future," *Religion Compass* 7.4 (2013): 103–14; Maxwell Davidson, *Angels at Qumran: A Comparative Study of 1 Enoch 1–36; 72–108 and Sectarian Writings from Qumran*, Journal for the Study of the Pseudepigrapha Supplement Series 11 (Sheffield: Sheffield Academic Press, 1992); Aleksander R. Michalak, *Angels as Warriors in Late Second Temple Jewish Literature*, Wissenschaftliche Untersuchungen zum Neuen Testament 330 (Tübingen: Mohr Siebeck, 2012); Eric Sorensen, *Possession and Exorcism in the New Testament and Early Christianity*, Wissenschaftliche Untersuchungen zum Neuen Testament 157, second series (Tübingen: Mohr Siebeck, 2002); Kevin P. Sullivan, *Wrestling with Angels: A Study of the Relationship between Angels and Humans in Ancient Jewish Literature and the New Testament* (Leiden: Brill, 2004); Graham H. Twelftree, *Jesus the Exorcist: A Contribution to the Study of the Historical Jesus*, Wissenschaftliche Untersuchungen zum Neuen Testament 54, second series (Tübingen: Mohr Siebeck, 1993); Guy Williams, *The Spirit World in the Letters of Paul the Apostle: A Critical Examination of the Role of Spiritual Beings in the Authentic Pauline Epistles*, Forschungen zur Religion und Literatur des Alten und Neuen Testaments 231 (Göttingen: Vandenhoeck & Ruprecht, 2009).

Fundamentally, the term describes a task performed by a divine being, not what a divine being *is*.[2]

The use of the term *angelos* increased in the Second Temple period on through the New Testament so that its meaning became more generic, akin to *daimonion*.[3] That is, it can be found on occasion outside the context of delivering a message in descriptions of a group of divine beings (e.g., Luke 15:10).

This widening of the term's semantics is shown in Hebrews 1:4–5; 2:7–9. In the second of these passages, the word *angelos* is used when the writer quotes Psalm 8:4–6, so that Hebrews 2:7 describes humankind as being "a little lower than the angels," whereas the Hebrew text of Psalm 8:5 has humanity being "a little lower than *elohim*." While the original Hebrew text could mean that humankind was created "a little lower than God [*elohim*]," the Greek translation that the writer of Hebrews is using (the Septuagint) interpreted *elohim* as plural, and translated the word with *angeloi* ("angels"). This shows us that *angelos* had become a word deemed appropriate to generally describe a member of the supernatural realm, just as *elohim* is used in the Old Testament.[4]

---

2. The difference between ontology (what a being is) and function (what a being does) is easily illustrated. The word "human" is an ontological term. Humans (regardless of gender) can be doctors, lawyers, mechanics, engineers, and messengers. All those terms describe functions or tasks. The word "angel" belongs to the latter classification.

3. As we'll see as the discussion continues, *daimōn* and *daimonion* are neutral terms, requiring context to determine if a good or evil spiritual being is in view. References to "angels" being evil or sinister are infrequent in the New Testament (Matt 25:41; 1 Cor 6:3; 11:10; 2 Cor 11:14; 2 Pet 2:4; Rev 9:11), and in no case are we told of a primeval angelic fall before or during the Genesis creation or before the fall of humankind. Such an idea comes from Church tradition and widely influential writings like Milton's *Paradise Lost*. References to "angels that sinned" look back to Genesis 6:1–4, the only passage in the Bible that describes a rebellion of a group of divine beings. More generally, phrases like "evil spirits" either convey the broad notion that the great enemy, the Devil or Satan, has divine allies, or might perhaps draw on the origin of evil spirits via the death of Nephilim giants in Second Temple Jewish literature (e.g., 1 Enoch). On that topic, see Archie T. Wright, *The Origin of Evil Spirits: The Reception of Genesis 6:1–4 in Early Jewish Literature*, Wissenschaftliche Untersuchungen zum Neuen Testament 198, second series (Tübingen: Mohr Siebeck, 2013). Lastly, Dale Martin's recent article contains some good analysis of how Christian thinking after the New Testament influences today's Christian demonology in ways that lacks biblical support. However, Martin inexplicably misses the connection of what Paul says about demons to Deut 32 and Israel's Old Testament experience with idolatry (i.e., Martin connects it only to Graeco-Roman idolatry). See Dale Basil Martin, "When Did Angels Become Demons?" *Journal of Biblical Literature* 129.4 (2010): 657–77. See the ensuing discussion and related sources in the footnotes along with chapter 38.

4. See the discussion in chapters 3 and 4. Some scholars argue that the word "angel" was used to downgrade or eliminate the idea of a divine council. This notion isn't coherent, since the Septuagint will also use *theos* ("god") to translate plural *elohim* or *elim* whether occurring alone (Exod 15:11; Psa 82:1b [Greek: 81:1b]; 95:3–4 [Greek: 94:3–4]; 97:9 [Greek: 96:9]) or in phrases like *beney elohim* (Psa 29:1 [Greek: 28:1]; Deut 32:43, with the Dead Sea Scrolls). See R. B. Salters, "Psalm 82:1 and the Septuagint," *Zeitschrift für die alttestamentliche Wissenschaft* 103.2 (1991): 225–39. This notion, usually made to defend the idea of a religious evolution to monotheism from polytheism on the part of the biblical writers, is also flawed with respect to the Qumran material, where there are nearly 180 instances of plural *elohim* or *elim* in the sectarian material, many of which occur in explicit divine council contexts. See Michael S. Heiser, "Monotheism and the Language of Divine Plurality in the Hebrew Bible and the Dead Sea Scrolls," *Tyndale Bulletin* 65.1 (2014): 85–100.

The two Greek terms translated "demon" in the New Testament are *daimōn* and *daimonion*. Our word "demon" is actually a transliteration of the Greek, not a translation. In classical Greek literature, which preceded the time of the New Testament, the term *daimōn* describes any divine being without regard to its nature (good or evil). A *daimōn* can be a god or goddesss, some lesser divine power, or the spirit of the departed human dead.[5] As such, it is akin to Hebrew *elohim* in its generic meaning.

The New Testament is silent on the origin of demons.[6] There is no passage that describes a primeval rebellion before Eden where angels fell from grace and became demons. The origin of demons in Jewish texts outside the Bible (such as 1 Enoch) is attributed to the events of Genesis 6:1–4. When a Nephilim was killed in these texts, its disembodied spirit was considered a demon. These demons then roamed the earth to harass humans. The New Testament does not explicitly embrace this belief, though there are traces of the notion, such as demon possession of humans (implying the effort to be re-embodied).

Not surprisingly, in the New Testament, the terms *daimōn* and *daimonion* are nearly always used negatively.[7] That is, they refer to evil, sinister powers.[8] This is likely due to the use of the terms in the Septuagint, though the influence of Second Temple Judaism may be a factor. The Septuagint translators use *daimōn* once (Isa 65:11) of a foreign god.[9] *Daimonion* occurs nine times to refer to idols (e.g., Psa 96:5 [Septuagint: 95:5]) and foreign gods of the nations whom Israel was not to worship (e.g., Psa 91:6 [Septuagint: 90:6]).[10]

In the New Testament, the verb equivalents to these nouns (*daimonao*, *daimonizomai*) refer to being possessed by a *daimōn* and are always negative.

---

5. J. E. Rexine, "*Daimōn* in Classical Greek Literature," *Greek Orthodox Theological Review* 30.3 (1985): 335–61.

6. Rev 12:7–17, a passage often referenced for such an idea, clearly situates the battle described there as following the birth of the messiah (Rev 12:5) and in association with the messianic birth. The major scholarly study on demonic origins in Jewish thought is Archie T. Wright, *The Origin of Evil Spirits: The Reception of Genesis 6:1–4 in Early Jewish Literature*, Wissenschaftliche Untersuchungen zum Neuen Testament 198, second series (Tübingen: Mohr Siebeck, 2013).

7. *Daimon* occurs once (Matt 8:31) whereas *daimonion* occurs over sixty times.

8. The one exception is Acts 17:18, where Greeks listening to Paul describe him by saying, "He seems to be a preacher of foreign divinities [*daimonion*]." The reference here is neutral.

9. The deity in question is Gad in the Hebrew Bible and Fortune in the Septuagint. See S. Ribichini, "Gad," in *Dictionary of Deities and Demons in the Bible*, 2nd ed. (ed. Karel van der Toorn, Bob Becking, and Pieter W. van der Horst; Leiden; Boston; Cologne; Grand Rapids, MI; Cambridge: Brill; Eerdmans, 1999), 339.

10. The nine Septuagint instances include two in the book of Baruch. The deity in view in Psa 91:6 (Greek: 90:6) is Qeteb. See N. Wyatt, "Qeteb," in *Dictionary of Deities and Demons in the Bible*, 673. The New English Translation of the Septuagint (NETS) renders *daimonion* as "demon." A foreign deity was, by definition (see Deut 32:8–9, 17) a "demon," a geographical guardian entity. See Chapters 4, 14, and 15.

Daimonion occurs in parallel to "unclean spirit" in several passages (e.g., Luke 8:29; 9:42; cf. Luke 4:33).

Oddly enough, only one verse in the Bible mentions Satan and demons together: "So if Satan also is divided against himself, how will his kingdom stand? For you say that I expel demons by Beelzebul" (Luke 11:18). The verse strongly implies that Satan has authority over demons, but does not make it clear that all demons are under his authority or how this authority emerged. The Old Testament is silent on the matter since the noun *saṭan* was not a proper name and was not used of the enemy in the garden.[11]

OBSERVATIONS ON PAUL'S VOCABULARY

The same ambiguity concerning the relationship between Satan and other divine beings hostile to God is found in Paul's writings. Since Paul mentions standing against the tactics of the devil in the same breath as a listing of other terms for supernatural enemies, Ephesians 6:11–12 informs us there is a relationship, but doesn't describe it in any specific way.

Similar passages that many Bible readers presume are clear in this regard are actually not. For example, 2 Corinthians 4:4 refers to "the god of this age" who has blinded humanity. Nearly all scholars identify this figure as Satan, but the name doesn't occur in the verse or the context.[12] Additionally, the phrase "god of this age" may refer to God himself. It is possible that the verse draws on Isaiah 6:9–10 (Septuagint), where it is God who has blinded the eyes of those who don't believe.[13]

Ephesians 2:2 speaks of "the prince of the power of the air" (ESV), another

---

11. See chapter 8. By the time of the New Testament, Satan had become a proper name. See G. H. Twelftree, "Demon, Devil, Satan," *Dictionary of Jesus and the Gospels* (ed. Joel B. Green and Scot McKnight; Downers Grove, IL: InterVarsity Press, 1992), 163–71. Paul regularly gives the Greek term a definite article, which, unlike the situation in Hebrew, marks the word as either a proper name or title. Beyond this observation, though, confusion reigns with respect to Second Temple Jewish thinking about Satan. As Williams notes: "Much literature from the period makes no specific mention of Satan (notably: Ben Sirach, Philo, and Josephus). Furthermore, even when Satan is mentioned, it is commonly as a *type* of angel, occurring frequently in the plural ('the Satans'). There was no standard nomenclature for this figure; we find no edifice which we may call the Jewish doctrine of Satan" (Williams, *Spirit World in the Letters of Paul the Apostle*, 88; emphasis added).

12. The identification with Satan is argued on two grounds: (1) the fact that the title here is similar to the epithet "ruler of this world" in the Gospel of John (John 12:31; 14:30; 16:11), whose identity would be difficult to reconcile with any other divine being than Satan; and (2) Paul's identification of the deception of people in the *eschaton* with Satan (2 Thess 2:9–10).

13. See Donald E. Hartley, "2 Corinthians 4:4: A Case for Yahweh as the 'God of this Age'" (paper presented at the 57th Annual Meeting of the Evangelical Theological Society, Valley Forge, PA, 2005); Hartley, "The Congenitally Hard-Hearted: Key to Understanding the Assertion and Use of Isaiah 6:9–10 in the Synoptic Gospels" (PhD diss., Dallas Theological Seminary, 2005).

verse associated with Satan—and which, upon closer examination, does not include any reference to the name or the devil.

It is difficult to know precisely what Paul was thinking here. Recall our earlier discussion of the original rebel of Genesis 3 who was cast down to "earth" (Hebrew: 'erets, a term that can refer to the ground or Sheol). It would be understandable to see that particular divine rebel as lord (first in rebellion and thus authority) of earth. This lordship could even extend to the "air" (the heavens), since that space was considered in ancient Israelite cosmology to be beneath God's domain, which was above the waters of the earth (Job 22:13; Amos 9:6; Pss 29:10; 148:4).[14]

However, if Paul was thinking more in terms of Graeco-Roman cosmology, this explanation fails since the air was "the region below the moon and above the earth."[15] The idea of Paul's using a Graeco-Roman backdrop for this phrase may get support from Paul's use of another term elsewhere: *stoicheia*. That Greek lemma can refer to one of four things: (1) basic principles of religious teaching (e.g., law); (2) rudimentary substances of the physical world; (3) astral deities (astrological myths); (4) spiritual beings in general.[16] Since this term is strongly rooted in Graeco-Roman cosmological thinking, it may be that Paul's reference to the "air" back in Ephesians is as well.[17]

---

14. See Michael S. Heiser, "Genesis and Ancient Near Eastern Cosmology," *Faithlife Study Bible* (ed. John D. Barry, Michael S. Heiser, Miles Custis, et al.; Bellingham, WA: Logos Bible Software, 2012); G. F. Hasel, "The Polemic Nature of the Genesis Cosmology," *Evangelical Quarterly* 46 (1974): 81–102; John H. Walton, *Ancient Near Eastern Thought and the Old Testament: Introducing the Conceptual World of the Hebrew Bible* (Grand Rapids, MI: Baker Academic, 2006), 165–78. The major scholarly study on ancient Israelite cosmology is Luis I. J. Stadelmann, *The Hebrew Conception of the World: A Philological and Literary Study*, Analecta Biblica 39 (Rome: Pontifical Biblical Institute Press, 1970).

15. Frank Thielman, *Ephesians*, Baker Exegetical Commentary on the New Testament (Grand Rapids, MI: Baker Academic, 2010), 123–24.

16. See D. G. Reid, "Elements/Elemental Spirits of the World," *Dictionary of Paul and His Letters* (ed. Gerald F. Hawthorne, Ralph P. Martin, and Daniel G. Reid; Downers Grove, IL: InterVarsity Press, 1993), 229. My listing is based on Reid's, but I have broken the possibilities down differently.

17. The usage of *stoicheia* in Heb 5:12 is a clear reference to religious teachings (the law). Second Peter 3:10, 12 refers more literally to elements of the physical world. There is no consensus among scholars on Paul's use of the term (Gal 4:3, 9; Col 2:8, 20). The question is whether Paul is using the term of spiritual entities/star deities in Gal 4:3, 9 and Col 2:8, 20. Three of these four instances append the word to "of the world" (*kosmos*; i.e., "*stoicheia* of the world"), but this doesn't provide much clarity. Paul's discussion in Gal 4 and Col 2 includes spiritual forces (angels, principalities and powers, false gods) in the context, which suggests *stoicheia* may refer to divine beings. He is contrasting *stoicheia* to salvation in Christ in some way. Since Paul is speaking to both Jews and Gentiles, he might also be using the term in different ways with respect to each audience. *Stoicheia* as law would make little sense to Gentiles, though it would strike a chord with Jews. My view is that in Gal 4:3 Paul's use of *stoicheia* likely refers to the law and religious teaching with a Jewish audience in view (cf. Gal 4:1–7). The audience shifts to Gentiles in 4:8–11, and so it seems coherent to see *stoicheia* in Gal 4:9 as referring to divine beings, probably astral deities (the "Fates"). Gal 4:8 transitions to pagans, since the Jews would have known about the true God. The reference to "times and seasons and years" (4:10) would therefore point to astrological beliefs, not the Jewish calendar. Paul is therefore denying the idea that the celestial *objects* (sun, moon, stars) are deities. His Gentile readers should

PAUL AND THE DEUTERONOMY 32 WORLDVIEW

Paul's writings reveal an awareness of the cosmic-geographical worldview that we've been discussing at length in this book.

One instance of *daimonion* in the Septuagint is particularly noteworthy as we begin exploring Paul's language. The term is used in Deuteronomy 32:17 to translate the "demons" (Hebrew: *shedim*), who are called *elohim* in that same verse, who had seduced the Israelites.[18] The reference is important in light of Paul's warning about fellowshiping with demons (*daimonion*) in 1 Corinthians 10:20–21 by eating meat sacrificed to idols. In that passage Paul quotes Deuteronomy 32:17. The clear implication is that Paul considered these beings real and dangerous.[19] This is why, in his earlier discussion of the issue of eating such meat, he acknowledged that there were other gods (*theoi*) and lords among people who did not belong to Yahweh and Jesus (1 Cor 8:1–6).[20] Paul was well aware of the divine council worldview that had the nations under lesser *elohim* and considered them a threat to believers, as they had been to Israel.

Taking Paul's comments in both 1 Corinthians 8 and 10 together (the subject matter is the same) helps us see that, for Paul, there was an overlap between the words *daimonion* and *theos* ("god").[21] The word *theos* was used of high-ranking spiritual beings who had authority both in pantheons and geographical domains on earth. The word *theos*, then, has some conceptual overlap with those divine beings who were set over the nations.

---

not be enslaved by the idea that these objects controlled their destiny. As a related issue, Paul's wording here cannot therefore be taken as a denial of the existence of other gods. Paul does deny their existence in 1 Cor 8:4–6, which must not be interpreted against the context of 1 Cor 10:20–21, as it relates to the same subject matter. Paul is just denying that celestial bodies are gods that control one's fate. This approach is also useful with respect to Col 2:8, 20, where the contexts seem to be pagan angel worship (i.e., worship of divine beings thought to have power over basic elements of the material world) and pagan asceticism. See E. Schweizer, "Slaves of the Elements and Worshipers of Angels: Gal 4:3, 9 and Col 2:8, 18, 20," *Journal of Biblical Literature* 107 (1988): 455–68; Clinton E. Arnold, "Returning to the Domain of the Powers: 'Stoicheia' as Evil Spirits in Galatians 4:3, 9," *Novum Testamentum* 38.1 (January 1996): 55–76.

18. The Septuagint also uses *daimonion* to translate *shedim* in its only other Old Testament occurrence: Psa 106:37. *Daimonion* is also the translation choice for references to "goat demons" (*se'irim*) in Isa 13:21 and "desert creatures" (*tsiyim*) in Isa 34:14. Recall from the discussion of Azazel in Lev 16 (the Day of Atonement) that Israelites believed the desert to be the realm of sinister evil and were sacrificing to "goat demons" (Lev 17:7).

19. See chapter 38 for more discussion of 1 Cor 10:20–21.

20. English translations wrongly put these terms in ironic quotes in 1 Cor 8 as though Paul were jesting. 1 Cor 10:20–21 shows us he wasn't. Paul's discussion in 1 Cor 10 actually tracks through Deuteronomy 32. See chapter 39 for a discussion of 1 Cor 10:20–21 and these points with sources for further study.

21. In classical Greek literature, not every *daimōn* could be referred to with *theos*. See Rexine, "*Daimōn*," 339.

The apostle's vocabulary elsewhere makes it clear that he understood and presumed the Deuteronomy 32 worldview:[22]

- "rulers" (*archontōn* or *archōn*)
- "principalities" (*archē*)
- "powers"/"authorities" (*exousia*)
- "powers" (*dynamis*)
- "dominions"/"lords" (*kyrios*)
- "thrones" (*thronos*)[23]
- "world rulers" (*kosmokratōr*)

These lemmas have something in common—they were used both in the New Testament and other Greek literature to denote *geographical domain authority*.

---

22. For a lengthy overview of Paul's adoption of this worldview, see Ronn Johnson, "The Old Testament Background for Paul's Principalities and Powers," (PhD diss., Dallas Theological Seminary, 2004). For brief discussions of individual terms see D. G. Reid, "Principalities and Powers," in *Dictionary of Paul and His Letters*, 746–752. Much of what we've discussed to this point with respect to contextualizing New Testament theology (chs. 31–36) by means of Old Testament theology, itself articulated within its own ancient Near Eastern context, presumes the Deut 32 worldview. Concepts such as the original goal of Eden, why the other nations have other gods, the divine sonship of Israel, Yahweh's covenantal relationship with Israel, and the need to reclaim the nations via a human, Davidic incarnation of Yahweh are inextricably tied to this worldview. As we saw in chapter 34, both testaments frame this theology in terms of the 70 nations of Gen 10, the world known to the biblical writers. We of course know that the world is a bigger place than these nations—and so did God. That God's vision included all nations of the world as we (and he) knew it is evidenced by the "universality" of humanity's lost condition and the command to evangelize (e.g., Rom 3:9, 23; 5:12, 18; Titus 2:11; Heb 5:9). The Deut 32 worldview is no more restricted to the known nations of Gen 10 and Israel than the gospel is so confined. The theology of the Deut 32 worldview is straightforward and applies to all nations of the earth at any time period. All nations whose God is not Yahweh are under the dominion of lesser gods. All people whose God is not Yahweh are enslaved to lesser gods who cannot provide salvation, and who are unjust and unloving. This spiritual dilemma and its solution (believing loyalty to Yahweh) are the same today as in biblical times. This parsing of the human, earthly condition is the result of humanity's rebellion (at various stages), Yahweh's just punishment of those nations, and his subsequent decision to revive his original Edenic vision through a new people, Israel, whom he would create from a couple of his choosing. They would in turn be the conduit through whom disinherited humanity could be redeemed. While specific details are often lacking because readers are centuries removed from the ancient Near Eastern context of the Old Testament discussed in this book, a number of early church writers had an inkling of the Deut 32 worldview and its relationship to the gods of other nations. The best resource overviewing the thinking of early Christian writers on this subject is Gerald R. McDermott, *God's Rivals: Why Has God Allowed Different Religions? Insights from the Bible and the Early Church* (Downers Grove, IL: InterVarsity Press, 2007). McDermott is professor of religion and philosophy at Roanoke College in Salem, Virginia. He is familiar with the idea of the divine council (e.g., p. 16 and his third chapter: "The Lord of Hosts: The Old Testament and the Real Existence of Other Gods").

23. There is only one instance of this lemma in the New Testament: "All things in the heavens and on the earth were created by him, things visible and things invisible, whether thrones [*thronoi*] or dominions or rulers or powers, all things were created through him and for him" (Col 1:16). The term is used in parallel to other lemmas that indicate geographical rule in supernatural contexts. See the discussion. Col 1:16 is of interest to scholars since it lists four lemmas: *thronoi – kuriotēs – archai – exousiai*. Scholars have tried to discern a coherent hierarchical ordering in the list (i.e., presuming a descent in rank), but without success or consensus. External usage of the terms provides no consistency in hierarchical meanings.

At times these terms are used of humans, but several instances demonstrate that Paul had spiritual beings in mind. We'll briefly survey Paul's terminology.

One of the Old Testament passages we looked at in addition to Deuteronomy 32:8–9 to understand Yahweh's decision to put the nations under the authority of lesser gods was Daniel 10. In that passage we saw that there were divine beings over the nations, called "princes" (*sar/sarim*) by Daniel, and that the Septuagint refers to Michael as one of the chief *archontōn* or *archōn*, depending on the manuscript evidence.[24]

Ephesians 6:12 includes a number of the lemmas listed above: "Our struggle is not against blood and flesh, but against the rulers [*archē*], against the authorities [*exousia*], against the world rulers [*kosmokratōr*] of this darkness, against the spiritual forces [*pneumatikos*] of wickedness in the heavenly places."

Paul refers to these hostile beings in the unseen realm earlier in Ephesians. He wrote that God raised Jesus from the dead and "seated him at his right hand in the heavenly places, far above every ruler [*archē*] and authority [*exousia*] and power [*dynamis*] and dominion [*kyrios*]" (Eph 1:20–21 ESV).[25] It was only after Christ had risen that God's plan was "made known to the rulers [*archē*] and authorities [*exousia*] in the heavenly places" (Eph 3:10 ESV). These cosmic forces are the "rulers [*archē*] and authorities [*exousia*]" disarmed and put to shame by the cross (Col 2:15). Had those "rulers" [*archōntōn*] known that the death of the messiah was necessary for God's plan to succeed, they never would have crucified Jesus (1 Cor 2:8).[26]

The reference to "dominion" in Ephesians 1:21 (*kyrios*; plural: *kuriotēs*) is related to the word Paul uses to describe how unbelievers have many gods

---

24. This is not to exclude a relationship of the divine powers to human foes of Israel and Yahweh. As we've seen with passages like Dan 7:20–28; Zech 14:1–5; and Isa 24:21–23, the Bible envisions conflict where human and divine involvement overlap. This perspective is of course prominent in the Dead Sea Scrolls, particularly in *The War Scroll* (1QM). Due to exaggerations and fantastic portrayals of spiritual warfare in popular Christianity and fiction, scholars are often hesitant to emphasize the supernatural element of Dan 10 and other passages. For example, see the discussion in David E. Stevens, "Daniel 10 and the Notion of Territorial Spirits," *Bibliotheca Sacra* 157 (2000): 410–31.

25. Interestingly, some Septuagint manuscripts have "powers" (*dynamis*; plural: *dynameis*) as the translation for the divine "host" in Dan 8:10. See also Rom 8:38 for supernatural powers.

26. Translation of the verse references in this paragraph are all from the ESV. The context of 1 Cor 2 is that of a divine plan—divine knowledge. While *archōn* (along with the rest of Paul's vocabulary) is found in the New Testament and elsewhere for human rulers, it makes little sense for Paul to see irony in the fact that humans didn't know God's mystery-plan involved the death and resurrection of the messiah. As Aune notes, "The term *archontes* used as a designation for angelic beings first occurs in the LXX Dan 10:13, and seven times in Theod. Dan 10:13, 20–21; 12:1, where the LXX has *stratēgos*, 'commander,' 'magistrate,' all translations of the Aram *śar*, 'prince.'" That the rulers here are evil supernatural powers of darkness is an interpretation found in church fathers such as Origen, Tertullian, and Justin (see D. E. Aune, "Archon," in *Dictionary of Deities and Demons in the Bible*, 82–85).

(*theoi*) and "lords" (*kurioi*), but for the believer there is only one God, Yahweh, and one Lord, Jesus (1 Cor 8:5). These gods and lords are considered real by Paul and are a threat to believers (1 Cor 10:20–21).

The picture that thus emerges from the New Testament has points of both clarity and ambiguity.[27]

It is clear that Satan is leader of at least some of the powers of darkness. As the original rebel, he likely ranked first (or worst) in terms of example in the minds of ancient readers. The fact that he is the one who confronted Jesus in the desert, an account we considered earlier, and offered Jesus the kingdoms of the world suggests as much. The lack of a clearly delineated hierarchy leaves the possibility that there are competing agendas in the unseen world, even where there exists the common goal of opposition to Yahweh and his people.[28]

A second point of relative clarity is that Paul grasped the Deuteronomy 32 worldview. This should be no surprise given Paul's command of the Old Testament. The world in which the newly inaugurated kingdom of God was now spreading was one dominated by invisible divine powers transparently described in the vocabulary of geographical rulership. We are not told how the terms relate to each other or precisely what they signify in a hierarchy, but the message of cosmic geography is plainly telegraphed.

THE "GLORIOUS ONES" IN PETER AND JUDE

Second Peter 2:10 and Jude 8 refer to the "glorious ones" (*doksas*). The term probably refers to divine beings of the council close to God's glorious presence, since Second Temple period texts describe such beings.[29] These passages in 2 Peter and Jude speak of (human) blasphemers who rail against the glorious ones. The 2 Peter passage adds the note that angels, though greater than those human blasphemers, would not dare to do such a thing. The wording suggests some distinction between angels and "glorious ones" in rank (and perhaps power). For example, 2 Enoch 21:3 identifies Gabriel, widely described as an archangel in biblical and other Second Temple period texts, as one of "the glorious ones of the Lord."[30]

---

27. See Williams, *Spirit World in the Letters of Paul the Apostle*, 127–40, for a survey of the interpretive problems and ambiguities.

28. Many New Testament scholars have commented on the New Testament's silence on how these divine beings might be related. See the companion website for further discussion.

29. See 1QH 10:8; 2 Enoch 22:7, 10; Martyrdom and Ascension of Isaiah 9:32; Philo, *Spec. Leg.* 1.45; T. Jud. 25:2; T. Levi 18:5.

30. Several New Testament scholars follow this trajectory. Bauckham writes: "The term δόξαι (lit. 'glories') for angels is attested in the Dead Sea Scrolls (נכבדים).... Probably they are so called because they participate in or embody the glory of God (cf. *T. Jud.* 25:2; *T. Levi* 18:5; Heb 9:5; Philo, *Spec. Leg.* 1.8.45).

Recall that, in terms of the divine council hierarchy of the Old Testament, "angels" would denote a low-level task or job description (transmitting a message as a messenger), as opposed to ruling over a geographical region, something assigned to "sons of God" in the Deuteronomy 32 worldview. In other words, in the spiritual world, just as in the human world, while divine beings (save for the unique Yahweh) are all of the same "species," some have higher rank than others. The "household" metaphor discussed in chapter 3 is illustrative. While a pharaoh's administration might number thousands, there was nevertheless an inner circle of individuals that had greater access, status, and delegated power. Hence "glorious ones" are likely named because of closer access to God's glory.

SACRED SPACE AND REALM DISTINCTION

The New Testament portrays the Christian life—even the very Christian *existence*—as prompting a spiritual turf war. But we often don't pick up on the messaging.

Sacred space and realm distinction are not just Old Testament concepts. We talked at length about these two concepts in earlier chapters in regard to the Israelite tabernacle and the temple. But New Testament language about them takes the reader in fascinating directions. Believe it or not, *you are sacred space.*

Paul in particular refers to the believer as the place where God now tabernacles—we are the temple of God, both individually and corporately. This is most transparently seen in English translations in two passages where Paul tells the Corinthians, "You are God's temple" (1 Cor 3:16), and, "Your body is

---

It is true that נבדים can also refer to illustrious men, noblemen (Isa 3:5; 23:8; Nah 3:10; Ps 149:8; 1QpHab 4:2; 4QpNah 2:9; 3:9; 4:4; 1QM 14:11), but in these cases the Septuagint does not use δόξαι, and one would expect a more idiomatic Greek rendering if this were Jude's meaning. It is in any case an unlikely meaning, especially in view of the parallel statement in v 10a. Clement of Alexandria already interpreted Jude's δόξαι as angels" (Richard J. Bauckham, *2 Peter, Jude*, Word Biblical Commentary 50 [Dallas: Word, 1998], 57). Bauckham's reference to Clement of Alexandria comes from the latter's *Comments on the Epistle of Jude* (*Ante-Nicene Fathers* 2:573): "They 'speak evil of majesty,' that is, of the angels" (cited in Gene L. Green, *Jude and 2 Peter*, Baker Exegetical Commentary on the New Testament [Grand Rapids, MI: Baker Academic, 2008], 76–77). Finally, J. N. D. Kelly observes: "This term cannot, any more than authority above and for much the same reasons, designate community leaders: this is quite out of keeping with the context, and there is no plausible instance of its bearing this sense…. In the light of the context (cf. 9) and 2 Pet. 2:10 f., which borrows from this verse, there can be no doubt that it here denotes a class of angelic beings; and this usage of the noun is supported by LXX Ex. 15:11. 'Glory' (*doxa*) originally stands for the numinous radiance which belongs to God Himself (e.g. Ex. 24:16 f.; 33:18–23; Ps. 19:1), but later the angels who surround Him come to be regarded as sharing in it (cf. Philo, *Spec. leg.* i. 8. 45: 'by thy glory I understand the powers which keep watch around thee')" (J. N. D. Kelly, *The Epistles of Peter and of Jude*, Black's New Testament Commentary [London: Continuum, 1969], 263).

the temple of the Holy Spirit" (1 Cor 6:19). The former speaks of the church corporately as the temple; the latter focuses on each believer individually.[31] Paul also relays the same message:

> [19] Consequently, therefore, you are no longer strangers and foreigners, but you are fellow citizens of the saints [lit.: holy ones] and members of the household of God, [20] built on the foundation of the apostles and prophets, Christ Jesus himself being the cornerstone, [21] in whom the whole building, joined together, grows into a holy temple in the Lord, [22] in whom you also are built up together into a dwelling place of God in the Spirit (Eph 2:19–22).

We are the place where God dwells—the same presence that filled the temple in the Old Testament.

The same concept is less obvious in other passages. For example, while most Christians will have heard of the tabernacle, most never discern that Paul transfers the language of the tabernacle to the believer to make the specific point that the same presence that oriented holy ground in Israel's camp indwells the believer. In 2 Corinthians the apostle writes:

> [1] For we know that if our earthly house, the tent, is destroyed, we have a building from God, a house not made by hands, eternal in the heavens. [2] For indeed, in this house we groan, because we desire to put on our dwelling from heaven (2 Cor 5:1–2).

Paul compares the believer's body—which he had called God's temple in his first letter to the Corinthians (1 Cor 6:19)—to a *tent*. The Greek word translated "tent" is *skēnos*, a term closely related to *skēnē*, the term used in 2 Corinthians 5:1–4 of Israel's tabernacle, and which is used in the Septuagint for the tabernacle (e.g., Exod 29:4).

The implications are startling. We have all likely heard the verse where Jesus says, "Where two or three are gathered in my name, I am there in the midst of them" (Matt 18:20). But put in the context of this other New Testament language, which in turn is informed by the Old Testament imagery of the tabernacle and temple, it means that wherever believers are and gather, the spiritual ground they occupy is sanctified amid the powers of darkness.

If we could see with spiritual eyes, we would see a world of darkness peppered with the lights of Yahweh's presence, spreading out to meet each other, inexorably pressing and spreading out to take back the ground of the disinherited nations from the enemy. Of course we would also see those lights surrounded by darkness.

---

31. This observation is made not only on the basis of the wordings in context, but also grammar. The second person verb form in 1 Cor 3:16 ("you are God's temple") is grammatically plural.

The imagery requires perspective. At one time, not long ago, there was one light, meandering its way through the domains of hostile gods. That light nearly went out, scattered to all parts of the known world in tiny embers. But then another solitary, but great, light shone in darkness (Isa 60:1; Matt 4:16). That light would turn the darkness into light (Isa 42:16), and the nations would be drawn to it (Isa 60:1–3).

The New Testament portrayal of the spiritual war doesn't hide the task from the reader. The people of God, in whom is the Name, the presence of Yahweh, are surrounded, as they have been before. The apostles understood that but were not faint of heart. There would be no surrender of holy ground in the midst of darkness. Some of the things they taught early believers to observe in fact commemorated the unseen conflict raging around them. Everyone had to choose a side.

CHAPTER 38

Choosing Sides

Any veteran who has experienced combat will tell you that war is a terrible thing. Caught in such a conflict, you must take sides. Many modern people, particularly in developed countries, like to think that diplomacy and neutrality provide a more enlightened path. But some wars—and some enemies—don't offer that option. When an enemy wants nothing but your defeat and annihilation, neutrality means choosing death.

The war raging in the unseen world for the souls of human imagers of Yahweh is that kind of war. Neutrality is not on the table. We've seen from the writings of Paul in particular that the advance of Yahweh's kingdom rule was cast as a turf war pitting him against hostile divine beings. That spiritual conflict is shown most dramatically in two unlikely places.

BAPTISM AS HOLY WAR

First Peter 3:14–22 is one of the more puzzling passages of the New Testament. Set against the backdrop of the divine council worldview, however, it's actually quite comprehensible.

> [14] But even if you might suffer for the sake of righteousness, you are blessed. And do not be afraid of their intimidation or be disturbed, [15] but set Christ apart as Lord in your hearts, always ready to make a defense to anyone who asks you for an accounting concerning the hope that is in you. [16] But do so with courtesy and respect, having a good conscience, so that in the things in which you are slandered, the ones who malign your good conduct in Christ may be put to shame. [17] For it is better to suffer for doing good, if God wills it, than for doing evil.

¹⁸ For Christ also suffered once for sins,
>> the just for the unjust,
> in order that he could bring you to God,
>> being put to death in the flesh,
> but made alive in the spirit,
> ¹⁹ in which also he went and proclaimed to the spirits in prison,

²⁰ who were formerly disobedient, when the patience of God waited in the days of Noah, while an ark was being constructed, in which a few—that is, eight souls—were rescued through water. ²¹ And also, corresponding to this, baptism now saves you, not the removal of dirt from the flesh, but an appeal to God for a good conscience through the resurrection of Jesus Christ, ²² who is at the right hand of God, having gone into heaven, with angels and authorities and powers having been subjected to him (1 Pet 3:14–22).

The overall theme of 1 Peter is that Christians must withstand persecution and persevere in their faith. That much is clear in this passage. But what's with baptism, the ark, Noah, and spirits in prison? And does this text say that baptism saves us?

To understand what Peter is thinking, we have to understand a concept that scholars have called *types* or *typology*. Typology is a kind of prophecy. We're all familiar with predictive verbal prophecy—when a prophet *announces* that something is going to come to pass in the future. Sometimes that comes "out of the blue," with God impressing thoughts on the prophet's mind that the prophet then utters. The prophecy is spelled out. Types work differently.

A type is basically an *unspoken* prophecy. It is an event, person, or institution that foreshadows something that will come, but which isn't revealed until after the fact. For example, in Romans 5:14 Paul tells us that Adam was a *typos* of Christ. This Greek word means "kind" or "mark" or *type*—it's actually where *typology* comes from. Paul was saying that, in some way, Adam foreshadowed or echoed something about Jesus. In Adam's case, that something was how his act (sin) had an effect on all humanity. Like Adam, Jesus did something that would have an impact on all humanity—his death and resurrection. Another example would be Passover, since it prefigured the crucifixion of Jesus, who was called "the lamb of God." The point is that there was some analogous connection between the type (Adam) and its echo (Jesus), called the *antitype* by scholars.

Peter uses typology in 1 Peter 3:14–22. Specifically, he assumes that the great flood in Genesis 6–8, especially the sons of God event in Genesis 6:1–4, *typified* or foreshadowed the gospel and the resurrection. For Peter, these events were commemorated during baptism. That needs some unpacking, since the points of correlation aren't apparent.

In an earlier chapter we saw the tight connections between Genesis 6:1–4 and the epistles of 2 Peter and Jude.[1] We discovered that 2 Peter and Jude communicated something about the flood and the sons of God that wasn't found in Genesis, but which came from the Second Temple book of 1 Enoch. Specifically, 1 Enoch 6–15 describes how the sons of God (called "Watchers" in that ancient book) who committed the offense of Genesis 6:1–4 were imprisoned under the earth for what they had done. That imprisonment is behind the reference to the "spirits in prison" in 1 Peter 3:19.[2]

Recall that the prison to which the offending divine beings were sent was referred to as Tartarus in 2 Peter 2:4–5. The Greek behind the terms is often translated "hell" or "Hades" in English, but those renderings are a bit misleading. Tartarus of course has no literal geography. This is the language of the spiritual realm. Tartarus was part of the underworld (biblical Sheol), a place conceived as being inside the earth because, in ancient experience, that is where the dead go—they were buried. Broadly speaking, the underworld is not hell; it is the afterlife, the place or realm where the dead go. That "place" has its own "geography." Some experience eternal life with God in the spiritual realm; others do not.[3]

In the 1 Enoch story, the Watchers appealed their sentence and asked Enoch, the biblical prophet who never died (Gen 5:21–24), to intercede with God for them (1 Enoch 6:4). God rejected their petition and Enoch had to return to the imprisoned Watchers and give them the bad news (1 Enoch 13:1–3; 14:4–5). The point to catch is that Enoch visits the spiritual world in the "bad section of town" where the offending Watchers are being held.

As was the case with 2 Peter 2:4 and its mention of being imprisoned in Tartarus, this story from 1 Enoch was on Peter's mind in 1 Peter 3. It is the key to understanding what he says.

---

1. See chapter 12.

2. I am aware that some scholars seek to argue that these imprisoned spirits are the spirits of people, namely, the people who died in the flood. The most thorough treatment of this issue and the larger topic of the meaning of 1 Pet 3 is Bo Reicke, *The Disobedient Spirits and Christian Baptism: A Study of 1 Peter 3:19 and Its Context,* Acta Seminarii Neotestamentici Upsaliensis 13 (Copenhagen: E. Munksgaard, 1946; repr., Eugene, OR: Wipf and Stock, 2005). Reicke (and other scholars of course) marshals solid evidence that reinforces a supernatural interpretation of the passage, one that was embraced in the early church and is found in the Apostles' Creed.

3. When terms like "hell," "Hades," "heaven," "Sheol," etc. are understood in this context—they all speak of the afterlife and its spiritual geography—there is no need to criticize the Apostles' Creed or other early Christian teaching as being unbiblical. The Apostles' Creed says Jesus "descended to Hades." Jesus did not go to hell, the place of punishment. Rather, the point is that he went to the realm of the dead—he died.

Peter saw a theological analogy between the events of Genesis 6 and the gospel and resurrection. In other words, he considered the events of Genesis 6 to be *types* or precursors to New Testament events and ideas.

Just as Jesus was the second Adam for Paul, *Jesus is the second Enoch for Peter*. Enoch descended to the imprisoned fallen angels to announce their doom. First Peter 3:14–22 has Jesus descending to these same "spirits in prison" to tell them they were *still defeated*, despite his crucifixion. God's plan of salvation and kingdom rule had not been derailed—in fact, it was right on schedule. The crucifixion actually meant victory over every demonic force opposed to God. This victory declaration is why 1 Peter 3:14–22 ends with Jesus risen from the dead and set at the right hand of God—*above all angels, authorities and powers*. The messaging is very deliberate, and has a supernatural view of Genesis 6:1–4 at its core.

So how does this relate to baptism? Our focus for answering that question is two terms in verse 21, that baptism is "an **appeal** to God for a good **conscience** through the resurrection of Jesus Christ."

The two boldfaced words need reconsideration in light of the divine council worldview. The word most often translated "appeal" (*eperōtēma*) in verse 21 is best understood as "pledge" here, a meaning that it has elsewhere.[4] Likewise the word "conscience" (*suneidēsis*) does not refer to the inner voice of right and wrong in this text. Rather, the word refers to the disposition of one's loyalties, a usage that is also found in other contexts and Greek literature.[5]

Baptism, then, is not what produces salvation. It "saves" in that it reflects a heart decision: a pledge of loyalty to the risen Savior. In effect, *baptism in New Testament theology is a loyalty oath*, a public avowal of who is on the Lord's side in the cosmic war between good and evil.[6] But in addition to that, it is also a visceral reminder to the defeated fallen angels. Every baptism is a reiteration of their doom in the wake of the gospel and the kingdom of God. Early Christians understood the typology of this passage and its link back to

---

4. BDAG, 285.

5. Ibid., 967–68. BDAG glosses the lemma this way: "attentiveness to obligation, conscientiousness" (p. 968). The entry and the secondary scholarship it cites for this meaning point to 1 Tim 1:5; 1 Cor 10:25, 27–29; Heb 9:9, 14 as New Testament examples. In these instances, it may be helpful to think of "conscience" as one's predilection or inner disposition in some behavioral direction (as opposed to a "moral gyroscope" that parses good and evil). Contemporary texts such as 1 Clement 2:4; 34:7 illustrate the former usage and meaning. See H. Osborne, "Συνείδησις," *Journal of Theological Studies* 32 (1931): 167–78; B. Reicke, *The Disobedient Spirits and Christian Baptism*, 174–82 (more external examples); Margaret E. Thrall, "The Pauline Use of Συνείδησις," *New Testament Studies* 14.1 (1967): 118–25; Paul W. Gooch, "'Conscience' in 1 Corinthians 8 and 10," *New Testament Studies* 33.2 (1987): 244–54.

6. For how this plays out in both believer's baptism and infant baptism (presuming the latter is divorced from the doctrine of salvation), see the companion website.

the fallen angels of Genesis 6. Early baptismal formulas included a renunciation of Satan *and his angels* for this very reason.[7] Baptism was—and still is—spiritual warfare.

RENEWING OUR VOW

The second historic Christian rite, observing the "Lord's Supper" or Communion, also has divine council associations, and again they are not so obvious. This time we need to begin in 1 Corinthians 8:1–6:

> [1] Now concerning food sacrificed to idols, we know that "we all have knowledge." Knowledge puffs up, but love builds up. [2] If anyone thinks he knows anything, he has not yet known as it is necessary to know. [3] But if anyone loves God, this one is known by him.
>
> [4] Therefore, concerning the eating of food sacrificed to idols, we know that "an idol is nothing in the world" and that "there is no God except one." [5] For even if after all there are so-called gods, whether in heaven or on earth, just as there are many gods and many lords,
>
> > [6] yet to us there is one God, the Father,
> > from whom are all things, and we are for him,
> > and there is one Lord, Jesus Christ,
> > through whom are all things, and we are through him.[8]

In 1 Corinthians 8 Paul was writing about whether it was permissible to eat food sacrificed to idols. He decided that it was allowable because "an idol is nothing" (8:4) and people were no better if they ate or abstained (8:8). However, he warned that believers who lack such knowledge should abstain (8:9).

Although Paul bases his decision on the fact that idols are nothing, his comments in verses 4–6 tell us that he knew the entities behind them were real. He knew his Old Testament.

Early in our study when I introduced the divine council, I noted that the *shema* of Deuteronomy 6:4, the theological creed of Israel, was worded in such a way that the existence of other gods was not denied ("the Lord *our* God is one"). Paul's wording in 1 Corinthians 8 has the same feel. In fact, most scholars believe that Paul specifically has the *shema* in mind.[9]

---

7. For example, see Tertullian: *On the Crown* 3; *On the Shows* 4; *On the Soul* 35.3. See Ansgar Kelly, *The Devil at Baptism: Ritual, Theology, and Drama* (Ithaca, NY: Cornell University Press, 1985), 94–105.

8. This passage is frequently translated with "gods" and "lords" in quotation marks, as though Paul wasn't serious about what he was saying. The Greek manuscripts have no such punctuation.

9. See, for example, Larry Hurtado, *One God, One Lord: Early Christian Devotion and Ancient Jewish Monotheism* (London: Continuum, 2003), 97–99. James also has the *shema* in view when he writes, "You

The book of Deuteronomy, in which the *shema* occurs, of course has several references to other gods as real entities, considering them to be demons (Deut 32:17). If the writer of Deuteronomy did not really believe there were other gods, then he would have to deny the existence of demons as well. The writer knew there were other real gods, and so the *shema* was demanding loyalty to Yahweh ("our God"), not denying the existence of other gods.[10]

We can be sure that Paul was thinking of the demonic entities of Deuteronomy 32:17 with regard to this issue since he quotes that verse in 1 Corinthians 10:14–22.[11]

> [14]Therefore, my dear friends, flee from idolatry. [15]I am speaking as to sensible people; you judge what I am saying. [16]The cup of blessing which we bless, is it

believe that God is one; you do well. Even the demons believe, and shudder!" (Jas 2:19). Note that James does not say the demons believe in God and therefore tremble. He says that they *believe that God is one*—and that is what frightens them. A fundamental theological point of the *shema* was that God had offered redemption to and through only *one* nation and community: Abraham's descendants. Israel had been created by supernatural intervention after God had disinherited the nations of the earth (Gen 10) at the Tower of Babel event (Gen 11:1–9). Deut 32:8–9, a passage at which we've looked many times in this book, described that disinheritance: "When the Most High gave to the nations their inheritance, when he divided mankind, he fixed the borders of the peoples according to the number of the sons of God. But the LORD's portion is his people, Jacob his allotted heritage" (ESV). After the judgment at the Tower of Babel, God called Abraham (Gen 12:1–3). The two events are juxtaposed back-to-back. When God called Abraham and promised the creation of his "portion," the nation of Israel, through Abraham and Sarah, he disinherited all other nations, allotting them to other heavenly beings, the sons of God. Those divine beings are elsewhere referred to as the host of heaven, gods (*elohim*), and demons (*shedim*) in Deuteronomy (Deut 4:19–20; 17:3; 29:24–26; 32:17). Old Testament theology puts these "sons of the Most High" (Psa 82:6) under judgment for not ruling justly and seducing the Israelites to worship them instead of the true God (Deut 29:24–26; 32:17; Psa 82). There are two important theological points related to the *shema* that touch on Jas 2:19. First, all the people of the nations under the dominion of lesser *elohim* were outside the plan of salvation. A Jewish follower of Jesus—the audience of the book of James (Jas 1:1–3)—knew and rightly affirmed the *shema*. Their faith in Jesus did not nullify the creed "The Lord our God is one" since Jesus was the incarnate Yahweh (see chs. 16–18). After the event of the cross, Abraham's seed was all believers, Jew and Gentile together (Gal 3:26–29). Believing "God is one" was still an expression of faith for a Jewish follower of Jesus that there was only one God who could provide salvation—and he had done just that through the work of Jesus. Second, the rebellious sons of God also knew what the *shema* meant. It reminded them that they were under judgment, sentenced to die like men (Psa 82:6–7; see ch. 30), and forever banished from the presence of the true God. That is what frightens them, not the reality of God's existence. See Christopher R. Bruno, *'God Is One': The Function of 'Eis Ho Theos' as a Ground for Gentile Inclusion in Paul's Letters*, Library of New Testament Studies 497; (London: Bloomsbury Publishing, 2013).

10. Deut 32:17 is regularly mistranslated in English versions, even producing results so confusing that they say the demons (*shedim*) both are and are not gods (e.g., ESV). The proper translation is reflected in the LEB: "They sacrificed to the demons, not God, *to* gods whom they had not known." See my article on this verse and its translation: Michael S. Heiser, "Does Deuteronomy 32:17 Assume or Deny the Reality of Other Gods?" *Bible Translator* 59.3 (July 2008): 137–45.

11. Scholars have recognized that, in 1 Cor 10, particularly in this section, Paul is tracing his argument by appealing to the story of Israel in Deut 32. See Guy Prentiss Waters, *The End of Deuteronomy in the Epistles of Paul*, Wissenschaftliche Untersuchungen zum Neuen Testament 221 (Tübingen: Mohr Siebeck, 2006), 131–47, esp. 134n12, where the author presents a long list of commentators who see an explicit connection between Deut 32:17 and 1 Cor 10:20.

not a participation in the blood of Christ? The bread which we break, is it not a participation in the body of Christ? [17] Because there is one bread, we who are many are one body, for we all share from the one bread. [18] Consider Israel according to the flesh: are not the ones who eat the sacrifices sharers in the altar? [19] Therefore, what am I saying? That food sacrificed to idols is anything, or that an idol is anything? [20] No, but that the things which they sacrifice, **they sacrifice to demons and not to God**, and I do not want you to become sharers with **demons**. [21] You are not able to drink the cup of the Lord and the cup of **demons**. You are not able to share the table of the Lord and the table of **demons**. [22] Or are we attempting to provoke the Lord to jealousy? We are not stronger than he is, are we? (1 Cor 10:14–22).

For Paul the pagan gods were demons. This makes perfect sense when considered in light of Deuteronomy 32:17, which makes exactly the same connection. It is interesting that Paul isn't completely categorical—he allows that meat sold in the market place can be eaten (1 Cor 10:25)—but is fearful of "provoking God to jealousy" under other circumstances. This phrase is an important clue, for it is lifted from Deuteronomy 32:16—the verse right before 32:17, where the gods are called demons:

> [15] And Jeshurun [Israel][12] grew fat, and he kicked;
> you grew fat, you bloated, and you became obstinate;
> and he abandoned God, his maker,
> and he scoffed at the rock of his salvation.
> [16] They made him jealous with strange gods;
> with detestable things they provoked him.
> [17] They sacrificed to the demons, not God,
> to gods whom they had not known,
> new gods who came from recent times;
> their ancestors had not known them (Deut 32:15–17).

It's pretty clear that Paul was worried about sacrificing to demons with respect to the whole issue of meat sacrificed to idols. The meat wasn't really the issue; being involved in the sacrifice was. Apparently some in the Corinthian church had gone beyond eating the meat to actual participation, assuming that since an idol was just a piece of wood or stone, their participation wouldn't offend God. Paul had to teach them that this wasn't true, and used the Lord's Table as an analogy (1 Cor 10:14–18).

---

12. See Sharon Pace Jeansonne, "Jeshurun," *The Anchor Yale Bible Dictionary* (ed. David Noel Freedman; New York: Doubleday, 1992), 3:771–72.

For Paul there was no middle ground. Participation at the Lord's Table meant solidarity with and loyalty to Yahweh. The Lord's Table commemorated not only Jesus' death (1 Cor 11:23–26) but the covenant relationship Yahweh had with the participants. Violating that relationship by participating in sacrifices to other gods was tantamount to siding with the gods of the nations.

DELIVERED UNTO SATAN

Baptism and the Lord's Table were rites of allegiance. The family of Yahweh was to keep itself whole and faithful to Yahweh, and those rites expressed that faithfulness. This context also helps us understand a controversial phrase in 1 Corinthians 5.

Within the Church, there were at times lapses of loyalty when members of the "household of faith" (Gal 6:10) transgressed the moral and doctrinal boundaries set by Yahweh. In such cases, Paul directed believers to remove fellow family members who were unrepentant from the church (1 Cor 5:9–13). More specifically, Paul demanded that the disloyal be "[handed] over … to Satan" (1 Cor 5:5). Paul further noted the goal of such a decision is "for the destruction of the flesh, in order that his spirit may be saved in the day of the Lord."

What did Paul mean by these phrases? With respect to the "destruction of the flesh," Paul often used the word "flesh" (*sarkos*) to refer to the physical body, but he sometimes used it to refer to the self-deception of trusting in our own works to merit God's favor, or an ungodly manner of life.[13] Since there is no indication that someone expelled from the church was going to die immediately as a result, this second usage makes the most sense in 1 Corinthians 5. Paul is insisting that the unrepentant person be dismissed from the church to live in his or her sin and endure the consequences of the behavior. Since salvation was not based in any way on human merit, the erring believer would be saved in the end, but care must be taken to avoid self-destructive sinful behavior from leading other believers astray.

But what about "handed over to Satan"? Recall that the Israelites viewed their land as holy ground and the territory of the non-Israelite nations as controlled by demonic gods. Israel was holy ground because that was where the presence of Yahweh resided. The opposite was true everywhere else.

In the last chapter, we saw that gatherings of believers were viewed the same way. God's presence was no longer in the Jerusalem temple, but in the

---

13. BDAG, 916; H. R. Balz and G. Schneider, *Exegetical Dictionary of the New Testament* (Grand Rapids, MI: Eerdmans, 1993), 3:231.

temple which is the body of Christ (1 Cor 3:16–17). The Corinthian church was therefore "holy ground"; outside that gathering was the demonic realm. To be expelled from the church was to be thrust into the realm of Satan.

The spiritual war brought on by the inauguration of the kingdom of God offers no neutrality. Just as Moses demanded "Who is on the LORD's side?" (Exod 32:26 ESV) in the wake of the golden calf debacle, so the question is put to every person today. There is salvation in no other name—the name of Jesus, who was and is the Name, the presence of Yahweh, who tabernacled on earth (John 1:14) in flesh for the salvation of the nations.

Section Summary

The kingdom of God is already a present reality, but isn't yet realized. John the Baptist announced it. He introduced its king. Jesus preached its arrival and demonstrated what life in God's Edenic world could and would be like: no disease, no infirmity, no demonic opposition.

Many people think of the New Testament as a recounting of the life of Jesus and the apostles sprinkled with a collection of letters sent by Paul to churches with odd names. While we follow these men and their lives and read the correspondence, the New Testament is so much more.

The New Testament marks the rebirth of a struggle thousands of years in the making. The people of God have been isolated and under foreign rule. The divine presence of the days of Moses, David, Solomon, and the prophets is nothing but memory. When angels visit Mary and Zechariah to announce the impending births of Jesus and John, centuries of divine silence are broken. Thirty years later, Judea will explode. The unseen spiritual conflict is even more volatile.

Every chapter of the New Testament provides a glimpse into this conflict. The cosmic geography of the Old Testament is evident in the New. Where Jesus goes and what he says and does when he gets there is framed by confrontation with unseen powers. The conflict pursues him unto death—as God had planned, and as Jesus provoked. The kingdom of God establishes a permanent beachhead at the foot of the cross and the door of the empty tomb.

The rest of the New Testament draws heavily on Old Testament motifs. Jesus is gone but present, just as Yahweh was in heaven invisible yet on earth in human form. The seed of Abraham, scattered to the winds in exile, turn out to function like spiritual cell groups secretly planted in every nation under the dominion of the hostile gods. The kingdom spreads slowly but relentlessly, one new believer at a time. Every church is a new pocket of resistance, every baptism another pledge of allegiance to the Most High, every celebration of the Lord's Supper a denial of fellowship with lesser masters and a proclamation of the success of Yahweh's mysterious plan.

The lines are drawn. The stakes are high. The enemy desperate. The fullness of the Gentiles will come, all Israel will be saved, and the Deliverer will come from the heavenly Zion.

It's just a matter of time.

PART 8

THE KINGDOM NOT YET

CHAPTER 39

Final Verdict

We've come to the place in the divine story line where the present must give way to the future. Many scholars and Bible students have proposed all sorts of things for interpreting what the Bible says about end times, but anything approximating precision is not possible.

The reason for this is straightforward. Old Testament prophecy for the messianic solution to the salvation of humanity and restoration of Eden was deliberately cryptic.[1] So it is with prophecy yet awaiting fulfillment. The biblical text is riddled with ambiguities that undermine the certainty of modern eschatological systems. The New Testament writers who speak about prophetic fulfillments *didn't* always interpret Old Testament literally. Much is communicated through metaphor framed by an ancient Near Eastern worldview. Consequently, our modern expectations about how a given prophecy will "work" are inherently insecure.[2]

Rather than offer yet another speculative system about end times, my goal over the next three chapters is to show you how the divine council cosmic-geographical worldview we have been exploring sheds significant light on how the long war against Yahweh ends. As with everything else in biblical theology, what happens in the unseen world frames the discussion.

Though the kingdom story of the Bible is rarely taught with it in mind, the divine council plays an important role throughout that story's unfolding. The scriptural pattern is that, when God prepares to act in strategic ways that propel his kingdom forward, the divine council is part of that decision making. The council is the vehicle through which God issues his decrees. The purpose of this particular chapter is to take a look back at the council's role

---

1. See chapter 28.
2. See the companion website for examples of these interpretive obstacles.

in the unfolding purposes of God and its final meeting, when God moves to initiate the consummation of his plan to restore Eden at the expense of the hostile powers of darkness.

EDEN, BABEL, SINAI, AND ISRAEL:
Acts in Council and Human Failure

From the very beginning of the human drama revealed in Scripture, the divine council of Yahweh was on the scene.[3] We saw at the beginning of our journey that Yahweh announced his will to create humanity: *Let us make humankind in our image and according to our likeness* (Gen 1:26). Yahweh created humankind as his imager, as he had created his divine family, so that they could participate in administering his affairs. In this case, that meant spreading his influence and the wonder of Eden throughout the rest of the earth. Humanity would multiply God's image through procreation (Gen 1:27–28; 5:1) to steward the vast planet and its life.

The original human imagers failed. Yahweh and his council next appear in the disastrous event at Babel. Yahweh comes down to observe the disobedience of his human imagers (Gen 11:6). He had spared a remnant after the great flood and repeated the instructions he'd given Adam and Eve (Gen 9:1). But instead of overspreading the earth, humanity had congregated at Babel (Babylon). Instead of taking Yahweh's influence and knowledge into the world, they sought to bring Yahweh to themselves.

In response, Yahweh said to his council, *Let us go down and confuse their language there* (Gen 11:7), and then did so. He also decided that he was done working with humanity. Once people dispersed, Yahweh disinherited them, putting them under the authority of lesser *elohim* (Deut 32:8–9).[4] He would now create his own people from a man and his wife too old to bear children, Abraham and Sarah. Israel would be Yahweh's portion on the planet (Deut 32:9). Through Abraham's descendants, the rest of the nations would be blessed (Gen 12:1–3).

The Israelites wound up in Egypt under hard bondage. God raised up Moses to deliver them and to be his agent of divine power against the gods of Egypt. After leading his people back to Mount Sinai, Yahweh and his council gave the fledgling nation of Israel the law.[5] All that was left at that point was to bring them to the land he had promised them. To that end, Yahweh went

---

3. See chapters 5 through 9.
4. See chapters 14 and 15.
5. Deut 33:1–2; Acts 7:52–53; Gal 3:19; Heb 2:2; See chapter 21.

with them in visible human form, the Angel in whom was the Name. But Israel failed.

At various times in the history of Israel's short-lived monarchy, the council is seen in fleeting glimpses. They are there when prophets are commissioned to urge loyalty to Yahweh and warn of punishment for rebellion (Isa 6:1–7; Ezek 1; Jer 1; 23:21–22). The prophet Micaiah pulls back the curtain of heaven, where we see Yahweh and his assembly of divine beings deciding the fate of Ahab (1 Kgs 22:13–28). Israel ultimately fails once more. Yahweh sends them, of all places, to Babylon as punishment.

ALL IS NOT LOST

The council re-emerges after the exile in three significant scenes we've looked at before.

While in exile, the prophet Daniel has a vision of a divine council scene. The vision is recorded in Daniel 7. As we discussed at length earlier, Daniel sees the enthroned God of Israel (the "Ancient of Days") amidst multiple thrones (Dan 7:9).[6] The divine court is present, this time to decide the future fate of earthly empires (Dan 7:9–12), portrayed by four beasts (Dan 7:1–8).

Once the decision is rendered—that the fourth beast must be destroyed and the other beasts will have their dominion diminished while they await destruction, a second Yahweh figure emerges, coming upon the clouds (Dan 7:13). God gives this divine "son of man" everlasting dominion over all "peoples, ... nations, and languages" (Dan 7:14). The appointed king shares his dominion with the "holy ones of the Most High" and "the nation of the holy ones of the Most High" (Dan 7:22, 27). Though set in the place of the people's exile—in Babylon—the vision communicates an ultimate victory of God and the reclamation of all nations through this son of man.[7]

The setting of Psalm 82 is not as clearly telegraphed as Daniel 7, but most scholars would place it during the exile.[8] As I've noted earlier, when the nations of the earth are taken back by Yahweh, the lesser *elohim* of those

---

6. See chapters 29 and 30.

7. The reference to "languages" in Dan 7:14 adds clarity to the reference to the division of nations at Babel, which division is correlated with multiplicity of languages (Gen 11:1–9).

8. This placement is often due to a preconceived notion of an Israelite evolution out of polytheism to monotheism, which allows Psa 82 to be cast as a "killing off" of the gods. I reject the evolutionary idea for a number of reasons. The presumption is flawed on several levels and results in a forced reading of Psa 82 and Deut 32:8–9. See Michael S. Heiser, "Does Divine Plurality in the Hebrew Bible Demonstrate an Evolution from Polytheism to Monotheism in Israelite Religion?" *Journal for the Evangelical Study of the Old Testament* 1.1 (2012): 1–24; Heiser, "Monotheism and the Language of Divine Plurality in the Hebrew Bible and the Dead Sea Scrolls," *Tyndale Bulletin* (forthcoming).

nations will be displaced by Yahweh's reconstituted council, his earthly sons and daughters made divine and set over the nations.[9] Those gods who had received their authority over nations from Yahweh but who had led people away from the Most High will have their authority terminated in Psalm 82. The gods themselves "will die like men" when Yahweh has reclaimed what is his (Psa 82:6–8).

Divine council members still loyal to Yahweh come into view once more as the exile of Judah is ending. As the sins of the Davidic dynasty and its people are pardoned, Yahweh directs his council in a series of grammatically plural commands:

1 "Comfort; comfort my people," says your God.

2 "Speak to the heart of Jerusalem, and call to her,

> that her compulsory labor is fulfilled, that her sin is paid for,
> > that she has received from the hand of Yahweh double for all her
> > sins" (Isa 40:1–2).[10]

The context of Isaiah 40 is a new beginning for Israel. God is acting to bring about a transition in Israel's status. She must return to Zion and await her coming king.[11] A voice within the council then cries out (again, in plural commands):

---

9. See chapter 35.

10. See chapter 31.

11. There is much more to this than the rebuilding of a temple and Zerubbabel's return. On Zerubbabel's lineage, see Derek Kidner, *Ezra and Nehemiah: An Introduction and Commentary* Tyndale Old Testament Commentaries 12 (Downers Grove, IL: InterVarsity Press, 1979). Kidner notes (pp. 40–41) of Zerubbabel: "He is known as the son of Shealtiel (3:2, et al.) who was Jehoiachin's eldest son. But the Heb text of 1 Chr 3:19 makes Zerubbabel the son of Pedaiah, who was a younger brother of Shealtiel. If this is the true text, it implies a levirate marriage of Pedaiah to the widow of Shealtiel, whereby the firstborn was reckoned as Shealtiel's to keep the family name in being (cf. Deut 25:5f.; Ruth 4:10). As Shealtiel's heir, he would be first in line for the throne." Scholars quite naturally draw from this lineage the idea that many Jews would have had hopes for a royal (Davidic) restoration, possibly in messianic terms. While it is true that Zerubbabel was in the line of David, the biblical material dating to the time of the return from exile and afterward bears abundant testimony to the fact that he was not the promised heir to the Davidic covenantal throne. Two items are, in my view, telling in this regard. First, while the prophet Zechariah casts Zerubbabel as God's agent for completing the temple (Zech 4:6–9), the prophet's eschatological outlook for the nation's destiny is more focused on Joshua the high priest (Zech 3:1–10; 6:9–15). "Joshua," of course, is in Hebrew Yeshua ("salvation"), the Hebrew equivalent of Jesus. Given the hindsight of the New Testament, there seems to be a play on words here if not a foreshadowing. Second, the name Zerubbabel means "seed of Babel." While neither the name nor the scriptural account of Zerubbabel amounts to a blemish on his character, it would seem that the name cryptically informs us of some theological messaging: Yahweh had taken his seed out of Babel (i.e., delivering them), but Yahweh would not have his ultimate Davidic king bear any attachment to Babylon. This may be why, although the nation was Yahweh's son, Matthew saw no analogy to Yahweh calling his seed out of Babylon (Israel, God's son, was there because of apostasy), but *did* see an analogy with Egypt (Hos 11:1; Israel was there because God gave Jacob instructions to go there; Gen 46:1–4). We also ought to be able to discern that this return would not be *the* kingdom of God because of the terms of

In the wilderness prepare the way of the LORD;
make straight in the desert a highway for our God (Isa 40:3 ESV).

A lone voice responds to the call in Isaiah 40:6.[12] The fact that the gospel writers quoted this passage with respect to John the Baptist and his message links the coming of the king with the messiah, Jesus of Nazareth.

With the coming of Jesus the restoration of the kingdom is inaugurated. It was formalized at Jesus' baptism, the beginning of his public ministry, and made irreversible at the crucifixion and resurrection. The divine son and servant succeeded—and will succeed—where Israel, God's human and corporate son and servant, failed.

Yahweh's rule on earth is progressing and advancing against unseen powers of darkness and humanity enslaved to those powers. The kingdom has a clear goal: the reclamation of the nations and restoration of Eden on a global scale. The result of accomplishing that goal will be the fulfillment of God's original intention of having a family-council of divine and human imagers. Humanity will become divine and displace the lesser *elohim* over the nations under the authority of the unique divine son, the resurrected Jesus.

We live in this period of advancement. We are already in God's kingdom, but not yet. Our bodies are earthly tabernacles for the glory that we have yet to fully experience. We are in the process of becoming what we are—the divine-human children and household-council of Yahweh.

When God once again moves to initiate the final phase of his plan, the council will again meet. We can see what has yet to happen when we read Revelation 4–5.

YAHWEH'S ELDERS IN COUNCIL

Scholars have long identified John's vision in Revelation 4–6 as a divine council scene.[13] One New Testament specialist in the book of Revelation notes:

---

the new covenant of Jer 31:31–33. Both Jeremiah and Isaiah describe kingdom living as a transformed society, one that cannot be accomplished without the presence of the Spirit and the divine messiah, as well as humans made divine. See J. J. M. Roberts, "The Divine King and the Human Community in Isaiah's Vision of the Future," in *The Quest for the Kingdom of God: Studies in Honor of George E. Mendenhall* (Winona Lake, Ind.: Eisenbrauns, 1983), 127–36.

12. In Isa 40:6, the traditional Hebrew text reads "and someone said" (literally, "a voice said"). The Dead Sea Scrolls read: "And I said." The latter has the prophet himself responding, which implies he is present in the council, a description that aligns with Isaiah's prophetic call in Isaiah 6. It also makes an application to a prophetic figure like John the Baptist more comprehensible. Many scholars consider the reading from the Dead Sea Scrolls to be superior and authentic. For the divine council context of Isaiah 40, see Cross, "The Council of Yahweh in Second Isaiah," 274–277; Seitz, "The Divine Council: Temporal Transition and New Prophecy in the Book of Isaiah," 234–235.

13. Joseph M. Baumgarten, "The Duodecimal Courts of Qumran, Revelation, and the Sanhedrin,"

The focus of the throne vision is God enthroned in his heavenly court surrounded by a variety of angelic beings or lesser deities (angels, archangels, seraphim, cherubim) who function as courtiers. All such descriptions of God enthroned in the midst of his heavenly court are based on the ancient conception of the divine council or assembly found in Mesopotamia, Ugarit, and Phoenicia as well as in Israel.[14]

Given the ground we've covered to this point, the description of John's vision will be quite familiar:

[1]After these things I looked, and behold, an open door in heaven, and the former voice that I had heard like a trumpet speaking with me was saying, "Come up here and I will show you the things which must take place after these things." [2]Immediately I was in the Spirit, and behold, a throne was set in heaven, and one was seated on the throne. [3]And the one seated was similar in appearance to jasper and carnelian stone, and a rainbow was around the throne similar in appearance to emerald. [4]And around the throne were twenty-four thrones, and seated on the thrones were twenty-four elders dressed in white clothing, and on their heads were gold crowns. [5]And from the throne came out lightnings and sounds and thunders, and seven torches of fire were burning before the throne, which are the seven spirits of God. [6]And before the throne was something like a sea of glass, like crystal, and in the midst of the throne and around the throne were four living creatures full of eyes in front and in back. [7]And the first living creature was similar to a lion, and the second living creature was similar to an ox, and the third living creature had a face like a man's, and the fourth living creature was similar to an eagle flying. [8]And the four living creatures, each one of them, had six wings apiece, full of eyes around and inside, and they do not have rest day and night, saying,

"Holy, holy, holy is the Lord God All-Powerful,
the one who was and the one who is and the one who is coming!"
(Rev 4:1–8).

The thrice-holy worship takes us back to Isaiah 6:3, an obvious divine council scene. Other points of similarity to other council visions include the creatures (cf. description of cherubim in Ezek 1; 10); wings on the creatures (cf. seraphim of Isa 6); God enthroned (Isa 6, Ezek 1, Dan 7), multiple thrones (Dan 7);

Journal of Biblical Literature 95 (1976): 59–78, esp. 65–70. Baumgarten writes: "It is surprising that scholars who deal with the exegetical problems associated with the twenty-four elders make no mention of the fact that the participation of the elders in the final judgment is a well-established Jewish concept with roots in biblical and apocalyptic thought. The heavenly tribunal itself is a familiar element of biblical imagery which has been compared with its cognates among the pagan cultures of the ancient Near East" (p. 67).

14. David E. Aune, *Revelation 1–5*, Word Biblical Commentary 52A (Dallas: Word, 1998), 277.

the gemstones, colors, and sea of glass (Ezek 1); divine spirits (1 Kgs 22). John's vision in fact combines earlier divine council features in this one vision.[15]

God is surrounded by twenty-four enthroned elders. The identification of these elders has produced much debate. It has been proposed that the twenty-four are

- heavenly beings, either cosmic counterparts to the twenty-four priestly divisions of Israel or divine representatives of the twelve tribes of Israel and the twelve apostles;
- glorified human believers representing all believers;
- Old Testament believers (cf. Heb 11); or
- nonhuman members of the divine council.[16]

The scene's description in Revelation 5 distinguishes the elders from angels (Rev 5:11) and specifically has the elders, not the angels, in close proximity to the throne encircling God as a council, imagery akin to Daniel 7.[17] Our discussion in chapter 35 about the divinization of humans after death or resurrection makes it possible that the elders are humans made divine. However, the inclusion of martyrs in the scene in Revelation 6:9–11 seems to require that the elders are also distinct from glorified believers. While it is true that both the elders and the martyrs are described in white robes (Rev 4:4; 6:11), the martyrs receive their robes subsequent to the description of the elders, and are not referred to as elders when that occurs.[18]

On one level, identification of the elders as human is quite consistent with other divine council material we've discussed, particularly the presentation of glorified believers by Jesus in the divine council (Heb 1–2).[19] Conversely, identifying them as divine doesn't impinge on the human presence in the council. Heaven and earth, divinity and humanity, are not easily separable when it comes to the divine council and God's plan for restoration of Eden.

The interpretive significance of seeing the elders as divine members of Yahweh's council is that such a reading dovetails with Old Testament divine council scenes involving the judgment of the nations and their gods.

---

15. G. K. Beale, *The Book of Revelation: A Commentary on the Greek Text*, New International Greek Testament Commentary (Grand Rapids, MI; Carlisle, Cumbria: Eerdmans; Paternoster Press, 1999), 320–22.

16. Aune lists these and other approaches (*Revelation 1–5*, 288–89).

17. See Aune, *Revelation 1–5*, 286.

18. Identification of the elders as divine beings versus humans is not essential to identifying the scene as a divine council session. Identification of the elders with the people of God is not erased if the elders are divine beings since the purpose of the council assembly is the final phase of God's triumph on earth and the fact that God's original intent was to include humans in his council rule. Heaven and earth, divinity and humanity, are not easily separable when it comes to the divine council and God's plan for humanity.

19. See chapter 36.

The choice of "elders" to describe the council derives from Isaiah 24:23, a passage that, not coincidentally, is apocalyptic in genre like the book of Revelation.

> [21] On that day the Lord will punish
>> the host of heaven, in heaven,
>> and the kings of the earth, on the earth.
> [22] They will be gathered together
>> as prisoners in a pit;
> they will be shut up in a prison,
>> and after many days they will be punished.
> [23] Then the moon will be confounded
>> and the sun ashamed,
> for the Lord of hosts reigns
>> on Mount Zion and in Jerusalem,
> and his glory will be before his elders (Isa 24:21–23 ESV).

Isaiah 24:23 describes an apocalyptic judgment on the divine enemies of Yahweh and the kings of earth aligned with them.[20] When their judgment is final, Yahweh will be glorified "before his elders." Scholars who have focused on this unusual language in Isaiah have drawn attention to the divine character of the elders by means of two trajectories: (1) comparative passages about elders in the Old Testament to establish that the term specifically refers to select members of a royal household; and (2) similarities in the descriptions of the elders in Revelation 4–5 and those of divine beings in other heavenly council scenes.[21]

---

20. The phrase "host of heaven" is at times used as frequent generic designation for divine beings—members of the nonterrestrial world, good or evil (e.g., 1 Kgs 22:19 and 2 Kgs 17:16, respectively). However, it is distinctly associated with those lesser *elohim* set over the nations who are enemies of Yahweh and his people (Deut 4:19; 17:3).

21. See John D. W. Watts, *Isaiah 1–33*, rev. ed., Word Biblical Commentary 24 (Nashville: Thomas Nelson, 2005), 389; Timothy M. Willis, "Yahweh's Elders (Isa 24,23): Senior Officials of the Divine Court," *Zeitschrift für die alttestamentliche Wissenschaft* 103.3 (1991): 375–85. Many scholars seek to identify the elders in this passage with Israel's human elders due to the reference to Zion and Jerusalem, as well as passages like Exod 24:9–11, where Moses, Aaron, Nadab, Abihu, and 70 elders saw the God of Israel. For that reason, some seek to translate "his elders" as "its elders" (i.e., the elders of Zion or Jerusalem). If this were the case, one would expect a feminine suffix pronoun to grammatically align with these feminine nouns. The form in Isa 24:23 is the plural noun ("elders") plus third masculine singular suffix. This form occurs in only one other place in the Hebrew Bible, Psa 105:22, where the context is clearly select court officials of the king's (Pharaoh's) household. Additionally, the references to Zion and Jerusalem do not require a literal reading, since those terms are also clearly attested eschatological *concepts* in apocalyptic contexts and, more generally, in New Testament biblical theology. See C. C. Newman, "Jerusalem, Zion, Holy City," *Dictionary of the Later New Testament and Its Developments* (ed. Ralph P. Martin and Peter H. Davids; Downers Grove, IL: InterVarsity Press, 1997).

The purpose of the council meeting is threefold: (1) exaltation of the Lamb that was slain (Rev 4:11; 5:11–12); (2) celebration of the Lamb's victory (Rev 5:1–5), an event that made his followers "a kingdom and priests to our God, and they shall reign on the earth" (Rev 5:10); and (3) opening of the seven seals (Rev 6).[22] The scene in Revelation 4–6 shows us that New Testament writers were attentive to the Old Testament pattern of divine council activity at momentous junctures in God's planning. The divine council scene in Revelation 4–6 launches Yahweh's final judgment on the earth described in Isaiah 24:23, the ultimate outcome of which aligns with Daniel 7, where the son of man obtains everlasting dominion and shares it with the holy ones and the people of the holy ones loyal to him and Yahweh.[23]

Revelation 4–6 sets the stage for the final confrontation between Yahweh and his people on the one hand and the powers of darkness and those under their dominion on the other. As we'll see in the next two chapters, the engagement is not only for the souls of humanity and the nations of the earth, but for mastery of the unseen realm itself.

---

22. Aune notes, "The book or roll with seven seals can be understood as containing the entire scenario of eschatological events through 22:5. The seven seals encompass the seven trumpets, while the seventh trumpet encompasses the seven bowls" (*Revelation 1–5*, 276).

23. In regard to the divine council scene in Rev 4–5, Baumgarten notes, "The judgment is not merely an episode, but serves as the framework which unifies the various apocalypses" (Baumgarten, "Duodecimal Courts," 66). Baumgarten specifically links the passage to the judgment of the gods of the nations in Psa 82 (p. 69).

CHAPTER 40

Foe from the North

THE EPIC SAGA OF THE BIBLE BEGAN WITH GOD'S ORIGINAL INTENTION TO rule over his new creation through human imagers, all the while being present with his heavenly imagers. Heaven had come to earth. We saw how it all went awry in the wake of God's decision to grant freedom to his imagers, both divine and human. The decision was necessary, for the creature could not truly be like the creator without sharing this attribute, the ability to truly exercise free will and choose between loyalty and rebellion.

What seems to us to be a long, drawn-out divine plan to restore that which was fallen was equally necessary. It might seem that God could have just stepped in after the fall and eliminated free will and the divine and human rebels who had abused it. Eden would be ensured and that would be that. While that would produce the desired end, the original *means*—free participation in God's creation by God's free-will agents, designed to be like him— would have been abandoned, amounting to a very flawed idea and spectacular failure. A resolution like that isn't fitting (or desirable) for the God of the Bible. God's original objective must come about in the way he intended.

Earthly geography, as many historians have pointed out, is a key part of human destiny. For ancient Israelites, geography had both literal and supernatural qualities. To this point, our discussion of both aspects has been oriented by two factors: (1) the cosmic-geographical worldview that emerged from the Babel incident (Deut 32:8–9), where Yahweh disinherited the nations and decided to raise up his own people from Abraham; and (2) the region of Bashan, the northernmost region of the promised land. In this chapter, we will focus on the second of those, since there was, in Israelite thinking, a psychological and supernatural dread of lands to the north. These fears were intertwined, in ancient thinking, with the great eschatological enemy known as the antichrist.

LITERAL GEOGRAPHICAL NORTH: Harbinger of Doom

Because it sat on the eastern Mediterranean Sea, Canaan found itself sandwiched between the homelands of ancient Near Eastern civilizations that would vie for control of the entire region: Egypt and Mesopotamia. Canaan, and therefore the people of Israel, would find itself being invaded from the north and south by foreign armies on the move. It would be occupied as a buffer zone between competing powers.

The Bible records a number of such incidents. But the most traumatic incursions into Canaan were always from the north. In 722 BC Assyria conquered the ten tribes of the northern Israelite kingdom and deported them to many corners of its empire. In a series of three invasions from 605 to 586 BC, Babylon destroyed the southern kingdom, comprising only two tribes, Judah and Benjamin. Both Assyria and Babylon invaded Canaan from the north, since they were both from the Mesopotamian region. The trauma of these invasions became the conceptual backdrop for descriptions of the final, eschatological judgment of the disinherited nations (Zeph 1:14–18; 2:4–15; Amos 1:13–15; Joel 3:11–12; Mic 5:15) and their divine overlords (Isa 34:1–4; Psa 82).[1]

It is hard to overstate the trauma of the Babylonian invasion. The northern tribes, too, had met an awful fate, the outcome of which was well known

---

1. See Joel Aaron Reemtsma, "Punishment of the Powers: Deut 32:8 and Psalm 82 as the Backdrop for Isaiah 34," (paper presented at the annual meeting of the Evangelical Theological Society, November 19, 2014; San Diego, CA; Ronald Bergey, "The Song of Moses (Deut 32:1–43) and Isaianic Prophecies: A Case of Intertextuality?" *Journal for the Study of the Old Testament* 28:1 (2003):33–54; Thomas A. Keiser, "The Song of Moses as a Basis for Isaiah's Prophecy," *Vetus Testamentum* 55 (2005): 486–500.

to the occupants of the kingdom of Judah. But Judah was David's tribe, and Jerusalem the home of Yahweh's temple. As such, the ground was holy and—or so the kingdom of Judah thought—would surely never be taken by the enemy. But Zion's inviolability turned out to be a myth. Jerusalem and its temple were destroyed by Nebuchadnezzar in 586 BC. The incident brought not only physical desolation but psychological and theological devastation.

The destruction of Yahweh's temple and, consequently, his throne, would have been cast against the backdrop of spiritual warfare by ancient people. The Babylonians and other civilizations would have presumed that the gods of Babylon had finally defeated Yahweh, the God of Israel. Many Israelites would have wondered the same thing—or that God had forsaken his covenant promises (e.g., Psa 89:38–52). Either God was weaker than Babylon's gods or else he had turned away from his promises.

Prophets like Ezekiel, Daniel, and Habakkuk, raised up by God during the exile, had a different perspective. Yahweh had *summoned* foreign armies under the command of other gods to punish his own people. Yahweh was in control. Spiritual disloyalty was what had led to the situation.

THE SINISTER, SUPERNATURAL NORTH

The word "north" in Hebrew is *tsaphon* (or *zaphon* in some transliterations). It refers to one of the common directional points. But because of what Israelites believed lurked in the north, the word came to signify something otherworldly.[2]

The most obvious example is Bashan. We've devoted a good deal of attention to the connection of that place with the realm of the dead and with giant clan populations like the Rephaim, whose ancestry was considered to derive from enemy divine beings. Bashan was also associated with Mount Hermon, the place where, in Jewish theology, the rebellious sons of God of Genesis 6 infamy descended to commit their act of treason.

But there was something beyond Bashan—farther north—that every Israelite associated with other gods hostile to Yahweh. Places like Sidon, Tyre, and Ugarit lay beyond Israel's northern border. The worship of Baal was central in these places. These cities of Phoenicia and Syria were Baal's home turf.[3] The

---

2. See Ludwig Koehler et al., *The Hebrew and Aramaic Lexicon of the Old Testament* (Leiden; New York: Brill, 1999), 1046–47 (esp. entry number 7); Cecelia Grave, "The Etymology of Northwest Semitic *sapanu*," *Ugarit-Forschungen* 12 (1980): 221–29.

3. One could also include the Hittites, since Jebel al-Aqra, Mount Zaphon, was also central to Hittite religion. See H. Niehr, "Zaphon," in *Dictionary of Deities and Demons in the Bible*, 2nd ed. (ed. Karel van der

fact that the center of Baal worship was just across the border was a contributing factor in the apostasy of the northern kingdom of Israel.

Specifically, Baal's home was a mountain, now known as Jebel al-Aqra', situated to the north of Ugarit. In ancient times it was simply known as *Tsaphon* ("north"; *Tsapanu* in Ugaritic). It was a divine mountain, the place where Baal held council as he ruled the gods of the Canaanite pantheon.[4] Baal's palace was thought to be on "the heights of *Tsapanu/Zaphon*."[5]

Baal was outranked only by El in Canaanite religion. However, Baal ran all of El's affairs, which explains why Baal was called "king of the gods" and "most high" at Ugarit and other places.[6] In Ugaritic texts, Baal is "lord of Zaphon" (*ba'al tsapanu*).[7] He is also called a "prince" (*zbl* in Ugaritic). Another of Baal's titles is "prince, lord of the underworld" (*zbl ba'al 'arts*).[8] This connection to the realm of the dead of course dovetails with our discussion of the themes associated with the serpent figure from Genesis 3. It is no surprise that *zbl ba'al* becomes Baal Zebul (Beelzebul) and Baal Zebub, titles associated with Satan in later Jewish literature and the New Testament.[9]

In short, when an Israelite thought of the north in theological terms, he or she thought of Bashan, Mount Hermon, and Baal. Later Jews would have made connections to the great adversary of Genesis 3.

This backdrop will help us understand how Jews living in the latter parts of the Old Testament period on through the Second Temple period and the New Testament era thought about end times—the time of God's final judgment of evil and the ultimate restoration of his rule. But for that we need to start with the concept of exile.

Toorn, Bob Becking, and Pieter W. van der Horst; Leiden; Boston; Cologne; Grand Rapids, MI; Cambridge: Brill; Eerdmans, 1999), 927.

4. Scholars disagree as to whether references to Baal's council should be taken as his own divine council, separate from El's council, or whether the rule of El's council as El's vice regent is in view. All agree the latter is certain, while the former notion of Baal also having a separate council is uncertain.

5. For Ugaritic texts, see *KTU* 1.4 v:55; vii:6; *KTU* 1.3 i:21–22; 1.6 vi:12–13; *KTU* 1.3 iv:1, 37–38; 1.4 v:23. See also W. Herrmann, "Baal," in *Dictionary of Deities and Demons in the Bible*, 133.

6. For Ugaritic texts, see *KTU* 1.16.Iiii:6,8; *KTU* 1.3.v:32; 1.4.Iv:43; 1.4.viii:50. See Nicolas Wyatt, "The Titles of the Ugaritic Storm-God," *Ugarit Forschungen* 24 (1992): 403–24; Herrmann, "Baal," in *Dictionary of Deities and Demons in the Bible*, 131–39; J. C. L. Gibson, "The Theology of the Ugaritic Baal Cycle," *Orientalia Roma* 53.2 (1984): 202–19.

7. See H. Niehr, "Baal Zaphon," in *Dictionary of Deities and Demons in the Bible*, 152–53.

8. The word *ba'al* in Ugaritic and Hebrew means "lord, master." Note the word *'arts* in the title. It is the common word for "earth, land" in Ugaritic, and also Hebrew (*'erets, 'arets*). We briefly discussed this word in chapters 10 and 11 with respect to the *nachash* ("serpent") being cast down to the earth/underworld.

9. See chapters 10–11. On Beelzebul, see Matt 10:25; 12:24 (cf. Mark 3:22; Luke 11:15) and Matt 12:27 (cf. Luke 11:18, 19). Beyond agreeing that there is certainly an association, scholars disagree on the precise etymological development and conceptual relationships between Baal-zebul, Baal-zebub (2 Kgs 1:2, 3, 6, 16) and Beelzebul. See W. Herrmann, "Baal Zebub," in *Dictionary of Deities and Demons in the Bible*, 154–56; E. C. B. MacLaurin, "Beelzeboul," *Novum Testamentum* 20:2 (1978): 156–60.

STILL IN EXILE

One of the great misconceptions of biblical study is that the return of the Jews from Babylon in 539 BC and the years following solved the problem of Israelite exile. *It didn't.* The prophets had envisioned the return of *all twelve tribes* from where they had been dispersed. That didn't happen in 539 BC or any other time framed by the Old Testament.

Jeremiah 23:1–8 is one of the clearest examples of this expectation:

¹ "Woe to the shepherds who destroy and scatter the flock of my pasture," declares Yahweh. ² Therefore thus says Yahweh, the God of Israel concerning the shepherds who shepherd my people, "You yourselves have scattered my flock, and you have driven them away, and you do not attend to them. Look, I will punish you for the evil of your deeds," declares Yahweh. ³ "Then **I myself will gather together the remnant of my flock from all the lands where I have driven them,** and I will bring them back to their grazing place, and they will be fruitful, and they will become numerous. ⁴ And I will raise up over them shepherds, and they will shepherd them, and they will no longer fear, and they will not be dismayed, and they will not be missing," declares Yahweh.

⁵ "Look, days are coming," declares Yahweh,
   "when I will raise up for David a righteous branch,
and he will reign as king, and he will achieve success,
   and he will do justice and righteousness in the land.
⁶ In his days **Judah** will be saved,
   and **Israel** will dwell in safety,
and this is his name by which he will be called:
   'Yahweh is our righteousness.'

⁷ "Therefore look, days are coming," declares Yahweh, "when they will no longer say, 'As Yahweh lives, who led up the Israelites from the land of Egypt,' ⁸ but 'As Yahweh lives, who led up, and **who brought the offspring of the house of Israel from the land of the north and from all the lands where he had driven them.'** Then they will live in their land."

Verse 3 is explicit—Yahweh promises to bring back his people from *all* the places where they have been scattered. Both kingdoms, Judah and Israel, will one day be brought back to the land (v. 6). The specific note that "the house of Israel" will be returned from "the land of the north" and "all the lands" where they were dispersed is an unambiguous reference to the first captivity of the ten "lost tribes" of Israel.

Other passages are clear in this regard as well. In Ezekiel 37, the famous vision of the dry bones, Yahweh says,

> [16] "Son of man, take a stick and write on it, 'For Judah, and the people of Israel associated with him'; [17] then take another stick and write on it, 'For Joseph (the stick of Ephraim) and all the house of Israel associated with him.' And join them one to another into one stick, that they may become one in your hand. [18] And when your people say to you, 'Will you not tell us what you mean by these?' [19] say to them, Thus says the Lord GOD: Behold, I am about to take the stick of Joseph (that is in the hand of Ephraim) and the tribes of Israel associated with him. And I will join with it the stick of Judah, and make them one stick, that they may be one in my hand. [20] When the sticks on which you write are in your hand before their eyes, [21] then say to them, Thus says the Lord GOD: Behold, I will take the people of Israel from the nations among which they have gone, and will gather them from all around, and bring them to their own land (Ezek 37:16–21 ESV).

Again, both Israel and Judah are mentioned, and Yahweh's people will be gathered from the *nations* (note the plural) in which they have been dispersed.

What this means is that *Jews living in the time of Jesus saw the nation as still being in exile.*[10] Ten of the tribes had not yet returned (and many Jews had stayed in Babylon when given the chance). Was Yahweh going to deliver them? Could the powers of darkness be finally overcome?

DELIVERANCE ... AND OPPOSITION

Part of the reason Jews expected a military deliverer in their messiah is that the prophets had taught that the regathering of all the tribes of Israel and Judah went hand in hand with the appearance of a great messianic shepherd-king. Ezekiel 37, the passage we just looked at that described the restoration of all the tribes, adds this element:

> [24] My servant David shall be king over them, and they shall all have one shepherd. They shall walk in my rules and be careful to obey my statutes. [25] They shall dwell in the land that I gave to my servant Jacob, where your fathers lived. They and their children and their children's children shall dwell there forever, and David my servant shall be their prince forever. [26] I will make a covenant of peace with them. It shall be an everlasting covenant with them. And I will

---

10. This psychological conditioning, brought on by biblical explanations of apostasy for the exile, was one of the reasons that absolute obedience to Torah became central to Judaism. Layers of law keeping were added to Torah to prevent violation. The restoration of the tribes (or more punishment) was at stake.

set them in their land and multiply them, and will set my sanctuary in their midst forevermore (Ezek 37:24–26 ESV).

In terms of biblical theology, this expectation was fulfilled in the inauguration of the kingdom of God and at Pentecost. Not only was the reclamation of the disinherited nations launched at that event, but it was accomplished *by means of pilgrim Jews from all the nations in which they had been left in exile, now converted to faith in Jesus, the incarnate Yahweh, and now inheritors of the Spirit and the promises of the new covenant.*

As Paul said in Galatians 3, anyone who followed Christ was a true offspring of Abraham—Jew or Gentile. Jews from every nation of exile had returned to the land to serve as catalysts for a greater regathering, the apostolic mission of the Great Commission. In Ephesians 4 Paul had cast Pentecost as the defeat of Bashan, the region to the north, ground zero for spiritual warfare in Israelite thinking. If we thought only in terms of Pentecost, it would look as if the dark lord of the dead (Baal Zebul)—identified with Satan by this time—was beaten.

But that would be a premature conclusion. It also wouldn't work with what followed Ezekiel 37's deliverance-from-exile and coming-shepherd-king prophecy. In the wake of all that good news, trouble would come—from the north.

GOG, MAGOG, AND BASHAN

The prophetic description in Ezekiel 38–39 of the invasion of "Gog, of the land of Magog" (Ezek 38:1–3, 14–15) is well known and the subject of much interpretive dispute, both scholarly and fanciful. One of the secure points is that Gog will come from "the heights of the north" (38:15; 39:2). While many scholars have focused on the literal geographic aspects of this phrasing, few have given serious thought to its mythological associations in Ugaritic/Canaanite religion with Baal, lord of the dead.

An ancient reader would have looked for an invasion from the north, but would have cast that invasion in a supernatural context. In other words, the language of Ezekiel is not simply about a human invader or human armies. An ancient reader would also have noticed that this invasion would come at a time when the tribes had been united and dwelt in peace and safety within the promised land—in other words, once the period of exile had ended.

The battle of Gog and Magog would be something expected after the initiation of Yahweh's plan to reclaim the nations and, therefore, draw his children,

Jew or Gentile, from those nations. *The Gog invasion would be the response of supernatural evil against the messiah and his kingdom.* This is in fact precisely how it is portrayed in Revelation 20:7–10.[11]

Gog would have been perceived as either a figure empowered by supernatural evil or an evil quasi-divine figure from the supernatural world bent on the destruction of God's people.[12] For this reason, Gog is regarded by many biblical scholars as a template for the New Testament antichrist figure.[13]

---

11. This passage is used and abused by all systems of eschatology. Critiquing those positions (as much as that is possible given prophecy's inherent ambiguities) is well beyond the scope of this chapter and even this book. See the companion website for more discussion. However, it is sufficient to make the point here that it is illegitimate Bible interpretation to posit the notion that the Gog and Magog of Rev 20:7–10 is a *different* Gog and Magog than in Ezek 38–39 in order to make one's explanation of end times work. We ought not to add to Scripture for the sake of a theological system. Any system must account for Rev 20:7–10 *and* the fact that the Jerusalem temple and restored Eden follow in Rev 21–22, just as Ezekiel's idealized temple follows in Ezek 40–48. The correspondences and sequencing are no accident. For scholarly discussion of Gog and Magog, see Sverre Bøe, *Gog and Magog: Ezekiel 38–39 as Pre-text for Revelation 19, 17–21 and 20, 7–10,* Wissenschaftliche Untersuchungen zum Neuen Testament 135 (Tübingen: Mohr Siebeck, 2001); William A. Tooman, *Gog of Magog: Reuse of Scripture and Compositional Technique in Ezekiel 38–39,* Forschungen zum Alten Testament 52, second series (Tübingen: Mohr Siebeck, 2011).

12. The connection "is also expressed in extra-biblical sources ... [of] an eschatological tyrant (1 Enoch 90:9–16; *Assumption of Moses* 8; 2 Baruch *(Syriac Apocalypse)* 36–40; 70; 4 Ezra 5:1–13; 12:29–33; 13:25–38" (see L. J. Lietaert Peerbolte, "Antichrist," in *Dictionary of Deities and Demons in the Bible,* 62). Some other conceptual links are illustrative. First, the Septuagint at times interchanges the names Gog and Og, the giant of Bashan. One scholar notes: "In the LXX[B] version of Deut 3:1, 13; 4:47, Gog stands for Hebrew Og (king of Bashan). On the other hand, P 967 reads Og instead of Gog in Ez 38:2" (see J. Lust, "Gog," in *Dictionary of Deities and Demons in the Bible,* 374). Second, the name "Gog" in Ezek 38–39 may reflect a personification of spiritual darkness if it derives from the Sumerian word *gûg* ("darkness"), though this is uncertain. See Daniel I. Block, *The Book of Ezekiel: Chapters 25–48,* New International Commentary on the Old Testament (Grand Rapids, MI: Eerdmans, 1997–1998), 433–31 (Block cites this possibility from a study by P. Heinisch, *Das Buch Ezechiel* (Bonn: Hanstein, 1923), 183. Third, the Septuagint text of Amos 7:1 mentions Gog as the king of the locust invasion described in that chapter. Locust imagery for invading armies is familiar in the Old Testament, but Rev 9 connects that language with demonic entities from the abyss. This is significant not only since the abyss (a Greek term, *abyssos*) is connected to the Underworld/Sheol, but also because the original offending sons of God of Gen 6 (cf. 2 Pet 2:4; Jude 6; 1 Enoch 6–11) were imprisoned in such a place. Rev 9 may therefore describe their release at the end of days to participate in a climactic confrontation with God and Jesus. This matrix of ideas may be designed to tell us that the Gog invasion does not describe an earthly enemy but a supernatural, demonic enemy. But as we have seen, both reality planes are frequently connected in the biblical epic. Fourth, the Nephilim giants are described as "lawless ones" (*anomōn*) in 1 Enoch 7:6, using the same Greek lemma used to describe the antichrist figure in 2 Thess 2:8. Fifth, Jewish tradition has the great flood (and so, the episode of Gen 6:1–4) coinciding astronomically with the appearance of the Pleiades. This is significant since the Pleiades are connected astronomically with the constellation Orion (the giant), which constellation is mentioned in an Aramaic Targum of the book of Job from Qumran, which uses *nephila* ("giant") to translate Hebrew *kesil* ("Orion"). See L. Zalcman, "Orion," in *Dictionary of Deities and Demons in the Bible,* 648; Zalcman, "Pleiades," in ibid., 657–58.

13. The foe-from-the-north theme is also picked up in Dan 11, a passage that many scholars believe in some way relates to the antichrist. Daniel's eschatological foe is connected to the north many times. The known invasion of Jerusalem by Antiochus IV (Epiphanes) in 167 BC follows many elements that are detailed in Dan 11. Antiochus attacked from the north (he was from the northern, Seleucid empire in Asia Minor). He committed the abominable act of profaning the temple by sacrificing a pig on the altar (cf. Dan 9:24–27) and made Jewish customs such as circumcision punishable by death. These offenses started

While Magog and "the heights of the north" aren't precisely defined in the Gog prophecy, the point is *not* about literal geography per se. Rather, it is the supernatural backdrop to the whole "northern foe" idea that makes any such geographical reference important. For sure ancient Jews would expect that the reconstituted kingdom of Yahweh would be shattered by an enemy from the north—as it had before. But ancient Jews would also have thought in supernatural terms. A supernatural enemy in the end times would be expected to come from the seat of Baal's authority—the supernatural underworld realm of the dead, located in the heights of the north. Gog is explicitly described in such terms. But there is another, similar thought trajectory in ancient Judaism and the early church that has been noted by scholars: The antichrist would come from the tribe of Dan, located in Bashan.[14]

The heart of the idea emerges from Genesis 49, part of the messianic mosaic. The right to rule Israel is linked to the tribe of Judah, and the one who holds its scepter is a "lion" (Gen 49:9–10). In contrast (Gen 49:17), Dan is referred to as a serpent, fitting imagery for Bashan, who "judges" his own people. Deuteronomy 33:22 picks up the theme: "Dan is a cub of a lion; he leaps from Bashan." Dan is an upstart inferior, who will attack from Bashan. Dan is thus an "internal outsider," an enemy of Yahweh's people. Those who interpreted these references in this way were also quick to point out that Dan is omitted from the list of tribes that yield the 144,000 believers in Revelation 7.

---

a rebellion in Jerusalem that led to a short period of Jewish independence. Therefore, those who saw the Gog enemy in Antiochus may also have been led to think of the new Jewish independent state as the final kingdom of God. History informs us clearly that it wasn't. Moreover, despite the elements of precision noted by scholars between the invasion of Antiochus IV and Dan 11, there are clear contradictions between the record of Antiochus's invasion and parts of Dan 11. Nearly two centuries later, Jesus still regarded the prophecy of the abomination of desolation (Dan 9:24–27) as yet to come (Matt 24:15–21). Regardless of the Antiochus issue, his association with the northern foe of Dan 11 nevertheless shows us that the foe-from-the-north motif is important. Later Jewish rabbis and early Christian scholars paid close attention to it.

14. The famous church father Irenaeus is an early source for this thinking (*Against Heresies* 5.30.2–3). However, it is in the writings of Hippolytus that the idea is most fully articulated. See Charles E. Hill, "Antichrist from the Tribe of Dan," *Journal of Theological Studies* 46.1 (1995): 99–117. Irenaeus tied this suspicion to the underworld and the fallen sons of God of Gen 6:1–4. Irenaeus knew that in 2 Pet 2:4 the word for the abyss in which these fallen entities were imprisoned was not the expected *abyssos*, but *tartaros*. This word was considered a lower realm than the normal underworld in Greek mythology (see BDAG, 991). Specifically, it was the place where the quasi-divine giant Titans were imprisoned. "Titans" (*titanos*) was the Greek word used in many Old Testament passages for various giant clan names (e.g., Rephaim). Irenaeus noticed that one of the variant spellings of this word (*teitan*) added up to "666" in Greek gematria (*Against Heresies* 5.30.3). (Gematria is the feature of some languages whereby letters of the alphabet were assigned numerical values, so that words convey numbers and vice versa). Irenaeus favored this answer for the number of the beast since it was *not* the name of a specific ruler or figure, but an evil tyrant, and since the name was connected to the demonic realm. See G. Mussies, "Titans," in *Dictionary of Deities and Demons in the Bible*, 873; G. K. Beale, *The Book of Revelation: A Commentary on the Greek Text*, New International Greek Testament Commentary (Grand Rapids, MI; Carlisle, Cumbria: Eerdmans; Paternoster Press, 1999), 718–20.

My point is not to argue for a specific view of the antichrist. All eschatological systems are speculative in many respects. The point is that the supernatural worldview of ancient Israel and Judaism must inform our own thinking. The cosmic enemy from the supernatural north, where the council of evil plotted against Yahweh's council, was a fixed part of the worldview of the biblical writers—especially when it comes to our next focus: Armageddon.

CHAPTER 41

The Mount of Assembly

EVEN PEOPLE WHO HAVE NEVER STUDIED THE BIBLE HAVE HEARD OF ARMA-geddon. Anyone who has ever investigated the term has undoubtedly read that it refers to a battle that will take place at or near Megiddo, the presumed geographical namesake for the term Armageddon. Further research would perhaps detect the fact that in Zechariah 12:11 the place name "Megiddo" is spelled (in Hebrew) with an "n" on the end, tightening the association between that place and the term Armageddon.

As coherent as all that sounds, it's wrong. As we'll see in this chapter, an identification of Armageddon with Megiddo is unsustainable. With respect to the word itself, the scriptural description of the event, and the supernatural concepts tied to both those elements, the normative understanding of Armageddon is demonstrably flawed.

THE MEANING OF "ARMAGEDDON"

The problems for the traditional identification begin with the term itself. In Revelation 16:12–16 we read:

> [12]And the sixth poured out his bowl on the great river Euphrates, and its water was dried up, in order that the way would be prepared for the kings from the east. [13]And I saw coming out of the mouth of the dragon and out of the mouth of the beast and out of the mouth of the false prophet three unclean spirits like frogs. [14]For they are the spirits of demons performing signs that go out to the kings of the whole inhabited world, to gather them for the battle of the great day of God the All-Powerful. [15](Behold, I am coming like a thief. Blessed is the one who is on the alert and who keeps his clothing, so that he does not walk around naked and they see his shamefulness!) And he gathered them to **the place called in Hebrew Armageddon.**

John, the author of Revelation, tells us explicitly that "Armageddon" is a *Hebrew* term. John does that in part because the book of Revelation is written in Greek. There's something about the Greek word translated "Armageddon" that required, for Greek readers, clarification that the term had been brought into the verse from Hebrew.

Those who can read Greek, or at least know the alphabet, will notice that the Greek term (Ἁρμαγεδών) would be transliterated into English characters as *h-a-r-m-a-g-e-d-o-n*. If you don't know Greek, you'll wonder right away where the initial "h" in the transliteration comes from. The "h" at the beginning of the term corresponds to the superscripted apostrophe before the capital "A" in the Greek letters—what is known as a rough breathing mark in Greek. The Greek language had no letter "h" and so instead used this mark to convey that sound.

As a result, the correct (Hebrew) term John uses to describe the climactic end-times battle is *harmagedon*. This spelling becomes significant when we try to discern what this *Hebrew* term means. The first part of the term (*har*) is easy. In Hebrew *har* means "mountain." Our term is therefore divisible into *har-magedon*, "Mount (of) *magedon*." The question is, what is *magedon*?

Two options have historically been offered for answering this question. The first is the traditional "Megiddo," which I mentioned at the start. The meaning of the phrase would be "Mount Megiddo." Many well-meaning Bible teachers accept this phrase after looking at pictures of Megiddo, like the one below:

The problem is that this is an archaeological *tell*—an artificial mound created by successive layers of building and occupation over millennia. It is not a natural formation. It is not a mountain, and there are no mountains in the entire region. The photograph shows just how *flat* the area of Megiddo actually is.

Revelation 19:11–21 informs us quite clearly that when Jesus returns bodily to earth, he will do so to end the conflict of Armageddon and defeat the beast, the antichrist. According to 16:16, this climactic event occurs at Armageddon. Students of biblical prophecy will find these verses very familiar.

Now let's take a look at Zechariah 12:9–11, recalling that 12:11 is the verse I mentioned at the beginning of the chapter, wherein we find the Hebrew for "Megiddo" spelled with a final *n*. If we read 12:11 in context, we will see that Armageddon cannot be at Megiddo, so the appearance of the final *n* in that verse cannot prove that the term points to that city:

> **9** "And on that day I will seek to destroy all **the nations that come against Jerusalem**.
> **10** "And I will pour out on the house of David and the inhabitants of **Jerusalem** a spirit of grace and pleas for mercy, so that, **when they look on me, on him whom they have pierced**, they shall mourn for him, as one mourns for an only child, and weep bitterly over him, as one weeps over a firstborn.
> **11** On that day the mourning in **Jerusalem** will be as great as the mourning for Hadad-rimmon in the plain of **Megiddo**" (Zech 12:9–11 ESV).

It is crystal clear that *the final conflict occurs at Jerusalem, not Megiddo*. Megiddo is referenced only to compare the awful mourning that will result.[1] Not only does Zechariah 12 place the final battle where the nations see the risen, pierced Christ at Jerusalem, but verse 11 tells us explicitly that *Megiddo is a plain, not a mountain*!

So where does this leave us? Does *magedon* point to Jerusalem? It would seem that it has to, in light of (1) the term *har-magedon*, which describes this final battle, and (2) Zechariah 12:9–11, which plainly sites the conflict at Jerusalem.

THE SUPERNATURAL MOUNT OF ASSEMBLY

In fact, *magedon* does indeed point to Jerusalem, in an especially dramatic way. *Har-magedon* is Jerusalem. The key is remembering that the term derives from Hebrew.

---

1. The mourning at Haddad-Rimmon on the plain of Megiddo refers to the untimely death of the beloved King Josiah on that plain (2 Chr 35:20–25).

To those who do not know Hebrew, "Megiddo" seems like an obvious explanation for *magedon* since both words have *m-g-d*. But in Hebrew there are actually two letters that are transliterated with "g" in Greek (and English translations). Here are the Hebrew letters behind "Megiddo":

mem – gimel – daleth

M – G – D

The same "m-g-d" can be represented another way, with a different Hebrew letter in the middle:

mem – ʿayin – daleth

M – ʿ – D

Neither Greek nor English has a letter (other than hard "g") that approximates the sound of *ʿayin*. That is why it is represented in academic transliteration as a backwards apostrophe. The sound of the letter *ʿayin* is made in the back of the throat and sounds similar to hard "g." Perhaps the best example of a Hebrew word that begins with the letter *ʿayin* in Hebrew but is represented by "g" in English transliteration is "Gomorrah" (*ʿamorah*).[2] That familiar word is not spelled with a Hebrew "g" (*gimel*) like the "g" in "Megiddo." It is spelled with *ʿayin*.

This means that the Hebrew phrase behind John's Greek transliteration of our mystery Hebrew term is actually *h-r-m-ʿ-d*. But what does that mean? If the first part (h-r) is the Hebrew word *har* ("mountain"), is there a *har m-ʿ-d* in the Hebrew Old Testament?

There is—and it's stunning when considered in light of the battle of "Armageddon" and what we discussed in the previous chapter about the supernatural north and antichrist.

The phrase in question exists in the Hebrew Bible as *har moʿed*.[3] Incredibly, it is found in Isaiah 14:13, a passage many readers will immediately recognize:

---

2. See the transliteration in James Swanson, *Dictionary of Biblical Languages with Semantic Domains: Hebrew (Old Testament)* (Oak Harbor, WA: Logos Research Systems, 1997). The *DBL* word number is 6686 (Strong's number 6017).

3. I know of one evangelical scholar who makes these connections. See Meredith Kline, "Har Magedon: The End of the Millennium," *Journal of the Evangelical Theological Society* 39.2 (June 1996): 207–22. Kline uses these points to argue in favor of a recapitulation view of the book of Revelation. Doing so allows him to see Rev 20:7–10 as an episodic repetition of Rev 16 and 19, thereby requiring the admission that the "thousand years" refrain of Rev 20:1–6 does not speak of a literal millennial kingdom following the Church Age, but actually *is* the Church Age. Hence he argues "the end of the millennium." My own eschatological views are not those of Kline's (amillennial), nor would my views align with any of the other systems. Nevertheless, Kline clearly grasped what was going on with the term Armageddon and sees the implications. See also C. C. Torrey, "Armageddon," *Harvard Theological Review* 31 (1938): 237–48. Greg Beale notes in

¹² **How you have fallen from heaven, morning star, son of dawn!**
You are cut down to the ground, conqueror of nations!

¹³And you yourself said in your heart,

"I will ascend to heaven;
I will raise up my throne above the stars of God;
and I will sit on the **mountain of assembly [*har moʿed*]**
on the **summit of Zaphon;**

¹⁴ I will ascend to the high places of the clouds,
I will make myself like the Most High."

¹⁵ But you are brought down to Sheol,
to the depths of the pit (Isa 14:12–15).

Back in chapter 11 we saw that the phrase *har moʿed* was one of the terms used to describe the dwelling place of Yahweh and his divine council—the cosmic mountain. The phrase obviously would have been filled with theological meaning to anyone who knew Hebrew and the Old Testament well. But why would Yahweh's dwelling place be called "the summit of Zaphon"? Didn't we just learn in the last chapter that was Baal's abode?

Recall that, in Psalm 68:15–16, Yahweh desired "Mount Bashan" as his own—that is, he wanted to defeat the forces of darkness and claim their customary abode as his own. The same is true of Zaphon. Look at what Psalm 48 says:

¹Yahweh is great and very worthy of praise
in the city of our God, in his holy mountain.
²Beautiful in elevation, the joy of the whole earth,
is **Mount Zion, in the far north** (Lit., "heights of the north"),
the city of the great king.

Psalm 48 makes a bold theological statement. It evicts Baal from his dwelling and boots his council off the property. The psalmist has Yahweh ruling the cosmos and the affairs of humanity, not Baal. Psalm 48 is a backhanded smack in the face to Baal.

So is Isaiah 14.

Both of these passages are textbook examples of how biblical writers

---

regard to Kline's analysis: "[Kline] demonstrates organic parallels with the immediate and broad contexts. Presupposing the correctness of deriving 'Armageddon' ultimately from *har mô ʿēd*, Kline's contextual analysis of Revelation is quite plausible" (see G. K. Beale, *The Book of Revelation: A Commentary on the Greek Text*, New International Greek Testament Commentary [Grand Rapids, MI; Carlisle, Cumbria: Eerdmans; Paternoster Press, 1999], 840).

adopt and then repurpose material found in the literature of other (pagan) cultures—in this case, Ugarit—to exalt Yahweh and to slight lesser gods. The Hebrew Bible has many examples, but they are obvious only to a reader of Hebrew who is informed by the ancient worldview of the biblical writers.

The result in the case of Armageddon is dramatic. When John draws on this ancient Hebrew phrase, he is indeed pointing to a climactic battle *at Jerusalem*. Why? Because Jerusalem *is* a mountain—Mount Zion. And if Baal and the gods of other nations don't like Yahweh claiming to be Most High and claiming to run the cosmos from the heights of Zaphon/Mount Zion, they can try to do something about it.

And of course they do. Armageddon is about how the unbelieving nations, empowered by the antichrist, empowered by the prince of darkness—Lord (*ba'al*) of the dead, prince Baal (*zbl ba'al*), Beelzebul—will make one last, desperate effort to defeat Jesus at the place where Yahweh holds council, Mount Zion, *Jerusalem*. Revelation and Zechariah agree.[4] Armageddon is a battle for all the supernatural and earthly marbles at Jerusalem. Megiddo doesn't fit the profile in any way.

A BATTLE OF GODS AND MEN:
Another Zechariah Connection

Zechariah 12:9–11 isn't the only passage in that Old Testament book that factors into the Armageddon event. Earlier, in chapter 30, we saw that Zechariah prophesied the coming of Yahweh with his holy ones, other divine beings of his council, in the final conflict against the wicked in all the nations who still stand against his rule:

> [3] Then Yahweh will go forth and fight against those nations, like when he fights on a day of battle. [4] On that day his feet will stand on the Mount of Olives, which faces Jerusalem on the east; and the Mount of Olives will be split in half, from east to west, by a very great valley; and half of the mountain will withdraw toward the north, and the other half toward the south. [5] And you will flee by the valley of my mountains, because the valley of the mountains

---

4. As far as the "n" at the end of the word *magedon*, John adopted the odd spelling found in Zech 12:11 not because he wanted to point to Megiddo as a location (since that verse clearly calls Megiddo a plain and the rest of the passage points to Jerusalem). Rather, he wanted to link the visible return of the Messiah in Zech 12:10 with the final cosmic-geographical conflict for the destiny of earth in Rev 16:16. In other words, by taking the familiar and theologically charged term *har mo'ed* and adding the "n" to it from Zech 12:11, John effectively unites the theological imagery of Isa 14:13 and Zech 12:10 with the battle he describes in Rev 16:16.

will reach to Azal, and you will flee like you fled from the earthquake in the days of King Uzziah of Judah. And Yahweh my God will come, and all the holy ones with him (Zech 14:3–5).

Yahweh is cast in human appearance in this passage ("his feet will stand on the Mount of Olives"). John draws on this passage and its imagery of a human Yahweh in Revelation 19:11–16, the climax of Armageddon:

> ¹¹And I saw heaven opened, and behold, a white horse, and the one seated on it was called "Faithful" and "True," and with justice he judges and makes war. ¹²Now his eyes *were* a flame of fire, and on his head *were* many royal headbands having a name written that no one except he himself knows. ¹³And *he was* dressed in an outer garment dipped in blood, and his name is called the Word of God. ¹⁴And the armies *that are* in heaven, dressed in clean, white fine linen, were following him on white horses. ¹⁵And out of his mouth came a sharp sword, so that with it he could strike the nations. And he will shepherd them with an iron rod, and he stomps the winepress of the wine of the furious wrath of God, the All-Powerful. ¹⁶And he has a name written on his outer garment and on his thigh: "King of kings and Lord of lords."

The incarnate Yahweh has the Name of the Most High. He is the Word of God in human form. He is accompanied by the armies of heaven. The language is obviously drawn from the Old Testament phrase "Lord of hosts," which refers to divine beings.

Traditional approaches to eschatology have recognized that Jesus returns with a divine ("angelic") army, but the divinization of the earthly children of God and their entrance into Yahweh's family council are often overlooked because of the unfortunate translation of *hagioi* ("holy ones") as "saints." The armies of heaven who witness the final demise of antichrist and his hordes are a combination of Yahweh's *elohim* and humans made divine:

> When the Son of Man comes in his glory and all the angels with him, then he will sit on his glorious throne (Matt 25:31).

> So that your hearts may be established blameless in holiness before our God and Father at the coming of our Lord Jesus with all his saints (1 Thess 3:13).

> And to you who are being afflicted, rest with us at the revelation of the Lord Jesus from heaven with his powerful angels (2 Thess 1:7).

> Behold, the Lord comes with ten thousands of his holy ones, ¹⁵to execute judgment on all (Jude 14–15 ESV).

Finally, there is a subtle addition to the description of Jesus' triumphant return in Revelation 19: "He will shepherd them with an iron rod" (v. 15). The language comes from Psalm 2:2, which John had quoted earlier, in Revelation 2:26–28, to refer to *human* believers made divine in the resurrection afterlife, who would rule and reign with Jesus over the nations:

> **26**The one who conquers and who keeps my works until the end, to him I will give authority over the nations, **27**and he will rule them with a rod of iron, as when earthen pots are broken in pieces, even as I myself have received authority from my Father. **28**And I will give him the morning star (Rev 2:26–28 ESV).

The implication, of course, is that the heavenly armies who return with Christ will be more than just nonhuman members of the divine council. The host will include believers who have been exalted into its membership, returned to displace the gods of the nations. Christian—do you know who you are? The day will come when the *elohim* will die like men—*and you will judge angels* (1 Cor 6:3).

CHAPTER 42

Describing the Indescribable

IN THE DISTANT PAST, GOD DISINHERITED THE NATIONS OF EARTH AS HIS coruling family, the original Edenic design, choosing instead to create a new family from Abraham (Deut 32:8–9). The disinherited nations were put under the authority of lesser *elohim, divine sons of God*. When they became corrupt, they were sentenced to mortality (Psa 82:6–8). The Old Testament is basically a record of the long war between Yahweh and the gods, and between Yahweh's children and the nations, to re-establish the original Edenic design.

The victory at Armageddon of the returning incarnate Yahweh over the Beast (antichrist) who directed the nations against Yahweh's holy city is the event that topples the *elohim* from their thrones. It is the day of Yahweh, the time when all that is wicked is judged and when those who believe and overcome replace the disloyal sons of God. The kingdom is ready for full, earthly realization under a reconstituted divine council whose members include glorified believers. The full mass of believing humanity will experience a new Edenic world in a resurrected, celestial state.

What was ruined by the fall is restored—and made irreversible—by the incarnation of Yahweh, his atoning death, and his resurrection. But all that is relatively easy to talk about when compared to passages that deal with what comes last and remains forever.

How do you describe the indescribable? Paul grasped the problem clearly. I still like the King James Version of his sentiments for their rhythmic, almost lyrical quality:

> Eye hath not seen, nor ear heard, neither have entered into the heart of man, the things which God hath prepared for them that love him (1 Cor 2:9 KJV).

How true. But in this last chapter, I want to try to sketch what the biblical writers were thinking when they wrote about the celestial bodies of resurrected believers and the eternal state of the new Eden.

CELESTIAL FLESH

We've devoted a good deal of attention to outlining the New Testament's use of sonship, family, and adoption terminology for believers (e.g., Gal 3:7–9, 23–28; John 1:11–12; 1 John 3:1–3; 2 Pet 1:2–4; Gal 4:4–6; Rom 8:15–23; Eph 1:4–5).[1] The logic of this language should be quite evident by now. In ages past the divine sons of God watched as Yahweh created the world (Job 38:7–8). Yahweh then announced to his council his intention to create humans who would be his imagers, a status his divine sons also shared (Gen 1:26–27). *We were designed to be embodied reflections of God.* That point of biblical theology was at the core of Paul's most extended discussion of what we will be in the new Eden, a place we cannot go to until we die in Christ and are raised with him. He wrote in 1 Corinthians 15:

> [35] But someone will say, "How are the dead raised? And with what sort of body do they come?" [36] Foolish person! What you sow does not come to life unless it dies. [37] And what you sow *is* not the body which it will become, but you sow the bare seed, whether perhaps of wheat or of some of the rest. [38] But God gives to it a body just as he wishes, and to each one of the seeds its own body. [39] Not all flesh *is* the same, but *there is* one flesh of human beings, and another flesh of animals, and another flesh of birds, and another of fish, [40] and heavenly bodies and earthly bodies. But the glory of the heavenly *bodies is* of one kind, and the *glory* of the earthly *bodies is* of another kind. [41] *There is* one glory of the sun, and another glory of the moon, and another glory of the stars, for star differs from star in glory.
>
> [42] Thus also *is* the resurrection of the dead. It is sown in corruption, it is raised in incorruptibility. [43] It is sown in dishonor, it is raised in glory. It is sown in weakness, it is raised in power. [44] It is sown a natural body, it is raised a spiritual body. If *there* is a natural body, *there* is also a spiritual *body.* [45] Thus also it is written, "The first man, Adam, became a living soul"; the last Adam *became* a life-giving spirit. [46] But the spiritual *is* not first, but the natural; then the spiritual. [47] The first man *is* from the earth, made of earth; the second man *is* from heaven. [48] As the one *who is* made of earth, so also *are* those *who are* made of earth, and as the heavenly, so also *are* those *who are* heavenly. [49] And just as we have borne the image of the *one who is* made of earth, we will also bear the image of the heavenly.
>
> [50] But I say this, brothers, that flesh and blood is not able to inherit the kingdom of God, nor can corruption inherit incorruptibility. [51] Behold, I tell you a mystery: we will not all fall asleep, but we will all be changed, [52] in a

---

1. See chapters 35–36.

moment, in the blink of an eye, at the last trumpet. For the trumpet will sound, and the dead will be raised imperishable, and we will be changed. [53] For it is necessary *for* this perishable *body* to put on incorruptibility, and this mortal *body* to put on immortality (1 Cor 15:35–53).

This passage generates a number of questions. The most fundamental is no doubt what Paul means by asserting that there is some sort of "heavenly body" (v. 40) that is "spiritual" (*pneumatikos*; v. 44) and immortal (vv. 52–53). Whatever he meant by that language has importance for every believer, since they "will also bear the image of the heavenly [second] man" (vv. 45–49).

There has actually been a good deal of scholarly attention paid to Paul's thoughts in 1 Corinthians 15.[2] In the ancient Hellenistic Graeco-Roman world of Paul, there was a belief that the afterlife dead had bodies that were not flesh and blood, but which were composed of "a finer, purer substance."[3] Many people during this time referred to this substance as *aether*, and believed that stars were also composed of it. This explains in part the propensity in extrabiblical writers to assert that the afterlife dead became stars or like stars. Since stars were thought to be divine members of the realm of the gods, the idea makes sense in its own context. Paul's thinking, however, transcends this equation.[4]

Paul was not dependent on Graeco-Roman paganism for thoughts about celestial immortality. The Old Testament contains kernels of the idea, and many Jewish literary works of the Second Temple period address the topic. Daniel 12:2–3 ties resurrection life to the heavens (and stars) without speculating on the nature of resurrection existence:

> [2]And many from those sleeping in the dusty ground will awake, some to everlasting life and some to disgrace and everlasting contempt. [3]But the ones

---

2. The most recent, lengthy scholarly treatment of this topic is M. David Litwa, *We Are Being Transformed: Deification in Paul's Soteriology, Beihefte zur Zeitschrift für die neutestamentliche Wissenschaft* 187 (Berlin: Walter de Gruyter, 2012), 119–71.

3. Litwa, *We Are Being Transformed*, 137. Litwa makes this point in an extended treatment of Stoic philosophical discussion of the "soul," the terms of which have several points of conceptual correspondence to Paul's description in 1 Cor 15. However, Litwa moves on to focus on distinctive elements of Paul's conception. In other words, Paul's idea of a "spiritual body" was not foreign to his culture, though his conception differed at points. Litwa notes that one of the key distinctions was that, for Paul, the spiritual body was immortal and incorruptible. He writes: "Although Cicero makes similar claims, other Stoic sources deny the immortality of the soul" (p. 139).

4. See Litwa, *We Are Being Transformed*, 139–46. See chapter 20 for the brief discussion of "star language" as it related to believers. The noted early church scholar Origen tried to frame the believer's glorification by appeal to the aether and the stars. See Alan Scott, *Origen and the Life of the Stars: The History of an Idea*, Oxford Early Christian Studies (Oxford: Oxford University Press, 1994).

having insight will shine like the brightness of the expanse, and the ones providing justice for the many will be like the stars forever and ever.

The New Testament contains similar thinking. Matthew 13:43 says, "Then the righteous will shine like the sun in the kingdom of their Father." The point of the celestial analogy is apparently that a believer's body will be like that of Jesus, since Jesus' appearance at the transfiguration is described in similar terms: "His face shone like the sun, and his clothing became bright as the light" (Matt 17:2). Second Temple Jewish sources describe the same idea with respect to the resurrected righteous.[5]

Ultimately, this sort of celestial language is trying to telegraph a simple but indescribably profound idea. In the eternal afterlife with God, believers will have the same sort of body that Jesus had after the resurrection. We will identify with the risen Jesus bodily as we identify with the Spirit currently: "He who is joined to the Lord becomes one spirit with him" (1 Cor 6:17 ESV).[6]

In our more modern language, we might say that the body Christ had after the resurrection was his earthly body, healed and transformed into a material form unbound by the limitations of human terrestrial existence. It was a "glorious body" (Phil 3:21), both of earth and not of earth. This resurrection transformation is the final, unimaginably literal expression of being conformed to the image of Christ (2 Cor 3:18). As one scholar summarizes:

> To be conformed to Christ's Glory body is evidently parallel to becoming "the same image" as a divine being (2 Cor 3:18). Thus this luminous corporeality of God known from the Hebrew Bible has been granted to Paul's converts through their participation in Christ. They are assimilated to the super body of the divine Christ. They share in the reality of Christ's divine body, which guarantees their participation in Christ's attributes of incorruptibility and immortality.[7]

---

5. See, for example, 1 Enoch 39:7 ("And I saw a dwelling place underneath the wings of the Lord of the Spirits; and all the righteous and the elect before him shall be as intense as the light of fire"); 104:1–4 ("I swear unto you that in heaven the angels will remember you for good before the glory of the Great One; and your names shall be written before the glory of the Great One. Be hopeful, because formerly you have pined away through evil and toil. But now you shall shine like the lights of heaven, and you shall be seen.... Be hopeful, and do not abandon your hope, because there shall be a fire for you; you are about to be making a great rejoicing like the angels of heaven"). The translation comes from James H. Charlesworth, ed., *The Old Testament Pseudepigrapha* (New Haven: Yale University Press, 1983), 1:85.

6. Paul is not espousing monism in 1 Cor 6:17. He is expressing unity with that spiritual being who is Yahweh, the Most High, who is a personal deity, the creator of all things visible and invisible (Col 1:15–17). Paul envisions unity of presence (i.e., joining in Yahweh's council in his abode) in a new earthly Eden, not absorption into an impersonal force in a nonterrestrial, immaterial dimension, indistinct from creation.

7. Litwa, *We Are Being Transformed*, 151.

GLOBAL SACRED SPACE

The book of Revelation frequently describes believers as those who "overcome" the assault of evil described in the book by retaining their faith in Christ, the Lamb of God who is the beginning and the end. On six occasions the term is used in conjunction with the reward of eternal life. The imagery invoked is unmistakable, as it is drawn from Old Testament descriptions of sacred space—first Eden, then the ark and the tabernacle, then the heavenly abode inhabited by the new, resurrected high priest, Jesus himself. To live in the new Eden means to occupy sacred space reserved for God and his family-council.

In Revelation 2:7, 11 Jesus says of those who conquer, "I will grant [to them] to eat of the tree of life, which is in the paradise of God.... [They] will not be hurt by the second death" (ESV). The reference to the tree of life is clearly Edenic. Revelation 2:11 is less transparent, but also echoes Eden. The first death refers to physical death, brought by Adam's sin and expulsion from Eden. Since all humans, believers and unbelievers, are resurrected before judgment, the second death is the final judgment (Rev 21:8). Those who continue to live with God do so in a new Edenic world.

Revelation 2:17 tells us that those who conquer receive "hidden manna" and "a white stone, and on the stone a new name written, that no one knows except the one who receives *it*." Manna, of course, was a food supernaturally provided during the wilderness wanderings (Exod 16). It was bread from heaven, an analogy to Jesus as the source of eternal life (John 6:31–58). It was "hidden" in the sense that it was reserved only for those who had believed to the end.[8] A pot of manna was placed "before the Lord" in the ark of the covenant in the holy of holies (Exod 16:33; Heb 9:4). According to Second Temple Jewish writings, manna was considered the food of angels and of the sons of God.[9]

The meaning of the white stone isn't completely certain. Based on parallels found in Second Temple period Jewish literature, the white stone was a symbol of legal acquittal or a token of membership among the righteous. The meaning is therefore very similar to conquering believers receiving white robes referenced in Revelation 3:5, which says: "The one who conquers in this way will be dressed in white clothing, and I will never erase his name from the book

---

8. See David E. Aune, *Revelation 1–5,* Word Biblical Commentary 52A (Dallas: Word, 1998), 189. *Second Baruch (Syriac Apocalypse)* 29:8 says, "And it will happen at that time that the treasury of manna will come down again from on high, and they will eat of it in those years because these are they who have arrived at the consummation of time" (cf. *Sibylline Oracles* 7.149). Translation is from Charlesworth, *Old Testament Pseudepigrapha,* 1:631.

9. Ibid., 189. See *Joseph and Aseneth* 16:14.

of life, and I will declare his name before my Father and before his angels." As we saw in chapter 36, Jesus in fact introduces us to the council. A white stone and a white robe were signs of membership in God's family.[10]

Revelation 3:12 draws on the temple. Jesus says, "The one who conquers, I will make him a pillar in the temple of my God. Never shall he go out of it, and I will write on him the name of my God, and the name of the city of my God, the new Jerusalem, which comes down from my God out of heaven, and my own new name." The language is familiar from passages like 1 Corinthians 3:16; 6:19, but still startling. Yahweh's temple was sacred space—and we are part of that temple. As we learned from the Old Testament, the temple was the abode of the Name, Yahweh's presence—and now we bear that Name.

Revelation 21:7 is the most explicit link between divine sonship and conquering evil and the nations: "The one who conquers will have this heritage, and I will be his God and he will be my son" (ESV). A "heritage" is of course an inheritance. Israel was Yahweh's inheritance, his portion (Deut 32:9). We are part of that (Gal 3:26–29) and also govern it as sons and daughters of his royal, divine household council. The inheritance of the believer is dominion with Christ and God.

REVERSAL OF THE CURSES

The Eden imagery at the end of the book of Revelation is obvious, as that can be the only context for the tree of life:

> [1] Then the angel showed me the river of the water of life, bright as crystal, flowing from the throne of God and of the Lamb [2] through the middle of the street of the city; also, on either side of the river, the tree of life with its twelve kinds of fruit, yielding its fruit each month. The leaves of the tree were for the healing of the nations. [3] No longer will there be anything accursed, but the throne of God and of the Lamb will be in it, and his servants will worship him....

---

10. Beale notes: "A white stone was commonly associated with a vote of acquittal (cf. 4 Macc. 15:26; Acts 26:10) or a favorable vote. Conversely, a black stone indicated guilt. A white stone sometimes was also used as a pass of admission to special occasions. Against this background, the meaning here probably refers to the reversal of the guilty verdict issued by the world's institutions against the overcomer because of refusal to participate in its idolatrous meals. Accordingly, the "white stone" becomes the invitation to take part in Jesus' supper (cf. 19:9). The notion that a banquet meal is in mind is supported by the reference to "manna." According to Jewish tradition, precious stones fell along with the manna (cf. *Midr.* Ps. 78.4). Some commentators have seen here the two precious stones on the shoulder pieces of the high priest's ephod, bearing the names of the twelve tribes (Exod 28:9–12). According to another Jewish tradition, these priestly stones were stored in the hidden ark, to be revealed in the messianic times (cf. 2 Bar. 6:7–8)." See G. K. Beale, *The Book of Revelation: A Commentary on the Greek Text,* New International Greek Testament Commentary (Grand Rapids, MI; Carlisle, Cumbria: Eerdmans; Paternoster Press, 1999), 252–53.

[14] Blessed are those who wash their robes, so that they may have the right to the tree of life and that they may enter the city by the gates....

[19] And if anyone takes away from the words of the book of this prophecy, God will take away his share in the tree of life and in the holy city, which are described in this book (Rev 22:1–3, 14, 19 ESV).

Notice that the tree of life is specifically now for "the healing of the nations," a clear reference to the reclaiming of the nations turned over to lesser gods at Babel (Deut 32:8–9). The effect is also described: "No longer will there be anything accursed." The curses upon earth and humanity brought on by the fall are reversed. The other two tree-of-life references naturally link the eternal life of the believer to being present in Eden—the place where God, the source of all life, dwells.

The Old Testament alludes to the reversal of the curse and the coming global kingdom in striking ways that echo the Edenic conditions:

- All those formerly sick or disabled will be restored to full health (Isa 29:18–19; 30:26; Mic 4:6–7).

- All will enjoy a supernatural abundance of milk, honey, fruit, and produce (Isa 4:2; 7:21–22; 25:6–9; 30:23–24; Joel 3:18; Amos 9:13–15).

- There will be peace throughout all creation (Hos 2:18; Isa 11:1–10; cf. Ezek 34:25–28); and all Israel (Isa 10:20; 52:6; Ezek 39:22).

- All nations (Isa 19:19–25; cf. Ezek 38:23) will know that Yahweh is God.

NO MORE SEA

One of my favorite verses in the Bible is Revelation 21:1. John writes:

Then I saw a new heaven and a new earth, for the first heaven and the first earth had passed away, and the sea was no more (ESV).

In the ancient world the sea was a thing of dread. It was unpredictable and untamable. It was a place upon which humans couldn't live. Consequently, the sea was often used as a metaphor for chaos, destruction, and death. The power and chaotic unruliness of the sea was symbolized in both the Old Testament and a wide range of ancient Near Eastern literatures with a dragon or sea monster, variously known as Leviathan and Rahab (e.g., Pss 74:14; 89:10).[11]

---

11. Leviathan is certainly not a literal prehistoric sea creature that survived into the time period of the Old Testament. The name is known from other Canaanite literature, such as that of Ugarit, and is referenced in the same ways as we find in the Hebrew Bible. It was a well-known chaos symbol across the known

Sea imagery conveys these ideas from the very beginning of the Bible. The waters of the primeval deep (Gen 1:2) must be calmed and restrained by God. The defeat of the gods of Egypt happens when the sea obeys its Maker (Exod 14). Jesus walks on the sea and instantly brings it into submission. To the ancient mind these incidents symbolized power over chaos and everything that might bring harm and death to humanity. Absence of chaos meant that everything was in perfect, divine order and calm.

This is why Revelation ends as it does, with God's return to permanently dwell with his family on a new earth. When Eden comes, *there is no more sea*. All that was originally intended in God's vision of a global Eden has come to pass. The final Eden has no death. The choices of God's free-will imagers that obstructed God's plan have been dealt with. All the imagers, human and divine, who dwell in the new Eden have chosen correctly—they have believed that Yahweh is the God of gods and that his way is best. Their will has aligned with his will. The "already, but not yet" has been realized. The "not yet" has given way to now and forever.

---

ancient world. See C. Uehlinger, "Leviathan," in *Dictionary of Deities and Demons in the Bible*, 2nd ed. (ed. Karel van der Toorn, Bob Becking, and Pieter W. van der Horst; Leiden; Boston; Cologne; Grand Rapids, MI; Cambridge: Brill; Eerdmans, 1999), 511–15; K. Spronk, "Rahab," in ibid., 684–86; C. H. Gordon, "Leviathan: Symbol of Evil," in *Biblical Motifs: Origins and Transformations* (ed. A. Altmann; Cambridge, MA: Harvard University Press, 1966) 1–9; John Day, *God's Conflict with the Dragon and the Sea*, University of Cambridge Oriental Publications 35 (Cambridge, UK: Cambridge University Press, 1985); M. K. Wakeman, *God's Battle with the Monster* (Leiden: Brill, 1973). Leviathan and chaos are important biblical-theological concepts that must be left for another time.

Epilogue

W<small>HEN WE BEGAN OUR JOURNEY</small>, I <small>SHARED WITH YOU MY OWN EXPERIENCE</small> of venturing into the mind of ancient Israelites and the Jews and Christians of the first century and how that made it impossible to look at the Bible as I had before. It ruined me in an agreeable way. But I can only say that with hindsight. At the time of that experience, I had already taught on the college level and was in the midst of one of the nation's most respected Hebrew Bible programs—and yet I hadn't been thinking clearly about Scripture. I hadn't seen much of what I've written in this book. I'd been blinded by tradition and my own predilection to keep certain things on the periphery when it came to the Bible. It was the worst possible time in my life to have everything put into upheaval, to have to rethink and reevaluate what I believed. It required that I be humbled, something that doesn't come easily to an academic.

The realization that I needed to read the Bible like a premodern person who embraced the supernatural, unseen world has illumined its content more than anything else in my academic life. One question I've been asked over the years when sharing insights that are now part of this book was one that I asked myself: *Why haven't I heard these things before?* It astonished me that I could sit under years of biblical preaching and teaching and never have anyone alert me to the important and exciting truths we've tracked here.

I've learned that the answer to that question is complex. Rather than dwell on it, God provoked me to do something about it. Most people aren't going to learn Greek and Hebrew (and other dead languages) as part of studying Scripture. Most aren't going to pursue a PhD in biblical studies, where they'll encounter the high-level scholarship that will force them to think about what the biblical text really says and why it says it in its own ancient context, far removed from any modern tradition. But everyone ought to reap some benefit from those disciplines. And so it has become my ambition to parse that data and synthesize it so that more people can experience the thrill of rediscovering the supernatural worldview of the Bible—of reading the Bible again for the first time.

The Unseen Realm is the first step in that effort. If you're like me, what you've read here will be fodder for thought for some time. And truth be told, it's just a starting point. My hope is that the book has alerted you to some terribly important principles that I've listed below: strategies for pursuing the biblical-theological ideas that run through Scripture. They're my short list of research principles that, even though they are self-evident, I need to be constantly reminded of.

1. **Let the Bible be what it is, and be open to the notion that what it says about the unseen realm might just be real.** The writers certainly thought it was. I would suggest that it's a good hermeneutical strategy to firmly grasp that they—the biblical authors—aren't *us* while we seek to understand *their* thoughts. That doesn't seem terribly profound, but it's critically important to reading Scripture as it was written.

2. **The content of the Bible needs to make sense in its own context, whether or not it makes sense in ours.** I can't help but think of our discussions of Genesis 6:1–4 here. That passage says what it says because of what it *addresses in the worldview of the writer.* Assigning a more "rational" (i.e., nonsupernatural) meaning to it in order to make it more palatable in a different context amounts to erasing its intended target. Even if some passages of Scripture don't make sense in our world, and we cringe at what they say, changing their context to remove our discomfort isn't sound hermeneutical method.

3. **How the biblical writers tie passages together for interpretation should guide our own interpretation of the Bible.** In academic jargon, this is referred to as intertextuality. It's important for understanding what a biblical writer was thinking and doing. It is how ideas are threaded through the canon. Most of our exegesis involves *breaking up* passages and verses into their constituent parts, whereas the biblical writers were *creating connections* between texts. Since the Bible is, unavoidably, something of an artifact to us, we have to pay careful attention to the parts. But too often we only gaze at the pieces in isolation and fail to observe how they are tethered to other pieces. Learning to pay attention to intertextuality is to follow an inspired breadcrumb trail where it leads.

4. **How the New Testament writers repurpose the Old Testament is critical for biblical interpretation.** In other words, the Septuagint is a big deal. It

does little good to remind ourselves that the New Testament is an inspired commentary on the Old Testament when we fail to discern just what Bible they were using (more often than not).

5. **Metaphorical meaning isn't "less real" than literal meaning (however that's defined).** Whether we like it or not, the biblical writers weren't obsessed with literalism the way we seem to be. Frankly, I've come to believe that every seminary and graduate school program in biblical studies ought to require a course on the hermeneutical methods of the biblical writers and first-century Judaism. It would be a wake-up call. Biblical writers regularly employ conceptual metaphor in their writing and thinking. That's because they were human. *Conceptual metaphor* refers to the way we use a concrete term or idea to communicate abstract ideas. If we marry ourselves to the concrete ("literal") meaning of words, we're going to miss the point the writer was angling for in many cases. If I use the word "Vegas" and all you think of is latitude and longitude, you're not following my meaning. Biblical words can carry a lot of freight that transcends their concrete sense. Inspiration didn't immunize language from doing what it does.

Finally, my prayer for readers is that God will use this book in your life the way he has used its content in my own spiritual journey: to marvel at the intricacy of the biblical narrative, to be blessed by the love of God for his human children, and to acknowledge the role of the unseen world in the inheritance of salvation (Heb 1:14).

Acknowledgments

THIS BOOK HAS BEEN A LONG TIME IN COMING. THE IDEA FOR IT AROSE WHILE I WAS in graduate school at the University of Wisconsin-Madison. I wanted to decode what I was learning about the need for reading the Bible in its own original context for non-specialists. There was too wide a chasm between how scholars read the Bible and how it was read in churches. Lay people and pastors were missing the many interpretive payoffs to serious exegesis of the text framed by the worldview of the writers, not to mention the beautiful coherence of the Bible's epic supernatural narrative. I wanted to bridge that gap in some way.

One of the first things I did toward preparing to write was create an informal online discussion group. I called it the Divine Council Study Group (DCSG). The original participants were James R. Black, Ronn Johnson, Doug Vardell, Stephen Huebscher, and Charles Kennedy. The discussions were stimulating and useful. They helped me discern many items that needed inclusion in what I would eventually write and produced questions that readers were sure to ask. The DCSG was also the impetus for the creation of a sweeping bibliography for all things related to the divine council worldview. The DCSG disbanded in 2004 after I graduated from my doctoral program and started work at Logos Bible Software, but it gave me direction to begin writing and start collecting material.

The book began shortly thereafter under the title *The Myth That is True.* In order to make myself accountable to produce something each month, I began writing portions in a monthly newsletter that I emailed to subscribers. That practice continued for almost eight years, during which time I abandoned the newsletter and started blogging. The first draft (or what I thought of as a first draft) was finished in 2012. Over those years I had a good deal of feedback from readers, far too many to mention all the names here. Some who proofread the initial manuscript version and otherwise encouraged me in the project include Mark Lutzow, Kevin Bucy, Tim Robinson, James Coke, Cathy Hawk, David Brewer, Brian Lopez, Cris Putnam, Ben Stanhope, Jonnathan Molina, Jeff Sievertson, Von Glitschka, Michael Krause, Kenneth Conklin, Keith Jentoft, Doug Overmyer, Anne Edsell, Russ White, Gearron Sublett, John D.

Barry, Eli Evans, Rick Brannan, Vincent Setterholm, Carl Jacques, Corby Amos, Mike Brant, Will Penland, Doug Van Dorn, Brian Godawa, Steve Runge, Carl Sanders, Stuart Whitaker, Neil van der Gugten, Mark Lundgren, Sharon Shipwash, John Dunn, Ron Dupree, Dennis Linscomb, Paul DeSilva, Margo Houts, Justin Blystone, Greg Lyle, Marc Wilson, Jay Bradley, Amy Bradley, Jeff Franklin, and Jessica Tyson. Mike Adamo, Dino Schulmeier, Melissa Nienhuis, and Eric Joel Ortiz specifically assisted me in organizing my cumulative divine council bibliography, currently numbering over three thousand items.

Dr. Bob Chisholm deserves special thanks for steering my first journal article ("Deuteronomy 32:8 and the Sons of God," 2001) related to the divine council through the review process. His endorsement and advice was crucial. Dr. Gerry Breshears was another scholar who saw very early on that what I was doing had value. He was a consistent encouragement to keep working on the draft. I'm thankful for David Burnett and his own research and its relation to the divine council worldview. David's the doctoral student I'll never have. It's been fun to watch him get absorbed by the material since he attended some of my early papers on the divine council at ETS meetings. My pastor, Dax Swanson, has also been a consistent voice of encouragement, not only for the project, but also for being able to teach the content to people in a local church context. I'm also thankful to all those who received advanced reader copies of *The Unseen Realm* and encouraged its readership through their endorsement.

The book that you now hold in your hands, though, would never have reached you without the commitment and input of several people that deserve special mention. During the course of my time at Logos I had dozens of conversations about the content with Dale Pritchett, a vice president with the company for many years until his retirement. Dale read through the initial *Myth That is True* draft on my website and, later, the uncorrected proofs for *The Unseen Realm* numerous times. He became what I can only describe as an evangelist for the material. His son Bob Pritchett, the CEO at Logos (now under the parent corporation, Faithlife), was one of Dale's converts. It was Bob who made the decision after reading the initial draft that the book couldn't remain a leisure project. He was the irresistible force behind the launch of *The Unseen Realm*. Bob wisely hired the Somersault Group to shepherd me through the editorial and promotional process. Those who read the early draft will quickly realize that my editor, Dave Lambert, did a wonderful job with the book. Dave is a seasoned editor, and I enjoyed the experience. Bob Banning, my copy editor, did amazingly thorough and insightful work. John Sawyer and Jeannette Taylor were equally proficient when it came to market analysis and promotional strategies. I learned a lot about publishing through their input. Their enthusiasm for the content was also encouraging. Emily Varner provided just the sort of competent guidance in getting the book exposure in the academic community that I'd hoped for. Bill Nienhuis, Publisher Relations Director at Faithlife/Logos served as liaison (read: my "handler") with respect to all parties. He made sure that none of us overlooked anything that needed to be done. Bill, I need you full time!

Finally, I'm grateful to my wife, Drenna. She makes everything I do possible.

Subject Index

NOTE: Entries in the subject index that consist of citations of Scripture refer to places where those verses are discussed. Quotations of all or part or a particular Scripture are cited in the Scripture index.

of David, 63–64

of Ezekiel, 237–238

of Gideon, 146–148

of Isaac, 137, 236

of Isaiah, 237–238

of Israel (Jacob), 137–140, 236

of Jeremiah, 238–239

of Joseph, 139–140

of Joshua, 145–146, 236

of Moses, 47, 130n6, 141–143, 151, 156–157, 236

of Noah, 235

of Samuel, 130–131, 223

validating, 239

divine image bearing, 40–43

divine judgment. *See* judgment

divine rebellion, 74, 78–79, 81n13, 82n15, 83n1, 84, 93–94, 109, 327

divine sonship, 96–97, 109, 307, 329n22, 381

diviner (*nochesh*), 87

divinization of believers, 48, 96, 159, 308n2, 311, 319–321, 378n4

doksas (glorious ones), 331–332

dominion mandate, 43, 58–59

dominions/lords (*kyrios*), 121, 329–331

dynamis (powers), 121, 329

E

Eden

ancient context of, 44–45

as divine abode, 44, 56, 75, 160–161

earth and, 49–50, 58–59, 123

expulsion from, 88, 90

final Eden, 383

as gardens and mountains, 44–45, 47, 75, 160–161

as heart of the seas, 160

human presence in, 47–48

life in, 89–90

location of, 49–51

as seat of the gods, 48, 75, 83, 160

Sinai and, 160–162

tabernacle and, 174–176

Ugarit and, 45–46

watery habitat of, 47, 49, 75

Edenic vision of Yahweh. *See also* plan of God; Yahweh

David and, 96

establishing new Eden, 383

failure of Israel in, 315

human participation and, 240–244, 254, 262–263, 267

Jesus and, 267

Moses and, 246

for new Edenic Earth, 43, 51

New Testament and, 261

opposition to, 215–216, 253

procreation and, 115, 186, 188n10, 315, 350

for reclaiming nations, 157, 260–261, 278–279, 296–302, 306–308, 322, 382

steadfastness of, 171

'edūt, 168–169

El

Baal and, 361

as chief deity of Ugarit, 46, 76, 227

lesser deities and, 83

as Most High, 76

as separate deity from Yahweh, 30n2

sons of, 81n10, 114n7, 280n8

worhsip of, 156

elders, 157–158, 161, 353–356

el-elyon (God Most High), 76

elohim. *See also* sons of God

as angels, 30

corrupt, 27–28, 58, 114, 290, 322

demons and, 30, 33–34

denial statements and, 34–35

divinity of, 29, 31–32

as family of God, 43

hierarchy among, 33n8, 34–35

human interaction with, 32

human view of, 28–29

incomparability with Yahweh, 34–35

under judgment, 158, 322

lesser, 114

as opponent of Jacob, 138–139

place of residence and, 29

polytheism and, 29–32

realness of, 32–35

shedim as, 280n7

as spiritual beings, 33n8

supernatural worldview and, 35

term usage, 26–27, 30–32, 323

Trinitarian view of, 28

worshipping, 34n11, 116

Scripture Index

NOTE: Biblical books are arranged in canonical order, followed by the books of 1 Enoch and 2 Enoch.

References to verses in the Septuagint are identified by (LXX) following the citation.

JOSHUA

JUDGES

OTHER CITATIONS

1 ENOCH

2 ENOCH

The Unseen Realm made accessible for everyone

What the Bible teaches
about the unseen world —
and why it matters

SUPER NATURAL

Michael S. Heiser

The Unseen Realm has opened the eyes of many readers to the supernatural worldview of the Bible. But not everyone is up to reading such a thorough academic book. In *Supernatural*, Dr. Michael S. Heiser presents the same content in a condensed format, making it easier to understand and digest. It's perfect for sharing with friends, family members, or congregants.

Visit **TheUnseenRealm.com**
to learn more.

LEXHAM PRESS

LEXHAM PRESS

—

WHAT DOES THE BIBLE REALLY TELL US ABOUT THE HEAVENLY HOST?

Everyone knows that angels have wings, usually carry harps, and that each of us has our own personal guardian angel, right? What the Bible really says about angels is overlooked or filtered through popular myths. In his latest book, *Angels*, Dr. Michael Heiser reveals what the Bible really says about God's supernatural servants. *Angels* is not guided by traditions, stories, speculations, or myths about angels. Heiser's study is grounded in the terms the Bible itself uses to describe members of God's heavenly host; he examines the terms in their biblical context while drawing on insights from the wider context of the ancient Near Eastern world.

—

LexhamPress.com/Angels

Learn more about Michael S. Heiser
and his books, blog, and research interests at
TheUnseenRealm.com.